STRATEGIES FOR READING AND STUDY SKILLS

ANNOTATED INSTRUCTOR'S EDITION

STRATEGIES FOR READING AND STUDY SKILLS

RICHARD PIROZZI
PASSAIC COUNTY COMMUNITY COLLEGE

ANNOTATED INSTRUCTOR'S EDITION

NTC Publishing Group
Lincolnwood, Illinois USA

Executive Editor: John T. Nolan
Developmental Editor: Sue Schumer
Interior and cover design: Ophelia M. Chambliss
Production Manager: Rosemary Dolinski

Credits and acknowledgments for reprinting copyrighted material are on pages 429–430, which represent a continuation of this copyright page.

Published by NTC Publishing Group.
© 1995 by NTC Publishing Group, 4255 West Touhy Avenue,
Lincolnwood (Chicago), Illinois 60646-1975 U.S.A.
All rights reserved. No part of this book may be reproduced, stored
in a retrieval system, or transmitted in any form or by any means,
electronic, mechanical, photocopying, recording or otherwise, without
the prior permission of NTC Publishing Group.
Manufactured in the United States of America.
Library of Congress Catalog Card Number: 94-67318

4 5 6 7 8 9 ML 9 8 7 6 5 4 3 2 1

CONTENTS

Preface to the Instructor   ix

Preface to the Student   xiii

Part 1   Study and Classroom Skills   1

Chapter 1   Getting Started   2

Setting Your Long-Range Goals   2
Managing Your Time   4
Getting Support at Home and at School   6
Setting Specific Study Goals and Improving
        Concentration   8
Finding a Place to Study   9
Managing Anxiety   10
Following Directions   11
It's Up to You   13

Chapter 2   Effective Classroom Note Taking   14

Introduction   14
Lecture 1: Effective Classroom Note Taking   14
Lecture 2: Introduction to the Middle East   22
Lecture 3: The Nursing Process   34

Chapter 3   Effective Test Taking   45

Lecture: Effective Test Taking   45
    Preparing for the Test   46
    Taking the Test   47
    What to Do after the Test   49

Part 2 Dealing Effectively with Textbook Material 59

Chapter 4   Vocabulary   60

Using the Context   61
    Punctuation   61
    Other Ways to Use Context   63
Using Word Parts   82
Using a Glossary   85
Using the Dictionary   92
Learning and Reviewing Vocabulary Words   95

Chapter 5   Finding Topics and Main Ideas   96

The Main Idea as the First Sentence   97
The Main Idea as the Last Sentence   98
The Main Idea between the First and Last Sentences   98
The Main Idea as Two Sentences   99
The Main Idea That Covers More Than One Paragraph   100
Unstated Main Ideas   101

Chapter 6   Finding Major and Minor Details   126

Identifying Details   126

Chapter 7   Recognizing Patterns of Organization   155

Simple Listing of Facts   155
    Form 1: Numbered within One Paragraph   156
    Form 2: Numbered over More Than
        One Paragraph   157
    Form 3: Unnumbered within One Paragraph   157
    Form 4: Unnumbered over More Than
        One Paragraph   158

Chronological Order 160
    Form 1: With Dates 160
    Form 2: Without Dates 162
Comparison and Contrast 162
    Form 1: Dealing with Similarities 163
    Form 2: Dealing with Differences 164
    Form 3: Dealing with Both Similarities
        and Differences 165
Cause and Effect 166
    Form 1: With Causes Stated First 167
    Form 2: With Effects Stated First 167

Chapter 8   Organizing Textbook Material   203

Outlining 203
Making Diagrams (Mapping) 216
Summarizing and Paraphrasing 227

Chapter 9   Using Inference   241

Reading between the Lines (Exercise 1) 241
Making "Educated Guesses" (Exercise 2) 245
Developing Inference Questions (Exercise 3) 272

Chapter 10   Five Steps to Effective Textbook Reading   282

Step 1   Overview the Textbook 282
Step 2   Preview Each Chapter before Reading 282
Step 3   Construct a Broad Topic Outline of the
           Chapter 283
Step 4   Turn Chapter Headings into Questions and
           Read to Find the Answers 287
Step 5   Review Answers to Questions Continually 294
Special Feature: Front Matter and Chapter 8 from the
    college textbook *Tools for Technical and*
    Professional Communication by Arthur H. Bell . . . 295

Part 3 Change-of-Pace Readings 327

Selection 1 "The Dark Menace"	328
Comprehension Questions	330
Selection 2 "The Experience of a Lifetime"	333
Comprehension Questions	334
Selection 3 "The Trajectories of Genius . . ."	338
Comprehension Questions	340
Selection 4 "Why Run?"	343
Comprehension Questions	346
Selection 5 "With No Parents, Ladeeta, 18, Presses On"	350
Comprehension Questions	356
Selection 6 "The Stono River Rebellion and Its Impact . . ."	360
Comprehension Questions	367
Selection 7 "The Decline and Fall" (Watergate)	371
Comprehension Questions	378
Selection 8 "Young Cassius Clay"	382
Comprehension Questions	397
Selection 9 " 'A Generation of Clumsy Feeble-Minded Millions' . . ."	402
Comprehension Questions	409
Selection 10 "A Historical Overview of the African American Literary Tradition"	413
Comprehension Questions	420

Index 427

Credits 429

PREFACE

To the Instructor

Although reading and study skills textbooks generally attempt to develop the same skills, those skills are presented and reinforced in various ways and at different levels of difficulty. In the end, it is those three factors—style of presentation, method of reinforcement, and level of difficulty—that will determine ultimately which particular textbook is most appropriate for a given audience. However, the effectiveness of any text depends in large measure on those individuals who use it. Instructors must put much of their own personalities into a given textbook, and students have to expend a substantial amount of time and effort while working their way through it.

Strategies for Reading and Study Skills takes a concise, easy-to-use, straightforward approach to college study. It seeks to help prospective and beginning students deal with their academic responsibilities and provides them with an introduction to the most important skills necessary for college survival. It does not pretend to offer a comprehensive treatment of all reading and study skills, but concentrates instead on the most crucial ones. Numerous examples and exercises are utilized to present, discuss and reinforce the skills. The material used for discussion and exercise purposes has been taken, for the most part, from a wide variety of introductory college textbooks. Because the exercise passages vary in reading level, length and subject matter, their usage can be tailored to the capabilities and interests of students. Throughout the text, an effort has been made to relate the exercises to the content areas by asking students to apply the skills to the textbooks that they are using in their other courses. In this way, students get a "feel" for the application of the skills so that the skills become more relevant and meaningful to them.

For ease of use, the textbook is divided into three parts. Part 1 deals with study and classroom skills, while Part 2 is concerned with textbook reading skills. The note taking exercises in Part 1 come particularly close to real-life college experiences, which should prove very useful to students. One of the unique features of the textbook is the inclusion in Part 2 of the front matter and an entire chapter from a college textbook, along with an integrated reading approach. The idea here is to introduce the student to an overall approach to textbook chapters that incorporates the specific reading and study skills developed throughout the semester. Certainly, that is the reality that must be confronted by students as they make their way through their various courses. Part 3 contains ten longer reading selections that deal with various topics of interest that will serve as a change of pace from the textbook material. Hence, the instructor has "a place to go" when students need a break from the usual routine. Also, a wide variety of test-like questions follow each of the selections thus providing additional test-taking practice.

The *Annotated Instructor's Edition* provides page-by-page suggestions and includes an Instructor's Manual at the back, containing assessment advice for each chapter and answers to the exercises. Instructors can, of course, adapt the material in the text to their own special needs by altering the sequence of chapters or by "picking and choosing" among the many exercises that are provided. In addition, the pages in the student edition are designed so that many of the exercises can be completed easily right in the books if the instructor so directs.

Acknowledgments

I am indebted to many people for their valuable assistance while I was writing this textbook. I owe a special thank you to Sue Schumer of NTC Publishing Group for believing in the project from the very beginning and sticking with it until its completion. Her gentle guidance and conscientiousness were extremely helpful and much appreciated. Professor Patricia Cowan, formerly of the nursing department at Passaic County Community College, was very helpful with the chapter on note taking. Barbara Austin had the difficult job of trying to understand my handwriting while typing the manuscript. The book has been classroom-tested here at Passaic County Community College, and my students were very willing to vocalize the strengths and weaknesses of the manuscript.

I am most appreciative of the many worthwhile suggestions offered through the years by Leila Gonzalez Sullivan, President of Middlesex

Community-Technical Colleges in Connecticut. No matter how busy her schedule, she has always agreed to help when asked. Professor Thomas Friedmann of Onondaga Community College, New York, was also very generous with his time and made many useful suggestions, as did Professor Rocco Blasi of Wright City College, Chicago.

In addition, the manuscript for *Strategies for Reading and Study Skills* was carefully read and evaluated by Brenda Armbrecht, Professor of Reading at DeKalb College, Georgia, and Phyllis Sherwood, Professor of English at Raymond Walters College, University of Cincinnati. Their input was very helpful and led to many improvements in the final product.

Finally, I want to thank my wife, Susan, for her consistent encouragement and for believing in me all of these years. Her unwavering support was a major factor in enabling me to complete the project and for that—and a host of other things too numerous to mention, this textbook is affectionately dedicated to her.

Richard Pirozzi

PREFACE

To the Student

As a beginning college student, I was deficient in reading and study skills. In fact, my standardized test scores were low enough to cause concern about my chances for success. Unfortunately, at that time there were no developmental skills courses to help me to survive, so I had to make up my mind to improve on my own. Once I did that, I was able to successfully complete my education.

I have designed *Strategies for Reading and Study Skills* (1) to *help* you improve the reading and study skills essential for your success in college and (2) to acquaint you with the responsibilities that go along with being a college student. It introduces you to those skills and then reinforces them through the use of exercises that vary in length and difficulty. Many of those exercises, such as those used in the chapter on note taking, will give you real-life college experience. In fact, many of the excerpts used throughout the exercises have been taken from a wide variety of college textbooks. Furthermore, you will be asked often to apply the skills that you are learning to specific content areas so that you will see the relevance of those skills. At the same time, you will become familiar with a variety of subject matter that should prove interesting to you.

You will notice that this textbook is divided into three parts. Part 1 deals with study and classroom skills, such as test taking and note taking, while Part 2 is concerned with textbook reading skills, such as finding the main idea and using inferences. Part 3 features ten reading selections from a variety of periodicals and books on various interesting topics, which should serve as a "change of pace" from textbook material.

Both this textbook and your instructor will provide you with much guidance and support, but it is ultimately up to you to devote the time and energy necessary for the development of the skills. In other words, read the introductory material and the directions very carefully, do all the exercises that are assigned and come to realize that what you are doing is valuable to your future. Your efforts will pay off in higher grades and in the personal satisfaction of knowing that you are becoming a much more efficient student.

Richard Pirozzi

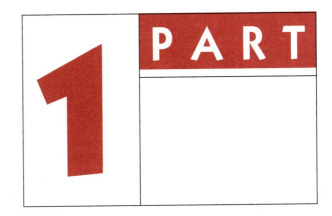

Study and Classroom Skills

STUDENTS DON'T READ

Getting Started

Chapter Objectives:
To provide students with a general introduction to college life including some of the most important issues that should be addressed by all new students. In addition, to present suggestions that are designed to promote students' success.

Discuss the benefits of a college education, while emphasizing the responsibilities of the college student. Students should consider the commitment and adjustments required, recognizing, however, that a college education is worth their effort. Relating personal accounts of experiences as a college student would be meaningful as well.

Going to college is a very challenging, rewarding experience that can change your life dramatically. Not only does a college education open up job opportunities, but it also should help you to better understand yourself and the world around you. If you take full advantage of the opportunity, you will become a more confident decision-maker—one who possesses a strong, positive self-image. In short, you will feel good about yourself as you enjoy the career and monetary benefits that are the byproducts of a college education.

Success in college, however, requires hard work and total commitment on your part. You must adjust to life as a student: attending classes, taking notes, completing assignments, studying, taking tests, and accepting the other responsibilities that go along with college life. Adding these duties to an already busy life is not easy, but it will pay off in the future.

Setting Your Long-Range Goals

As a start, you should clarify why you are attending college. In other words, what are the long-range goals you hope to achieve as a result of successfully completing your college education? These goals, by necessity, are rather broad and few in number, usually involving the completion of a degree program and a career choice. When you set these goals at the very beginning, you can focus on them as you make your way through college, which should help to motivate you and result in better day-to-day decision making. In other words, they give you something to aim for—a reason to plan and work hard. Remember that these are goals that may take several years to accomplish; therefore, you must be willing to make sacrifices today for the rewards you will receive tomorrow. Sometimes it is not easy to wait for the fruits of your labor, but your efforts will be well worth it in the end. Try to be patient!

Once you have set your long-range goals, you are then ready to come up with various strategies for their accomplishment. These strategies involve short-term goals that determine and guide your daily activities and give you a picture of how well you are progressing toward your ultimate goals. For example, the accomplishment of a specific study goal, the completion of an assignment, the mastery of a textbook chapter, or a high grade on a test are steps that will lead to success in the long run. These short-term goals must be continually evaluated and are subject to change as circumstances dictate, but you are in a better position to make the "right" decisions if you keep your long-range goals in mind. In the end, the setting of goals will help to make you more disciplined, add structure to your life, increase your motivation and self-confidence, and provide you with constant feedback as to how well you are progressing.

In the space provided, list your long range goals:

Long-Range Goals

_____

_____

_____

_____

_____

_____

> Provide examples of long-range goals. Ask each student to vocalize his or her goals for the rest of the class. Note any patterns that emerge and write them on the blackboard.
>
> The students' participation is very important at this point so that they overcome early any reluctance to responding orally in class. Remind them that their individual responses can be very helpful to each other. Finally, emphasize that responding in class is, in fact, one of the college student's responsibilities.

Managing Your Time

Now that you have determined your reasons for attending college, take a moment to think about other responsibilities that could interfere with the accomplishment of your long-range college goals. In the time schedule that follows, put an X in the boxes for the hours each day that you must devote to those responsibilities that fall outside school.

Students need to realize that, despite schedules crowded with competing interests, school must be incorporated into their routine every day. In addition, beginning students often do not recognize that college involves much more than just attending classes. Be sure to emphasize that fact. Check with students individually to review and comment on their schedules. Follow up with a class discussion of problems and possible solutions associated with time management.

Time Schedule

	Mon.	Tues.	Wed.	Thurs.	Fri.	Sat.	Sun.
5:00 A.M.							
6:00							
7:00							
8:00							
9:00							
10:00							
11:00							
12:00 P.M.							
1:00							
2:00							
3:00							
4:00							
5:00							
6:00							

	Mon.	Tues.	Wed.	Thurs.	Fri.	Sat.	Sun.
7:00 P.M.							
8:00							
9:00							
10:00							
11:00							
12:00 A.M.							
1:00							
2:00							
3:00							
4:00							

Now that you have filled in the hours for your weekly activities, you probably are amazed at how busy you are. Nevertheless you must set aside hours each day for college responsibilities if you are to succeed. These responsibilities not only involve attending classes and completing assignments, but also studying for tests on a daily basis. With that in mind, return to the time schedule to include your class times and to fill in the hours each day that you intend to devote to assignments and studying. Spread your study hours throughout the week; those hours should total twice as many as those that you spend in class. Set aside hours when you are generally the most wide awake and ones that are free from distractions. Although the hours you need each week will vary according to your workload, you must make college part of your daily routine by trying to adhere to your schedule. If you do not, you may fall behind and endanger your chances of successfully meeting your long-range goals. *You must discipline yourself and live by a very strict study schedule because, in college, no one forces you to do anything.* Are you willing to make the commitment? Good!

As you look at your time schedule, you probably wonder just how you are going to get everything done. Careful management of your

Explain to students that college responsibilities require a significant commitment of their time. Possibly, this commitment could cause resentment, since time spent on studies is time spent away from friends and family. Thus, it is important that students understand the significance of communicating their long-range objectives to others and asking for their support.

Emphasize the necessity of becoming familiar with the college environment as quickly as possible. Ask students to bring to class information regarding office hours and office locations for all of their instructors. In addition, verify that they have made contact with their counselors and/or advisors. Reinforce the importance of getting help immediately when problems arise.

limited time is essential. Each day make a list of the things that you have to do and then number them in order of importance. For example, if that day you must complete an assignment that is due the next day or prepare for a test that is scheduled that week, by necessity, these activities rank at the top of your list. Your other activities should come after them and even might have to be put aside temporarily. In other words, sometimes you have to make choices by doing the most important, pressing things first before turning to other responsibilities.

Getting Support at Home and at School

Another key to success in college is having as much moral support as possible both at home and at school. Take the time to discuss your long-range goals with your family, friends, and the significant others in your life, and ask for their understanding and support. Emphasize how important college is to you, but also assure them that you will continue to set aside time to be with them. Remember that this undertaking is a major adjustment for you *and* for those around you, because they may not be able to have as much of your attention as before.

In the space provided, list the names of the important people in your life. Then, after you have discussed your long-range goals with one of these people, place a check mark after that name. Work through your list until you have communicated with each person.

Important People

_____

_____

_____

_____

_____

_____

In addition to getting support at home, you need to identify those offices at school, and the people who work in them, that can lend you a helping hand. As quickly as possible, find out the locations and functions of the various offices at your college, such as the registrar's office and others dealing with financial aid and the academic areas. Make sure that you know who your counselor is. Most colleges assign students to counselors and/or advisors. Because counselors are there specifically to help students deal with both academic and nonacademic problems, get to know your counselor and/or advisor quickly. Also, make a point of knowing the office hours and locations of all your instructors so that you can meet with them outside class.

Fill in the following list with the most important offices at your college along with their locations and functions. At the top of the list, record the name and office location of your counselor and/or advisor, along with the date on which you first contacted this person. Read your college catalog and ask questions to get the information needed to complete this exercise. Remember that you need to become a part of your college environment immediately so that you feel you belong and know where to go for help.

Counselor's Name: _____

Office Location: _____

Date Contacted: _____

Other Offices	Locations	Functions

Setting Specific Study Goals and Improving Concentration

To improve your concentration, study and complete assignments in one- or two-hour blocks, and then take a break. When you alternate subjects during each study block, you do not become fatigued or bored. For example, you may spend half your time working mathematics problems, and then turn to one of your reading assignments.

The importance of goal-setting in general was already discussed earlier in this chapter. Remember to set specific study goals *each* time you sit down to study or complete assignments to help you to focus on what you need to do and to improve your concentration. As you accomplish these specific goals, you build your self-confidence because you know you are making progress. Possible study goals could include mastering one or two mathematics problems, reading and understanding a section of a given textbook chapter, learning the parts to the human circulatory system, memorizing the causes and results of the Civil War, or being able to comprehend and use a particular part of a computer program. Keep in mind that you never should study without a specific purpose, and you should not be satisfied until that purpose has been realized.

Now look back at your time schedule. Use it to help you prepare a list of specific study goals that you want to accomplish the next time you sit down to study or complete assignments. It may be helpful for you to consult your course outlines or syllabi to help you plan. Be sure to set goals for each of your study blocks throughout the week. Space for your list follows.

Specific Study Goals

> Students must appreciate the importance of being goal-oriented. Use your own examples from athletics and other areas to help bring home this critical point. Also, provide additional examples of possible study goals.

Date & Time   *Goal*

_____   _____

_____   _____

_____   _____

_____   _____

Have students read aloud in class their specific study goals. In a general discussion, compare strategies and highlight similarities.

Finding a Place to Study

Have a definite place at home where you can study without being distracted. Although the area need not be large, it should be big enough so that you can spread out your books and work comfortably. Make sure you have enough light to read; otherwise, your eyes may tire very quickly. Having a specific study area not only makes you more comfortable as you do your school work, but it also makes it easier to discipline yourself. You know that when you arrive there, you get down to serious business!

In addition to working at home, you, of course, can complete assignments and study at school and at a variety of other places. At school, make use of the library, vacant classrooms, or any other accessible places to accomplish some of your study goals. Also, take advantage of any free time you may have while, for example, waiting in the doctor's office or for your car to be repaired. Because of your busy life you need to take advantage of any available time that suddenly develops, so take at least some of your books with you wherever you go. Now take a moment to list, in order of importance, the places at home and elsewhere that you can do your school work.

Study Places

Home   Elsewhere

_____

_____

_____

_____

_____

_____

In a class discussion, ask each student to describe the place he or she intends to study regularly. Emphasize that if one really wants to study, a place can be found.

Managing Anxiety

Stress—an unavoidable human experience—is not necessarily a bad thing, as long as we do not permit it to overwhelm us, and we direct it toward positive results. Athletes certainly use stress to achieve their ends with remarkable success. As a student, it is normal to feel anxious about instructors, tests, papers, and most importantly, grades.

However you must work at controlling anxiety so that you can accomplish your goals. Any kind of exercise, such as walking, cycling, or running, is a wonderful way to eliminate excess stress while, at the same time, contributing to physical well-being; so take a half-hour a day to clear your mind and help your body. Various relaxation techniques like deep, slow breathing, listening to music, or doing anything else that you find soothing also can be very useful. During particularly stressful periods try talking with your counselor, a caring instructor, or a trusted friend who may make suggestions or recommend useful relaxation techniques. Sometimes just talking about your fears and feelings calms you down.

Most importantly, especially when you are stressed, concentrate on your specific study goals and particularly on your long-range goals so that you direct the stress toward positive ends. *Believe in yourself* and,

Ask students to list and then read aloud those general experiences that tend to make them anxious. Look for patterns such as "the fear of the unknown" that can be discussed as a class. Emphasize the importance of employing relaxation techniques and of seeking help from others when anxiety becomes overwhelming.

like an athlete, focus all your energies on accomplishing what you have set out to do. Take a few moments now to list the methods you intend to use to control excessive anxiety.

Methods to Control Excessive Anxiety

_____

_____

_____

_____

_____

Have students offer their favorite methods and, as a class, discuss their effectiveness.

Following Directions

In the exercise, carefully follow the list of directions.

Exercise

1. Read all of the following directions before doing anything.
2. Take out a piece of lined notebook paper.
3. Write your name in the upper-left-hand corner of the paper.
4. Write the date in the upper-right-hand corner of the paper.
5. On the first line of your paper, write the number 1,256,000.
6. Subtract 556 from the above number.
7. Take one-third of the remainder. Multiply it by 10.
8. Add 400 to the total.
9. Skip this exercise.

If you attempted to complete the exercise, you did not follow the directions. Direction number one states clearly that you should read *all* of the directions *before* doing anything. If you had done that, you would have read direction number nine that tells you to skip the exercise. This is a trick designed to illustrate how we do not follow directions.

Explain to students that the fact that the sample text exercise involved mathematics could have brought on anxiety, which sometimes causes one not to follow directions. Once again, emphasize the importance of controlling anxiety.

It is helpful to relate some of your own experiences with students who did not follow directions. Also, ask students about their own experiences.

Unfortunately, we all, at times, are guilty of not following directions the way we should, and it costs us time, money, and sometimes, even our lives. For students, not following directions can result in missed, incomplete, or incorrect assignments, careless mistakes on tests, and lower grades at the end of the semester. So, when you are given written directions for a test or exercise, make it a habit to read the instructions at least twice, and underline the key words that will help you focus on what needs to be done. When the directions are oral, give the person who is talking your undivided attention. Stop whatever you are doing, control excessive anxiety, and look directly at the speaker. Too often students miss important instructions because they are anxious, talking, daydreaming, or looking for a pen. Take the advice of one of my students. "When oral directions are being given, students must *Stop, Look,* and *Listen*!"

If you are confused by the directions or are not sure what exactly to do, ask questions. Instructors generally want to help you to understand, so do not be afraid to approach them. In fact, they will often give you very valuable information if they know that you need assistance. With so much at stake in college, do not leave anything to guesswork or make questionable assumptions that will come back to haunt you later. Following directions carefully can make the difference between passing and failing! Now list the four important suggestions regarding following directions that were just mentioned.

Suggestions

1. _____

2. _____

> What suggestions regarding following directions did students list? Ask individuals to share their lists aloud with the class. See the Instructor's Manual, Chapter 1 Answers.

3. _____

4. _____

It's Up to You

You now have some general suggestions that can help you as you begin your college education. In the following chapters you will be introduced to various reading and study skills that will make your journey a little easier. Look on the coming experience as a challenge that will improve your life and make you a more complete person. When the going sometimes gets tough, remember your long-range goals and keep your focus on their accomplishment. Use any of the resources available at your college, such as caring individuals, orientation programs, and various workshops, to guide and assist you. Get to know your instructors and, particularly, your counselor and/or advisor so that you will feel comfortable enough to approach them to discuss problems or to seek their advice on such things as course, program, and career selection. If possible join an organization or a club so that you meet other students and become an active part of your new environment. You have made a very important decision to pursue a college education, so become totally involved in its successful completion.

In your notebook, make a list of the most important suggestions mentioned in this chapter. Be sure to include those that you find to be particularly helpful and that you intend to follow very closely. From time to time while you are studying, recite your list aloud so that you remember it.

Summarize the chapter as you review the students' lists of the most important suggestions.

CHAPTER 2

Effective Classroom Note Taking

Chapter Objective:
To introduce effective classroom note taking through suggestions and practice opportunities, including actual college lectures.

Introduction

As you know, this chapter deals with effective classroom note taking. The suggestions that follow will be given to you as a lecture by your instructor so that you can get some firsthand experience at taking notes. You will have an opportunity to read the lecture material after you have taken notes.

When you take notes, try to record what you consider to be the most important information. At this point do not become overly concerned if you miss some material. After the lecture you will be given an opportunity to compare what you have written down to both model notes and the lecture material. Although your notes do not have to look exactly like the model notes, you should have included similar information, so listen for and record the important points. Now take out a notebook and close your textbook in preparation for the lecture.

Lecture 1

Effective Classroom Note Taking

One of the most important skills college students must develop is the ability to take lecture notes effectively. Although many instructors base their tests on both the textbook and on the information they cover in class, some place greater emphasis on the material they present in their lectures. Particularly for those instructors, you must be able to take notes that include at least the most important points. The fact that some instructors are disorganized and others talk very quickly complicates the process. Nevertheless note taking is a skill that you can sharpen considerably by following some suggestions and by practicing. While this chapter provides you with both, it is only a beginning that you need to reinforce by the continuous practice you will get in most of your content courses. In short, you will have much on-the-job training as you proceed through college.

For this initial note taking experience, students should not read the lecture material first. Because many students are not accustomed to taking notes, prevent their feeling discouraged by giving the lecture at a much slower pace than usual.

Preparation for the Lecture

Note taking is a four-step process involving: (1) preparation for the lecture, (2) listening and taking notes, (3) correcting and/or rewriting your notes, and (4) reviewing your notes on a continuous basis. You should start by recognizing that, for the most part, note taking is not an enjoyable experience. It is hard work that requires total concentration and good listening skills. Listening skills include hearing, evaluating what you hear, and reacting to what you hear by deciding what to write down. You must attend each class on time with a positive attitude and a willingness to pay close attention to what is being said—no matter how boring it may seem or how tired you may be. This is not always easy to do, but it is absolutely necessary if you are to accomplish your long-range goals.

Before you go to a lecture, be sure to review the material from the previous lecture and to read your textbook assignment so that you are prepared to listen and understand what the instructor will be covering. You need to arrive on time because instructors often summarize the previous lecture before introducing the new material. Coming late to class is not only impolite, it can cause confusion and result in incomplete notes. Make sure that you bring a few pens and pencils with you and that you use a large notebook with wide pages so that you have plenty of room to make corrections and add notes at a later time. Title and date each lecture so that you can find the material easily when you want to review.

Listening and Taking Notes

To listen and take notes effectively, sit where you can see and hear the instructor clearly and in a position that enables you to write quickly and comfortably. As soon as class begins, direct your complete attention toward the instructor to the exclusion of everyone and everything else.

Since writing down every word spoken by the instructor is almost impossible, you have to know how to separate important from unimportant information. In most cases, when the instructor raises his or her voice, repeats the same information, writes material on the board, gives a definition, or provides you with a list of points, the information is important enough to be included in your notes. Try to learn the personal lecturing style of each of your instructors so that you are able to recognize when each emphasizes certain material. For example, some instructors actually tell you what is important, while others give you hints with statements like, "If I were you, I would learn that point." Still others may pound on the lectern or tap a piece of chalk on the board to stress something. Learn these individual traits as early in the semester as possible to help you decide what information belongs in your notes.

If the instructor speaks very quickly, you may need to use abbreviations like the following.

- Mex. (instead of Mexico)
- 3 (the number instead of three the word)
- def. (instead of definition)
- 1/1/93 (instead of January 1, 1993)
- JFK (instead of John Fitzgerald Kennedy)
- ex. (instead of example)
- pts. (instead of points)
- good s. skills = better grades (instead of "good study skills will result in better grades")

It does not matter what abbreviations you use as long as *you* can understand them later when you correct and add to your notes. Furthermore do not worry about grammar, incomplete sentences, spelling, or punctuation when you take notes under time pressure. Just be sure that you are able to make sense of them after the lecture. Remember to leave plenty of space in your notebook so that you have room for additional information.

Finally, do not hesitate to ask questions if you are confused by lecture material or if you are having difficulty keeping up. Most instructors are very willing to help you if they realize that you are having trouble, so let them know quickly. You will not get assistance unless you ask for it, and there is too much at stake for you not to speak up!

Correcting and/or Rewriting Your Notes

An essential habit you need to develop is to go back over your notes as soon after class as you can—certainly no later than that same day. You need to correct and make sense of your notes while the lecture is still fresh in your mind. As you go through your notes, check, star, or highlight in some way the most important parts so that you can spot them easily when you review. A good method is to rewrite your notes, using your textbook to add relevant points and fill in gaps. If you discover trouble spots, go to your instructor for clarification or additional information.

Reviewing Your Notes on a Continuous Basis

In most classes your notes are at least as important as your textbook, so you must familiarize yourself with them on a continuous basis. Make sure that you review them during each study block, paying particular attention to those areas that you have checked, starred, or highlighted. *Reciting* your notes to yourself or out loud may help you to learn and remember the most important information.

Because you will accumulate many pages of notes over the course of a given semester, make it a practice to study your notes on an ongoing basis; do not wait until the night before a test to try to learn them. As mentioned, reviewing your notes from previous lectures also helps you listen and take better notes in future lectures. Note taking, then, is a nonstop process!

Exercise 1

Compare your notes first to the model notes on pages 18–21 and then to the lecture material.

In Exercise 1, make certain students compare their notes to the model notes *before* looking at the lecture material. Point out some of the shortcuts used in the model notes, and inquire about crucial information the students might have omitted.

Exercise 2

In your notebook list the most important note-taking suggestions mentioned in this chapter. Your instructor may collect your list or ask you to read it aloud in class.

In going over student lists in Exercise 2, summarize the most important note-taking suggestions.

Model Notes—Lecture 1

Model Notes

Effective Classroom Note taking
　　　　　　　　　　　　Date

V. import. skill → tests
Must get down most import. pts.
Difficult — some instruct. disorganized
　　　　　　　　 " talk quickly
Can develop skill — by following suggestions
　　　　　　　　　 by practicing (content courses)

* 4 steps

1.) prep. for lect.

2.) list. and taking notes

3.) correcting/rewriting notes

4.) reviewing

Prep For Lect.
Note: not enjoyable — hard work, tot. concentration, good listen. skills
listening: hearing
　　　　　　 evaluating
　　　　　　 reacting

Attend every class on time with
positive attitude — no matter how
tired or bored
         ↑   ↑
necessary for long-range goals

Review previous lect. & read assign.
before lect.

Arrive on time ⟨ instructors summarize
                 avoid confusion and
                 incomplete notes

Bring pens & pencils
Use large notebook with wide pages
title & date each lect.

<u>Listening and Taking Notes</u>

Sit where you can see and hear
instruct.
Position — write quickly & comfort.
Direct complete attention to instruct.
exclude everyone/thing else
Can't write down every word —
separate import. from un important

Important: instruct. raises voice, repeats, writes on board, gives def., lists pts.

Also learn lect. style of instruct. ↗ quickly
  ↓ some tell you what is important
     others give hints
     others pound lectern, tap chalk

{ Use abbrev. like: mex — Mexico
→ I have to   3 — three
  understand them   def — definition
  no matter which   1/1/93 — January 1, 1993
  ones I use.   JFK — John Fitzgerald Kennedy
                         ex. — example
                         pts. — points
                         = — equals as in
                         good s. skills = better grades

Don't worry about gram., incomplete sent.
↓ punct., spell. *so long as I can make sense of notes.
↓ *Leave space in note for addl. info.

Ask instruct. quest. if confused or can't keep up
  ↓ must ask for asstst

<u>Correcting / Rewriting Notes</u>
Get back to notes quickly (same day)
Make corrections — make sense while fresh
  Check
  Star   } most import pts.
  Highlight
Rewrite if necess = aid to learning and remem.
Use text for more info. or gaps
Ask instruct for help ↑↑

  <u>Reviewing</u>
Continuous (every study block)
Pay attention to stars, checks, highlights.
Don't wait until test — study every day

Review notes from prev. lect to help in upcoming classes.

* Nonstop process!

It is easier for students to follow the second lecture by providing them an outline.

As they answer the questions, make sure that students look only at their notes and spell all answers correctly. Later in reviewing the questions and answers, try to determine why some mistakes were made.

Exercise 3

Your instructor is going to deliver another practice lecture, which begins below. It is titled "Introduction to the Middle East." Listen very carefully and take notes using the note-taking suggestions just covered. Afterwards, you will use your notes to answer questions that focus on the most important points. You then will be given an opportunity to compare your notes to model notes and to the actual lecture material. Although your notes do not have to look exactly like the model notes, they at least should contain almost the same information.

Lecture 2

Introduction to the Middle East

Meaning and Countries of the Middle East

There has not been complete agreement as to what this region of the world should be called. It has been referred to over the years as the Near East, the Middle East, and even Southwest Asia. For our purposes, we will call it the Middle East.

There has also been much disagreement regarding what countries are part of the Middle East. For example, some historians include Pakistan, whereas others do not. Most everyone agrees, however, that the countries we will be studying are part of the region. They are the non-Arab Jewish state of Israel, the non-Arab Islamic states of Turkey and Iran, and the Arab Islamic states of Egypt, Iraq, Jordan, Lebanon, Syria, and Saudi Arabia. The capitals of these countries are as follows:

Israel: Jerusalem and Tel Aviv (Because of the Israeli occupation of Jerusalem in the June 1967 war, there is much controversy over the country's capital. Israel claims Jerusalem as its capital, whereas most of the world community recognizes Tel Aviv, which was the capital of Israel before the 1967 war. You will be expected to know the names of both capitals.)

Turkey: Ankara

Iran: Teheran

Egypt: Cairo

Iraq: Baghdad

Jordan: Amman

Lebanon: Beirut
Syria: Damascus
Saudi Arabia: Riyadh

Importance of the Middle East

The Middle East region is important for religious, historical, strategic-geographic, and economic reasons. It has religious significance because the three great monotheistic (belief that there is only one God) religions—Judaism, Christianity, and Islam—were born in the Middle East. The region has historical importance because many world events have taken place there, and it has been a part of many great civilizations, including the Persian, Roman, Arab, and Turkish empires. The strategic-geographic significance of the Middle East stems from the fact that the region is a part of the continents of Asia, Africa, and Europe. In fact, it is located at the crossroads of these three continents. Finally, the Middle East has economic importance because of its substantial oil resources.

Physical Characteristics of the Middle East

As far as the physical geography of the Middle East is concerned, the region does consist of mostly dry land. With the exception of oil, it is rather poor in natural resources. Furthermore, it is important to recognize that the entire region is *not* oil rich. Such countries as Saudi Arabia, Iran, and Iraq have much oil, whereas Egypt, Syria, and Turkey have relatively little. The principal food crop grown in the area is wheat, and the leading industrial crop is cotton.

People of the Middle East

The people of the Middle East can be divided into three major groups, according to the language they speak. It should be stressed that these three categories are very broad and that there is much variety within each group. Those people who speak the Arabic and Hebrew languages make up the largest group, which is known as the Semites. An Arab can be defined as one whose native language and culture are Arabic and who identifies with Arab problems or ways of life. Although Hebrew is the official national language of Israel, it is not sufficient to define a Jew as one who speaks Hebrew. Many Jews (including Israelis) speak languages other than Hebrew. For our purposes, we will define a Jew as a follower of the Jewish religion who identifies with Jewish problems and life.

The second major language grouping consists of those Middle Eastern people who speak Turkish. Finally, the third group is made up of Iranians, who speak the Persian language.

How People of the Middle East Live

Approximately 75 percent of the Middle Eastern people are farmers, 20 percent live in the cities, and 5 percent are nomads (wanderers). Life on the farm can be characterized as primitive, with high disease, illiteracy, birth and death rates. The cities, which have both rich and poor sections, are the centers of political activity. Arab nomads of the Middle East are called Bedouins and are ruled by hereditary leaders known as sheikhs. The nomadic population of the region has been declining for many years.

Questions

See the Instructor's Manual, Chapter 2 Answers.

1. Name six Arab countries and three non-Arab countries.

Arab	Non-Arab
Egypt	Israel
Iraq	Turkey
Jordan	Iran
Lebanon	
Syria	
Saudi Arabia	

2. Name the capitals of the following countries.

   Israel: _Jerusalem & Tel Aviv_
   Iran: _Teheran_
   Turkey: _Ankara_
   Syria: _Damascus_

Saudi Arabia: _Riyadh_

Iraq: _Baghdad_

3. When did Israel occupy Jerusalem? (month and year)

   June, 1967

4. List and explain four reasons why the Middle East is important.

   Religious

   Historical

   Strategic-Geographic

   Economic —

5. *True or false:* The Middle East is rich in natural resources.

   False

6. Define *monotheistic*.

   Belief that there is only one God

7. Name the three great monotheistic religions.

   Judaism

   Christianity

   Islam

8. The Middle East was part of many great empires. Name three.

   Persian

   Roman

   Arab & Turkish

9. The Middle East is part of what three continents?

   Asia

   Africa

   Europe

10. *True or false:* Because of its many rivers, the Middle East consists mostly of wetlands.

    False

11. Name three oil-rich countries of the Middle East.

    Saudi Arabia

    Iran

    Iraq

12. Name three Middle Eastern countries that have very little oil.

    Egypt

    Syria

    Turkey

Lecture 2: Introduction to the Middle East   27

13. What is the principal food crop grown in the Middle East?
    Wheat

14. What is the leading industrial crop in the Middle East?
    Cotton

15. Name the three major language groupings of people in the Middle East.
    Semites
    Turkish
    Persian

16. What is the largest language grouping in the Middle East?
    Semites – speak Arabic and Hebrew

17. Define *Arab*.

    on whose native language and culture are Arabic and who identifies w/ Arab problems or ways of life

18. Define *Jew*.

    a follower of the Jewish religion who identifies with Jewish problems and life

19. The Semites consist of those people who speak what two languages?

    Arabic
    Hebrew

20. What is the official national language of Israel?

    Hebrew

21. Iranians speak _Persian_.

22. Approximately _75_ percent of the Middle Eastern people

    are farmers; _20_ percent live in the cities, and _5_ percent are nomads.

23. Define *nomad*.

    wanderers

24. *True or false:* Life on the farm is characterized by high disease rates, low birth rates, and high death rates.

    false

25. Where are the centers of political activity in the Middle East?

    cities

26. What are the Arab nomads of the Middle East called?

    Bedouins

27. What are the hereditary leaders of the nomads called?

    sheikhs

As the students compare their notes with the model notes for Exercise 4, emphasize again the various shortcuts illustrated. See whether students recognize that the word "principal" has been misspelled. Point out that these kinds of mistakes are common in a pressure situation and that should be corrected immediately after class.

28. *True or false:* The nomadic population of the Middle East is on the increase.

    false

29. What is another name for the Middle East?

    Near East
    SW Asia

30. *True or false:* Oil is the most important natural resource in the Middle East.

    true

Exercise 4

Compare your notes first to the model notes on pages 31–33 and then to the lecture material.

Because Exercise 5 involves a more difficult lecture, it is very important that students read the material first and receive an outline. For variety, consider asking another instructor to give the lecture.

Once again, students should use only their notes to answer the questions. Point out the shortcuts used in the model notes. Also, be sure to ask students how well they did in answering the questions.

Exercise 5

You are about to be given another practice lecture by your instructor. This one deals with "The Nursing Process." Beginning on page 34 you will find the lecture material—this time read it *before* your instructor delivers the lecture. Your reading will familiarize you with the subject matter.

Both the lecture and the corresponding questions were made up by a faculty member from a college nursing program. Once again, listen to the lecture very carefully and take notes as best you can. After the lecture you will use your notes to answer the questions so that you can determine how well you did at note taking. You will then have a chance to compare your notes to model notes and to the lecture material to make sure that you have written down the most important information. Remember that the model notes were supposedly taken in a pressure situation, and therefore, would need to be corrected, added to, or rewritten as soon after the lecture as possible.

Model Notes—Lecture 2

Model Notes
Introduction to the Middle East
Date:

Meaning and Countries

Has been called Near East, M. East and Southwest Asia. We should call it M.E. Disagreement over countries included, we will study:
Israel (non-Arab Jewish)
Turkey and Iran (n-Arab Islamic)
Egypt, Iraq, Jordan, Lebanon, Syria and Saudi Arabia (Arab Islam)

Capitals
Jerusalem and Tel Aviv * Know both
↑ occupied by Is in June 67 war. Is. claims as cap.
↑ pre 67 cap. world recog as cap of Is

Turkey - Ankara
Iran - Teheran
Egypt - Cairo
Iraq - Baghdad
Jordan - Amman
Lebanon - Beirut
Syria - Damascus
S. Arabia - Riyadh

Importance of M.E. → check spell

1. religious — 3 great monotheistic (belief in one God) religions born there: Judaism, Christianity and Islam.
2. historical — many import. world events and part of many great empires (Persian, Roman, Arab and Turkish)
3. strategic - geographic — part of continents of Asia, Africa and Europe. Located at crossroads of
4. Economic — much oil

Physical Characteristics

Mostly dry land. Poor in natural resources (except oil)
Entire region not oil rich — S. Arabia, Iran, and Iraq have much oil, but Egypt, Syria, and Turkey have little.
Principle food crop — wheat Leading indust. ~~cotton~~ Leading indust — cotton

People

Three major lang. groups (very broad much variety in each) 1. Semites (largest) Those that speak Arabic and Hebrew languages
*Arab (def) — one whose native lang. and culture is Arabic and who identifies with Arab problems or ways of life. Hebrew is off. national lang. of Israel, but can't define Jew as one who speaks Hebrew. Many Jews (including Israelis) speak other lang.

Lecture 2: Introduction to the Middle East

ways of life
Hebrew is off. national lang. of Israel. but can't define Jew as one who speaks Hebrew. Many Jews (including Israelis) speak other lang.

  * Jew (def.) - follower of the Jew. religion who identifies with Jew. problems and life.

2 - Turks - speak Turkish
3 - Iranians - speak Persian

How they Live
 Approx. 75% farmers. 20% live in cities. 5% are nomads (wanderers)
Life on farm is primitive - high disease, illiteracy, birth, death rates.
 Cities — rich and poor sections
   — centers of pol. activity

Arab nomads called Bedouins. Ruled by hereditary leaders called Sheikhs. Nomad pop. declining

Lecture 3

The Nursing Process

The nursing process is an organized, systematic approach designed to meet the health care needs of patients. More specifically, it is a way of thinking and solving medical problems. Its purpose, in short, is, first, to help identify patient problems; second, to develop a plan to help the patient deal with those problems; third, to evaluate the care given to the patient.

There are five steps, or phases, involved in the nursing process: assessment, analysis, planning, implementation, and evaluation. For the most part, the steps correlate with the scientific method of problem solving as follows:

Nursing Process	*Scientific Method of Problem Solving*
Assessment	Recognize and define problem; collect data
Analysis	Develop hypothesis
Planning	
Implementation	Test assumptions
Evaluation	Evaluate; formulate conclusions

Assessment Phase

In the assessment phase of the nursing process, the nurse collects both objective and subjective data. The objective data is derived from whatever the nurse can see, hear, feel, or smell, such as heart rate, blood pressure, respiration, and perspiration. Data can be gathered from resources like the patient's medical record, diagnostic tests, journals, and by means of a physical examination. Subjective data, on the other hand, is based on what the patient says or how he or she expresses feelings. This information generally comes from interviewing the patient and asking open-ended questions like: "How are you feeling?". As you can see, the patient is the primary source of data for the nursing assessment.

Analysis Phase

The analysis phase involves careful study of the data and identification of the problem. It is important to recognize that the etiology, or contributing factors, as well as the problem, must be uncovered so that proper care can be planned. The problem is expressed as a nursing diagnosis that is based on the patient's response rather than just on the medical diagnosis. After arriving at a diagnosis, the nurse then must develop goals that are patient specific, measurable, and have a definite time frame.

Planning Phase

In the planning phase, the nurse prioritizes and organizes nursing care. Included in this phase are possible nursing actions, or interventions, that correspond to the following categories.

Possible Nursing Interventions	*Categories*
Talking with or hugging a patient	Psychological support
Teaching progressive muscle relaxation or how to deep breathe	Teaching needs
Giving a bath or back care	Hygiene
Removing sharp objects or preventing falls	Protective measures
Bringing in another health care team member, such as a clinical nurse specialist or dietitian	Referrals
Providing a proper diet or help with walking	Physical needs
Administering medications and treatments; *not* prescription of drugs	Medical regimen
Providing adequate ventilation or proper temperature	Environmental adaptations

Not all of these categories or interventions necessarily have to be included in each patient's plan of care, but the nurse will often use many of them.

Implementation Phase

During the implementation phase, the nurse plan of care, including interventions, is put into action or practice. It is important to emphasize here that there always must be a scientific rationale as to why the nurse is doing something. In other words, the plan must make scientific sense, or it is virtually useless. Once again, you can see the close relationship between the nursing process and the scientific method.

Evaluation Phase

Evaluation is an ongoing phase designed to determine if the patient's health care needs are being met, or the goals are being attained. If not the nurse must find out what went wrong so that corrective action can be taken. For example, the diagnosis or interventions could have been wrong or inappropriate, which of course, would explain why the plan did not work.

In summary, the nursing process is a continuous cycle that allows modification of patient care as circumstances change. It is not just a series of steps to be taken once, but rather it is a circle requiring that the phases be revisited often to make adjustments. The process serves as a nationwide framework that is used to develop nursing curriculums, guide programs, and most importantly, help one to make decisions in the field. In short, it should guide everything that the nurse does!

See Instructor's Manual, Chapter 2 Answers.

Questions

1. Which step of the scientific method of problem solving correlates with the development of a nursing diagnosis?
   a. recognizing a problem
   b. collecting data
   c. developing a hypothesis
   d. testing assumptions

2. When using the nursing process, the purpose of writing goals is which of the following?
   a. to identify the individual's responses to nursing interventions
   b. to pinpoint health problems that require nursing interventions
   c. to guide nursing interventions
   d. to differentiate the nurse's role from the physician's

3. During which phase of the nursing process does the nurse identify the individual's progress toward achieving goals?
   a. assessment
   b. analysis
   c. planning
   d. evaluation

4. Which of the following information collected by the nurse is classified as subjective data?
   a. palms cold and clammy
   b. heart rate 120, respiratory rate 24
   c. "I cannot seem to catch my breath."
   d. urine is amber colored

5. Which of the following is a correctly written goal?
   a. teach the patient how to administer own insulin injection
   b. maintain normal bowel elimination
   c. the patient will identify three foods that are high in potassium within two days
   d. the nurse will turn the patient every two hours

6. Teaching a patient how to walk using crutches is an example of what phase of the nursing process?
   a. assessment
   b. analysis
   c. implementation
   d. evaluation

7. An example of a medical diagnosis, in contrast to a nursing diagnosis, is which of the following?
   a. ineffective breathing pattern: hyperventilation related to anxiety
   b. fluid volume deficit related to excessive diarrhea
   c. potential for infection related to open skin (leg cuts)
   d. congestive heart failure and high blood pressure

8. Which characteristic is a distinguishing feature of nursing diagnoses?
   a. builds on medical diagnosis
   b. identifies a response to illness
   c. represents an exhaustive list of all patient health care problems
   d. must be established with patient collaboration

9. What is the primary source of data for a nursing assessment?
   a. the patient
   b. the medical record
   c. the patient's family
   d. the physician

10. Hypothesis development in the scientific method correlates with which phase of the nursing process?
    a. assessment
    b. analysis
    c. evaluation
    d. implementation

11. The focus of the evaluation phase of the nursing process should be on determining which of the following?
    a. if all of the nursing interventions have been completed
    b. if nursing care was implemented safely
    c. the patient's satisfaction with the care received
    d. whether the health care needs of the patient have been met

12. The following goal was set for Mrs. Whitcomb: Drink six 8-ounce glasses of liquid every 24 hours for 4 days. Which evaluation statement indicates the goal was met?
    a. drank 48 ounces of liquid of own choosing today
    b. drank 48 ounces of liquid in 4 days
    c. drank 8 ounces of liquid every day for 4 days
    d. drank 48 ounces of liquid every day for 4 days

13. The nursing interventions selected by the nurse must be based upon which of the following?
    a. scientific rationales
    b. patient preference
    c. nursing intuition
    d. physician orders

14. Which nursing intervention would provide the patient with psychological support?
    a. administering a medication
    b. referral to a dietitian
    c. talking and listening
    d. helping walk to the bathroom

15. The word "etiology" refers to which of the following?
    a. problems
    b. planning
    c. contributing factors
    d. patients

16. Medical regimen refers to which of the following?
    a. administering medications
    b. prescribing drugs
    c. providing treatments
    d. both a and c

17. The nursing process is used for the following.
    a. to develop curriculums
    b. to guide programs
    c. to make decisions in the field
    d. all of the above

18. Providing the patient with a proper diet falls under which category?
    a. medical regimen
    b. physical needs
    c. hygiene
    d. teaching needs

19. Which one phase of the nursing process does not correlate exactly with the scientific method of problem solving?
    a. evaluation
    b. analysis
    c. implementation
    d. planning

20. What is the purpose of the nursing process?
    a. to help identify patient problems
    b. to develop a plan to help the patient deal with those problems
    c. to evaluate the care that is given
    d. all of the above

Model Notes—Lecture 3

Model Notes

The Nursing Process

Date:

An organ. system. approach to meet health care needs of patients.
 ↓ way of thinking & solving med. prob.
 ↓ Purpose: 1) ident. patient problems
   2) develop. plan to help pat. deal with these probs.
   3) evaluate care given

5 steps/phases: Scientific Meth. of Problem Solving
 Assessment ←→ Recog/define prob. Coll. Data
 Analysis ←→ Hypothesis develop.
 Planning
 Implementation ←→ test assumpt.
 Evaluation ←→ Eval. Formulate Conclus

Ass. Phase

Nurse collects objective & subjective data

- Object. data = what nurse sees, hears, feels, smells (heart rate, blood press., resp., sweat)

  Data Resources: pat's med. record
  diag. tests
  journals
  phy. exam

- Subject data = what pat. says (expresses feelings)

  Comes from interview pat. using open-ended quest. (i.e. How are you feeling?)

  * Pat. = primary source of data for nurs. assess.

  Analysis Phase
  ↳ study of data & ident. of problem.
     Etiology (def. = contrib. factors) as well as prob. must be uncovered.

Prob. expressed as nurse. diag — based on pat's response not just med. diag.

After diag. the nurse develops goals which are: patient specific
    measurable
    with def. time frame

Planning Phase
↳ nurse prior & organizes nursing care

Includes possible nursing actions or interventions

Poss. Nurse Intervent.	Categories
talking with/hugging pat.	psych. support
teach progress. muscle relax or how to deep breathe	teach needs
bath/back care	hygiene
remove sharp objects/ prevent. falls	protect. measures

- bringing in another health care team mem. — referrals
  nurse specialist / dietitian

- providing prop. diet / walking help — physical needs

- admin. meds & treatments, not prescript. of drugs — med. regimen

- providing adequate vent. / prop. temp. — envir. adapt.

↓

Not all necess. but nurse often uses many of them.

Implement Phase
Nurse care plan (interventions) put into action * must be based on scientific rationale.

Evaluation Phase
Ongoing →
- → Patients' health care needs being met?
- → Goals being attained?

If not, corrective action taken!

Summary

Process a continuous cycle — not just series of steps ← must be revisited to make adjustments.

Process nationwide framework to:
　develop nursing curr.
　guide programs
most import* help one make decisions in field

Guides everything nurse does!

CHAPTER 3

Effective Test Taking

Chapter Objectives: To present suggestions on taking tests more effectively and avoiding some common mistakes. Also, to give students an additional note taking experience for practice.

The suggestions that deal with effective test taking will be given as a lecture by your instructor so that you have one last practice note-taking experience. Read the material before the lecture begins just like you did for the lecture on "The Nursing Process." Reading before you get to class helps to familiarize you with the subject matter, thereby making it easier for you to listen and take notes.

When you take notes, use the tips and practice the skills that you learned in Chapter 2. When the lecture is over, you will be asked to use your notes to answer questions that show you how well you did with your note taking. The questions also demonstrate some of the very points made in the lecture. After you have finished the questions and your instructor has helped you grade them, you can look again at the actual lecture material to compare it to your notes.

When delivering the lecture, provide any personal experiences that reinforce the suggestions. Encourage students to relate their own experiences and suggestions regarding test taking.

Lecture

Effective Test Taking

Obviously, studying for and taking tests is one of the most difficult tasks performed by college students. To do well requires many hours of hard work, much skill, great care, and a little luck. In fact, test preparation is a nonstop process that includes all of the responsibilities of college life: attending every class, effective note taking, reading all assignments, and continuous review. Success on tests also depends on avoiding careless and costly mistakes. Unfortunately students sometimes prepare well, but end up with low grades because they do not follow directions or because they make foolish errors.

The following suggestions are designed to help you to prepare better for tests and also to avoid some of the more common blunders committed by students. The suggestions are divided into three parts: preparing for the test, taking the test, and what to do after the test.

Preparing for the Test

As already mentioned, test preparation is continuous and involves all of your academic responsibilities. In short, right after you complete a test, you begin preparing for the next one by going to class, taking notes, reading assignments, and reviewing constantly. If you wait until the last minute to prepare, you may be contributing to your own confusion and heightening your own anxiety level.

When your instructor announces that a test is scheduled, make sure that you find out what material will be covered, the type of test that you will be taking, and the length of time the test will be. You cannot prepare adequately if you do not know what to study, and it surely helps to be aware of the kinds of questions that you will have to answer. Tests are objective, essay, or a combination of objective and essay.

If the test is going to be an objective one—that is, true-false, multiple-choice, matching, or fill-in—you need to learn as much specific information as you possibly can. For essay tests, you probably do not have to know every detail. However the more facts you know, the better your answers will be because you will be able to support your statements. You also have to be ready to write out your answers, so as a way of preparing, try to guess the essay questions and write out answers in advance. Furthermore some instructors provide a list of *possible* essay questions for tests. In those instances, it especially pays to write out, or at least outline, answers beforehand.

Avoid going into a test in an overtired state. When you are exhausted you are likely to be anxious and to make careless mistakes. Get enough sleep and eat well so that you can function effectively. Test taking requires great mental effort, so you must be in top form. Finally, when you have prepared well, you can go into the test with a positive attitude, knowing that you have done everything you could and truly believing that "nothing is going to stop you now."

Taking the Test

Make sure that you arrive a few minutes early for the test so that you have time to relax and calm down before it starts. Take a minute to close your eyes and think about your long-range goals. Do not permit other students to make you insecure or nervous! If you have prepared adequately, you can be confident that you will do well. One way to boost your confidence and lower your anxiety level is to look over the entire test before you start so that you see that you know many of the answers.

Chapter 1 stressed the importance of following directions, and doing so in a test situation certainly is crucial. So remember to read written directions at least twice and to underline the key words to help you focus and understand them. Also give your undivided attention to your instructor's oral directions. Finally immediately ask for clarification if you become confused. Of course to get complete directions from the instructor, you must be on time!

As part of the directions, make sure you are aware of the time limit for a test. You have to plan carefully so that you complete all of the questions. Begin with the questions to which you know the answers. You do not want to waste too much time on the ones that may give you trouble. Hopefully with the time limit in mind, you can deal with the troublesome ones later on. Also be aware of the point value of *each* question. Some questions may be worth more than others, and if that is the case, spend more time on those that are worth the most.

Objective questions. As already mentioned, tests are either objective, essay, or a combination of both. Objective questions, which include true-false, multiple-choice, matching, or fill-in, measure your knowledge of very specific information. These kinds of questions require that you read every word very carefully because instructors sometimes omit, add, or change a word that affects the meaning of a statement. For true-false and multiple-choice questions, watch for extreme words like *all, always, every, never, none,* and *only* that are likely to make a statement false or incorrect. Furthermore in a multiple-choice test, make sure that you read *all* of the choices before you select your answer. Look carefully at possibilities that state "all of the above" or "none of the above" for they are often the correct answers. Also when two answers are very similar, that may mean that one of them is likely to be correct. When all else fails, focus on the longest, most complete answer for it could be the right one.

When you deal with matching questions, study both lists carefully so that you know exactly what you are matching. Use the list that contains items with the most information as your base, and try to match those items with the shorter ones on the other list. Cross out items as you match them, and make sure that you know whether you can use an item more than once. In most cases, you cannot.

With fill-in questions, you must determine how many words are needed for each blank. Although a given blank almost always calls for only one word, you cannot make that assumption automatically. If you cannot recall the exact word or words you need to complete a statement, use similar ones. When you finish a question, read it over very carefully to see that it makes sense.

In most instances, do not change your original answer to an objective question; your first response to a question is usually a correct one. Of course if you are *absolutely sure* that you have made a mistake, correct your answer, but do not make a habit of changing your mind. As already mentioned, after you answer all the questions you know, tackle the ones that are giving you difficulty. On most tests you will not lose points for guessing, so do not leave any questions unanswered. Read each question very thoroughly because sometimes one question supplies an answer to another question. Use these suggestions either to help you to eliminate some of the possibilities or point you toward the correct answer. In short, even if you have no idea as to the appropriate answer, it pays to guess as long as you will not be penalized for it: in most cases you will not be penalized.

Essay questions. To do well on an essay test, you not only need to know the information, but you must be able to get your ideas down on paper in a neat, coherent fashion. Your first step is to read each essay question carefully, making sure that you know exactly what the instructor wants. Be aware of the meanings of the following words that are often found on essay tests.

- *Analyze:* to divide into parts and point out the relationship among those parts; in short, to examine very thoroughly
- *Compare:* to examine the characteristics of things or persons in order to determine similarities and differences
- *Contrast:* to examine the characteristics of things or persons in order to determine differences
- *Criticize:* to evaluate something or someone by indicating positive and negative points
- *Define:* to provide a meaning

- *Describe:* to give the characteristics or qualities of something or someone
- *Discuss:* to provide details about something or someone
- *Enumerate:* to provide a listing
- *Evaluate:* to judge the positive and negative aspects of something or someone
- *Explain:* to provide details and make understandable
- *Identify:* to give the characteristics and importance of something or someone
- *Illustrate:* to make clear by providing examples
- *Interpret:* to explain the meaning of something

If you are not sure what the instructor expects you to do, by all means ask him or her.

When you are certain you know what your instructor wants, you are ready for step two, which involves outlining or making a list of all the points you have learned. Sometimes students are so worried about forgetting something that they quickly start answering an essay question just to get the information out of their minds and onto the paper. Because that method often results in sloppy, confusing answers, take the time to first clear your mind before writing out your answer through outlining. The outline or list need not be elaborate, but just enough so that you feel confident that you will not forget what you know.

The third step entails writing out your answer in complete sentences by referring back to your outline or list. Pretend that the person grading your paper knows nothing about the topic—that way you will not leave any gaps in your answers. Also when the test combines both objective and essay questions, you sometimes can use the details contained in the objective questions to help you answer the essay questions. Finally, if you are running short of time and cannot write out a complete essay answer, you may be forced instead to use your outline or list as your answer. At least the instructor will see that you know the information, and he/she may give you partial credit. Never leave an answer blank, because you certainly will not get any points for that.

What to Do after the Test

Always set aside a few minutes to review your test before you turn it in to your instructor. Do not be in a rush to leave the room! Carefully check the front and back of each test page to be certain that you have not missed any questions. Look over the objective questions and your answers to catch careless mistakes. Read your essay answers to make sure that they are clear and legible.

When your graded test is returned to you, find out why any of your answers are wrong. Everyone makes mistakes occasionally, but you want to learn from yours so that you do not make them a second time. Finally, keep all of your test papers handy for review purposes: instructors may ask similar questions on a midterm or final examination. If you are not permitted to keep your papers, make notations in your notebook and textbook to indicate what information was covered by the questions so that you can refer back to it.

Objective Questions

See Instructor's Manual, Chapter 3 Answers. Many of the questions, such as numbers 6, 12, and 16, are tricky in order to demonstrate some of the suggestions and warnings given in the lecture. In reviewing them, point out the "tricks" to students as you reinforce the most important suggestions.

1. Preparation for tests is a _____ process involving all the responsibilities of college life.

2. The responsibilities of college life include which of the following:
   a. attending every class
   b. effective note taking
   c. reading all assignments
   d. continuous review
   e. all of the above
   f. none of the above

3. List two reasons students sometimes end up with low grades even though they prepare well for a test.

   _____

   _____

   _____

   _____

4. Try not to save all of your preparation for the last minute because that can contribute to _____ and

   _____ .

5. When your instructor announces that a test is scheduled, make sure that you find out which of the following?
   a. what material will be covered
   b. the type of test that you will be taking
   c. how long it will be
   d. all of the above
   e. none of the above

6. *True or false:* An objective test consists of true-false, multiple-choice, matching, essay, or fill-in questions.

7. One way to prepare for an essay test is to guess the

   _____ and write out _____ .

8. *True or false:* If you are overtired for a test, it can lead to anxiety and careless mistakes.

9. It is important to take a test with a _____ attitude.

10. You should arrive a few minutes early when you are scheduled to take a test for which of the following reasons?
    a. so that you can study
    b. so that you can talk with your classmates
    c. so that you can ask the instructor questions
    d. so that you can get a good seat
    e. all of the above
    f. none of the above

11. Why is it important to look over the entire test before starting?

    _____

    _____

    _____

    _____

12. *True or false:* You should read written directions once and underline the key words as a way of helping you to understand.

13. What should you do if you become confused by the directions to a test?

   _____

   _____

   _____

   _____

14. To save time on a test, which of the following should you do?
    a. do the questions that you know the answers to last
    b. read the questions very quickly
    c. do the questions that you know the answers to first
    d. try to do the questions that you do not know the answers to
    e. all of the above
    f. none of the above

15. Why should you be aware of the point value of each question on a test?

   _____

   _____

   _____

   _____

16. *True or false:* Questions that contain words such as *all, every, never, none,* and *only* are always false or incorrect.

17. Why should you carefully read every word in an objective question?
    a. instructors sometimes omit a word
    b. instructors sometimes add a word
    c. instructors sometimes change a word
    d. all of the above
    e. none of the above

18. _____ , _____ , _____ , _____ , _____ , and _____ are extreme words that are likely to make a statement false or incorrect.

19. *True or false:* When taking a multiple-choice test, make sure that you read all of the choices before selecting your answer, and look carefully at possibilities that state "all of the above" or "none of the above" for they are always the correct answers.

20. When taking a multiple-choice question test, which of the following should you keep in mind?
    a. It is unnecessary to read all of the choices.
    b. If answers are similar, one must be the right answer.
    c. You should never guess.
    d. When all else fails, focus on the longest, most complete answer for it could be the right one.
    e. All of the above.
    f. None of the above.

21. List four suggestions for matching questions.

22–34. *Matching:* Place the letter of the correct definition from List II next to the appropriate word in List I.

List I   **List II**

___ Interpret   a. to judge the positive and negative aspects of something or someone

___ Explain   b. to make clear by providing examples

___ Criticize   c. to provide a meaning

___ Compare   d. to examine the characteristics of things or persons in order to determine differences

___ Define   e. to provide a listing

___ Illustrate   f. to evaluate something or someone by indicating positive and negative points

___ Identify   g. to give the characteristics and importance of something or someone

___ Evaluate   h. to explain the meaning of something

___ Enumerate   i. to provide details and make understandable

___ Analyze   j. to provide details about something or someone

___ Contrast   k. to examine the characteristics of things or persons in order to determine similarities and differences

___ Describe   l. to divide into parts and point out the relationship among those parts; in short, to examine very thoroughly

___ Discuss   m. to give the characteristics or qualities of something or someone

35. List three suggestions for fill-in questions.

_____

_____

_____

_____

_____

_____

36. *True or false:* You should never change your original answers to objective test questions.

37. *True or false:* In most instances, it is a good idea to guess if you do not know the answer to a question.

38. Read each objective question very thoroughly because sometimes it will supply an _____ to another question.

39. What two factors determine how well you do on an essay test?

    _____

    _____

    _____

    _____

    _____

    _____

40. List the three steps you should use when you answer an essay question.

    _____

    _____

    _____

    _____

    _____

    _____

41. *True or false:* If you are not sure what the instructor expects you to do on an essay test by all means ask a classmate.

42. Which of the following apply when you write out your answer to an essay question?
    a. use complete sentences
    b. refer back to your outline or list
    c. pretend that the person grading your paper knows nothing about the topic
    d. all of the above
    e. none of the above

43. You can sometimes use the details contained in the

    _____ to help you answer the essay questions.

44. What should you do if you are running out of time and cannot write out an essay answer?

45. *True or false:* You should never leave an essay answer blank.

46. After you finish a test, why should you check carefully the front and back of each page?

47. After you complete a test, you should look over the _____ questions and your _____ so that you can catch _____ _____, and read your _____ answers to make sure that they are _____ and _____ .

48. Why is it important to find out the reasons why any of your test answers are wrong?

49. What should you do if you are not permitted to keep your old test papers?

50. *Essay Question:* In your notebook, write an essay that includes the most important test-taking suggestions mentioned in this chapter.

PART 2

Dealing Effectively with Textbook Material

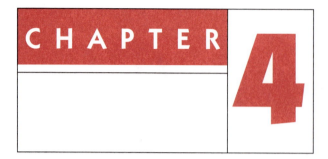

CHAPTER 4

Chapter Objectives: To stress the importance of vocabulary development and to introduce the various methods that can be used to find and learn word meanings.

Vocabulary

An inescapable chore in your college education is to learn new words. Facing that fact and approaching the task in a systematic way is crucial for several reasons. First, on tests instructors will often ask you to define at least the key terms used in their particular subject areas. Second, the more words you know, the easier you will understand both textbook and lecture material. Third, in a general sense, broadening your vocabulary will enable you to become a more effective reader, listener, writer, and speaker. Not only will you comprehend better, but you will also have more words at your disposal to fulfill your responsibilities as a student. Finally, when you graduate you will be better equipped to understand and deal with the world around you.

   This chapter explores four ways of finding the meanings of unfamiliar words: using the context, using word parts, using a glossary, and using the dictionary. The method you employ will depend upon the given situation, and sometimes, on your personal preference. However, when you are comfortable with all the methods, you increase your chances of finding word meanings quickly and efficiently.

Using the Context

Context refers to the setting or the surrounding words in a sentence that give a particular word its specific meaning. As you know, many words have several different possible meanings depending upon how they are used in a given situation. For example, if you are asked to define the word *run,* you probably would say something like "to go someplace rapidly by moving one's legs more quickly than when walking." However, if you are provided with a particular context, such as "She had a run in her stocking.", "The river runs along the southern border.", or "The army will run the blockade.", the meaning of *run* changes dramatically. In short, as a reader you must focus on the context because it can help you to determine specific word meanings.

Punctuation

There are different ways that the context can be useful. The easiest one is when a writer actually provides you with a meaning by separating it from the rest of the sentence through the use of various punctuation marks, such as colons, commas, dashes, and parentheses. In fact, textbooks sometimes use boldface type or italics for key words when they are first defined in context. We will discuss each of the punctuation methods in turn.

Colons

Read the following passages in which the writers use colons.

> The human mind has a number of ingenious ways of dealing with anxiety that do not remove the original problem but that do provide temporary relief from its effects. These various methods of coping have been termed *defense mechanisms:* automatic responses that help one to alleviate or avoid the painful feelings of emotional conflict. (*Essentials of Life and Health,* CRM Books)

The meaning of *defense mechanisms,* which is provided right after the colon, is "automatic responses that help one to alleviate or avoid the painful feelings of emotional conflict."

> In cases of disease or injury, physicians often perform a *splenectomy:* a surgical procedure involving the removal of the spleen, which is located in the upper left part of the abdomen.

Other examples of punctuation, like quotation marks, can be brought up as well.

Once again you find the meaning of *splenectomy* immediately following the colon and right before the comma: "a surgical procedure involving the removal of the spleen."

Commas

Now look at the way the following writers have used the comma to help define a word.

> The monkey was raised with a surrogate, or substitute, mother.

The meaning of the word *surrogate,* which is "substitute," is set off by commas.

> This and chilblains, which is a mild form of frostbite, are a common source of discomfort, particularly to older people who live in cold, damp climates where homes are not always equipped with central heating. (*Introduction to Patient Care,* Beverly W. Du Gas)

Chilblains is also defined between the commas: "a mild form of frostbite."

Dashes

In the following excerpts the writers employ dashes to signal definitions.

> In psychology, such swallowing whole is often called socialization—the process of assimilating and internalizing the rules of one's culture. (*Essentials of Life and Health*)

The definition of *socialization* follows the dash—"the process of assimilating and internalizing the rules of one's culture."

> But the most logical approach, recycling, remains underutilized. It has been estimated that recycling—the reprocessing of used materials for reuse—could provide two-fifths of the materials required in our own manufacturing sector. (*Contemporary Business,* Louis E. Boone and David L. Kurtz)

In this example, the definition of *recycling* is located between two dashes—"the reprocessing of used materials for reuse."

Parentheses

Finally look at how parentheses can be used.

> The problem of pediculosis (head lice infestation) has reached high levels in the United States.

Pediculosis is defined within the parentheses that immediately follow it: "head lice infestation."

> Neurotic behaviors associated with anxiety include phobias (intense fear of an object or situation that the person consciously recognizes as no real danger), obsessive-compulsive behavior (the persistent intrusion of unwanted thoughts, urges, or actions that one is unable to stop even though one may perceive them as absurd), and hypochondriasis (a preoccupation with the body and with fear of presumed diseases, even though the individual is in good health), (*Essentials of Life and Health*)

In this paragraph, the words *phobias, obsessive-compulsive behavior,* and *hypochondriasis* all are defined within the parentheses that immediately follow each.

Other Ways to Use Context

Although punctuation may make it easier to spot the definitions of words, there are other ways, including synonyms, antonyms, examples, and general sentence clues, in which context can help you to determine word meanings. Of course, the punctuation marks just covered often are used in combination with these.

Synonyms

These are words that have the same, or almost the same, meaning.

> Although the Senator clearly was culpable, it was several years before she would actually admit that she was blamable for what happened.

Because *culpable* and *blamable* are synonyms, you can figure out that culpable must mean "deserving of blame."

> Ismail the Magnificent was one of the most ostentatious Egyptian leaders. In fact, he was so showy that he had huge monuments constructed in his honor.

Ostentatious and *showy* are synonyms; therefore ostentatious means "always showing off."

Antonyms

These are words that have the opposite, or almost the opposite, meaning.

> The cathedral was rather ornate, while most of the other architecture of that period was very simple.

Ornate and *simple* are antonyms, so ornate must mean "flashy" or "highly decorative."

> Whereas this particular chemical is detrimental, all of the others used in the experiment are harmless.

Because there is a clear contrast made between *detrimental* and *harmless*, the definition of detrimental is "harmful" or "dangerous."

Examples

> Alcohol, tranquilizers, cocaine, marijuana, opium, and LSD are all psychoactive drugs.

To use examples to figure out word meanings, you at least must know what they have in common. For example, alcohol, tranquilizers, cocaine, marijuana, opium, and LSD all affect the mind; therefore *psychoactive* means "affecting the mind."

> Scientists have concluded that the following are carcinogens: tobacco, asbestos, saccharin, and most air and water pollutants.

If you are aware of the fact that all of the examples above cause cancer, then the definition of *carcinogens* must be "substances that cause cancer."

General sentence clues

> Some criminologists believe that the incarceration of criminals for life has caused problems for the correctional system.

When all else fails, you may be able to determine word meanings by looking carefully at the general sense of the sentence and at some of the key words in it. In this example the use of the words *criminologists, criminals for life,* and *correctional system* plus the general subject matter of the sentence enables us to conclude that *incarceration* means "imprisonment."

> Because they are softer, some metals are more malleable than others, which makes them easier to work with.

The words *softer, metals,* and *easier to work with* along with the general sense of the sentence help us uncover the meaning of *malleable,* which is "bendable" or "flexible."

Exercise 1

Using the context, try to determine the meaning of the words that appear after each of the following passages. Remember first to see if you can find the actual definition between punctuation marks. If you cannot, use one or more of the other contextual methods discussed. Be prepared to indicate the particular methods that you used to find the various word meanings.

See Instructor's Manual, Chapter 4 Answers.

Be sure to have students specify the context method that they used to find word meanings.

1

Urethritis, inflammation of the urethra, is usually an ascending infection. If may be caused by a bacterial or viral infection or by trauma from an indwelling catheter or repeated cystoscopic examinations.

(*Textbook of Medical-Surgical Nursing,* Lillian S. Brunner and Doris S. Suddarth)

urethritis: _____

2

Nomads—Bedouins, or desert Arabs—dwelt with their herds in the neighborhood of Mecca.

(*The Middle East: A History,* Sydney Nettleton Fisher)

Bedouins: _____

3

Breathing in is called inspiration or inhalation.

(*Principles of Anatomy and Physiology*,
Gerard J. Tortora and Nicholas P. Anagnostakos)

inspiration: _____

4

Over five million are of Mexican origin or descent. A growing number of this group, especially the younger people in urban areas, prefer the name "Chicano" rather than "Mexican-American" or Hispano.

(*Business: Its Nature and Environment*,
Raymond E. Glos, Richard D. Steade, and James R. Lowry)

Chicano: _____

5

An unusual type of capitalism is laissez-faire: a term borrowed from the French that means the noninterference of government in the business sector.

laissez-faire: _____

6

Slavery established a ground for the seeds of racism. When, during the late eighteenth century, abolitionists (people who opposed slavery) increasingly denounced the slave trade, advocates of slavery were forced to find new arguments to defend their actions.

(*Patterns of Civilization: Africa,*
The Institute for Contemporary Curriculum Development)

abolitionists: _____

advocates: _____

7

In familiar situations, people learn to follow scripts—the rules governing who will do what and when.

(*Introduction to Psychology,* James W. Kalat)

scripts: _____

8

What was needed was a way to identify the sphere of influence of a city: the area whose inhabitants depend on the central city for jobs, recreation, newspapers, television, and a sense of common community.

(*Sociology,* Rodney Stark)

sphere of influence: _____

9

When researchers first glance at a distribution, they probably look for the range—the difference between the lowest and highest values.

(*Business Communications,* William C. Himstreet, Wayne Murlin Baty, and Carol M. Lehman)

range: _____

10

Philanthropic (charitable) organizations also finance health services, particularly for specific groups in the population, such as the Shriners' hospitals for children and the charitable clinics and hospitals run for the poor.

(*Introduction to Patient Care*)

philanthropic: _____

11

Much of the violent crime in the United States is committed by recidivists, and it is simply amazing that our society lets these habitual criminals back on the street.

recidivists: _____

Using the Context 69

12

Many people with dental malocclusion (crooked teeth) are very self-conscious about their appearance.

malocclusion:_____

13

A loan made to finance the purchase of residential real estate is typically secured by means of a mortgage against such property. The real estate mortgage, in one form or another, has probably been used as long as the right of private property has been recognized. The borrower in such a loan transaction is called the mortgagor; the lender, the mortgagee.

(*Principles of Finance,*
Carl A. Dauten and Merle T. Welshans)

mortgage:_____

mortgagor:_____

mortgagee:_____

Most students—like many people—will define "mortgage" as the loan itself. Make sure that they understand that the mortgage serves as the security for the loan. Use other examples, such as the relationship of the automobile loan to the title of ownership, to bring home the point.

14

The medication was for delirium tremens, a condition induced by alcohol withdrawal and characterized by excessive trembling, sweating, anxiety, and hallucinations.

(*Health Psychology,* Linda Brannon and Jess Feist)

delirium tremens:_____

15

From ages 1 to 2, we can see the beginnings of social play, but still it is mostly parallel play: Two or more infants play at the same time in the same place, but almost independently.

(*Introduction to Psychology*)

parallel play:_____

16

Homeostasis in all organisms is continually disturbed by stress, which is any stimulus that creates an imbalance in the internal environment.

(*Principles of Anatomy and Physiology*)

stress:_____

homeostasis:_____

17

Real wages—or what the wage earner's income would actually buy, even allowing for the losses due to unemployment—are estimated to have risen about 50 percent in the industrialized countries between 1870 and 1900.

(*A History of the Modern World*, R. R. Palmer and Joel Colton)

real wages:_____

18

However, people sometimes learn to dislike themselves because others criticize and reject them. They become distressed by the incongruence (mismatch) between their self-concept and their ideal self.

(*Introduction to Psychology*)

incongruence: _____

19

Ecology is usually defined as the study of the interactions between organisms and their environment. "Environment" is given a very broad meaning here; it is taken to embrace all those things extrinsic to the organism that in any way impinge on it—not only light, temperature, rainfall, humidity, and topography, but also parasites, predators, mates, and competitors. Anything not an integral part of a particular organism is considered part of the organism's environment.

(*Elements of Biological Science,* William T. Keeton)

ecology: _____

environment: _____

extrinsic: _____

20

My brother uses many different condiments on his food, but his favorite ones are mustard, ketchup, and relish.

condiments:_____

21

The major constituent of urine is water. The amount of urine excreted daily by an adult may vary from 500 to 2500 ml (milliliters). The exact amount depends on liquid intake and the amount of water lost through perspiration. Heavy perspiration decreases the volume of urine formed. Coffee, tea, or alcoholic beverages have a diuretic (stimulate formation of urine) effect.

(*Introductory Chemistry,* Robert J. Ouellette)

constituent:_____

excreted: _____

diuretic: _____

Using the Context 73

22

When negotiations do break down, disagreements between union and management representatives may be settled by mediation—the process of bringing in a third party, called a mediator, to make recommendations for the settlement of differences. The final step in settling union-management differences is arbitration—the process of bringing in an impartial third party, called an arbitrator, who renders a binding decision in the dispute. The impartial third party must be acceptable to the union and to management, and his or her decision is legally enforceable. In essence, the arbitrator acts as a judge, making a decision after listening to both sides of the argument.

(*Contemporary Business*)

mediation:_____

arbitration:_____

23

When the fort was enveloped by the Indians on all sides, it was only a matter of time before it fell.

enveloped:_____

24

The chemist converted the liquid into gas by heating it over a slow flame.

converted: _____

25

Whereas Professor Harrington is quite loquacious, Professor Metz is considered to be rather taciturn because he barely says a word.

loquacious: _____

taciturn: _____

26

Both Ottoman strength and the weakness of Ottoman adversaries accounted for these rapid conquests. When the expansion began, *ghazis,* warriors for the faith, were attracted in large numbers to Osman's forces, for he was struggling against Islam's chief enemy at the time—Byzantium.

(*The Middle East Today,* Don Peretz)

adversaries: _____

ghazis: _____

Using the Context 75

27

The scientist was found dead in the hot tub which she used for laboratory experiments. The cause of death was officially attributed to hyperthermia: excessively high body temperature.

hyperthermia:_____

28

Wages paid to employees may be based on the amount of output produced by the worker (a piece wage), the amount of time spent on the job (a time wage), or some incentive added to a time wage or piece wage to reward the employee with extras (such as time off or bonus money) for exceptional performance.

(*Contemporary Business*)

piece wage:_____

time wage:_____

incentive:_____

29

The patient will undergo surgery for a brain aneurysm—a bubble in an artery—sometime tomorrow, and barring complications, should be released from the hospital in two weeks.

aneurysm:_____

30

Swallowing, or deglutition, moves food from the mouth to the stomach.

(*Principles of Anatomy and Physiology*)

deglutition: _____

31

A learning disability—a disorder of one or more of the basic psychological processes used in spoken or written communication—may cause an inability to listen, speak, think, read, write, or calculate. Under federal law, a child is considered learning disabled and entitled to special tutorial assistance if there is a "severe discrepancy" between his or her expected and actual achievement in school.

(*The New York Times*, 7/3/80)

learning disability: _____

discrepancy: _____

32

The physicians decided to treat the cancer with radiation rather than drugs. This change in treatment plans was for the purpose of palliation: to relieve the pain without curing.

palliation: _____

33

Interest groups have generally used two methods to pursue their goals through the judicial process. The first is to initiate suits directly on behalf of a group or class of people whose interests they represent (such suits are commonly referred to as "class actions"). The second method is for the interest group to file a brief as a "friend of the court" (amicus curiae) in support of a person whose suit seeks to achieve goals that the interest group is also seeking.

(*Political Science: An Introduction*,
Richard L. Cord, James A. Medeiros, and Walter S. Jones)

class action:_____

amicus curiae:_____

34

The term "triage" was first described in the *Annals of Military Medicine* as the process of sorting the sick and wounded on the basis of urgency and type of condition presented so that the patient can be properly routed to the appropriate medical area. It is, therefore, right that triage be used in the emergency situations encountered daily in the streets.

(*Principles and Practice of Respiratory Therapy*,
J. A. Young and Dean Crocker)

triage:_____

35

Since the time of John Locke, David Hume, David Hartley, and other British philosophers of the 1660s and 1700s, association (the linking of sensations or ideas) has been regarded as central to all thought processes.

(*Introduction to Psychology*)

association: _____

36

The President and his cabinet have vacillated repeatedly in their public remarks on the foreign-aid bill, sometimes supporting it, while at other times speaking out against it.

vacillated: _____

37

Nicodemus—named for an African prince who became the first slave in this country to buy his freedom—was a mecca for black people during its heyday in the late 1870s. Posters boasting the town's virtues drew men and women who just a few years before had been slaves.

("New Promise for Nicodemus," Angela Bates, *National Parks,* July/August 1992)

Nicodemus: _____

Using the Context 79

38

A shaman, or medicine man, is treating Paiakan's wife for an illness, using plants from the "pharmacy" of the forest. Some of the men are going off on a hunting trip. Women and children bathe in the river as butterflies of brilliant colors swirl across a blue sky. Time seems to stand still, before it races on.

("I Fight For Our Future," Hank Whittemore, *Parade Magazine,* April 12, 1992)

shaman:_____

pharmacy:_____

39

The epidermis, or outer layer of skin, which is made up of dead cells, becomes thickened and leathery. Sebaceous (oil) glands in the face can become greatly enlarged, as if the person had acne.

(*The New York Times,* 10/28/92)

epidermis:_____

sebaceous:_____

40

Gastroenteritis—the word stands for inflammation of the stomach and intestine—has many causes. But in most cases the actual cause is not identified.

(*The New York Times*, 1/9/92)

gastroenteritis:_____

41

Using the words "passed away" instead of died, "senior citizen" instead of aged, "maintenance technician" instead of janitor, and "sanitation worker" instead of garbage collector are all examples of euphemisms.

euphemisms:_____

42

He concluded that love has three main dimensions: intimacy (how well you can talk with and confide in your partner), passion (erotic attraction and the feeling of being in love), and commitment (an intention to continue in the relationship).

(*Introduction to Psychology*)

intimacy:_____

passion:_____

commitment:_____

43

A flexible and inexpensive form of electronic mail is facsimile transmission, or fax. A fax machine reads a document that has been inserted into the machine and transmits the document (text, pictures, and graphics) over telephone lines to another fax machine that receives the message and prepares a printed copy of the document.

(*Business Communications*)

facsimile transmission:_____

transmits:_____

44

The term *ghetto* originated in Venice, where the section of the city in which Jews were required to live was, in late medieval times, called the "borghetto." This word derived from the Italian word *borgo,* which meant "borough," which is a major section of a city. *Borghetto* was the diminutive form meaning "little borough." Over time the word was shortened to *ghetto,* and its use spread to all European languages. Today the term is often applied to any neighborhood occupied by an ethnic or racial minority.

(*Sociology*)

borgo:_____

borghetto:_____

diminutive:_____

ghetto:_____

Exercise 2

Using your textbooks or other sources, bring to class ten examples of words that you were able to define from the context in which they appeared. Your instructor may decide to distribute them to the rest of the class for discussion purposes.

This exercise is effective because it shows students the relevance of context to their work in other classes and to reading in general, as well. Choose some of the examples to distribute to the class.

Using Word Parts

In some instances your knowledge of word parts (roots, prefixes, suffixes) can help you determine the meanings of unfamiliar words. A root is the basic part, or stem, from which words are derived. For example, the root *tang* means "touch," and the word tangible is formed from it. A prefix is a word part or group of letters added *before* a root or word to change its meaning or to create a new word. For instance if we add the prefix *in*—which means "not"—to tangible we get intangible. Thus, we change the meaning from touchable to untouchable. Finally, a suffix is a word part or group of letters added *after* a root or word to create another word or to affect the way a word is used in a sentence. As you saw in the example above, the suffix *ible,* meaning "capable of being," can be added to the root *tang* to form tangible or intangible. Thus, the word intangible is made up of the prefix *in* (not), the root *tang* (touch), and the suffix *ible* (capable of being), which add up to the literal meaning "not capable of being touched." The more roots, prefixes, and suffixes that you know, the greater the likelihood that you will be able to use at least some of them to figure out word meanings.

Exercise 3

Use class discussion to help students who are struggling in figuring out definitions or coming up with examples of their own.

Following are tables that list some of the more common word parts, their meanings, and an example for each. When possible, use the word parts to help you to figure out the definitions of the examples that are unfamiliar to you. Write your definitions in the spaces provided. Also try to come up with an example of your own for each of the roots, prefixes, and suffixes. If you have difficulty coming up with some of the definitions or examples, your instructor or classmates may help you when this exercise is discussed in class.

when this exercise is discussed in class.

Roots

Root	Meaning	Example	Definition	Your Example
aqua	water	aquatic		
audi	hear	audible		
auto	self	autobiography		
bene	good, well	benign		
bio	life	biography		
chron	time	synchronize		
cred	believe	credible		
culp	blame	culprit		
derm	skin	dermatology		
geo	earth	geology		
graph	to write	polygraph		
log	speech	dialog		
micro	small	microbiology		
mort	death	mortal		
ped	foot	pedicure		
phob	fear	claustrophobia		
phon	sound	phonics		
poly	many	polygamy		
port	to carry	transport		
pseud	false	pseudonym		
psych	mind	psychology		
script	to write	Scripture		
spec	to look	spectacles		
therm	heat	hyperthermia		

Prefixes

Prefix	Meaning	Example	Definition	Your Example
a-	not, without	atheist		
ante-	before, in front of	anterior		
anti-	against, opposite	antiseptic		
bi-	two	bilingual		
circum-	around	circumference		

Prefix	Meaning	Example	Definition	Your Example
con-	together, with	congregate		
contra-	against	contraception		
extra-	more than	extraterrestrial		
hyper-	over	hyperactive		
hypo-	under	hypodermic		
il-	not	illegitimate		
im-	not	immobile		
in-	not	inoperative		
inter-	between	interstate		
intra-	within	intrastate		
ir-	not	irrational		
mal-	bad	malignant		
mis-	wrong	misadvise		
mono-	one	monologue		
non-	not	nonprofit		
post-	after	posterior		
pre-	before	prejudice		
pro-	for	proponent		
re-	back, again	recede		
retro-	backward	retroactive		
semi-	half	semiconscious		
sub-	under	subservient		
super-	over	supernatural		
trans-	across	transfer		
tri-	three	tripod		
un-	not	uncivil		

Suffixes

Suffix	Meaning	Example	Definition	Your Example
-able	capable of	readable		
-ar	relating to	solar		
-en	made of	golden		
-er	person who	adviser		
-ful	full of	plentiful		
-fy	to make	pacify		
-hood	condition	bachelorhood		
-ible	capable of	edible		
-ize	to make	sterilize		

Suffix	Meaning	Example	Definition	Your Example
-less	without	penniless		
-logy	study of	sociology		
-ment	state of being	harassment		
-or	person who	conductor		
-ward	direction	westward		

Exercise 4

You now are aware of the definitions for all of the examples provided by the textbook. In your notebook, make up a sentence using each one of them.

For these exercises, call upon students to read their sentences aloud. Make corrections "gently" because these exercises may be difficult for many students.

Exercise 5

Now taking *your* examples, write a sentence in your notebook using each one of them.

Using a Glossary

Glossaries often are found in the back matter—or sometimes within the chapters themselves—of content textbooks dealing with such subjects as business, health, psychology, and sociology. A glossary is alphabetized and provides definitions for the most important terms used in the textbook. Unlike a dictionary, which generally lists several meanings and provides additional important information about each word, a glossary only gives the one meaning that is appropriate for the specific subject matter of that textbook. It also provides definitions for specialized combinations of words generally not found in the dictionary. For example in the sample glossary on the following pages, you will find a definition for *boundary ambiguity*. Although the dictionary does give separate meanings for each of these words, it does not define them when they are used together, as does this particular glossary. In short, glossaries are useful tools because they provide you with a rapid means of finding the appropriate definitions of the most important terms used in a given subject area.

Chapter 4 Vocabulary

Select a few terms from the glossary provided and ask students to define them. Discuss as a class how dictionaries and glossaries differ.

See Instructor's Manual, Chapter 4 Answers.

Exercise 6

Find the meanings of the following words using the pages from the partial glossary beginning on page 88. Write out the definition.

exaggeration principle: _____

_____

_____

_____

anticipatory socialization principle: _____

_____

_____

_____

coping strategies: _____

_____

_____

_____

double bind paradox: _____

_____

_____

_____

allocation principle for resources: _____

_____

_____

deviation amplifying feedback is sometimes called: _____

_____

_____

_____

concrete-symbolic dimension: _____

_____

_____

_____

aftermath phase of violence: _____

_____

_____

_____

cognitive coping strategies: _____

_____

_____

_____

deviation dampening feedback is sometimes called: _____

_____

_____

_____

Glossary

Abstraction dissociated from an object; something relatively nonspecific, generalized, intangible, or obscure—as opposed to being specific, tangible, and concrete.

Abuse an act carried out with the intention of, or perceived as having the result of, hurting another person.

Acute anxiety an intense, usually short-term, emotional response to a stressful situation; generally alleviated when the situation is addressed and coping mechanisms are activated (*see* Anxiety).

Acute stage of family stress the time when a family first confronts a stressor situation; energy is directed toward minimizing its impact by dealing with emotions and collecting information about the problem.

Affect the external expression of emotion; in the family, healthy affect includes expressions of intimacy and nurturance (pronounced af´fect).

Aftermath phase of violence the time when tension is released, and the batterer is contrite and seeks forgiveness.

Alliances the connections that occur when two or more individuals become unusually close and align themselves as a unit (subsystem) within the family.

Allocation the process of assigning resources to various places, situations, or processes, in order to attain goals.

Allocation principle for resources on Foa's model, the closer resources and goals are, the greater the likelihood that the resources can be used to attain the desired goals.

Altruism selfless concern for others, and unselfish behaviors that foster the welfare of others.

Ambivalence feeling two opposite affective states or desires at the same time.

Analogic message message that defines the nature of the relationship between the sender and receiver and is part of a communication that gives digital messages animated life (*see* Digital message).

Anticipatory socialization learning about a role before making a transition into it; prior knowledge and accurate expectation lead to ease of transition.

Anticipatory socialization principle the enhancement of development—through disclosure of information, advice, and experience—for persons involved in a transition.

Anxiety a negative emotion that includes distress or uneasiness of mind caused by apprehension of danger or misfortune.

Artificial reproduction a response to infertility that involves conception of a child through means other than sexual intercourse.

(*Family Science,* Wesley R. Burr, Randal D. Day, and Kathleen S. Bahr.)

Authority (power)-based decision making a method in which the powerful people (usually the males or the parents) determine what to do; useful where there are young children or when an adult is temporarily or permanently incapacitated.

Basic level of fusion the degree to which a given family is customarily involved in its emotional systems to the detriment of its intellectual systems (*see* Fusion).

Boundaries the physical, mental, or emotional barriers between parts of a family system or between the family system and its environment.

Boundary ambiguity occurs when families are uncertain about who is in or out of the family and who is performing what roles within the family system.

Boundary confusion confusion about the rights and obligations associated with family status positions.

Boundary permeability the flexible condition that allows family systems to merge and adjust understood roles while meeting all members' needs.

Calibration the process of monitoring and assessing outputs to see if they are within acceptable standards.

Chronic anxiety an uneasiness, distress, or apprehension that endures for long periods of time.

Chronic anxiety principle the higher the level of chronic anxiety in a relationship system, the greater the strain on people's adaptive capabilities.

Closed family paradigm a cluster of fundamental beliefs about the family that emphasizes continuity, steadiness, and conventional ways of doing things.

Cognitive coping strategies things families can do mentally (intellectually) to help them cope with stress.

Cohesion an established pattern of togetherness, integration, or connectedness between or among people.

Commune "any group of five or more adult individuals (plus children, if any) the majority of whose dyads are not cemented by blood or marriage, who have decided to live together . . . [to focus] upon the achievement of community . . ." (Zablocki, 1980).

Communication a symbolic, transactional process that involves creating and sharing meanings through consistent patterns.

Compartmentalized roles expected behavior patterns with little or no flexibility that can prevent family members from acting or thinking in new ways.

Competition vying with others for supremacy.

Competitive communication messages sent within the family system that produce feelings of competition.

Conceptual framework the context within which ideas are related and have their meaning; the concepts that make up a particular theory or theoretical perspective.

Concrete-symbolic dimension refers to whether a resource is tangible or intangible. Examples of concrete resources are tangibles like houses, cars, stocks, and contracts. Examples of symbolic resources are intangibles like information, status, creativity, and respect.

Conjugal love the love between husbands and wives (*see also* Romantic love).

Consensus-seeking method of decision making a method by which a family keeps working until they find a decision that is emotionally acceptable to everyone.

Conservatism the belief system where people emphasize protecting and maintaining traditional ways of doing things.

Constructivism the philosophical belief that individuals "construct," or create, at least some of their perceptions of reality.

Content regarding rituals, it refers to what is actually done.

Cooperation willingly working or acting together for a common purpose or benefit.

Cooperation principle cooperation will facilitate the attainment of family goals, while competition will disrupt that attainment.

Cooperative communication messages sent in a family system that produce feelings of support and relationship enhancement.

Coping strategies processes, behaviors, or patterns of behaviors that families use to adapt to stress: getting help from others, trying to be adaptable, and learning to accept new realities.

Cybernetic human systems are cybernetic when they behave as if they can think, process information, make choices that influence their life course, and engage in purposive action.

Cycles in the family realm, a complex series of behaviors that ultimately leads to the starting point (*see* Vicious cycles).

Deliberateness a conscious effort to effect change in the family; for example, to reverse a family trend.

Determinism the belief that everything that happens has certain causes and science can discover them; assumes when cause-and-effect patterns are not discernible it is because science has not yet progressed enough to identify the laws that are operating.

Developmental tasks a task that arises at or about a certain period in the life of an individual, successful achievement of which leads to happiness and success with later tasks, while failure leads to unhappiness, disapproval by society, and difficulty with later tasks.

Deviation amplifying feedback the process whereby responses are intended to maintain or increase signaled changes because they are perceived as desirable (sometimes called *positive feedback loops* or *variety feedback loops*).

Deviation dampening feedback the process whereby responses are attempts to decrease or eliminate signaled changes because they are perceived as undesirable (sometimes called *negative feedback loops* or *constancy feedback loops*).

Dichotomy a variable that has two categories or conditions.

Differentiation being able to distinguish the self from the extended family (*see* Fusion).

Digital message the actual words and content of the message.

Disabling rules rules that can cause family members to interact in unhealthy and damaging ways, interfering with the ability to accomplish family goals.

Discipline grows out of the sets of assumptions known as perspectives that discipline scholars to think and study in a particular way; that is, a psychological perspective leads scholars to choose the discipline of psychology within which to work.

Disenchantment also called disillusionment; the loss of emotional attachment and a psychological violation of explicit but unverbalized contracts.

Distance regulation the process by which family members signal when joinings and separations are optimal, tolerable, or intolerable (*see* Emotional distance).

Distinctiveness of rituals the separation by families of their family rituals from their undesirable characteristics or chronic problems (such as alcoholism); when this is done successfully, families are able to disrupt the transition process.

Double bind paradox in family communication, the situation where two conflicting demands are transmitted to a family member, followed by a third demand for family closeness.

Ecosystem in the family realm, the community and environment that surround a family unit.

Egoism concern for self so great that it precludes concern for others (*see* Altruism).

Emotional boundaries the barriers by which we regulate how close emotionally we allow another person to get; in healthy individuals this process is managed almost unconsciously to produce some superficial relationships, some close relationships, and a few intimate relationships.

Emotional coping strategies things families can do to deal with the strong emotional reactions that arise out of stressor events.

Emotional cutoff the process of trying to eliminate, deny, or avoid emotional involvement with the parental family, even though strong involvement and reactivity still exist.

Emotional distance the process used by a family member in transition who disengages emotional, and sometimes physical, attachments to a family system.

Epigenesis principle what is done in earlier transitions and stages tends to influence what can be—and tends to be—done in later transitions and stages.

Epistemology the part of philosophy that deals with how knowledge is acquired and how we can know it is valid; "how we know what we think we know."

Equifinality the idea that "many beginnings can lead to the same outcome, and the same beginning can lead to quite different outcomes" (Bavelas & Segal, 1982).

Exaggeration principle under stress, a family has a natural tendency toward exaggerating its own special character; in problem solving, families will try harder to do more of the same.

Exceptions families have rules that allow the system to deal with the unexpected and regulate necessary behavior even when an important family rule cannot be followed.

Using the Dictionary

The dictionary is a very valuable tool not only for finding word meanings, but also because it provides additional important information about each word, including correct spelling, pronunciation, part of speech (noun, pronoun, adjective, verb, adverb, conjunction, preposition), various endings, and derivation (origin). The derivation, or etymology, of a word refers to its historical development, including what language it came from.

As you know, the dictionary is alphabetized. At the top of each page two boldfaced words appear; these are the first and last entries on that page. Thus, if the word you are looking up fits alphabetically between the guide words on a particular page, you can find it there.

Let us look at a typical entry taken from *The Random House Dictionary*.

> **prim·i·tive** (prim′ i tiv), *adj* [L. *primitivus*, from *primus*, first] **1** being the first or earliest of the kind **2** characteristic of early ages or of an early state of human development **3** simple or crude — *n* **4** a person or thing that is primitive **5** a naive or unschooled artist — **prim′·i·tive·ly**, *adv* — **prim′·i·tive·ness, prim′·i·tiv′·i·ty**, *n* — **prim′·i·tiv′·ism**, *n*

The word *primitive* is located on the dictionary page between the guide words **primary accent** and **principle.** Right after the correct spelling of the word comes the pronunciation (in parentheses). Most dictionaries provide a pronunciation key for the symbols that they use, which usually is located either at the front or on the bottom of the individual pages. The next entry tells us the part of speech; *primitive* is an adjective. The derivation of the word—located within the brackets—is Latin from *primitivus* which comes from *primus,* meaning first. Five definitions follow, the last two of which are for when *primitive* is used as a noun. Finally, the various endings are provided. These endings change the part of speech of the word to an adverb or a noun. Most dictionaries furnish a key in the back that explains the abbreviations used for such things as parts of speech and derivation.

As you can see, dictionaries provide much valuable information about words that can be very useful as you make your way through college. If you do not own a dictionary, purchase one immediately, and refer to it often. In fact, you should buy two dictionaries—an unabridged, hardcover one for use at home and a smaller, paperback one to carry with you while you are at school! Also, the school library has very large dictionaries that come in very handy when you are studying there.

Exercise 7

Use your dictionary to answer the following questions.

1. Which of the following words would you find on a page with the guide words **narrative–natural**?

   narrow   narthex   natural history
   nativism   natural gas   nascent
   nasalize   narrator   naturalism
   narrate   nationwide   natty

2. Find and write down the correct spellings for the following words.

   nationalise: _____   salamandar: _____

   premrose: _____   slouche: _____

   envesion: _____   bressiere: _____

   Finding the correct spelling for the words may be difficult for students, so explain to the class that this often requires trial and error.
   See Instructor's Manual, Chapter 4 Answers.

3. Write out the pronunciation guide for each of these words.

   chamois: _____   mullah: _____

   kamikaze: _____   hacienda: _____

   ubiquitous: _____   decimate: _____

4. Indicate the parts of speech for the words below.

   confluence: _____   deposit: _____

   insolvable: _____   truly: _____

   within: _____   an: _____

5. Provide the derivation for each of the following words.

   terrapin: _____   laudable: _____

   voodoo: _____   geriatrics: _____

   tapioca: _____

6. Give the various endings for these words.

   demolish: _____   asphyxiate: _____

   vibrate: _____   condense: _____

   obfuscate: _____   sage: _____

7. Write out the definitions for the words listed below.

   apathy: _____

   bourgeois: _____

   conservative: _____

   entrepreneur: _____

   heterogeneous: _____

   homogeneous: _____

   liberal: _____

   metabolism: _____

   neurosis: _____

   physiological: _____

   psychosis: _____

   prognosis: _____

   verbose: _____

   whimsical: _____

   zealous: _____

Learning and Reviewing Vocabulary Words

Whether you use the context, word parts, a glossary, or the dictionary to find the meanings to the most important words that you encounter in college, it is a good idea to keep a written record of them either in a notebook or on note cards. Writing them down helps you to learn, remember, and review them for tests without having to look them up again. In addition to writing down the definitions, always include the sentences in which the words appeared so that you are aware of the context and indicate what textbooks or other sources they came from.

Exercise 8

Following the format below, start a vocabulary notebook by recording in your notebook 25 unfamiliar words that you come across while reading your textbooks or various other sources. If you prefer, you may use note cards instead.

Model

Name of textbook or other sources: _____

Word	Context	Definition
____	____	_____
____	____	_____
____	____	_____
____	____	_____
____	____	_____
____	____	_____
____	____	_____

As in Exercise 2, this exercise illustrates the relevance and practical applications of this text material. If time permits, suggest that students share their vocabulary notebook words with other classmates taking the same content classes.

Emphasize strongly the importance of learning the key terminology in every single course and the value of the vocabulary notebook for accomplishing that.

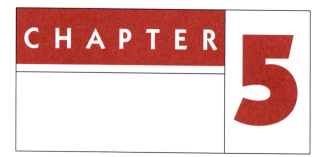

Finding Topics and Main Ideas

Chapter Objectives: To emphasize the importance of topics and main ideas and to provide suggestions for finding them. Also, to introduce and help students differentiate between major and minor details.

Paragraphs are made up of sentences that serve as main ideas, major details, and minor details. The main idea is very important because it is the summary statement that discloses the overriding theme of most—if not all—of the remaining sentences in a paragraph. Thus, it provides the general overall message of a given paragraph. Details, on the other hand, are much more specific; they provide additional information or support for the main idea. As a reader you must be able to recognize the main idea of every paragraph so that you can uncover the message the author wants to give you.

When you look for the main idea, first find the topic of a paragraph. The topic, which is not a sentence, can be stated in a word or a phrase that can serve nicely as a title. It is so related to the main idea that it usually is mentioned in that sentence. In short, the topic is the subject matter of the sentences in a paragraph, and it is therefore the answer to the question: *What (who) is this paragraph about?*

Once you know the topic of a paragraph, you must try to find the sentence or sentences that provide the general message regarding that topic. Sometimes that message is not stated explicitly in any sentence, so you have to put it into your own words. Whether stated or unstated, always express the main idea in sentence form. It answers the question: *What is the overall message regarding the topic of this paragraph?*

Occasionally, certain phrases and words, such as "in short," "in brief," "in summary," "in fact," "clearly," "thus," "yes," and "as these examples show," introduce the main idea. Be on the look out for them. Major and minor details, which will be discussed thoroughly in the next chapter, are sometimes preceded by the words "for example" or "for instance," because details generally are examples or instances of something. Look carefully for the main idea directly above those words! Finally, simple lists of sentences that begin with such words as "first," "second," "third," and "finally" are often major details, and you usually can find the main idea just before the first item on those lists. A "simple listing of facts" is a common pattern of organization.

Emphasize the relationship between the topic and the main idea. Feel free to add to the list of words that introduce main ideas and those that often come before details.

The Main Idea as the First Sentence

In most instances the main idea is stated somewhere in a paragraph, but not always in the same place. The most obvious location to look for it is in the first sentence, as in the following paragraph.

> A database is similar to a filing system. It is useful for compiling non-numerical data that is to be used as a basis for a list (like a mailing list), that is to be sorted, or to be a source of information. For example, a database is a good tool for sorting and preparing a mailing list, and it is a particularly good tool for performing special operations on the list. For example, if you wanted to mail the same letter to many people (maybe 100 or more) with different addresses and have each correct address typed on each letter, or if you wanted to sort the letters alphabetically or according to zip code and produce mailing labels as well, then a database program is what you need.
> (*Fundamentals Of Computer Education,* Janice L. Flake, C. Edwin McClintock, and Sandra Turner)

We can state the topic of this paragraph simply as "A Database" because that is what the paragraph is about. It answers the question: What (who) is this paragraph about? We can find the main idea by asking and answering the second question: What is the overall message regarding "A Database"? The first sentence provides the overall message regarding the topic: "A database is similar to a filing system." That sentence generalizes or sums up the rest of the paragraph, which consists of details that tell us how or why a database is similar to a filing system. Take note that two of the detail sentences are preceded by the words "for example," which may help readers to locate the main idea.

The Main Idea as the Last Sentence

Finding the main idea would be very easy if it were always the first sentence, but unfortunately, that is not the case. Look at the following paragraph where the main idea is presented in the last sentence.

> In the public mind, anthropology is often seen as a search for the world's "last surviving Stone Age tribes," lost cities, or the bones of remote human ancestors. But with fewer such tribes, cities, and bones left to discover, so the conventional reasoning goes, anthropologists will soon be left with nothing to do. As it turns out, nothing could be farther from the truth; anthropologists will be busy far into the future studying their own and other cultures. (*Cultural Anthropology,* William A. Haviland)

Once again, by asking and answering the two questions that we have been using, we should be able to locate the topic and main idea. The paragraph is about "Anthropology" so that is its topic. In this case the last sentence serves as the overall message regarding that topic: "Anthropologists will be busy far into the future studying their own and other cultures." Notice how the author begins the paragraph by telling us how the public views anthropology, but then informs us that that view is not true by stating that ". . . nothing could be farther from the truth. . . ." He then proceeds to give his overall message, which of course, is the main idea. Authors sometimes use that negative technique to lead us to the overriding point that they wish to make, so watch carefully for it. Another technique used commonly by authors is to begin a paragraph or paragraphs by asking a question. They then proceed to answer the question with a general statement that often is the main idea. You will encounter examples of these techniques in some of the passages in Exercise 1.

The Main Idea Between the First and Last Sentences

The main idea also can be located somewhere between the first and last sentences.

> Discuss your job offer with several professors who are knowledgeable about the employer or the work itself. You might also ask the opinion of several of the people whom you interviewed when you were exploring your interests and comparing them with career profiles. Still, regardless of how many outside opinions you seek out, the final decision is yours and it may be the most

profound one of your life. We do not mean to imply that you will be locked into this employer or career for the rest of your life. You may change employers several times during your career if competitors offer faster advancement, greater challenge, more responsibility, or (naturally) more money. Furthermore, you may decide to pursue an altogether different career some time in the future, as time and experience change your preferences, interests, and personal priorities. Those things change naturally as part of the adventure called life. Whatever your present or future goals, though, we wish you good luck and good job hunting! (*Introduction to Business,* Joseph T. Straub and Raymond F. Attner)

The topic of this paragraph can be stated as "Deciding Whether to Accept a Job Offer" because that is what most of the sentences are about. With regard to the main idea, most of the details point to the sentence: "Still, regardless of how many outside opinions you seek out, the final decision is yours and it may be the most profound one of your life." It is the only statement in the paragraph that sums up the overall message regarding the topic, and it is supported by details located on both sides of it. Remember that the main idea can be found in any sentence of a paragraph.

The Main Idea as Two Sentences

Sometimes a writer uses two sentences to express the main idea, as in the following example.

> All living things must reproduce their kind. Single-celled organisms may split in half; other simple animals send reproductive cells out into their watery environment in hopes that these cells will encounter and unite with similar cells from another animal of the same species. In the higher levels of organisms, reproduction occurs when males introduce sperm directly into the female body. What is unique about humans as higher animals is that this act can be separated from reproduction—people can participate in sexual activity without being motivated to produce offspring. This is because the sexual act not only brings pleasure but also represents an ultimate statement of love and affection for another human being. (*Essentials of Life and Health*)

The topic of the paragraph is "Reproduction," and one of the main ideas is stated in the first sentence: "All living things must reproduce their kind." That statement is followed by details that provide examples of how various living things reproduce. However, the author adds a second message in the middle sentence that states: "What is unique about humans as higher animals is that this act can be separated from reproduction—people can participate in sexual activity without being motivated to produce offspring." That statement, in turn, is followed by a detail that explains why people participate in sexual activity. If a reader did not spot that second main idea, he or she would come away from the paragraph with only half a message, which of course, would result in an incomplete understanding.

When an author uses two sentences to express the main idea, those sentences can be located almost anywhere in a given paragraph. For instance, they can be together, such as the first or last two sentences, or as in our example, they can be separated by details. Therefore, you must look carefully at each paragraph you read to determine: if there are two sentences that sum up the details, or if two general statements seem to be a logical continuation of each other, or if the overall message of a particular paragraph changes and goes in a somewhat different direction. Obviously, it is much easier to deal with a main idea stated in only one sentence.

A Main Idea That Covers More Than One Paragraph

There are occasions when a main idea provides the overall message for more than one paragraph.

> A market is people—but people alone do not make a market. A car dealer would be unimpressed by news that 60 percent of a marketing class raised their hands in response to the question: "Who wants to buy a new Mazda RX7?" More pertinent would be the answer to this question: "How many of them have the funds for the down payment?" A *market* requires not only people and willingness to buy but also purchasing power and authority to buy.
>
> A successful salesperson quickly learns how to pinpoint which individual in an organization or household has the authority to make particular purchasing decisions. Without this knowledge, too much time can be spent convincing the wrong person that the product or service should be bought. (*Marketing*, David L. Kurtz and Louis E. Boone)

The topic here can be stated as "A Market" because that is what both paragraphs are about, while the best statement of the overall message is found in the last sentence of the first paragraph: "A market requires not only people and willingness to buy but also purchasing power and authority to buy." Notice how the first paragraph provides details regarding "people," "willingness to buy" and "purchasing power" as aspects of a market, while the second paragraph is concerned with "authority to buy." The main idea statement thus sums up, in a very concise way, the overall message of both paragraphs, even though it is located in a rather strange place. Needless to say, a main idea covering more than one paragraph can be found almost anywhere, so it may not be easy to recognize. Therefore, make sure that the statement you select is broad enough to take in at least most of the details of the combined paragraphs.

Unstated Main Ideas

As mentioned, there are times when the overall message of a paragraph or paragraphs is not stated. In other words, only details are provided, with no sentence general enough to sum them up. On these occasions, you have to look carefully at the details to determine what they have in common. For example, read the following paragraph.

> In Susan's case, there was not unanimity regarding high quality teaching skills, and little evidence was to be found regarding either scholarship or strong commitment to the College. In addition, reports from the counseling staff were not favorable, indicating student complaints and a failure to cooperate in meeting with counselors to discuss student problems. These reports fly in the face of the highly positive student comments found in the clinical evaluation questionnaires. Furthermore, two of the three tenured faculty in the Nursing Department do not support Susan's retention, which in itself can be very damaging to any program. They view her as lacking expertise in any particular area and as not genuinely committed to students. Although the Director of Nursing supports the reappointment, she is not at all certain that Susan is tenurable. In fact, during my discussions with the Director, she was rather emphatic in stating that Susan is not in the same league as two of the other three untenured faculty in that program.

The topic of the paragraph is "Susan" because virtually all of the sentences deal with her. In other words, "Susan" is clearly the answer to the question: What (who) is this paragraph about? However, no one statement sums up the sentences by answering the question: What is the overall message regarding "Susan"? In a situation like this we first must determine how the details are similar to uncover the main idea. Because almost all of the sentences present negative points regarding Susan's performance as a faculty member, an accurate main idea can be expressed something like: "Susan is not a high quality faculty member," or "Susan is only a mediocre faculty member." When you deal with unstated main ideas, of course, you do have leeway regarding your choice of words, as long as they express, in a general sense, the

Chapter 5 Finding Topics and Main Ideas

message supported by the details in the paragraph. Most of the time paragraphs have stated main ideas, but when they do not, you must still come away with an overall message.

Exercise 1

Find the topics and main ideas of the following passages. Remember, the topic is the subject matter that you state in a word or phrase that can serve as a title. It is the answer to the question: What (who) is this paragraph about? On the other hand express the main idea as a sentence: it answers the question: What is the overall message regarding the topic of this paragraph? When you look for the main idea, you must determine whether it is stated. If it is unstated make up a sentence that expresses best the overall message supported by most of the details. Also remember that stated main ideas sometimes involve two sentences rather than just one.

> Because the passages vary in difficulty and subject matter, you can select those appropriate to the skill level and interests of your students. Have students discuss and justify their topic and main idea selections.
> See Instructor's Manual, Chapter 5 Answers.

1

Using word processing in the classroom is not without its problems. At first, students' lack of familiarity with the keyboard will make text entry slow. In many schools, keyboarding skills and touch typing are being introduced in the elementary school curriculum. Even when students can type reasonably well, word processing requires a lot of individual computer time. And giving adequate computer time can be a problem, because few elementary schools have more than one or two computers per classroom. Also, having something go wrong on the word processor can be frustrating to students. Selecting software with plenty of safety features can minimize problems, and peer instruction can relieve pressure on the teacher.

(*Fundamentals of Computer Education*)

Topic: _____

Main Idea: _____

_____

2

Most of us think of teachers as persons who work directly with students and facilitate their learning. In addition, however, teachers spend considerable time managing the instructional process. Teachers are responsible for preparing lesson plans; collecting attendance data; developing, administering, and scoring tests; analyzing student-performance data and prescribing the next appropriate instructional activity; completing periodic grade reports; and preparing reports for the central office.

(*Fundamentals of Computer Education*)

Topic: _____

Main Idea: _____

_____

3

For years it was believed that our natural resources were free goods which, although wasted and exploited, would be replenished by nature. This nation did not recognize that it was destroying the ability of nature to maintain a balanced ecological system. Today many of our lakes and streams are too polluted to support plant and fish life. In strip-mine areas, the wasted land lies barren. Energy sources that took nature thousands of years to create are consumed within minutes. As indicated by these few examples, a realistic program of environment and energy conservation should be adopted by every business.

(*Business: Its Nature and Environment*)

Topic: _____

Main Idea: _____

_____

In Exercise 1, note that Selections 2 and 3 employ the negative technique discussed. Selections 7, 8, 18, and 19 are examples of passages that begin with a question. Those questions should help lead students to the topic and main idea. Remind students to review the chapter introduction, in which both the opening question and the negative technique are discussed.

Many students might regard Selection 4 as sexist, which could lead to some lively classroom discussion. Ask students to offer their opinions and supporting reasoning regarding this passage. (Note that the source of this passage was published in 1973, as indicated in the credits at the end of this textbook.)

4

Fundamentally, history is the story of men's efforts to get along with one another. It is as simple as that. But men have not found the problem of getting along together a simple one. At times they have tried to solve it with clubs and knives and arrows, with guns and tanks and poison gas. They have also sought through peaceful intercourse to overcome fear and suspicion of one another to the end that each might enjoy the fruits of his daily labor with some degree of security and safety.

(*World History*, Joseph Reither)

Topic: _____

Main Idea: _____

_____

5

Architecture, sculpture, and painting are the most permanent of the arts. Music and dance are the most perishable. Cave paintings and pyramids survive, but the music and dance of the ancient world are lost completely. Even with the music of much later times, where we have a great deal of material, we "have" it in a strikingly incomplete way. People think they know how a Beethoven sonata should sound, and they may indulge in fine points of criticism of someone's performance of it—but when we stop to think, we should ask: How did it actually sound to Beethoven? How do we know? It will be well to take up some of these questions at the outset of our study of music history, in order to understand some of its problems and peculiarities.

(*A History of Art and Music,* H. W. Janson and Joseph Kerman)

Topic: _____

Main Idea: _____

_____

6

Whenever Mary Jane and her husband have an argument, she begins to feel dizzy and to experience tight feelings in her chest. Jim has missed most of his major exams this semester—he always seems to get the flu or a bad cold at the wrong time. Gary sometimes wakes in the middle of the night with asthma attacks and has to be rushed to the hospital—adding another problem to his already stressful life. Ruth's doctors are puzzled by the fainting spells she has from time to time—usually after losing her temper and screaming at her children.

(*Essentials of Life and Health*)

Topic: _____

Main Idea: _____

_____

7

What makes people happy? The answer is more elusive than you might expect. Common sense tells us that people are happy when more good things than bad things happen to them. You are happy when you earn a promotion at work or a good grade at school, when you win an award, or when you receive a compliment. You are also happy when you rid yourself of a worry that made you unhappy—remember the opponent-process principle. For example, you become happy when you discover that the $500 fine you received for overdue library books was a mistake.

However, such events make people happy only for a little while. Most people do not become permanently depressed because of a single tragic event, and hardly anyone becomes permanently happy because of a single good event. A person who won a lottery a few years ago is not significantly happier than most other people are; a person whose spinal cord was badly injured a few years ago is only a little less happy than others are. As the novelist Fyodor Dostoyevsky wrote concerning his years in prison, "Man is a creature that can get used to anything, and I think that is the best definition of him!"

(*Introduction to Psychology*)

Topic: _____

Main Idea: _____

_____

8

What is the particular problem you have to resolve? Defining the problem is the critical step. The accurate definition of a problem affects all the steps that follow. If a problem is defined inaccurately, every other step in the decision-making process will be based on that incorrect point. A motorist tells a mechanic that her car is running rough. This is a symptom of a problem or problems. The mechanic begins by diagnosing the possible causes of a rough-running engine, checking each possible cause based on the mechanic's experience. The mechanic may find one problem—a faulty spark plug. If this is the problem, changing the plug will result in a smooth-running engine. If not, then a problem still exists. Only a road test will tell for sure. Finding a solution to the problem will be greatly aided by its proper identification. The consequences of not properly defining the problem are wasted time and energy. There is also the possibility of hearing "What, that again! We just solved that problem last month, or at least we thought we did."

(*Introduction to Business*)

Topic: _____

Main Idea: _____

_____

Unstated Main Ideas

9

There is a reason the Olympics are held every four years. It takes time to develop champions worthy of the ideal. And there is something in the human spirit that compels these athletes to go for the gold—no matter how often they may have gone for it in the past. Consider the two American athletes, a man and a woman, who made their last dash to Olympic glory as part of gold-medal relay teams whose performances stood the track stadium on its collective ear. The anchorman on the men's team that set a world record was only an alternate when the games began. A team member's injury gave him his chance. No matter. With baton in hand, his heart and feet carried him away from the field to sweet victory—which he then dedicated to his fallen teammate.

(*The New York Times*, 8/13/92)

Topic: _____

Main Idea: _____

_____

10

College students have to go to class for several hours each day. When in class, they are expected to listen very carefully to instructors and take many pages of notes. Also, they are required to spend much time reading some rather difficult textbooks that deal with various subjects. In addition, students have to put aside a few hours each day in order to do homework and to study in preparation for tests which come all too often. On top of all of this, they are often required to write essays and research papers.

Topic: _____

Main Idea: _____

_____

11

Analogies can hamper thinking, however. Once you think of things in terms of one relationship, it can be hard to think of them in terms of any other. You can forget that any pair of items has many possible relationships. Suppose someone said that a teacher's use of chalk is like a bookkeeper's use of a quill pen. In this case, the *teacher/chalk* relationship is no longer simply that between a person and a tool the person uses. The analogy with the bookkeeper and the quill pen suggests that there is something old-fashioned and out-of-date about a teacher using chalk.

Or, suppose that someone said that a teacher and chalk were like an artist and paint. Now the chalk is no longer being thought of as a tool at all (whether old-fashioned or not), but as an artistic medium through which something pleasing is created.

In short, an analogy can be a trap if you think it sums up all the relationships between two objects. You can, however, open up your thinking if you use analogies imaginatively to help you find and think about relationships.

(*Developing Creative and Critical Thinking,* Robert Boostrom)

Topic: _____

Main Idea: _____

_____

12

We can remember as preteens or early teenagers talking about love with our peers and wondering how we would know when it happened. At times we felt certain that what we were feeling was love—only to decide, in light of the broken romance, that is was just "infatuation." Occasional discussion with adults elicited a series of homilies about not letting the heart rule the head. A married cousin, perhaps speaking from experience, advised, "Never date anyone you wouldn't consider marrying." The point was clear: one might fall in love with someone with whom marriage was inappropriate. Parental words of wisdom ranged from "It's as easy to fall in love with a rich person as a poor one" to "Don't worry about it. When love hits, you'll know it." None of this advice seemed very helpful. Even so, we all knew that whatever love was, it was *very* serious.

(*Marriage and the Family,* Marcia Lasswell and Thomas Lasswell)

Topic: _____

Main Idea: _____

_____

13

The departments of anesthesiology and internal medicine usually assume the medical direction of the respiratory therapy department. Historically, many respiratory therapy departments have been organized under the direction of anesthesiologists. This was due in part to the fact that the pulmonary physiologic abnormalities of patients require a basic understanding that practitioners of both fields have in common. In addition, there is similarity in the equipment used in both fields. Another important factor is the presence of the anesthesiologist in the hospital for extended periods of time. Thus, his availability for such day-to-day tasks is considered somewhat ideal.

(*Principles and Practice of Respiratory Therapy,*
J. A. Young and Dean Crocker)

Topic: _____

Main Idea: _____

_____

14

Mendel was a monk, and later the abbot, at the monastery of Brünn, in what is now Czechoslovakia. For his experiments he used ordinary garden peas, which he grew in the monastery garden. Peas have one great advantage for genetic experiments: they can be cross-fertilized or self-fertilized, as the experimenter wishes. The shape of a pea flower is such that the pollen of one flower usually fertilizes the egg of the same flower; however, by removing the male flower parts and transferring pollen by hand from one plant to another, any given pea plant may be used to fertilize any other plant.

(*Exploring Biology,* Pamela S. Camp and Karen Arms)

Topic: _____

Main Idea: _____

_____

15

You are most certainly entitled to your opinions, and as a student, you are often expected to evaluate what you read. However, you must be careful not to let your beliefs interfere with learning. I am writing about this problem from personal experience. One of my students once refused to read a chapter on the dangers of cigarette smoking because she believed that these dangers have been greatly exaggerated. I explained to her that in college, students are often required to read, learn, and remember information even if they do not agree with it. Furthermore, I stressed that not only would she have to read that particular chapter, but that the class would be tested on that material as well. After some thought, the student was able to overcome her personal feelings, and in fact, she did well on the test. This was a difficult task and one that seemed to her to be unfair. It is not an easy matter to have to control your opinions or to ignore life experiences that contradict what you read. Your viewpoint, preferences, and experiences are very important, but you must try to keep an open mind when reading textbooks.

Topic: _____

Main Idea: _____

_____

16

Suppose your school or department has budgeted $1500 to buy software, and you have been asked to recommend purchases. You already have a good supply of software for using the computer as a tool, and now you want to buy some instructional software. You have catalogs from about ten software publishing companies listing hundreds of programs for your computer, with prices ranging from $25 to over $500. But your school's experience in basing its software selection on catalog descriptions has not been altogether successful. Of the six programs purchased last year, only one is in demand by students and teachers. The others seem to be collecting dust in the closet.

This year you want to become more selective. When possible, you plan to order software for a 30-day preview. And to decide on those that are worth previewing, you want to read several reviews written by educators like yourself.

Where can you find reliable software reviews? What criteria are appropriate for the evaluation of software? How can you proceed in reviewing educational software?

(*Fundamentals of Computer Education*)

Topic: _____

Main Idea: _____

_____

17

The danger of their work makes police officers especially attentive to signs of potential violence and lawbreaking. Throughout the socialization process, the recruit is warned to be suspicious, to be cautious, and is told about fellow officers who were shot and killed while trying to settle a family squabble or write a ticket for speeding. In 1990, seventy-six officers were killed in the line of duty, a figure much lower than the average yearly number. The folklore of the corps emphasizes that officers must always be on their guard. They must look for the unusual, including everything from persons who do not "belong" where they are observed to businesses open at odd hours. They must watch for and interrogate persons, including:

- those known to the officer from previous arrests, field interrogations, and observations;
- emaciated-appearing alcoholics and narcotics users, who may turn to crime to pay for their habit;
- anyone who fits the description of a wanted suspect;
- known troublemakers near large gatherings;
- persons who attempt to avoid or evade the officer, who are visibly "rattled" when near the officer, and who exhibit exaggerated unconcern over contact with the officer;
- "lovers" in an industrial area (make good lookouts);
- persons who loiter about places where children play or around public restrooms;
- persons wearing a coat on a hot day;
- cars with mismatched hubcaps, or dirty cars with clean license plates (or vice versa);
- uniformed "deliverymen" with no merchandise or truck

With these as examples, it is not hard to understand how police officers become suspicious of everyone and all situations.

(*The American System of Criminal Justice,* George F. Cole)

Topic: _____

Main Idea: _____

_____

18

With human beings, why does mothering often seem to come naturally to women but not to men? People, like monkeys, are influenced by early socialization experiences—messages and experiences provided for us by other people to direct our growth in particular directions. Girls are frequently given dolls before they are old enough to stand, and practice caretaking roles to prepare them for the traditional feminine roles they will assume once they are adults. It is not surprising that many women seem to take to the mothering role "naturally" once they have children. If the Pittsburgh Steelers had all been urged into changing diapers and caring for younger siblings in their preteen years, and then been given jobs as baby-sitters during adolescence, they, too, might "naturally" fit the mothering role.

(*Psychology,* Spencer A. Rathus)

Topic: _____

Main Idea: _____

_____

19

What, then, are the realities? There is a distinction which it is important to make in any discussion of Islam. The word "Islam" is used with at least three different meanings, and much misunderstanding can arise from the failure to distinguish between them. In the first place, Islam means the religion taught by the Prophet Muhammad and embodied in the Muslim revelation known as the Qur'ān. In the second place, Islam is the subsequent development of this religion through tradition and through the work of the great Muslim jurists and theologians. In this sense it includes the mighty structure of the Sharī'a, the holy law of Islam, and the great corpus of Islamic dogmatic theology. In the third meaning, Islam is the counterpart not of Christianity but rather of Christendom. In this sense Islam means not what Muslims believed or were expected to believe but what they actually did—in other words, Islamic civilization as known to us in history. In discussing Muslim attitudes on ethnicity, race, and color, I shall try to deal to some extent at least with all three but to make clear the distinction between them.

(*Race and Slavery in the Middle East,* Bernard Lewis)

Topic: _____

Main Idea: _____

_____

20

If you visit a mental hospital, you will notice that many patients stroll up to the nurses' stations several times a day, toss pills from small paper cups into their mouths; and swallow them with some water. Some patients have been taking the same pills for up to twenty years. Some patients take the pills to help them cope with feelings of anxiety that arise from day to day, some to lift themselves out of fearsome depressions, some to reduce violent agitation. Occasionally patients take pills because they, and perhaps the hospital staff, are afraid to find out what will happen if they do not take the pills.

(*Psychology*)

Topic: _____

Main Idea: _____

_____

21

You go to the beach, looking forward to an afternoon of swimming and surfing. Someone tells you that a shark attacked two swimmers yesterday and has just been sighted close to shore. Do you venture into the water? What if the shark attack occurred a month ago, and no shark has been seen in the area since then? Now would you go in? What if no shark has attacked anyone in this area, but someone saw a small shark there a few days ago?.

What if no shark has ever been seen within 50 miles of this particular beach, but recently you read a magazine story about shark attacks?

How much fear and caution is normal? Staying out of the water because you see a shark is perfectly reasonable. Staying out of the water because of sharks you have read about is, by most people's standards, excessively cautious. If you refuse even to look at photographs of the ocean because they might remind you of sharks, you have a serious problem indeed.

It is normal to have a certain amount of fear and to avoid situations that might provoke fear. But excessive fear and caution are linked to some of the most common psychological disorders.

(*Introduction to Psychology*)

Topic: _____

Main Idea: _____

_____

22

What is striking about crime in the United States is that the problem is so much greater than it is in other industrialized countries. In per capita terms, about ten American men die by criminal violence for every Japanese, Austrian, German, or Swedish man; about fifteen American men die for every English or Swiss man; and over twenty for every Dane. More than 150 countries, both developed and undeveloped, have lower murder rates than the United States, as shown in Figure 1.2. When we look at robbery rates, the data are even more dismaying. The robbery rate for New York City is five times greater than London's and, incredibly, 125 times higher than that of Tokyo. In the 1980s crime in the United States stabilized at a very high level; however, by the 1990s arrests for drug sales and possession had skyrocketed, causing dislocations in many parts of the criminal justice system. As the twentieth century draws to a close, our thoughts turn to the future. Will crime remain at today's levels? What will be the focus of criminal justice policies?

(*The American System of Criminal Justice*)

Topic: _____

Main Idea: _____

_____

23

Whereas anatomy and its branches deal with structures of the body, physiology deals with FUNCTIONS of the body parts—that is, how the body parts work. As you will see in later chapters, physiology cannot be completely separated from anatomy. Thus you will learn about the human body by studying its structures and functions together. Each structure of the body is custom-modeled to carry out a particular set of functions. For instance, bones function as rigid supports for the body because they are constructed of hard minerals. Thus the structure of a part often determines the functions it will perform. In turn, body functions often influence the size, shape, and health of the structures. Glands perform the function of manufacturing chemicals, for example, some of which stimulate bones to build up minerals so they become hard and strong. Other chemicals cause the bones to give up minerals so they do not become too thick or too heavy.

(*Principles of Anatomy and Physiology*)

Topic: _____

Main Idea: _____

_____

24

Two geographic features of the Middle East have been significant in all periods of history. Its location has given it an important, sometimes strategic, position between Africa and Eurasia, and between the Mediterranean world and the Asia of India and the Far East. Nations, tribes, traders, armies, and pilgrims—peoples on the move—have traversed the Middle East, finding the land bridge convenient and along the way discovering the wealth of the area and the civilization of its people.

The second important geographic feature is the relative magnitude of the Middle East. Arabia, the central land mass of the Middle East, embraces an area about the same size as that of the United States east of the Mississippi River plus Texas and California. The southern shore facing the Indian Ocean from Aden to Muscat is as far as from new Orleans to Boston; on the west, the Red Sea is as wide as Lake Erie is long, and the distance from Aden to Port Said is nearly the same as from New York to Denver. Northward from Arabia proper to the Turkish frontier is another 400 miles. When Egypt, Iran, and Turkey are added, the area becomes equivalent to that of the continental United States.

(*The Middle East: A History*)

Topic: _____

Main Idea: _____

_____

25

Many reasons have been advanced to account for nonreporting of crime. Some victims of rape and assault fear the embarrassment of public disclosure and interrogation by the police. Increasingly, evidence reveals that much violence occurs between persons who know each other—spouses, lovers, relatives—but the passions of the moment take on a different character when the victim is asked to testify against a family member. Another reason for nonreporting is that lower socioeconomic groups fear police involvement. In some neighborhoods, residents believe that the arrival of the law for one purpose may result in the discovery of other illicit activities, such as welfare fraud, housing code violations, or the presence of persons on probation or parole. In many of these same places the level of police protection has been minimal in the past, and residents feel that they will get little assistance. Finally, the value of property lost by larceny, robbery, or burglary may not be worth the effort of a police investigation. Many citizens are deterred from reporting a crime by unwillingness to become "involved," go to the station house to fill out papers, perhaps go to court, or to appear at a police lineup. All these aspects of the criminal process may result in lost workdays and in the expense of travel and child care. Even then, the stolen item may go unrecovered. As these examples suggest, multitudes of people feel that it is rational not to report criminal incidents because the costs outweigh the gains.

(*The American System of Criminal Justice*)

Topic: _____

Main Idea: _____

_____

Exercise 2

You now have been introduced to both stated and unstated main ideas. As you know, a stated main idea can be a first sentence, a last sentence, or located somewhere in between. It can also cover more than one paragraph, or it sometimes can be expressed as two sentences. An unstated main idea can be determined by readers if they analyze the details in terms of an overall message that is being conveyed.

Use your textbooks and various other sources, such as periodicals, to bring to class examples of all of the different kinds of main ideas. Your instructor may make copies and distribute them to the rest of the class for discussion.

Use this exercise to review the various skills and strategies needed to find topics and main ideas. You should encourage students to bring in a variety of examples to discuss—from newspaper and magazine articles as well as textbooks from other courses. At this point, you could also refer students to some readings in Part 3 as a change of pace.

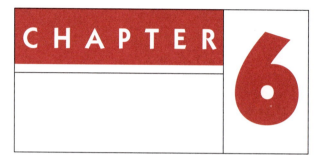

Finding Major and Minor Details

Chapter Objectives: To improve understanding of major and minor details and to provide suggestions for finding them.

Discuss strategies for recognizing major and minor details in written material. Emphasize that test questions in content courses often concern details, thus recognizing and differentiating among them is very important.

Identifying Details

The last chapter stated that paragraphs consist of various sentences that serve as main ideas, major details, and minor details. As you know by now, main ideas sum up what the rest of the sentences are telling us, and they provide the writer's overall message. In short, main ideas are supported in varying degrees by most, if not all, of the details in a given paragraph. However, some details are more important than others in terms of how directly they support the main idea. Major details are most important because they explain further the main idea and give direct support to it. Minor details provide additional information about the major details and support the main idea only indirectly. For example, look at one of the introductory paragraphs from Chapter 5.

> All living things must reproduce their kind. Single-celled organisms may split in half; other simple animals send reproductive cells out into their watery environment in hopes that these cells will encounter and unite with similar cells from another animal of the same species. In the higher levels of organisms, reproduction occurs when males introduce sperm directly into the female body. What is unique about humans as higher animals is that this act

can be separated from reproduction—people can participate in sexual activity without being motivated to produce offspring. This is because the sexual act not only brings pleasure but also represents an ultimate statement of love and affection for another human being. (*Essentials of Life and Health*)

Recall that the topic of the paragraph is "Reproduction" and that there are two stated main ideas. The first one—"All living things must reproduce their kind."—is followed by three sentences that tell us how single-celled organisms, other simple animals, and higher levels of organisms reproduce. These are major details because they lend direct support to the main idea. The second main idea, "What is unique about humans as higher animals is that this act can be separated from reproduction—people can participate in sexual activity without being motivated to reproduce offspring.", also is followed by a major detail that explains the reasons why the sexual act among humans can be separated from reproduction. That detail says that it has to do with pleasure, and it is also a statement of love and affection for another human being. Once again the sentence provides direct support for the main idea. Notice that no other sentences explain further the major details; therefore the paragraph does not have any minor details. Minor details do not have to be included!

Let us look at one more example from Chapter 5.

In Susan's case, there was not unanimity regarding high quality teaching skills, and little evidence was to be found regarding either scholarship or strong commitment to the College. In addition, reports from the counseling staff were not favorable, indicating student complaints and a failure to cooperate in meeting with counselors to discuss student problems. These reports fly in the face of the highly positive student comments found in the clinical evaluation questionnaires. Furthermore, two of the three tenured faculty in the Nursing Department do not support Susan's retention, which in itself can be very damaging to any program. They view her as lacking expertise in any particular area and as not genuinely committed to students. Although the Director of Nursing supports the reappointment, she is not at all certain that Susan is tenurable. In fact, during my discussions with the Director, she was rather emphatic in stating that Susan is not in the same league as two of the other three untenured faculty in that program.

As you remember, the topic of the paragraph is "Susan," and the unstated main idea is something like "Susan is not a high quality faculty member." Four major details directly support the main idea by supplying reasons.

I. Major Details
   A. In Susan's case, there was not unanimity regarding high quality teaching skills, and little evidence was to be found regarding either scholarship or strong commitment to the College.
   B. In addition, reports from the counseling staff were not favorable, indicating student complaints and a failure to cooperate in meeting with counselors to discuss student problems.
   C. Furthermore, two of the three tenured faculty in the Nursing Department do not support Susan's retention, which in itself can be very damaging to any program.
   D. Although the Director of Nursing supports the reappointment, she is not at all certain that Susan is tenurable.

Major details B, C, and D are followed in turn by minor details that support them directly by providing clarification and/or additional information.

II. Minor Details
   1. These reports fly in the face of the highly positive student comments found in the clinical evaluation questionnaires.
   2. They view her as lacking expertise in any particular area and as not genuinely committed to students.
   3. In fact, during my discussions with the Director, she was rather emphatic in stating that Susan is not in the same league as two of the other three untenured faculty in that program.

Although these minor details do support the main idea at least indirectly, their primary function is to supply more information about the major details—to explain them further.

When you try to find major and minor details, ask yourself two questions. First: What details directly support the main idea? You can locate major details by answering that question. Second: What details support the major details by supplying more information about them? The answer helps you uncover minor details. Focusing your attention on these questions along with the ones used to find topics and main ideas enables you to recognize the relationship among the various sentences in a paragraph. This should improve your comprehension. The following exercises will give you the opportunity to analyze paragraphs so that you can identify topics, main ideas, major details, and minor details.

Exercise 1

For this exercise, first find the topic and main idea for each passage by answering the two questions we used in the last chapter. After you have written down the topics and main ideas, locate and write out the major and minor details. Focus your attention on the two questions suggested in the previous paragraph to help you uncover and classify the details.

1

Ann's first reaction to being told that she had only about a year to live was shock. She refused to believe that the diagnosis was correct, and even after obtaining several other medical opinions, she still refused to accept that she was dying. In other words, her initial reaction was one of *denial*.

(*I Never Knew I Had a Choice*,
Gerald Corey and Marianne Schneider Corey)

Topic: _____

Main Idea: _____

_____

Major Details: _____

_____

Minor Details: _____

_____

Select passages appropriate to students' ability levels and interests. Have students discuss and justify their choices for topics, main ideas, major details, and minor details. Be certain they recognize the relationship among them.

Regarding Selection 22 specifically, note that inferences will be covered in depth in Chapter 9. If Selections 3 and 25 are to be used, consider a brief preliminary discussion of a "simple listing of facts" as one pattern of organization. Patterns of organization will be covered in depth in the next chapter.

See Instructor's Manual, Chapter 6 Answers.

2

In addition to borrowing words from other languages, we create words as we need them. For example, we "blend" breakfast and lunch to form *brunch* and smoke and fog to form *smog.* We "compound" words by putting them together to label new concepts like *downtime* and *spinout,* and we make new words from the first letters of other words, as in the acronyms *scuba* (*s*elf-*c*ontained *u*nderwater *b*reathing *a*pparatus) and *radar* (*ra*dio *d*etecting *a*nd *r*anging). Business creates trademark words such as *Xerox* and *Kleenex,* and we use them in a much more general way. Words, words, everywhere! You can see why the language is so rich!

(*The Language of Learning,* Jane N. Hopper and Jo Ann Carter-Wells)

Topic: _____

Main Idea: _____

_____

_____

_____

Major Details: _____

_____

_____

_____

Minor Details: _____

_____

_____

_____

3

A college student purchases a stereo. A home owner buys several cans of house paint. A manufacturer of tires purchases raw rubber, sulphur, and other materials and ultimately sells tires to automobile owners. A mining company sells coal to an electric utility company. All of the above have at least two things in common. First, they are quite ordinary transactions, occurring countless numbers of times. Second, they involve sales of goods. Thus we can hardly question the relevance of studying the law of sales.

(*Business Law,* alt. ed., Rate A. Howell, John R. Allison, and N. T. Henley)

Topic: _____

Main Idea: _____

_____

Major Details: _____

_____

_____

_____

Minor Details: _____

_____

_____

_____

4

Commercials in which screen stars, sports heroes, and prominent figures from all walks of life are used as salespeople are a proven type of commercial. The main concern in this type of commercial is to avoid staginess and artificiality. A viewer is all too ready to disbelieve the words of your prominent personality unless you phrase the message in comfortable, conversational language that fits your star salesperson. Keep the testimonial brief, natural, and believable, for even professional actors are not always capable of adjusting to selling roles.

(*Advertising Copywriting,* Philip Ward Burton)

Topic: _____

Main Idea: _____

_____

Major Details: _____

_____

_____

_____

Minor Details: _____

_____

_____

_____

5

With the arrival of spring in a Canadian forest, a male white-throated sparrow whistles a song that sounds rather like "Sam Peabody, Peabody, Peabody." He repeats the song thousands of times and with such clarity and consistency, we might wonder how he does it, and what good it does him. We might also wonder why male swamp sparrows and white-crowned sparrows living in the same forest have distinctive songs of their own. Do all those birds automatically "know" what they are supposed to sing the first time they do it, or do they learn something from their surroundings that influences the way they sing? Questions of this sort lead us into the world of animal behavior studies.

(*Biology*, Cecie Starr)

Topic: _____

Main Idea: _____

_____

Major Details: _____

_____

_____

_____

Minor Details: _____

_____

_____

_____

6

About six out of ten homes in the United States have cable TV through which they receive all television programs. These programs consist of broadcast transmissions that can ordinarily be received over the air (via a TV antenna), cable-originated programs (both nationally telecast shows, like MTV, and locally originated and telecast shows), distant broadcast stations (which beam their signal up to a satellite where it is then bounced down to other markets), and subscriber-paid, noncommercialized programming (such as HBO). Although there is an abundance of programs and stations that can be viewed, there is currently no defined and accepted geographic area which can be called a Cable TV Market.

(*Introduction to Advertising Media*, Jim Surmanek)

Topic: _____

Main Idea: _____

_____

Major Details: _____

_____

_____

_____

Minor Details: _____

_____

_____

_____

7

Being naked sun-worshippers may be normal, even desirable behavior for some primitive peoples. It may also be considered positive activity among certain North American and European beach goers. But try doing it in the parking lot at the local mall and you will doubtless be arrested and held for psychiatric observation. Similarly, a lot of behavior that is permissible at a rock concert or at a showing of a cult horror film would be considered strange—even "sick"—at a college faculty meeting. Our point: what is considered psychologically healthy or unhealthy, or normal or abnormal behavior can vary according to culture and according to situations within a culture.

(*Healthy for Life,* Brian K. Williams and Sharon M. Knight)

Topic: _____

Main Idea: _____

_____

Major Details: _____

_____

_____

_____

Minor Details: _____

_____

_____

_____

_____

8

We'll start by saying that without exception *every* relationship of any depth at all has conflict. No matter how close, how understanding, how compatible you are, there will be times when your ideas or actions or needs or goals won't match those of others around you. You like rock music, but your companions prefer Beethoven; you want to date other people, but your partner wants to keep the relationship exclusive; you think a paper you've done is fine, but your instructor wants it changed; you like to sleep in on Sunday mornings, but your roommate likes to play the stereo—loudly! There's no end to the number or kinds of disagreements that are possible.

(*Looking Out/Looking In,* Ronald B. Adler and Neil Towne)

Topic: _____

Main Idea: _____

_____

Major Details: _____

_____

_____

_____

Minor Details: _____

_____

_____

_____

9

If you are a smoker now, and have been smoking for some time, you may feel that you're just too far along to give it up. In fact, however, it is almost never too late to quit. A study of elderly smokers—people in their 60s, 70s, and beyond—contradicts the widely held belief that by the time smokers reach old age the habit has either already taken its toll or those who survive that long have somehow become immune to the dangers of cigarettes. Smoking is a killer at any age, and the study showed that no matter how long people smoked, there were real benefits to giving up cigarettes, and the benefits began to appear very quickly.

(*Healthy for Life*)

Topic: _____

Main Idea: _____

_____

Major Details: _____

_____

_____

_____

Minor Details: _____

_____

_____

_____

10

Radio is meant to be heard, and television is made to be seen and heard. That means you have to write for the ear or for the ear and eye. Simplification is the key to broadcast writing. Because it is harder to absorb the spoken word than the written word, concepts need to be pared down to the bare bones. Sentences must be shorter, speech more colloquial, and complex issues distilled to their essence. One of the major advantages of using broadcast media is its repeatability. Listeners may hear or see a message many times in the course of a single day or a single week. Even so, you must learn to write as though your audience will only hear or see your message one time.

(*Handbook for Public Relations Writing,* Thomas Bivins)

Topic: _____

Main Idea: _____

_____

Major Details: _____

_____

_____

_____

Minor Details: _____

_____

_____

_____

11

There is a great irony about graduate education. People get into graduate schools by having been good students. They succeed in graduate school by learning to cease being students. Until graduate school, one is a consumer of knowledge—and one succeeds by learning what other people think about various matters. In graduate school, a person must become a producer of knowledge and succeeds by having his or her own thoughts about these same matters.

(*Sociology*)

Topic: _____

Main Idea: _____
_____

Major Details: _____
_____
_____
_____

Minor Details: _____
_____
_____
_____

12

Business is a major force in American life. It affects us in our daily activities. It is always present—in newspaper stories or on television and radio broadcasts. Business provides most of the jobs that enable people to earn money, and it offers the goods and services that people spend that money on. As a result of the dominant role business plays in our lives, people have a natural curiosity to learn more about it. People take up the pursuit of business to be able to understand the "hows and whys" more thoroughly.

(*Introduction to Business*)

Topic: _____

Main Idea: _____

_____

Major Details: _____

_____

_____

_____

Minor Details: _____

_____

_____

_____

13

More televised violence than at any time in the medium's history is flowing into American homes. It's coming from many more sources than ever before—home video, pay-per-view, and cable, as well as from the broadcast networks and stations. The overwhelming weight of scientific opinion now holds that televised violence is indeed responsible for a percentage of the real violence in our society. What is new is that psychologists, child experts, and the medical community are just now beginning to treat televised violence as a serious public health issue—like smoking and drunk driving—about which the public needs to be educated for its own safety and well-being.

("How Much Violence?" Neil Hickey, *TV Guide,* August 22, 1992)

Topic: _____

Main Idea: _____

_____

Major Details: _____

_____

_____

_____

Minor Details: _____

_____

_____

_____

14

Context clues are probably the most commonly used means of understanding unknown or partially known words. To use context clues effectively, you must try to understand the writer's point of view and his style as well as considering the subject matter of the written work. For example, the mournful tone of Edgar Allan Poe is unlike the brisk tone set by Rudyard Kipling. The vocabulary and sentence patterns used by Charles Dickens are different from those used by Ernest Hemingway. But the importance of style and vocabulary extend beyond literature. If you are reading a biology book and come to an unknown word, your guess about its meaning would be different from the guess you would make if you were reading an auto repair manual. Your use of the context clues will be influenced by your knowledge of the subject matter and your understanding of just how the author is trying to transmit his message to you.

(*The Language of Learning*)

Topic: _____

Main Idea: _____

_____

Major Details: _____

_____

_____

_____

Minor Details: _____

_____

_____

_____

15

All of us are individuals. We have different personalities. We think differently. We all have different needs, wants, values, expectations, and goals in life. We are not made from the same mold. We all want to be treated as a special person because we are unique. We all are at different places in our lives. We perceive things differently depending on where we are at various times. Being liked may be important to us today; a year from now it may be more important to us to be recognized for what we have accomplished. Looking at today's workforce brings the concept of individuality into sharp focus. "Baby boomers," senior citizens, the newly arriving "baby busters," bring their own needs, goals, and values to the workplace.

(*Introduction to Business*)

Topic: _____

Main Idea: _____

_____

Major Details: _____

_____

_____

_____

Minor Details: _____

_____

_____

_____

16

Robert Morris was perhaps the foremost business and financial leader in the nation in 1787. This Philadelphia merchant owned scores of ships that traded throughout the world; he engaged in iron manufacturing, speculated in land in all parts of the country, and controlled the Bank of North America in Philadelphia, probably the nation's largest financial institution at the time. He earned his title "the patriot financier" by underwriting a large share of the debts of the United States during and after the Revolutionary War. Later in his life, his financial empire collapsed, probably because of overspeculation, and he died in debt. But at the time of the Convention, he stood at the center of America's financial structure.

(*The Irony of Democracy,* Thomas R. Dye and Harmon Zeigler)

Topic: _____

Main Idea: _____

_____

Major Details: _____

_____

_____

_____

Minor Details: _____

_____

_____

_____

Identifying Details | 145

17

Many college students encounter difficulties in keeping intimate relationships alive. You can make choices that will increase your chances of developing lasting friendships: be tolerant of differences between your friends and yourself; learn to become aware of conflicts and deal with them constructively; be willing to let the other person know how you are affected in the relationship; stay in the relationship even though you may experience a fear of rejection; check out your assumptions with others instead of deciding for them what they are thinking and feeling; be willing to make yourself vulnerable and to take risks; and avoid the temptation to live up to others' expectations instead of being true to yourself.

(*I Never Knew I Had a Choice*)

Topic: _____

Main Idea: _____
_____

Major Details: _____
_____
_____
_____

Minor Details: _____
_____
_____
_____

18

The nomination of Geraldine Ferraro for vice president of the United States in 1984 brought out many conflicting points of view. There seemed to be widespread agreement among Americans that it was a welcome step toward the full participation of women in positions of power and influence. In fact, 78 percent of Americans told Gallup interviewers they approved of the nomination. Still, there was a lot of disagreement over the net effects of Representative Ferraro's candidacy on voters. Many suggested that it would make little or no difference. Others claimed it might well get Walter Mondale elected. And others saw negative effects on voters. Then in the aftermath of President Reagan's landslide victory, many grumbled that a lot of people hadn't really voted for him but simply had rejected a woman for so high an office.

(*Sociology*)

Topic: _____

Main Idea: _____

_____

Major Details: _____

_____

_____

Minor Details: _____

_____

_____

_____

19

Some people are very comfortable with touching themselves, with touching others, and with being touched by others. They require a degree of touching to maintain a sense of physical and emotional well-being. Other people show a great deal of discomfort in touching themselves or allowing others to be physical with them. They may bristle and quickly move away if they are touched accidentally. If such people are embraced by another, they are likely to become rigid and unresponsive. For instance, in Jerry's own family of origin there was very little touching among members. He found that he had to recondition himself to feel comfortable with being touched by others and in touching others. In contrast, Marianne grew up in a German family characterized by much more spontaneous touching. Between the two of us there are differences in the amount of touching that we seek and require.

(I Never Knew I Had a Choice)

Topic: _____

Main Idea: _____

_____

Major Details: _____

_____

_____

Minor Details: _____

_____

_____

_____

20

The Founding Fathers—those fifty-five men who wrote the Constitution of the United States and founded a new nation—were a truly exceptional elite, not only "rich and well-born" but also educated, talented, and resourceful. When Thomas Jefferson, then the nation's minister in Paris, first saw the list of delegates to the Constitutional Convention of 1787, he wrote to John Adams, the minister to London. "It is really an assembly of demigods." The men at the Convention belonged to the nation's intellectual and economic elites; they were owners of landed estates, important merchants and importers, bankers and financiers, real estate and land speculators, and government bond owners. Jefferson and Adams were among the nation's very few notables who were not at the Constitutional Convention.

(*The Irony of Democracy*)

Topic: _____

Main Idea: _____

_____

Major Details: _____

_____

_____

_____

Minor Details: _____

_____

_____

_____

21

Many people express some very real fears as they begin to recognize and accept their sexuality. A common fear is that if we recognize or accept our sexual feelings, our impulses will sweep us away, leaving us out of control. It's important to learn that we can accept the full range of our sexual feelings yet decide for ourselves what we will *do* about them. For instance, we remember a man who said that he felt satisfied with his marriage and found his wife exciting but was troubled because he found other women appealing and sometimes desired them. Even though he had made a decision not to have extramarital affairs, he still experienced a high level of anxiety over simply having sexual feelings toward other women. At some level he believed that he might be more likely to *act* on his feelings if he fully accepted that he had them. It was important that he learn to discriminate between having sexual feelings and deciding to take certain actions and that he learn to trust his own decisions.

(*I Never Knew I Had a Choice*)

Topic: _____

Main Idea: _____

_____

Major Details: _____

_____

_____

_____

Minor Details: _____

_____

_____

_____

22

When you make an inference, you go beyond the facts at hand to reach a conclusion. For instance, from the expression on the face of a friend, you may infer you said something that hurt her feelings. Or, you might hear the slosh of car tires on the street outside and infer that it's raining. Or, you might smell smoke and infer that the bread in the toaster is burning. Anytime you draw a new idea out of the facts at hand, you're making an inference.

These three examples are not only inferences but also examples of inductive reasoning. When you reason inductively, you draw a conclusion that seems likely or probable, but it isn't necessarily so. Take, for example, the inference that your friend was hurt by something you said. The inference makes sense, but suppose you then learned that she was wearing shoes that were too tight. With that new information, your inductive conclusion seems less certain. And that's the way it is with induction: it's always possible that a new fact will cause you to reach a new conclusion.

(*Developing Creative and Critical Thinking*)

Topic: _____

Main Idea: _____

_____

Major Details: _____

_____

_____

_____

Minor Details: _____

_____

_____

23

I was one very bored nine-year-old on that rainy Saturday morning, and my grandfather's pocket watch seemed to beg for investigation, so I pried it open. For as long as I could remember it had hung from a hook in the back of my father's bureau, its ticking so quiet I had to lean in to hear it. But now, with its intricate innards exposed, the magic of its operation would be made plain to me. With care, I placed the parts in a long row in the exact order in which I had removed them (the better to reconstruct the movement later). Tiny screws and pins so small they stuck to my skin, toothed wheels, and thin mounting plates all lifted out so cleanly they seemed to have agreed to fit together just so. As I pulled it apart, it all seemed so sensible. Watching it tick and whirr, I found the shape and interplay of the parts perfectly obvious, so very normal. It stopped running when the first screw was out.

It is still hanging in my parents' home, but in the living room now. My mother arranged the more attractive parts, the case, the front, the engraved back, some gears, and some jeweled pins, on a background of dark blue velvet and framed it all behind glass. Very pretty, I think, but certainly not a watch anymore.

(*Sociological Ideas,* William C. Levin)

Topic: _____

Main Idea: _____

_____

Major Details: _____

_____

_____

Minor Details: _____

_____

_____

24

A mere decade or so ago, we might have thought medical science was well on its way to wrapping up some of the dread diseases of the past. Bubonic plague, which had swept medieval Europe, was no longer considered a problem. Syphilis, which had afflicted the Spanish colonizers of the New World, seemed to be behind us. Yellow fever, once a killer in American port cities, had disappeared. Tuberculosis and smallpox seemed to have been overcome.

Then, almost as punishment for our complacency, *new* diseases began to appear. One of the authors owns a 1975 medical dictionary. Here are three now-familiar diseases that I found that were not listed in it: *Lyme disease,* a disease transmitted by ticks, first recognized in 1975; *AIDS,* the famous sexual disease of acquired immunological deficiency named in 1982; and *chronic fatigue syndrome (CFS),* another immune system disease, characterized by extreme tiredness, first detected in 1984.

(*Healthy for Life*)

Topic: _____

Main Idea: _____
_____

Major Details: _____
_____
_____
_____

Minor Details: _____
_____
_____

25

Reflecting is a special kind of thinking. In the first place, it's both *active* and controlled. When ideas pass aimlessly through your head, that is not reflecting. When someone tells you a story and it suddenly brings to mind something that happened to you, that is not reflecting either. Reflecting means focusing your attention. It means weighing, considering, choosing. Suppose you're going home, and when you get there, you turn the knob, the door opens, and you step in. Getting into your home does not require reflection. But now suppose that when you turn the knob, the door does not open. To get into the house, some reflecting is in order. You have to think about what you are going to do. You have to imagine possibilities and consider alternatives.

The second way that reflecting is different from some other kinds of thinking is that it's *persistent*. It requires continuous effort. Suppose you're still trying to get through your front door. You check your pocket for the key. You walk around the house looking for an open window. You go to a phone to call a family member who has a key. Such behavior is evidence of persistent reflective thinking. And if someone asked you what you were doing, you might say that you were trying to figure out how to get into your house. But suppose, instead, you went to a nearby record store and thumbed through the new releases. Someone asked you what you were doing and you said that you were trying to figure out how to get into your house. That would not make sense. You are only reflecting as long as you stick to the problem or task.

The third way that reflecting is different from some other kinds of thinking is that it's *careful*. It aims at making sense. This doesn't mean that reflecting cannot be imaginative. A great deal of reflection could go into writing a science-fiction story about people who can move through solid objects. The ability to walk through walls could make sense in a science-fiction story. But it wouldn't make much sense in trying to get through your locked front door. Such imagining would be a kind of thinking, but it would not be reflection.

(*Developing Creative and Critical Thinking*)

Topic: _____

Main Idea: _____

_____

Major Details: _____

_____

_____

_____

Minor Details: _____

_____

_____

_____

_____

Exercise 2

Refer to specific passages already used in Chapter 5.

In Exercise 1 in Chapter 5, you found the topics and main ideas for the passages. For additional practice, you may want to find the major and minor details for each of those same passages.

Exercise 3

Your instructor may ask you to find the major and minor details in some of the passages that students brought to class as part of Exercise 2 in Chapter 5.

CHAPTER 7

Recognizing Patterns of Organization

Chapter Objectives: To introduce patterns of organization—simple listing of facts, chronological order, comparison and contrast, and cause and effect. In addition, to provide suggestions for recognizing those patterns of organization.

As you know from the last two chapters, distinguishing between main ideas, major details, and minor details is not always easy. This is particularly true when the author has not placed the details in any specific order. However, sometimes writers do organize details into patterns, making them easier to locate. Those patterns of organization tend to flow from the main idea, so focusing on it can help you recognize the specific pattern that is present. This also works in reverse; knowing the different patterns when you see them can lead you to the main idea. In addition, there are certain *signal words* that tip you off when a particular pattern is used. The four patterns of organization that you will explore in this chapter are: simple listing of facts, chronological order, comparison and contrast, and cause and effect.

Emphasize that patterns, when present, make it easier to recognize and learn details. Caution students that sometimes no pattern will be present, while at other times writers may use more than one. Also mention any additional patterns you think students should recognize.

Simple Listing of Facts

The following signal words should help you to recognize a simple listing of facts.

also	finally	in addition	other
another	first, second, third, etc.	last	part
examples	1, 2, 3, etc.	list	several
factors	following	many	types

> When introducing the "simple listing of facts" pattern, emphasize how important it is to determine the purpose of the list indicated in the main idea, which usually precedes the list.

Simple listing of facts, which can take at least four different forms, is just what it sounds like: a list of major details that include such things as characteristics, examples, reasons, or types of something. Familiarize yourself with the signal words to help you recognize the pattern.

Form 1: Numbered within One Paragraph

A number of factors may interfere with parent-child communication about sex. First, American society, like all others, has many cultural, religious, and legal rules that define appropriate adult-child communication and interaction. Second, different child and family experts recommend conflicting child-rearing methods. Third, to some, parent-child discussion of sexuality borders on violation of incest taboos. Fourth, parents may have forbidden their children to use the words needed for a coherent and meaningful discussion; the resultant embarrassment on the part of one or both may overshadow the intended messages. Finally, it may seem simplest to parents and teachers to deny or even punish any sexual or erotic interests, communications, or behaviors by children. (*Marriage and the Family*)

In most forms of simple listing, the main idea is found right before the first major detail on the list, as is the case in the example above. Pay particular attention to the signal words used by the writer, which tip you off to the presence of the pattern: "factors," "First," "Second," "Third," "Fourth," and "Finally." Now let's identify the main idea and the details from the example.

Main Idea: A number of factors may interfere with parent-child communication about sex.

Numbered simple list:

First, American society, like all others, has many cultural, religious, and legal rules that define appropriate adult-child communication and interaction.

Second, different child and family experts recommend conflicting child-rearing methods.

Third, to some, parent-child discussion of sexuality borders on violation of incest taboos.

Fourth, parents may have forbidden their children to use the words needed for a coherent and meaningful discussion.

Finally, it may seem simplest to parents and teachers to deny or even punish any sexual or erotic interests, communications, or behaviors by children.

Form 2: Numbered over More Than One Paragraph

The different definitions of moderate drinking for men and women are based on physiological differences. It is not a myth that women typically get drunk faster than men do when they both drink the same amount. There are several reasons for this.

First, women generally weigh less than men do, so the same amount of alcohol is concentrated in a smaller body mass.

Second, women typically have a higher percentage of body fat and less body water than men do. Since alcohol dissolves much more readily in water than in fat, the difference in body composition means that when alcohol enters a woman's body, it becomes more concentrated, and therefore has a more potent effect, than the same amount of alcohol would in a man's body.

Third, there is an enzyme in the stomach that metabolizes alcohol before it gets into the bloodstream, and that enzyme is about four times as active in men as in women. So even if a man and a woman weigh the same, have the same proportion of body fat and drink the same amount, more pure alcohol is likely to reach a woman's blood and brain than a man's. (*The New York Times*, 8/5/92)

In this form of the pattern, the simple list is numbered, but it covers several paragraphs as illustrated by the example. Once again, the main idea can be found right before the list, and the signal words "several," "First," "Second," and "Third" let the reader know that there is a list.

Main idea: There are several reasons why women get drunk faster than men.

Numbered simple list:

First, women generally weight less than men do, so the same amount of alcohol is concentrated in a smaller body mass.

Second, women typically have a higher percentage of body fat and less body water than men do.

Third, there is an enzyme in the stomach that metabolizes alcohol before it gets into the bloodstream, and that enzyme is about four times as active in men as in women.

Form 3: Unnumbered within One Paragraph

A culture cannot survive if it does not satisfy certain basic needs of its members. The extent to which a culture achieves the fulfillment of these needs will determine its ultimate success. "Success" is measured by the values of the culture itself rather than by those of an outsider. A culture must provide for the production and distribution of goods and services considered necessary for life. It must provide for biological continuity through the reproduction of its members. It must enculturate new members so that they can become functioning adults. It must maintain order among its members. It must likewise maintain order between its members and outsiders. Finally, it must motivate its members to survive and engage in those activities necessary for survival. (*Cultural Anthropology*)

Although the list in the example above is not numbered, the repetition of the words "A culture must," "It must provide," "It must enculturate," "It must likewise," and "Finally, it must" indicate the presence of the list.

Main idea: A culture cannot survive if it does not satisfy certain basic needs of its members.

Unnumbered simple list:

A culture must provide for the production and distribution of goods and services considered necessary for life.

It must provide for biological continuity through the reproduction of its members.

It must enculturate new members so that they can become functioning adults.

It must maintain order among its members.

It must likewise maintain order between its members and outsiders.

Finally, it must motivate its members to survive and engage in those activities necessary for survival.

Form 4: Unnumbered over More Than One Paragraph

In general, there are three ways in which the computer can be used to manage the instructional process. At the minimum, the computer is used to keep records of students' progress. Students do most of their work with traditional instructional materials, except that students write their pre- and posttest responses on optical scanning sheets that are fed into a scanner for scoring. Then the data are transmitted to the computer for analysis and storage. Summary statistics for the whole class, as well as individual student records, can be printed out as needed—for parent-teacher conferences, reports to the central office, or the preparation of individual education plans and report cards.

The computer can also be used to generate and administer the pre- and post-tests. The student can actually take the test on the computer. The computer can be programmed to analyze the student's response and, according to that analysis, select the next question. Students do not have to suffer through a test above their ability. The number of questions and the time spent in testing are minimized. In more sophisticated CMI systems, the computer can be programmed to prescribe instruction according to test results. For example, in using a computer-managed reading program, the student may be asked to read a specific story in the reading textbook and return to the computer to take a comprehension test.

Finally, the computer can be used to provide the instruction as well as to manage it. For example, the management component of the program can be linked to a tutorial program so that the level of each student's placement within the tutorial depends on previous test results. The tutorial is interactive, provides feedback about whether the student's answers are correct, and can branch to higher or lower levels of difficulty depending on the student's responses through *adaptive testing. (Fundamentals of Computer Education)*

The appearance of the signal words "Three," "also," and "Finally" plus the repetition of the words "the computer is used," "the computer can also be used," and "the computer can be used" make it clear that simple listing is present in this example.

Main idea: In general, there are three ways in which the computer can be used to manage the instructional process.

Unnumbered simple list:

At the minimum, the computer is used to keep records of students' progress.

The computer can also be used to generate and administer the pre- and post-tests.

Finally, the computer can be used to provide the instruction as well as to manage it.

In addition to these various forms of simple listing of facts, writers sometimes use a combination of numbered and unnumbered details as in the following example.

There are several strengths and capabilities of the Co-op program. First, the Co-op program is an academic program that allows a student to experience gratification, motivation and self-confidence while involved in the work setting. Secondly, students have an opportunity to directly apply the knowledge learned in the classroom, and are more apt to learn content if they are engaged in it. And thirdly, students can field test their career choices prior to completing their degree program.

Another important strength of the program is that both the experienced and inexperienced student-employee will benefit from the Human Relations Seminar which is part of the Co-op program. Students are provided an opportunity to discuss such topics as communication in the workplace; job performance; organizational structure; employee rights, unions; power; ethics, and other related topics while completing their work experiences.

In addition, students participating in the Co-op program are enabling themselves to gain new perspectives about the world around them, perspectives that they might not otherwise be exposed to had they not experienced the Co-op program. (*Strategic Plan For The Cooperative Education Program,* Passaic County Community College, New Jersey)

After the first sentence, which is the main idea, notice how the writer makes use of the words "First," "Secondly," and "And thirdly" to number the first three details on the list, but then turns to the words "Another" and "In addition" to complete it. This writing style is not at all unusual, so be on the lookout for it.

Chronological Order

The following signal words should help you to recognize chronological order.

after	events	later	steps
before	finally	next	then
beginning	first	once	when
dates	last	repeat	year

When introducing the "chronological order" pattern of organization, discuss with students how chronological order differs from simple listing of facts. Point out that the element of time determines chronological order, whereas simple listing permits changing the order of the details because no particular time sequence applies.

Remind students to be aware of the purpose *of a given chronological order, as well. In other words, what is it that is being organized in time sequence?*

In chronological order, major details involving dated or undated events, directions, or steps are presented in time order. For example, historical material, which usually includes dates, often presents events in the order in which they occurred as in the following passage.

Form 1: With Dates

What is now known as the United Kingdom is made up of England, Wales, Scotland, and Northern Ireland. The union took place over three centuries, beginning in 1536 when King Henry VIII, the son of Henry VII, a Welsh prince, merged England and Wales under a single government.

Scotland was joined to England in the early 17th century by King James I, who was the first to refer to the union as the United Kingdom. James had become King James VI of Scotland in 1567 when his mother, Mary Queen of Scots, gave up the throne; he became King James I of England after his cousin, Queen Elizabeth, died in 1603.

In 1707, after a century of strife between the two nations, the Scottish Estates narrowly ratified an Act of Union with England, formally creating the Kingdom of Great Britain with a unified Parliament in Westminster.

In 1800, the island of Ireland was joined to Great Britain, forming what became officially known as the United Kingdom of Great Britain and Ireland.

But in 1921, the largest part of Ireland won its independence as the Irish Free State, now known as the Republic of Ireland. The northern six counties of Ireland, a mostly Protestant region, remained part of the United Kingdom and that province is now known as Northern Ireland.

The Channel Islands and the Isle of Man are not part of the United Kingdom but direct dependencies of the Crown, with their own legislative systems.

The population of Great Britain is about 57 million. Of that total, about 5.2 million live in Scotland, 2.8 million in Wales, and 1.6 million in Northern Ireland. (*The New York Times,* 3/3/92)

Once again, it helps to identify the main idea, which often precedes the chronological order: "What is now known as the United Kingdom is made up of England, Wales, Scotland, and Northern Ireland." Notice how all of the events that support the main idea are dated.

Events:

The union took place over three centuries, beginning in 1536 when King Henry VIII, the son of Henry VII, a Welsh prince, merged England and Wales under a single government.

Scotland was joined to England in the early 17th century by King James I, who was the first to refer to the union as the United Kingdom.

In 1707, after a century of strife between the two nations, the Scottish Estates narrowly ratified an Act of Union with England, formally creating the Kingdom of Great Britain with a unified Parliament in Westminster.

In 1800, the island of Ireland was joined to Great Britain, forming what became officially known as the United Kingdom of Great Britain and Ireland.

But in 1921, the largest part of Ireland won its independence as the Irish Free State, now known as the Republic of Ireland. The northern six counties of Ireland, a mostly Protestant region, remained part of the United Kingdom and that province is now known as Northern Ireland.

With regard to a sequence of undated events, directions, or steps in a given system or process, the time ordering of the details often involves at least some other signal words as is the case in the following passage.

Form 2: Without Dates

To perform the Heimlich maneuver, stand behind the victim, make a fist with one hand, then press the fist, thumb-side in, against the victim's abdomen. The fist must be slightly above the navel and well below the rib cage. Next, press the fist into the abdomen with a sudden upward thrust. Repeat the thrust several times if needed. The maneuver can be performed on someone who is standing, sitting, or lying down.

Once the obstacle is dislodged, be sure the person is seen at once by a physician, for an inexperienced rescuer can inadvertently cause internal injuries or crack a rib. It could be argued that the risk is worth taking, given that the alternative is death. (*Biology*)

Although the main idea is unstated, it is apparent from the details that the passage is tracing the steps to the Heimlich maneuver, which is designed to dislodge obstacles and, thereby, prevent choking. In a sense, then, the pattern of organization in this example has led us to the main idea. The use of the signal words "then," "Next," "Repeat," and "Once" help in locating the major details in the pattern that, of course, provide the steps to the maneuver.

Steps:

To perform the Heimlich maneuver, stand behind the victim, make a fist with one hand, then press the fist, thumb-side in, against the victim's abdomen.

Next, press the fist into the abdomen with a sudden upward thrust.

Repeat the thrust several times if needed.

Once the obstacle is dislodged, be sure the person is seen at once by a physician, for an inexperienced rescuer can inadvertently cause internal injuries or crack a rib.

Comparison and Contrast

The following signal words should help you to recognize comparison and contrast.

alike	difference	on the other hand
between	disagree	same
common	distinction	similarity
compare	distinguish	unlike
contrast	like	whereas
debate	likeness	

When introducing the "comparison and contrast" pattern of organization, emphasize the point that the main idea should indicate exactly what is being compared and contrasted.

Comparison and contrast, which takes three forms, organizes details dealing with similarities and/or differences between two or more events, ideas, persons, things, etc. Once again, you need to locate the main idea because it lets you know exactly what is being compared and contrasted.

Form 1: Dealing with Similarities

The Arab countries have a common culture, and the predominant language spoken by their populations is, of course, Arabic. From a geographical perspective, they are all located in the Middle East—which is a region extending over parts of the three continents of Africa, Asia and Europe. Furthermore, much of their territory is made up of desert with the obvious problems that result from a lack of water. Islam is the religion of choice for the vast majority of the Arab people even though there are different sects. Most important of all, their historical experience throughout the centuries has been similar, with the western nations exercising much economic and political control over them right up until the 20th century. In sum, the similarities among the Arab countries far outweigh any differences that may exist which helps to explain why they are treated by the rest of the world as a separate and distinct region.

The last sentence, which is the main idea, tells us that the passage deals with the similarities among the Arab countries. Those similarities are mentioned by the other sentences that are the major details in the paragraph. Notice how the signal words "common," "similar," and "similarities" also help us to recognize the pattern.

Similarities:

The Arab countries have a common culture, and the predominant language spoken by their populations is, of course, Arabic.

From a geographical perspective, they are all located in the Middle East—which is a region extending over parts of the three continents of Africa, Asia and Europe.

Furthermore, much of their territory is made up of desert with the obvious problems that result from a lack of water.

Islam is the religion of choice for the vast majority of the Arab people even though there are different sects.

Most important of all, their historical experience throughout the centuries has been similar, with the western nations exercising much economic and political control over them right up until the 20th century.

Form 2: Dealing with Differences

The term *insomnia* refers to getting less sleep than one needs. Different people need different amounts of sleep. Sleeping 6 hours a night might constitute insomnia for one person; it might be normal for another. People who are tired and inefficient during the day are not getting enough sleep at night. Those who are alert and active during the day are sleeping enough, regardless of exactly how many hours they spend in bed at night.

    It is convenient to distinguish three main types of insomnia: People with onset insomnia have trouble falling asleep. Those with termination insomnia awaken early and cannot get back to sleep. Those with maintenance insomnia awaken repeatedly during the night, though they get back to sleep each time. In many cases onset insomnia and termination insomnia are related to an internal biological rhythm that is out of synchrony with the outside world. At 11:00 P.M. a person with onset insomnia may feel as if it were still only 6:00 P.M. At 2:00 A.M. a person with termination insomnia may already feel as if it were 7:00 A.M. In such cases, therapy is a matter of trying to readjust the biological rhythms so the person can feel sleepy and wakeful at the normal times. (*Introduction to Psychology*)

In this passage, the signal word "distinguish," used in the first sentence of the second paragraph—which is the main idea—alerts us to the fact that differences among three types of insomnia are going to be presented. The differences are made clear by the major details.

Differences:

People with onset insomnia have trouble falling asleep.

Those with termination insomnia awaken early and cannot get back to sleep.

Those with maintenance insomnia awaken repeatedly during the night, though they get back to sleep each time.

Form 3: Dealing with Both Similarities and Differences

An American entering Japan for the first time would not immediately be aware of all of the differences that exist between the United States and Japan. The physical environment of Tokyo is not really all that different from Chicago or New York. Masses of people, traffic moving at a hectic pace, overcrowded streets, skyscrapers, professionals carrying attaché cases, department store windows displaying the latest fashions—except for the language and oriental features of the people, Tokyo is like any other world-class city.

However, one would not have to be in Japan very long for the differences in behavior to become more and more apparent. For Japan, a society built on an ancient culture, has survived through its amazing capacity to absorb the new, to adapt itself to new situations and conditions, but at the same time to cling to values that have developed over nearly two thousand years of history. The result is that although there are similarities between Japan and the United States, there are also major differences—differences that relate to the land, differences in the character of the people, and differences in the history of how land and people have produced the values that characterize each culture. (*Crime and Justice in Two Societies,* Ted D. Westermann and James W. Burfeind)

In the passage about Japan, the use of the signal words "differences," "different," "like," and "similarities" indicate that the comparison and contrast deal with both similarities and differences, and they, in turn, are introduced in each paragraph by a separate main idea.

First main idea: An American entering Japan for the first time would not immediately be aware of all of the differences that exist between the United States and Japan.

Similarities:

The physical environment of Tokyo is not really all that different from Chicago or New York.

Masses of people, traffic moving at a hectic pace, overcrowded streets, skyscrapers, professionals carrying attaché cases, department store windows displaying the latest fashions—except for the language and the oriental features of the people, Tokyo is like any other world-class city.

Second main idea: However, one would not have to be in Japan very long for the differences in behavior to become more and more apparent.

Differences:

For Japan, a society built on an ancient culture, has survived through its amazing capacity to absorb the new, to adapt itself to new situations and conditions, but at the same time to cling to values that have developed over nearly two thousand years of history.

The result is that although there are similarities between Japan and the United States, there are also major differences—differences that relate to the land, differences in the character of the people, and differences in the history of how land and people have produced the values that characterize each culture.

> Since the "cause and effect" pattern of organization is difficult for many students to comprehend, offer additional "real world" examples of cause and effect relationships. Again, emphasize the significance of signal words and the main idea in recognizing this pattern of organization.
>
> When introducing Form I, point out that both the cause and the effects are mentioned in the first sentence, which happens often with this pattern.

Cause and Effect

The following signal words should help you to recognize cause and effect.

affects	consequences	reason
because	effect	result
brings out	leads to	therefore
cause	reaction	

This particular pattern involves the presentation of causes, or reasons, along with their effects, or results. To use a simple example, say someone sticks you with a pin, and you jump. Then sticking you with the pin is the cause, while the effect is your jump. When you read, notice that the causes sometimes come before the effects, while at other times, the effects are mentioned first. Also, it is very common to have both causes and effects within the same sentence. Once again finding the main idea and any signal words should help you to recognize this pattern.

Form 1: With Causes Stated First

Medicinal drugs have allowed the medical profession to alleviate suffering and extend life for individuals who only a few decades ago would have either existed in pain or died. There is no doubt that chemistry and medicine will be wedded for all future time. The picture is not without its unfortunate features. Side effects of drugs administered even by qualified physicians do cause some suffering and even death. The dependence of some members of society on medicinal drugs has become so great it approaches a national scandal. In addition the younger generation has become so accustomed to a society in which legal drugs are prevalent that for some it is easy to slip into addiction to illicit drugs. (*Introductory Chemistry*)

Although the main idea of this passage is unstated, the overall message is something like: "Medicinal drugs have had both good and bad effects." Notice that the overall cause "medicinal drugs" is mentioned first and that it is followed by first the positive and then the negative effects of their use. The signal words "effects" and "cause" make it obvious that this pattern is being used.

Good Effects:

Medicinal drugs have allowed the medical profession to alleviate suffering and extend life for individuals who only a few decades ago would have either existed in pain or died.

Bad Effects:

Side effects of drugs administered even by qualified physicians do cause some suffering and even death.

The dependence of some members of society on medicinal drugs has become so great it approaches a national scandal.

In addition, the younger generation has become so accustomed to a society in which legal drugs are prevalent that—for some—it is easy to slip into addiction to illicit drugs.

Form 2: With Effects Stated First

What causes unethical conduct in business? Although the cause of every unethical action cannot be identified, there appear to be two major contributors. One major cause appears to be from the pressure to succeed in business. Trying to get ahead, reaching for the next rung on the ladder, greed, and personal interest are replacing acceptable ethical behavior. In recent years Michael Milken, the high priest of junk bonds and the recipient of a $550 million pay package in 1987, was indicted and let go by his firm. And Ivan Boesky, the stock speculator who told an applauding university audience at Berkeley that "greed is healthy," had time to contemplate his ethics at Lompoc Federal Prison Camp in California when he was convicted of inside trading.

Competition also can be a cause of unethical business practices. Some firms slip into questionable business practices as a way to keep pace with competitors, who may in turn have established their dominant market position by using under-the-table practices to attract and retain large numbers of important customers. Companies on the edge of bankruptcy may employ dubious means to get or keep customers whose business can make the difference between survival and financial failure. (*Introduction to Business*)

In this passage, the main idea first states the effect—"unethical [business] action"—and then lets us know that there are two major causes for it: "Although the cause of every unethical action cannot be identified, there appear to be two major contributors." The use of the signal word "cause" makes it easy to locate the two reasons for unethical business action.

Causes:

One major cause appears to be from the pressure to succeed in business.

Competition also can be a cause of unethical business practices.

Exercise 1

See Instructor's Manual, Chapter 7 Answers.

You have been introduced to four patterns of organization: simple listing of facts, chronological order, comparison and contrast, and cause and effect. In each of the following passages, identify the topic, main idea, and dominant pattern of organization. Also write out the major details from each of the patterns, paying particular attention to the signal words that the writer used to help you to find them.

1

Analysts can find endless reasons for the retro craze. For the networks, certainly, repackaging what's already in the vaults is far cheaper than producing new shows, a consideration to be taken seriously in times of lean budgets. And on a broader sociological level, viewers might understandably be eager to escape an unsettling present—pocked with problems ranging from economic recession to AIDS—and return to what they perceive, even if inaccurately, as less complicated and decidedly safer times.

(*The New York Times,* 11/22/91)

Topic: _____

Main Idea: _____

_____

Pattern of Organization: _____

Major Details: _____

_____

_____

_____

_____

_____

_____

2

Products you buy are created by the work of many businesses. Think of a loaf of bread: first a farmer grew the wheat with the help of fertilizer supplied by a chemical company; when it was ripe, he harvested it using a machine he bought (with the help of a bank) from a manufacturer. He trucked the wheat to a mill, which ground it into flour and sold it to a bakery. That company brought the flour by train to its plant, where it was combined with other ingredients bought from other suppliers to make bread. The bakery then wrapped the bread in plastic bought from yet another company. Using the trucks it bought from a truck manufacturer, the bakery transported the bread to a retail store, where you were able to purchase it.

(*Introduction to Business*)

Topic: _____

Main Idea: _____
_____

Pattern of Organization: _____

Major Details: _____
_____
_____
_____
_____
_____

3

When most people talk about stress, it is usually in terms of pressure they are feeling from something happening around them or to them. Students talk about being under stress because of poor exam performance or an impending deadline for a major paper. Parents talk about the strain of raising teenagers and the financial burdens of running a household. Teachers talk about the pressure of maintaining professional currency while still managing to keep on top of duties connected with classroom teaching. Doctors, nurses, and lawyers talk about meeting the endless demands of their patients and clients.

(*Stress and Health*, Phillip L. Rice)

Topic: _____

Main Idea: _____

_____

Pattern of Organization: _____

Major Details: _____

4

Barbara and Marvin were both very successful in their community. Marvin was a physician, and Barbara operated a thriving dress shop. As the years passed, Marvin was consumed by his job. He spent an enormous amount of time keeping himself on top of its many demanding problems. He expected Barbara to entertain guests and to be there for him when he was gone weekends and nights. She was expected to be the "model wife." At another level, Barbara perceived her husband as rejecting, cold, and insensitive to the changes that were occurring in her life. Each time there was an insensitivity, or indiscretion, Barbara would say to herself, "Oh, well. It doesn't matter." She reports arising one morning and realizing that in fact it did not matter. She would sit in the counseling session, staring blankly into space, searching for words to describe the emptiness.

(*Family Science*)

Topic: _____

Main Idea: _____

_____

Pattern of Organization: _____

Major Details: _____

_____

_____

_____

_____

_____

_____

Cause and Effect 173

5

Crack cocaine arrived on the streets of New York, southern California, and Florida in 1985. Selling for ten to twenty dollars a vial, it became an immediate hit among users. Drug treatment centers were soon seeing addicts who had been using cocaine for several months only, not years. Beginning in mid-1986 the police of cities such as Washington, New York, Miami, and Los Angeles started to see sharp increases in murder, robbery, and other violent crimes in those neighborhoods where crack was in widespread use. New York's drug treatment centers were soon overwhelmed, and hospitals were registering an increase in the number of cocaine-addicted babies being born. In early 1987 Drug Enforcement Administration and Border Patrol officials reported increased drug trafficking on the Mexican border and the interception in Florida of large quantities of cocaine flown in from Colombia and Peru.

(*The American System of Criminal Justice*)

Topic: _____

Main Idea: _____

_____

Pattern of Organization: _____

Major Details: _____

_____

_____

_____

_____

_____

6

Michelle and Kim have much in common, even though they really are not close friends. It all started on that day in 1975 when they were born. Not only was the date and hour the same, but they came into this world while their mothers were in Columbia Presbyterian Hospital. Most of their early years were spent in Manhattan, and they graduated from the same elementary and high schools. In high school their level of activity in sports and social affairs was high, and both were honor students. From a physical standpoint, they are now approximately the same height, with blond hair and blue eyes. Their personalities are also very much alike: they are outgoing, vivacious, and easy to get along with. In fact Michelle and Kim are two of the most popular girls around, and it is a real joy to spend time with them! Is it any wonder that they are expected to be very successful no matter what they decide to do in life?

Topic: _____

Main Idea: _____

_____

Pattern of Organization: _____

Major Details: _____

_____

_____

_____

_____

_____

_____

7

The effects of overcrowding on animals have been extensively studied by social and natural scientists. At the very least, overcrowding among animals results in the disturbance of normal social interactions, such as courtship, mating, and maternal behavior. Usual dominant-submissive relationships cease to function, with the result that a stable group organization can no longer be maintained. At the worst, the prolonged stress of overcrowding can stimulate extreme tension and hyperactivity, culminating in death.

(*Cultural Anthropology*)

Topic: _____

Main Idea: _____
_____

Pattern of Organization: _____

Major Details: _____
_____
_____
_____
_____
_____
_____
_____

8

What do people do as a result of their fear of crime? As suggested earlier, many take what they believe are precautions by curtailing activities that they think may place them in a dangerous situation. Others attempt to reduce potential property loss by installing systems of one kind or another—more locks, window grilles, and alarms—that turn the home into a fortress. Those who can afford to do so may take refuge in apartment houses or residential enclaves that offer continuous surveillance, doormen or gatekeepers, and patrols. Still others flee to the suburbs or to the countryside, where is seems to them that crime is not a problem.

(*The American System of Criminal Justice*)

Topic: _____

Main Idea: _____

_____

Pattern of Organization: _____

Major Details: _____

_____

_____

_____

_____

_____

_____

9

Sexual motivation, like hunger, depends on both a physiological drive and available incentives. Again as with hunger, the sex drive increases during a time of deprivation, at least up to a point, and it can be inhibited for social and symbolic reasons, including religious vows.

However, the sex drive differs from hunger in important ways. Many people experience little sex drive in the absence of such incentives as a loving partner or erotic stimuli. Moreover, people differ greatly in the incentives that arouse them sexually. Some people are aroused by the sight of shoes or undergarments, the feel of rubber or leather, the experience of inflicting or receiving pain, and other preferences that most people do not share and find hard to understand.

(Introduction to Psychology)

Topic: _____

Main Idea: _____

_____

Pattern of Organization: _____

Major Details: _____

_____

_____

_____

_____

_____

_____

10

Love Canal was a 16-acre chemical dump site for the Hooker Chemical Company of Niagara Falls, New York. The company used the abandoned canal to dispose of nearly 20,000 tons of chemical wastes over a period of roughly ten years, ending in 1953. Hooker Chemical then covered the canal and sold it to the local school district for $1. Families built homes on the site over the next 20 years. But no one told them the open field in their midst contained the seeds of deadly destruction: it was to be a park for the children. Officials did not begin to seriously investigate the problem until 1976, and they did not take any substantive action until 1978, when they developed a relocation plan that allowed 237 families at the center of Love Canal left to seek homes elsewhere. Unfortunately, 700 families on nearby streets were not included in the relocation plans. They were left alone to worry about their safety and their fate.

(*Stress and Health*)

Topic: _____

Main Idea: _____

_____

Pattern of Organization: _____

Major Details: _____

_____

_____

_____

_____

_____

_____

11

Managers can do several things to uncover clues to poor morale. One approach is to check company records on tardiness, absences, quality rejects, and comments received during exit interviews. Another approach is to observe and listen: employees' comments to each other, direct remarks to their supervisors, and informal communications through body language are all clues to work attitudes. As an example, one ride attendant at a sprawling amusement park confided: "Whenever we think the higher-ups aren't listening to us or giving us the attention we deserve, we just screw up the roller coaster. The big boys come running to find out what went wrong, which gives us an hour or so to talk to them and get things off our chests. After the problem is fixed and they leave we feel better, like they know we're alive, and things run fine until we start feeling ignored again. Then another breakdown happens." The investigating managers did not read the situation for what it was, a morale problem masquerading as a mechanical one.

A more formal way to check on morale is by conducting an employee attitude or opinion survey. This is a questionnaire that lets workers express their feelings about their jobs anonymously. It is thorough. All workers can be given the questionnaire if management wishes. It is a way to gather honest responses about employee morale.

(*Introduction to Business*)

Topic: _____

Main Idea: _____

_____

Pattern of Organization: _____

Major Details: _____

_____

_____

_____

12

Corrupt police officers have been described as falling into two categories: "grass eaters" and "meat eaters." "Grass eaters" are persons who accept payoffs that the circumstances of police work bring their way. "Meat eaters" are persons who aggressively misuse their power for personal gain. "Meat eaters" are few, though their exploits make headlines; "grass eaters" are the heart of the problem. Because "grass eaters" are many, they make corruption respectable, and they encourage adherence to a code of secrecy that brands anyone who exposes corruption as a traitor.

(*The American System of Criminal Justice*)

Topic: _____

Main Idea: _____

_____

Pattern of Organization: _____

Major Details: _____

_____

_____

_____

_____

_____

_____

_____

_____

13

Good writers learn the craft of writing in much the same way that other skilled artisans or professionals learn their trades. Each of them typically follows a four-stage plan.

The first stage involves learning how to use the *tools of the trade.* For the writer these tools are the basic rules of language, including grammar, punctuation, and capitalization, as well as number, spelling, and syntax conventions.

In the second stage the writer learns the *proper techniques* for efficient and coherent combination of these basic tools. These techniques involve learning how to use words skillfully and precisely, how to write effective sentences and paragraphs, and how to develop appropriate style and tone.

After learning these techniques, the writer needs a *plan of action.* For example, what procedures or strategies are known to be effective in writing a business letter? The third stage, then, involves learning and applying strategies for producing the desired result.

Finally, in the fourth stage, the writer practices *applying the tools, techniques, and strategies* in varying situations. In this way writers improve their skills in producing satisfactory results.

(*Essentials of Business Communication,* Mary Ellen Guffey)

Topic: _____

Main Idea: _____

_____

Pattern of Organization: _____

Major Details: _____

_____

_____

_____

_____

14

What motivates someone to become anorexic? First, many women who become anorexic have always prized self-control. Their extreme weight loss demonstrates extreme self-control and thereby raises their self-esteem.

Second, by becoming so thin that they lose their secondary sexual characteristics, including breast development, they stop being attractive to men. At least some young women with anorexia have a fear of sex and a fear of accepting an adult role. By becoming extremely thin, they can retreat into looking like, acting like, and being treated like little girls again.

Third, maintaining a dangerously low weight is a way of rebelling quietly and of attracting attention. Before the onset of the disorder, most anorexic girls are described as having been obedient, conforming, and highly intelligent perfectionists—girls who never gave their parents or teachers any trouble. Perhaps as a result, their parents and others took them for granted and gave them little attention. Their severe weight loss makes the parents and friends suddenly attentive and concerned. The anorexic girl comes to enjoy the attention; she becomes reluctant to lose it by gaining weight.

There are probably other reasons behind anorexia. As with most complex human behaviors, anorexia is based on a combination of motivations, not just one.

(*Introduction to Psychology*)

Topic: _____

Main Idea: _____

_____

Pattern of Organization: _____

Major Details: _____

_____

_____

_____

15

What makes us tick? What makes us the way we are? Way down deep, are humans good, bad, or somewhere in between?

The 17th-century philosopher Thomas Hobbes argued that humans are by nature selfish. Life in a state of nature, he said, is "nasty, brutish, and short." To protect ourselves from one another, we must be restrained by a watchful government.

The 18th-century political philosopher Jean-Jacques Rousseau disagreed. He maintained that humans are good by nature but have been corrupted by "civilized" governments. Although he conceded that society could never return to "noble savagery," he believed that education and government should promote the freedom of the individual. Rational people acting freely, he maintained, would advance the welfare of all.

The debate between those two viewpoints survives in modern theories of personality. Some theorists, including Sigmund Freud, have held that people are born with sexual and destructive impulses that must be held in check if civilization is to survive. Others, including Carl Rogers, have held that people will achieve good and noble goals once they have been freed from unnecessary restraints.

(Introduction to Psychology)

Topic: _____

Main Idea: _____

_____

Pattern of Organization: _____

Major Details: _____

_____

_____

_____

_____

16

Many people in our society drink alcohol because it serves as a *social lubricant.* They have a drink or two before dinner and meet their friends at cocktail parties. Executives meet over drinks to discuss business. Alcohol makes them feel more relaxed and less self-conscious. It frees people to say and do things they would otherwise suppress. A friend of mine, after a few too many beers, once kissed a policeman for no apparent reason. (The policeman was still laughing as we walked away.) Even the *expectation* of becoming slightly intoxicated loosens people's inhibitions and helps them keep the conversation moving. The prevalence of alcohol in so many settings is one reason that people with a drinking problem have trouble giving it up.

Alcohol serves a similar social function when it is used for *celebration.* Beer and stronger drinks often flow freely when friends get together to celebrate such happy events as winning a bowling tournament, completing a project, or just making it to Friday night.

Some people use alcohol or other drugs not only to celebrate the good times but also to escape the bad times. Their motive is *escape.* Many depressed people become alcohol abusers or drug addicts.

Young people, especially males, sometimes use drugs or alcohol to *attract attention,* to demonstrate to their friends how completely stoned or drunk they can get. They may even brag about how much damage they are doing to themselves.

A less common motivation for using alcohol or other drugs is *self-handicapping*—putting oneself at a disadvantage in order to have an excuse for failure. One experiment was set up to make it appear that students had succeeded on a series of tasks, even though they themselves knew their success had been an accident. Then they were asked to choose between two drugs before continuing with a similar series of tasks. One drug, they were told, would improve their performance and the other would impair it. Most of the students opted for the drug that would impair their performance. Apparently they expected to do poorly anyway (because their earlier success had been mostly a matter of luck), and they wanted to have a ready-made excuse for their failure. People who are doing poorly in their studies or in their work may turn to alcohol or other drugs for the same reason.

(*Introduction to Psychology*)

Topic: _____

Main Idea: _____

_____

Pattern of Organization: _____

Major Details: _____

17

Once the buying motives have been identified, the next step is to create a promotional strategy—the communication ingredient in the marketing mix. A promotional strategy is composed of the four elements of the promotional mix: personal selling, advertising, publicity, and sales promotion. The promotional strategy is developed with an understanding of the communication process, which includes sender, encoding, message, medium, decoding, target market, feedback, and noise.

The first element of the promotional mix is personal selling. It is a personal attempt to persuade the prospective customer to buy a product. Salespersons use a seven-step sales approach that includes prospecting, preapproach, approach, presentation, objections, closing, and follow-up.

The second element of the promotional mix is advertising. Advertising is any nonpersonal message paid for by an identifiable sponsor for the purpose of promoting products, services, or ideas. There are two types of advertising: product (intended to promote demand for a product or service) and institutional (done to enhance a company's public image). Once the type of advertising is determined, marketers have to select the medium for presenting the message. They may select from among direct mail, newspaper, radio, outdoor advertising, television, and magazines. Regardless of the media used, all advertising must be done within legal guidelines that prohibit false or misleading advertising claims.

The third element of the promotional mix is publicity. It is nonpaid, nonpersonal communication to promote the products, services, or image of the company. The development of a publicity element of the promotional mix requires the firm to take advantage of all opportunities to present material to independent media. Types of publicity include news publicity, business feature articles, finance releases, and emergency releases.

Sales promotion is the fourth element of the promotional mix. It involves marketing activities, other than personal selling and advertising, that stimulate consumer purchasing and dealer effectiveness. Specific types of sales promotion devices are directed at the middleman: point-of-purchase displays, cooperative advertising programs, specialty advertising, trade shows, and push money. Other types are intended for the consumer: coupons, samples, premiums, special services, contests and sweepstakes, trading stamps, and refund offers.

(*Introduction to Business*)

Topic: _____

Main Idea: _____
_____

Pattern of Organization: _____

Major Details: _____
_____
_____
_____
_____
_____
_____
_____
_____
_____
_____
_____

18

Gases are easily distinguishable from liquids and solids. They have no characteristic shape or volume and can be contained in any size or shape vessel. The volumes of solids and liquids have clearly visible boundaries. A gas, on the other hand, completely fills any container in which it is placed and is bounded only by the walls of the container. If a colored gas such as bromine is placed in a transparent container, the gas can be seen to be distributed evenly throughout the container. If the same quantity is transferred to a larger or differently shaped container, the distribution is still uniform. The intensity of the color of the gas will, of course, diminish in the larger container.

At normal atmospheric pressure and temperature the densities of gases are in the range of 0.0002 to 0.004 g/ml. Therefore it is more convenient to state the densities of gases in terms of grams per liter.

Gases are highly compressible. Under high pressure the volume of a gas can be decreased by a factor of nearly 1000. It is this feature of high compressibility that allows industry to place large volumes of gases in cylinders under pressure. The gas in tanks used by a welder would occupy a volume several thousand times larger than the tank of gas at normal atmospheric pressure.

Gases undergo considerable expansion when heated under constant pressure. The density of gases thus decreases when heated, and this is the reason that hot air rises.

(*Introductory Chemistry*)

Topic: _____

Main Idea: _____
_____

Pattern of Organization: _____

Major Details: _____
_____
_____

In Selection 18 the contrast is implied. With the exception of the first paragraph, the writer gives only the characteristics of gases. This requires the reader to complete the contrast by inferring how liquids and solids differ. Emphasize these differences to students, and mention again that inferences will be covered in Chapter 9.

19

Let us trace the movement of blood through the human circulatory system, beginning with that returning to the heart from the legs or arms. Such blood enters the upper right chamber of the heart, called the **right atrium** (or auricle). This chamber then contracts, forcing the blood through a valve (the tricuspid valve) into the **right ventricle,** the lower right chamber of the heart. Now, this blood, having just returned to the heart from its circulation through tissues, contains little oxygen and much carbon dioxide. It would be of little value to the body simply to pump this deoxygenated blood back out to the general body tissues. Instead, contraction of the right ventricle sends the blood through a valve (the pulmonary semilunar valve) into the **pulmonary artery,** which soon divides into two branches, one going to each lung. In the lungs, the pulmonary arteries branch into many small arteries, called arterioles, which connect with dense beds of capillaries lying in the walls of the alveoli. Here gas exchange takes place, carbon dioxide being discharged from the blood into the air in the alveoli and oxygen being picked up by the hemoglobin in the red cells of the blood. From the capillaries, the blood passes into small veins, which soon join to form large **pulmonary** veins running back toward the heart from the lungs. The four pulmonary veins (two from each lung) empty into the upper left chamber of the heart, called the **left atrium** (or auricle). When the left atrium contracts, it forces the blood through a valve (the bicuspid or mitral valve) into the **left ventricle,** which is the lower left chamber of the heart. The left ventricle, then, is a pump for recently oxygenated blood. When it contracts, it pushes the blood through a valve (the aortic semilunar valve) into a very large artery called the **aorta.**

After the aorta emerges from the anterior portion of the heart (the upper portion, in humans standing erect), it forms a prominent arch and runs posteriorly along the middorsal wall of the thorax and abdomen.

Numerous branch arteries arise from the aorta along its length, and these arteries carry blood to all parts of the body. Each of these arteries, in turn, branches into smaller arteries, until eventually the smallest arterioles connect with the numerous tiny capillaries embedded in the tissues.

Very little, if any, exchange of materials occurs across the walls of the arteries or veins, which are apparently impermeable to the substances in the blood and tissue fluid. In the capillaries, oxygen, nutrients, hormones, and other substances move out of the blood into the tissues; such waste products as carbon dioxide and nitrogenous wastes are picked up by the blood, and substances to be transported, such as hormones secreted by the tissues, or nutrients from the intestine and liver, are also picked up.

Selection 19 can serve to remind students that chronological order does not always involve only historical events and dates.

From the capillary beds the blood runs into tiny veins, which fuse to form larger and larger veins, until eventually one or more large veins exit from the organ in question. These veins, in turn, empty into one of two very large veins that empty into the right atrium of the heart: the **anterior vena cava** (sometimes called the superior vena cava), which drains the head, neck, and arms, and the **posterior vena cava** (or inferior vena cava), which drains the rest of the body.

(*Elements of Biological Science*)

Topic: _____

Main Idea: _____

_____

Pattern of Organization: _____

Major Details: _____

20

The decade that had begun in exhilaration and hope was dissolving into bitterness and hate. "Before my term is ended," Kennedy had said in 1961, "we shall have to test anew whether a nation organized and governed such as ours can endure. The outcome is by no means certain." Convinced that the inequalities in American society were a source of danger to American life, Kennedy tried to get America moving toward his New Frontier, carrying the poor and nonwhites with him. He was murdered. After his death his brother Robert made himself the peculiar champion of the outcasts and victims of American life. He was murdered. Martin Luther King was the eloquent advocate of nonviolence in the pursuit of racial justice. In April 1968 an assassin killed him. Some Americans regarded these murders as isolated aberrations. Others began to lose faith in a society that destroyed the three men of the decade who seemed most to embody American idealism.

The panorama of American life, especially after 1963, became one of epithets, demonstrations, sit-ins, marches, burnings, riots, shootings, bombings. Frustrated minorities, feeling the "system" hopelessly rigged against them, turned to violence, if only because they could see no other way to get a hearing for just grievances. Political philosophers offered rationales for violent action. The experience of a generation of war doubtless habituated people to killing; and the war in Vietnam, by legitimizing violent methods in a dubious cause abroad, justified for some the use of violence in better causes at home. Television transmitted the techniques of protest, encouraging habits of instant reaction and hopes of instant results.

(*The National Experience,* John M. Blum et al.)

Topic: _____

Main Idea: _____

_____

Pattern of Organization: _____

Major Details: _____

In Selection 20, make sure students can distinguish among all the causes and effects.

21

Today's computers can be roughly divided into microcomputers, minicomputers, mainframes, and supercomputers, with each group characterized by size, price, speed of operation, and memory/processing capabilities.

Microcomputers are the smallest, least costly, and most popular computers on the market. Microcomputers range from around $100 to several thousand dollars and vary as widely in power, with some models rivaling minicomputers and older mainframes in capabilities. Businesses use microcomputers for everything from preparing spreadsheets to performing desktop publishing.

Thanks to the microprocessors' compactness, microcomputers are small enough to fit on top of a desk or, in some cases, a briefcase. In business applications, the microcomputer may function as a stand-alone unit or be hooked up with other microcomputers or a mainframe to expand their capabilities. Because of their low price, microcomputers are sold like appliances in department, discount, and computer-specialty stores. The availability of low-cost, easy-to-use programs plays a major role in consumer acceptance of microcomputer brands.

Minicomputers were first developed during the 1960s to perform specialized tasks such as handling data communications. Today's minicomputers rival some mainframes in power and are used in word processing, industrial automation, and multioperator applications.

Minicomputers are smaller, cheaper, and easier to maintain and install than are mainframes but are in declining demand because of the increasing power of the microcomputers. However, several operators linked to the same minicomputer can still access resources such as printers and disk storage faster than a network of microcomputer operators can. Minicomputer prices range from around $50,000 to several hundred thousand dollars.

Mainframe computers are large, fast systems capable of supporting several hundred input and output devices such as keyboards and monitor screens. Large businesses, universities, banks, and hospitals rely on mainframe computers for their tremendous operational speed and processing capacity. For example, minicomputers could not possibly handle the thousands of reservation orders that travel agents make each day with an airline, but mainframe computers can and do. Mainframe computers range in price from several hundred thousand dollars to several million dollars.

A mainframe computer produces considerable heat so its environmental temperature and humidity must be controlled by special systems. Besides the environmental costs, mainframe computers require large support staffs. Typically, the computer vendor (seller) trains the user's staff and provides maintenance support. In turn, the staff operates and programs the mainframe computer.

Supercomputers are the fastest, most expensive computers manufactured. They can run numerous different calculations simultaneously, thereby processing in a minute what would take a personal computer several weeks or months. Scientists at Sandia National Laboratory in New Mexico built a super computer consisting of 1,024 processors. Each processor has the computing capability of a computer and is assigned a separate part of one massive problem, which is worked by all the processors simultaneously. Called the "hypercube," this supercomputer solves problems 1,000 times faster than does a typical mainframe computer.

Most supercomputers are used for scientific work, particularly for creating mathematical models of the real world. Called **simulation,** this process is especially useful in seismology, oil exploration, weather forecasting, and predicting the spread of pollution. Supercomputers cost millions of dollars and only a few are produced each year.

(*Four Software Tools Plus,* Tim Duffy)

Topic: _____

Main Idea: _____

_____

Pattern of Organization: _____

Major Details: _____

_____

_____

_____

_____

22

On December 1, 1955, Mrs. Rosa Parks, a seamstress in Montgomery, Alabama, boarded a city bus at the end of a long day of work. After paying her fare she walked down the aisle, passing through the "white section" of the bus as required by law, and took the last seat open in the "colored section." Two stops later the white section filled up, leaving a white man standing in the aisle. At that point the bus driver, J. P. Blake, asked Mrs. Parks and three other black passengers to vacate their seats, which make up the front row of the colored section. No one moved. Blake said, "You all make it light on yourselves and let me have those seats." The other three black passengers, a man and two women, rose and stood in the aisle. But Mrs. Parks didn't. Blake told her that if she didn't move he would call the police and have her arrested for violating Montgomery's bus segregation law. She told him to go ahead because she was not going to move. Thereupon Blake left the bus and phoned the police. When two officers confronted Mrs. Parks, she asked them, "Why do you push us around?" One of them answered, "I don't know, but the law is the law and you're under arrest."

Mrs. Parks was taken to the police station, booked, and fingerprinted. She was then permitted to call her mother, whose first response was "Did they beat you?" After her daughter had reassured her and explained her situation, her mother called E. D. Nixon, a local black leader. Nixon soon arrived at the jail to try to arrange bail for Mrs. Parks. Meanwhile, something of immense importance was taking place in another part of the city.

After talking with Mrs. Parks, Nixon had phoned Jo Ann Robinson, a professor of English at Alabama State University, then an all-black school. Robinson was a leader of the newly organized political affairs committee at the Dexter Avenue Baptist Church. She, in turn, called several other women on the Alabama State faculty who also were on the committee. At midnight they gathered in Robinson's office, under the pretext of grading exams, and began drafting a leaflet:

> Another Negro woman has been arrested and thrown into jail because she refused to get up out of her seat on the bus and give it to a white person.... Until we do something to stop these arrests, they will continue.... The next time it may be you, or your daughter, or mother. This woman's case will come up Monday. We are, therefore, asking every Negro to stay off the buses on Monday in protest of the arrest and trial.

As they worked on the leaflet, the professors realized that there was nowhere they could get it printed—whites owned all of the printing shops. So they stayed through the night and ran off copies on the mimeograph machines at Alabama State. Around 3 A.M., Robinson called Nixon and told him what she and her associates were doing. He was enthusiastic about their plan and agreed to organize a meeting that evening at her church. So, at 5 A.M. Nixon phoned the new pastor of the Dexter Avenue Baptist Church, a 26-year-old from Atlanta by the name of Martin Luther King, Jr. When asked to endorse a one-day boycott of the buses, King said, "Brother Nixon, let me think about it and you call me back." An hour later Nixon called King again. The young minister said he would be willing to take part. Nixon replied, "I'm glad you agreed because I already set the meeting up to meet at your church."

The rest is history.

(*Sociology*)

Topic: _____

Main Idea: _____
_____

Pattern of Organization: _____

Major Details: _____
_____
_____
_____
_____
_____
_____
_____
_____

(Use additional paper as needed.)

23

It is probably impossible to separate completely what is inherited and what is learned in any behavior pattern. Behavior is not a simple combination of these two elements, but is the outcome of a fusion between them. So far as the part played by learning can be distinguished, however, the learning process is one well worth studying. Before we examine some commonly recognized categories of learning, we should mention several factors that complicate its study.

First, it is often difficult to determine whether improvement in the performance of a behavior pattern is due to experience or simply to greater maturity or to a different physiological condition. For example, observations that young birds just leaving the nest cannot fly well, but improve rapidly over the next few days, have led to the widespread belief that the birds must learn to fly and that they improve with practice. But, as repeated experiments have demonstrated, when young birds are reared in narrow tubes or other devices that prevent them from flapping their wings and are released at an age when they normally would already have "learned" to fly, they are able to fly as well as control birds raised under normal conditions. In other words, it is not practice that causes the flight of a newly fledged bird to improve; it is greater maturity. Numerous other examples could be cited of improvement that appears to be a result of learning but is really a result of maturation. Furthermore, injections of hormones have sometimes caused behavior patterns to change in ways previously thought to be produced only by learning experiences; hence one must be exceedingly careful to rule out physiological changes as a possible cause before asserting that a particular behavioral change is due to learning.

A second complication in studying the learning ability of animals is that an animal may readily learn something in one context and be completely incapable of learning it in some other context. Thus one may erroneously conclude that the animal cannot learn something when, in fact, the negative results are simply a product of the experimental situation used.

Another difficulty in determining what an animal can learn is that a particular behavior can often be learned only during a rather limited critical period in its life. If the animal does not encounter the necessary learning situation during the critical period, it may never learn the behavior. Exposure to the learning situation before or after the critical period may be ineffective in producing learning. For example, during his studies of the development of Chaffinch song, Thorpe demonstrated that, unless young Chaffinches hear a Chaffinch song during a certain period in their development, they never learn to sing properly, despite frequent later exposure to singing Chaffinches. Critical periods are seldom so rigid in human beings, but there is abundant evidence that various types of learning ability are greatest at certain ages. For example, children between the ages of two and ten can learn languages far more easily than adults.

Still another difficulty is that one cannot always tell immediately whether or not learning has occurred. There may be considerable delay between exposure to the learning situation and the performance of a behavior pattern that shows effects of learning. For example, if young Chaffinches only a few weeks old are allowed to hear a tape recording of a singing adult for a few days and are then raised in isolation, they will sing a nearly normal Chaffinch song when they first begin to sing the following spring. Exposure to the song during their first summer, long before they themselves are old enough to sing, results in learning, but the proof does not come until months later.

Much caution is needed in any attempt to compare the learning capabilities of different species. As might be deduced from the differences between their nervous systems, superficially similar learning in different species may actually involve different underlying mechanisms and fulfill entirely different functions in the lives of the animals. Thus, as shown by T. C. Schnierla of Columbia University, rats and ants can learn to run the same maze, but they do so in very different ways; rats appear to learn a "map" of the maze as a whole, whereas ants appear to learn the maze as a series of separate problems, one at each choice point. Mastery of the maze tends to improve the performance of rats when they are subsequently placed in new mazes, but it actually seems to hinder the performance of ants in new mazes. In other words, rats not only learn the particular maze but can also generalize to some extent from this experience and thus develop increased competence at running other mazes, whereas ants learn only the particular maze and this achievement makes their behavior in new mazes less flexible.

(*Elements of Biological Science*)

Topic: _____

Main Idea: _____

_____

Pattern of Organization: _____

Major Details: _____

Exercise 2

If you want to incorporate composition practice at this time, you may have students write paragraphs using each of the four patterns of organization covered in this chapter.

Use your textbooks or other sources to find examples of the four patterns of organization and bring them to class. Your instructor may make copies of your examples and distribute them to your classmates for purposes of discussion.

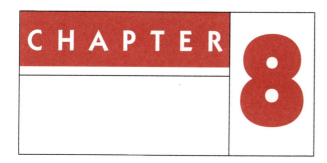

Organizing Textbook Material

Chapter Objective: To introduce outlining, mapping, underlining, summarizing, and paraphrasing.

Outlining

You have had much practice finding topics, main ideas, major and minor details, and patterns of organization. You will use these skills for outlining—a very helpful study technique that shows clearly the relationship among the various sentences in a given paragraph or passage. And understanding the relationship will help you understand textbook material much better. We will use the following format for outlining.

Topic

  I. Main Idea
     A. Major Detail
         1. Minor Detail
         2. Minor Detail
     B. Major Detail
         1. Minor Detail
         2. Minor Detail
 II. Main Idea
     A. Major Detail

Reinforce that outlining aids comprehension. When done correctly, outlining gives a clear picture of the relationship among the various sentences (main ideas, major details, and minor details) in a paragraph or passage.

    Tell students once they are confident at outlining, they may use phrases rather than whole sentences. They will be doing that later in this chapter when they diagram, summarize, and paraphrase. Caution the students, however, not to omit any words that have a major effect on the meaning.

        1. Minor Detail
        2. Minor Detail

As you can see, the topic is centered at the top of the page. The one or, occasionally, two main ideas are preceded by Roman numerals and placed at the margin. Capital letters come before the major details and are indented under the main idea. Arabic numbers are used to designate the even more indented minor details. Recall that details are considered major when they *directly* support the main idea, while others are called minor because they lend direct support to the various major details. Of course, the number of major and minor details varies from paragraph to paragraph. To save time you may use phrases or key words rather than complete sentences when you outline. However, just as when you take lecture notes, you have to be able to make sense of them later. Now read the following passage and then look carefully at the outline that follows it.

> There are three types of noise that can block communication. The first, external noise, includes those obvious things that make it difficult to hear, as well as many other kinds of distractions. For instance, too much cigarette smoke in a crowded room might make it hard for you to pay attention to another person, and sitting in the rear of an auditorium might make a speaker's remarks unclear. External noise can disrupt communication almost anywhere in our model—in the sender, channel, message, or receiver.
>   The second type of noise is physiological. A hearing disorder is probably the most obvious type of physiological barrier, although many more exist. Consider, for instance, the difficulty you experience as a listener when you are suffering from a cold or are very tired. In the same way, you might speak less when you have a sore throat or a headache.
>   Psychological noise refers to forces within the sender or receiver that make these people less able to express or understand the message clearly. For instance, an outdoorsman might exaggerate the size and number of fish caught in order to convince himself and others of his talents. In the same way, a student might become so upset upon learning that she failed a test that she would be unable (perhaps unwilling is a better word) to clearly understand where she went wrong. (*Looking Out/Looking In*)

Students should note that the simple list in this passage is only partially numbered, a common writing practice introduced in Chapter 7.

Noise That Can Block Communication

I. There are three types of noise that can block communication.
    A. The first, external noise, includes those obvious things that make it difficult to hear, as well as many others kinds of distractions.

1. For instance, too much cigarette smoke in a crowded room might make it hard for you to pay attention to another person, and sitting in the rear of an auditorium might make a speaker's remarks unclear.
2. External noise can disrupt communication almost anywhere in our model—in the sender, channel, message or receiver.
   B. The second type of noise is physiological.
      1. A hearing disorder is probably the most obvious type of physiological barrier, although many more exist.
      2. Consider, for instance, the difficulty you experience as a listener when you are suffering from a cold or are very tired.
      3. In the same way, you might speak less when you have a sore throat or a headache.
   C. Psychological noise refers to forces within the sender or receiver that make these people less able to express or understand the message clearly.
      1. For instance, an outdoorsman might exaggerate the size and number of fish caught in order to convince himself and others of his talent.
      2. In the same way, a student might become so upset upon learning that she failed a test that she would be unable (perhaps unwilling is a better word) to clearly understand where she went wrong.

As you may have noticed, the passage is organized by a simple listing of facts pattern. The main idea, which in this case covers three paragraphs, states that "there are three types of noise that can block communication," which of course, lets you know that there are likely to be three major details. Two of the three major details are numbered, making them easy to locate, and the relevant minor details follow neatly after each of them. Although paragraphs are not always written in a specific pattern of organization, when they are, outlining becomes a much simpler task because the major and minor details are easier to recognize.

Now read the next example and the outline that follows it.

George Bush sought and received the support of the international community in his efforts to turn back Iraqi aggression in Kuwait. To that end, he consulted with his allies and the United Nations before taking any actions. Also, the economic stranglehold on Iraq made it difficult for that nation to sustain the battle. More specifically, the oil and trade embargo prevented much needed revenue and goods from coming into the country which had grave effects on the economy. In fact, the population was virtually starving, which lowered its morale and affected its will to fight. Furthermore, Saddam Hussein did not possess the sophisticated weaponry that his adversaries had, nor was his military leadership sufficiently schooled in techniques and strategies. This explains why his troops were so badly outmaneuvered on the battlefield. Add to all of these reasons, the fact that Iraq had just fought a long, draining eight year war with Iran which depleted the country's resources and sapped its strength. In short, there were several important factors that contributed to the defeat of Iraq in the recent Persian Gulf War.

The Defeat of Iraq

I. In short, there were several important factors that contributed to the defeat of Iraq in the recent Persian Gulf War.
   A. George Bush sought and received the support of the international community in his efforts to turn back Iraqi aggression in Kuwait.
      1. To that end, he consulted with his allies and the United Nations before taking any actions.
   B. Also, the economic stranglehold on Iraq made it difficult for that nation to sustain the battle.
      1. More specifically, the oil and trade embargo prevented much needed revenue and goods from coming into the country which had grave effects on the economy.
      2. In fact, the population was virtually starving which lowered its morale and affected its will to fight.
   C. Furthermore, Saddam Hussein did not possess the sophisticated weaponry that his adversaries had, nor was his military leadership sufficiently schooled in techniques and strategies.
      1. This explains why his troops were so badly outmaneuvered on the battlefield.
   D. Add to all of these reasons, the fact that Iraq had just fought a long, draining eight year war with Iran which depleted the country's resources and sapped its strength.

The last sentence in the passage is the main idea: "There were several important factors that contributed to the defeat of Iraq in the recent

Persian Gulf War." Those factors, which amount to four, represent the major details (A. to D.) that directly support the main idea. The words "also," "furthermore," and "add to all of these reasons" help you find them. All of the major details except the last one have supporting minor details that provide more specific information.

Remember from Chapter 5 that occasionally a paragraph has two main ideas. Although this happens infrequently, you should be prepared to outline such a paragraph. Read the following example and then study carefully the outline that comes after it.

> The investors were motivated by varying considerations. Some saw the syndicate as a chance to make money. Others were guided by the desire to safeguard a local hero, or simply have a bit of fun. Regardless, the contract signed by Cassius Clay and cosigned by his parents was fair and generous for its time. Clay received a $10,000 signing bonus and, for the first two years, a guaranteed draw of $333 a month against earnings. The sponsoring group had options to extend the contract for up to four additional twelve-month periods. Earnings would be split fifty-fifty for the first four years and sixty-forty in Clay's favor thereafter. All management, training, travel, and promotional expenses, including a trainer's salary, would come out of the syndicate's end. And 15 percent of Clay's income would be set aside in a pension fund, which he could not touch until he reached age thirty-five or retired from boxing. (*Muhammad Ali: His Life and Times,* Thomas Hauser)

The Motivations of Investors
and
Cassius Clay's Contract

I. Investors were motivated by varying considerations.

   A. Some saw the syndicate as a chance to make money.

   B. Others were guided by the desire to safeguard a local hero, or simply have a bit of fun.

II. Regardless, the contract signed by Cassius Clay and cosigned by his parents was fair and generous for its time.

   A. Clay received a $10,000 signing bonus and, for the first two years, a guaranteed draw of $333 a month against earnings.

      1. The sponsoring group had options to extend the contract for up to four additional twelve-month periods.

   B. Earnings would be split fifty-fifty for the first four years and sixty-forty in Clay's favor thereafter.

C. All management, training, travel and promotional expenses, including a trainer's salary, would come out of the syndicate's end.

D. And 15 percent of Clay's income would be set aside in a pension fund, which he could not touch until he reached age thirty-five or retired from boxing.

Notice that there are two topics in the paragraph that involve "the motivations of the investors" and "Cassius Clay's contract." (Cassius Clay was Muhammad Ali's name at the time that he signed the contract.) The two main ideas flow logically from the topics and are given direct support by different major details that explain what exactly the motivations of the investors were and why Clay's contract was fair and generous. Notice that there is only one minor detail in the entire paragraph, which comes after the first major detail under the second main idea.

Outlining gives you a clear and complete picture of an entire paragraph's structure, thereby showing how all of its sentences are logically related to each other. It enables you to focus on the major and minor details, making it easier to find main ideas. Recognizing patterns of organization, when they are present, also will help you to distinguish between the various sentences. Although outlining can be time consuming, the technique is well worth the effort because the careful thought you put into it will surely bring about much better comprehension.

Writing the outlines on the chalkboard or displaying them with an overhead projector would be very helpful to students.

See Instructor's Manual, Chapter 8 Answers.

Exercise 1

Read the following two paragraphs and then fill in the outline for each.

1

There are several approaches to preventing accidents. *Persuasion* and *education* are aimed at changing people's skills, attitudes, values, and emotions. Driver-education classes, campaigns for stricter gun laws, and counseling for drunk drivers are examples of efforts at persuasion and education. *Laws* are generally more successful than persuasion. We have laws, for example, requiring the use of seatbelts, infant car seats, and motorcycle helmets, and we have laws against drunk driving. Historically, the most successful programs of accident prevention have been *passive*. That is, they do not require people to take any action in order to be protected. For example, milk is pasteurized; drinking water is treated; and cars come equipped with headrests, seatbelts, and shatterproof windshields. Let's take a look at some specific suggestions on passive protections from agents of harm.

(*Essentials of Life and Health*)

Topic

_____

_____

I. Main Idea: _____

_____

A. Major Detail: _____

_____

_____

_____

1. Minor Detail: _____

_____

B. Major Detail: _____
   _____
   _____
   _____

   1. Minor Detail: _____
      _____
      _____

C. Major Detail: _____
   _____
   _____
   _____

   1. Minor Detail: _____
      _____
      _____

   2. Minor Detail: _____
      _____
      _____

   3. Minor Detail: _____
      _____
      _____

2

Learning how to drive can be a very frustrating, humbling experience for many people. This is because there are so many different things to think about and do all at once. Two hands, two feet, two eyes, two ears, and one brain just don't seem adequate for the job. Learning how to drive also can be a very frightening experience for those who tend to crumble in the face of adversity. Cars seem to come at you from all directions, and other drivers are not exactly patient. They blow their horns continuously while making all kinds of bizarre faces—to say nothing about some of the terminology they use to describe you. Their behavior makes one seriously contemplate the benefits of walking!

Topic

_____

_____

I. Main Idea: _____

_____

_____

    A. Major Detail: _____

    _____

    _____

        1. Minor Detail: _____

        _____

        _____

II. Main Idea: _____

A. Major Detail: _____

_____

_____

_____

1. Minor Detail: _____

_____

_____

_____

2. Minor Detail: _____

_____

_____

_____

Exercise 2

Outline each of the passages in your notebook using the format that we have been following. Remember that the number of major and minor details will vary and that sometimes there could be more than one main idea. As already mentioned, *you may feel more comfortable using phrases instead of complete sentences when outlining.* Therefore, if you wish, you may use just key phrases or perhaps abbreviate the sentences as long as none of the meaning is lost.

To guide the students, you may write the outlines on the chalkboard or display them on an overhead projector.

See Instructor's Manual, Chapter 8 Answers.

1

Lipids are found in many living organisms, and they are categorized into three groups: simple lipids, compound lipids, and derived lipids.

Simple lipids contain the elements carbon, hydrogen, and oxygen. Examples are fats and oils such as butter, margarine, and corn, olive, peanut, and safflower oils. Other simple lipids are waxes such as beeswax and lanolin.

Compound lipids are composed of carbon, hydrogen, oxygen, nitrogen, and phosphorus. They include the phospholids, which are found in cell membranes, and the glycolipids in brain and nerve cells.

Finally, there are the derived lipids containing only carbon, hydrogen, and oxygen. These include the steroids found in the male and female sex hormones and cholesterol and the fat-soluble vitamins A, D, E, and K.

(*Body Structures and Functions,*
Elizabeth Fong, Elvira B. Ferris, and Esther G. Skelley)

2

Cars can be deadly weapons. Every year, half of all the people who die from injuries and half of those with permanent spinal cord injuries are hurt in car accidents. Cars are especially dangerous in the hands of people who are drunk. As we saw in Chapter 5, a blood alcohol level of 0.10 percent or higher means that a person is legally drunk and should not drive. Nevertheless, half of all drivers killed are drunk, and of these, nearly one-quarter were convicted of a moving violation within the previous three years. In other words, many drunk drivers have a history of dangerous driving.

(*Essentials of Life and Health*)

3

U.S. law is usually divided into two basic types: criminal and civil. A **criminal law** defines an action as a crime and specifies a penalty. Serious crimes are called felonies, and less serious ones are labeled misdemeanors (the precise line between these varies from state to state). In principle, all criminal actions are against the public order. If Smith assaults Jones, the government (not Jones) will prosecute Smith. In contrast, under **civil law,** the government provides a code regulating conduct for settling disputes between private persons. For example, if Jones buys a car from Smith and the car suddenly falls apart, Jones may sue Smith for damages under provisions of state civil law regulating contracts and liability. Because civil law sanctions are less severe than criminal law punishments, civil law standards of proof are less demanding.

(*Understanding American Government,* Robert Weissberg)

4

An item on the television news connects the use of saccharin with cancer. A diet book that recommends eating large amounts of pineapple becomes a best seller. A suburban supermarket begins to offer alfalfa sprouts and cakes of tofu to its customers.

As these examples suggest, Americans are now more interested in food and nutrition than they ever have been. We are concerned about whether certain foods may be hazardous to our health, and many Americans have initiated changes in their eating habits to maintain their health. The federal government, aware of the growing public concern about nutrition and health, has released a number of health-promotion pamphlets, including "Objectives for the Nation," a list of seventeen nutritional goals. As a nation, we seem to be obsessed with keeping our weight down, and we are more likely than ever to choose "diet" soft drinks—and even "sugarless" chocolates and chewing gum. Our changing tastes in food have led some of us to sample new foods—yogurt, for example. Whatever we eat, we probably wonder whether we're eating the right thing. Increasingly, we are concerned about nutrition.

(*Essentials of Life and Health*)

5

The experience of the Amish is one example of the way a subculture is tolerated by the larger culture within which it functions. As different as they are, the Amish actually practice many values that our nation respects in the abstract: thrift, hard work, independence, a close family life. The degree of tolerance accorded to them may also be due in part to the fact that the Amish are white Europeans, of the same race as the dominant culture. American Indian subcultures have been treated differently by whites. There was a racial difference; the whites came as conquerors, and Indian values were not as easily understood or sympathized with by the larger culture. The nation was less willing to tolerate the differences of the Indians, with results that are both a matter of history, as well as very much a current concern.

(*Cultural Anthropology*)

6

The occupation of prostitute takes several basic forms. Most female prostitutes work as streetwalkers, soliciting clients in public places such as streets and hotel lobbies. These women are generally poorly educated and include a high proportion of minority-group members, teenage runaways, and older prostitutes who are nearing the end of their careers. Other women work in brothels, which are today disguised as "massage parlors" or "clubs"; these prostitutes have higher status and better earnings than the streetwalker, and they face less danger from their clients or the police. Still others work as call girls, operating out of hotel rooms or apartments, either on their own or through an "escort agency." These are usually the better-educated prostitutes, who may regard the occupation as a potential avenue to higher social status as the mistress or even the wife of a wealthy man. Male prostitutes catering to homosexuals solicit clients on certain streets, in some gay bars, and occasionally through "escort agencies." Male prostitutes catering to women generally work through private introductions and try to establish regular relationships with a small number of clients rather than transient relationships with many women.

(*Society: A Brief Introduction,* Ian Robertson)

> Exercise 3: Distribute some of the better outlines prepared by students and discuss them as a class. This can serve as a good motivational, reinforcement, and confidence-building exercise.

Exercise 3

In your notebook, outline three paragraphs from textbooks that you are using in your other courses. If you are currently not using textbooks, use any book or periodical that you choose.

Making Diagrams (Mapping)

Outlining is only one way of organizing the information in a paragraph or passage. Although outlining shows clearly the relationship between main ideas, major details, and minor details, you may prefer to use diagrams to organize material. Whereas outlining generally involves complete sentences or longer phrases, diagraming—sometimes called mapping—uses key words or phrases. For example, one of my students constructed the following diagram on unfamiliar words (*Table 8.1 on page 217*) so that he could picture the different ways to find the meanings of difficult words. Notice how the connecting lines illustrate the relationship among the various methods.

That same student drew the diagram on overviewing (*Table 8.2 on page 218*) to depict the technique as a means of familiarizing oneself with a textbook.

As you may have guessed by now, there is not one set way of diagraming a paragraph. The student's diagrams use connecting lines to show relationships. However, because of the nature of the material involved, he made no effort to distinguish the comparative level of importance of each of the items. As you know from your work with main ideas, major details, and minor details, the information contained within a paragraph is often not of equal weight. To show the relative importance you can use various sized shapes, such as boxes, circles, or triangles. Obviously, you will find the most significant information in main ideas, so the forms you use for them should be the largest, followed by the ones used for major details, and finally, by those you use for the minor details. Use lines or arrows to connect the related words or phrases. A typical diagram is structured something like the one in Table 8.3 on page 219.

Remember that a paragraph will occasionally contain more than one main idea, and the number of major and minor details will vary from paragraph to paragraph. Because the shapes hold only a little information, you must condense sentences into concise phrases or words to fit.

Table 8.1

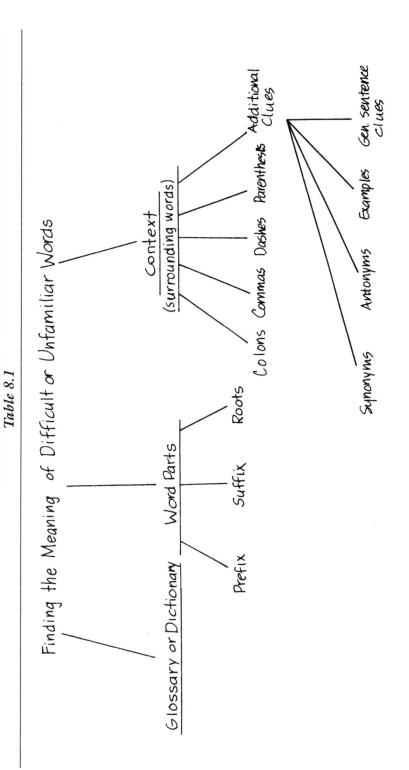

Emphasize that a wide variety of diagrams is acceptable as long as their organization reflects the importance of elements in relationship to one another. As with outlining, a diagram should show the relationship among the different ideas expressed in a given paragraph.

Table 8.2

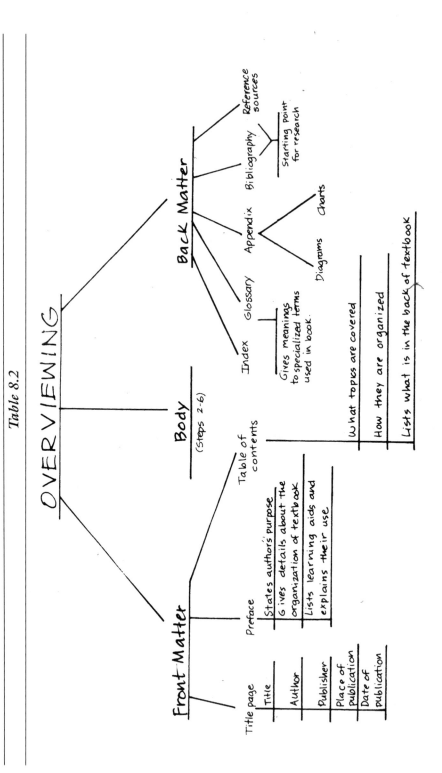

Table 8.3

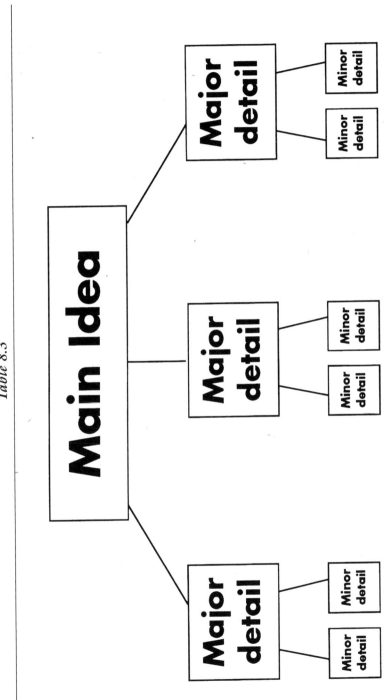

For example, look again at this passage on noise that was outlined at the beginning of this chapter.

There are three types of noise that can block communication. The first, external noise, includes those obvious things that make it difficult to hear, as well as many other kinds of distractions. For instance, too much cigarette smoke in a crowded room might make it hard for you to pay attention to another person, and sitting in the rear of an auditorium might make a speaker's remarks unclear. External noise can disrupt communication almost anywhere in our model—in the sender, channel, message, or receiver.

The second type of noise is physiological. A hearing disorder is probably the most obvious type of physiological barrier, although many more exist. Consider, for instance, the difficulty you experience as a listener when you are suffering from a cold or are very tired. In the same way, you might speak less when you have a sore throat or a headache.

Psychological noise refers to forces within the sender or receiver that make these people less able to express or understand the message clearly. For instance, an outdoorsman might exaggerate the size and number of fish caught in order to convince himself and others of his talents. In the same way, a student might become so upset upon learning that she failed a test that she would be unable (perhaps unwilling is a better word) to clearly understand where she went wrong. (*Looking Out/Looking In*)

See table 8.4 below for an example of a box diagram for this passage.

Table 8.4

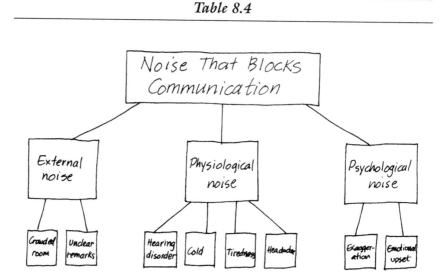

Notice that the key ideas from the major details, which are of equal importance, are housed in the same sized boxes. The minor details, which vary in number, are smaller and connected by lines to the respective major details. The diagram makes it easy to see how the material flows from main idea to major details to minor details. The relationship among the various pieces of information is pictured clearly, making learning and remembering easier. Again, recognizing patterns of organization, such as simple listing, helps you to diagram with more speed.

Reviewing the following paragraph on Cassius Clay's contract, a diagram that includes two main ideas can be constructed without much difficulty.

> The investors were motivated by varying considerations. Some saw the syndicate as a chance to make money. Others were guided by the desire to safeguard a local hero, or simply have a bit of fun. Regardless, the contract signed by Cassius Clay and cosigned by his parents was fair and generous for its time. Clay received a $10,000 signing bonus and, for the first two years, a guaranteed draw of $333 a month against earnings. The sponsoring group had options to extend the contract for up to four additional twelve-month periods. Earnings would be split fifty-fifty for the first four years and sixty-forty in Clay's favor thereafter. All management, training, travel, and promotional expenses, including a trainer's salary, would come out of the syndicate's end. And 15 percent of Clay's income would be set aside in a pension fund, which he could not touch until he reached age thirty-five or retired from boxing. (*Muhammad Ali: His Life and Times,* Thomas Hauser)

Following is a sample box diagram of the paragraph.

Table 8.5

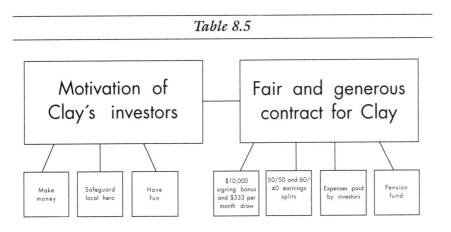

Point out to your students that the key ideas from the two main ideas are connected by a line. One minor detail has been excluded because it is not really important. To make a diagram manageable, information may be reduced.

Exercise 4

Reviewing paragraphs 1 and 2 that follow—the same two you outlined in Exercise 1—construct a box diagram for each paragraph. Use the diagrams in Table 8.6 (page 225) and Table 8.7 (page 226) as models. Remember to use only the most important information and to reduce it into concise phrases or words. Note that in Table 8.7, there are no boxes for minor details, which in paragraph 2 add little information.

1

There are several approaches to preventing accidents. *Persuasion* and *education* are aimed at changing people's skills, attitudes, values, and emotions. Driver-education classes, campaigns for stricter gun laws, and counseling for drunk drivers are examples of efforts at persuasion and education. *Laws* are generally more successful than persuasion. We have laws, for example, requiring the use of seatbelts, infant car seats, and motorcycle helmets, and we have laws against drunk driving. Historically, the most successful programs of accident prevention have been *passive*. That is, they do not require people to take any action in order to be protected. For example, milk is pasteurized; drinking water is treated; and cars come equipped with headrests, seatbelts, and shatterproof windshields. Let's take a look at some specific suggestions on passive protections from agents of harm.

(*Essentials of Life and Health*)

> **2**
>
> Learning how to drive can be a very frustrating, humbling experience for many people. This is because there are so many different things to think about and do all at once. Two hands, two feet, two eyes, two ears, and one brain just don't seem adequate for the job. Driving also can be a very frightening experience for those who tend to crumble in the face of adversity. Cars seem to come at you from all directions, and other drivers are not exactly patient. They blow their horns continuously while making all kinds of bizarre faces—to say nothing of some of the terminology they use to describe you. Their behavior makes one seriously contemplate the benefits of walking!

> Ask for student volunteers to draw their diagrams on the blackboard or you may want to display them on an overhead projector.

Exercise 5

Turn back to the six passages that you outlined in Exercise 2. In your notebook, construct a diagram for each using whatever form (boxes, circles, or triangles) you like. Remember you must condense the main ideas, major details, and minor details into brief phrases or words. Also use forms of equal size for information of equal importance and draw lines or arrows to link related information.

Exercise 6

In your notebook construct diagrams for any three paragraphs from textbooks you are using in your other courses. If you currently are not using additional textbooks, use any books or periodicals of your choice. Keep in mind that recognizing patterns of organization and locating main ideas, major details, and minor details help you uncover the most important information.

Table 8.6

Paragraph 1 Diagram Model

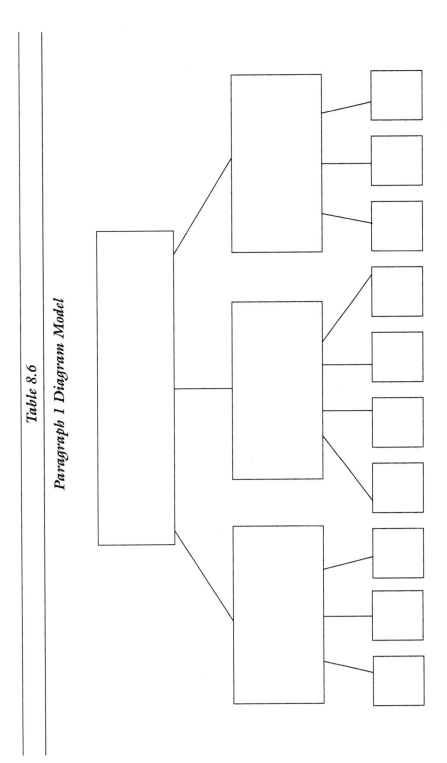

Chapter 8 *Organizing Textbook Material*

Table 8.7
Paragraph 2 Diagram Model

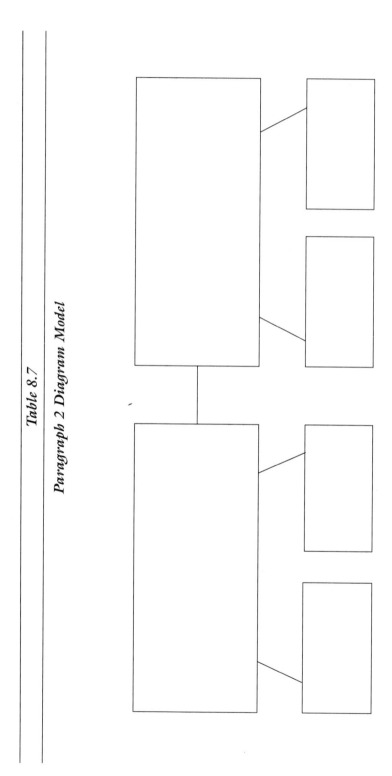

Summarizing and Paraphrasing

So far, you used outlining and diagraming (mapping) to organize textbook material. As you know, outlining often involves the use of whole sentences, whereas diagraming focuses on key words or phrases. In both instances, you write out all or many of the actual words of the writer. Although these techniques help you to recognize the relationship among the various sentences and ideas in a passage, they do not necessarily result in a thorough and complete understanding of what you have read.

If you truly understand reading material, you should be able first to interpret it, then to condense or shorten it, and finally to put it into your own words. When you condense information, you are *summarizing* the main points by using many of the writer's own terms. Putting the information into your own words is called *paraphrasing*—a skill you used in Chapter 5 when you wrote out unstated main ideas. In short, paraphrasing involves substituting your own words—not your opinions—for the author's, except for certain key terminology, essential to the meaning of the material. We often use both summarizing and paraphrasing in our every day lives. For example, when you try to explain to someone what happened in class or what a particular movie or television program was about, you are summarizing and paraphrasing. In those instances, you generally use your own words to provide a short description without relating, word-for-word, everything that occurred.

Given the vast amount of information normally presented in a typical college reading assignment, you need to find a way to reduce the information to manageable proportions. Summarizing and paraphrasing, when you do it correctly, should make textbook material easier to learn and remember. To summarize you must be able to pick out the most important information, usually found in main ideas, major details, and context definitions. Underlining is a technique that helps you focus better by getting you more actively involved in your reading, while enabling you to highlight the information you need for your summary.

Underlining is very useful for several reasons. First, the physical act of underlining forces you to be more attentive, thereby aiding your concentration; you are less likely to daydream or fall asleep. Second, in determining what you should underline, you first must evaluate carefully what you are reading, resulting in better comprehension. Third, because underlining involves increased concentration, thought, and evaluation, it helps you remember. Finally, when done properly,

---

Ask students how many of them underline in their textbooks. Emphasize the importance of underlining as a way of improving concentration, comprehension, and retention. You may want to have students underline the introduction to this chapter to determine their understanding of this skill.

underlining helps you to locate quickly only the most important information when you review; you need not read the material in its entirety again. In short, make it a habit to underline, particularly when you are dealing with textbook material.

The major problem with underlining is that students sometimes underline too much, finding it difficult to determine what is important. You can avoid this problem by underlining only the information you find in main ideas, major details, and context definitions. Use patterns of organization and context clues to help you locate them.

After underlining and summarizing material, you can then attempt to paraphrase it. To do this correctly, you must understand fully what the writer is saying, otherwise you may omit important information and lose some of the meaning. For example, look one last time at the passage on noise used to illustrate outlining and diagraming.

> <u>There are three types of noise that can block communication. The first, external noise, includes those obvious things that make it difficult to hear, as well as many other kinds of distractions.</u> For instance, too much cigarette smoke in a crowded room might make it hard for you to pay attention to another person, and sitting in the rear of an auditorium might make a speaker's remarks unclear. <u>External noise can disrupt communication almost anywhere in our model—in the sender, channel, message, or receiver.</u>
>
> <u>The second type of noise is physiological. A hearing disorder is probably the most obvious type of physiological barrier, although many more exist.</u> Consider, for instance, the difficulty you experience as a listener when you are suffering from a cold or are very tired. In the same way you might speak less when you have a sore throat or a headache.
>
> <u>Psychological noise refers to forces within the sender or receiver that make these people less able to express or understand the message clearly.</u> For instance, an outdoorsman might exaggerate the size and number of fish caught in order to convince himself and others of his talents. In the same way, a student might become so upset upon learning that she failed a test that she would be unable (perhaps unwilling is a better word) to clearly understand where she went wrong. (*Looking Out/Looking In*)

Notice how the main idea and the details (some of which are organized by the simple listing pattern of organization) have been underlined to make them stand out. A summary of the passage would read something like the following.

External, physiological, and psychological noise can block communication. External noise, which includes distractions that make it difficult to hear, can disrupt communication in the sender,

---

Sidebar: Remind students that when they diagrammed they were forced to condense or shorten material in order to accommodate limited space on the various forms. Explain that they will apply the same skill when summarizing. Paraphrasing, on the other hand, will take them one step beyond by having them condense the material in their own words, rather than those of the author. Paraphrasing requires much practice because students often lose or omit some of the writer's meaning in the translation. Encourage their efforts at developing this skill.

channel, message, or receiver. There are many physiological barriers, such as a hearing disorder. Psychological noise refers to forces within the sender or receiver that make these people less able to express or understand the message.

Although the information has been condensed, many of the writer's words have been repeated, which by itself, does not necessarily mean that true understanding has taken place. Therefore, if we were to go one final step and paraphrase the passage, we might end up with something like the following.

Outside distractions, physical problems, and mental factors can all interfere with communication. Distractions can disrupt the sender, channel, message, or receiver. Any kind of a physical disorder, such as a hearing or speaking problem, makes it difficult to communicate. Finally, forces within the mind of the sender or receiver can have a negative effect on a message.

As you can see, very few of the writer's words have been used to paraphrase the passage, but the most important information has been included through the use of other, perhaps more familiar, terms. The ability to paraphrase demonstrates a more complete understanding of whatever you are reading because you are able to translate the material into words that are more meaningful to you, which should make it easier to learn and remember.

Until this point the skills of summarizing and paraphrasing have been separated for purposes of discussion. However you may want to combine them as they become more familiar to you. For example, look at the following passage, paying particular attention to the sentences that have been underlined.

One of the first women to make a career in psychology was Mary Calkins. When Henry Durant founded Wellesley College in 1870, he decided to hire only women to teach the all-female student body. But he could find no woman with an advanced degree in psychology. Finally, in 1890, he hired a bright young woman, Mary Calkins, who had a B.A. degree in classics, to teach psychology, promising that he would pay for her graduate education in psychology. Then the problem was to find a graduate program that would accept a female student. After much debate and stiff resistance, nearby Harvard University finally agreed to let her attend graduate classes, although at first it would not allow her to register officially as a student. In 1895, when she passed the final examination for the Ph.D. degree, one of her professors remarked that she had performed better on the examination than had any other student in the history of the department.

> <u>The Harvard administration, however, was still unwilling to grant a Ph.D. degree to a woman.</u> It suggested a compromise. <u>It would grant her a Ph.D. degree from Radcliffe College, the recently established women's undergraduate college associated with Harvard. She refused,</u> declaring that to accept the compromise would violate the high ideals of education. She never gave in, and neither did Harvard. <u>Although Mary Calkins never received a Ph.D. degree, she became a pioneer in psychological research, inventing a technique of studying memory, known as the paired-associates method, that is still used today.</u> (*Introduction to Psychology*)

Remember that the goal here is to first reduce the amount of information by eliminating unimportant material. So concentrating on the topic, main ideas, major details, and context definitions is crucial. Next the information should be translated into the reader's own words—except those words used by the writer that are crucial to the meaning of the passage. A summary that has been paraphrased could possibly look like the following.

> Henry Durant founded Wellesley College in 1870 and hired Mary Calkins to teach psychology. Because she did not have a degree in that field, she tried to get into a graduate program. After much resistance because she was a woman, Harvard agreed to have her attend classes. Although she passed the Ph.D. exam with a performance that was the best ever, Harvard refused to give her the degree because she was a woman. Instead it offered to have Radcliffe College, which was an undergraduate woman's college associated with Harvard, grant her the degree. She refused to accept the offer and never received her Ph.D. However she still contributed to the field by inventing a way of studying memory called the paired-associates method that is still used today.

Notice how only certain key words, such as the names of the schools, the names of individuals, and specialized terms like "paired-associates method," are included. Nevertheless, the information is condensed and different words are used without losing the basic meaning of the passage. Thus, the material should be easier to understand, learn, and remember. Make it a practice to underline, summarize, and paraphrase your reading assignments whenever you can.

Exercise 7

In your notebook first summarize and then paraphrase the following passages. Remember to pay close attention to topics, main ideas, major details, and context definitions and to use underlining to highlight the most important information. Also remember to condense or shorten the material when you summarize it. When you paraphrase, use mostly your own words.

Student volunteers should read their summaries and/or paraphrasing aloud in class in order to promote discussion. Make corrections gently and praise what has been done correctly.

See Instructor's Manual, Chapter 8 Answers.

1

Almost all human children, even many retarded children, acquire language skills in their first few years regardless of whether their parents make any real effort to teach them. Although closely related to humans genetically, chimpanzees have no language. Why not? Researchers have tried to teach chimpanzees some approximation of human language, partly to discover the differences between chimpanzees and humans, partly to discover what learning a language requires, and partly to deepen their understanding of language itself.

(*Introduction to Psychology*)

2

According to a survey of people who watched one of the 1980 presidential debates between Jimmy Carter and Ronald Reagan, most of those who planned to vote for Carter thought Carter won the debate, and most of those who planned to vote for Reagan thought Reagan won. Few people changed their attitudes toward the candidates as a result of watching the debate.

In fact, it is difficult to change people's attitudes, especially deeply held attitudes. Still, political candidates try to convince us to vote for them, and advertisers try to induce us to buy their products.

What are the most effective ways of persuading people to change their attitudes? The effectiveness of persuasion depends on *who* says *what, how* he or she says it, and to *whom*.

(*Introduction to Psychology*)

3

People change. From moment to moment we aren't the same. We wake up in the morning in a jovial mood and turn grumpy before lunch. We find ourselves fascinated in a conversational topic one moment, then suddenly lose interest. One moment's anger often gives way to forgiveness the next. Health turns to illness and back to health. Alertness becomes fatigue, hunger becomes satiation, and confusion becomes clarity.

We also change from situation to situation. You might be a relaxed conversationalist with people you know but at a loss for words with strangers. You might be patient when explaining things on the job and have no tolerance for such things at home. You might be a wizard at solving mathematical problems but have a terribly difficult time putting your thoughts into words.

Over longer stretches of time we also change. We grow older, learn new facts, adopt new attitudes and philosophies, set and reach new goals, and find that others change their way of thinking and acting toward us.

(*Looking Out/Looking In*)

4

Have you ever wondered how scientists are able to launch the space shuttle at just the right speed so it will orbit the earth and return safely? Whether there is life on other planets? Why human organ transplants have become more successful than ever before? Or what causes cancer? If you have, then you have begun to think as a scientist does.

Scientists are curious. They are always asking questions and seeking answers. Scientists try to solve problems and learn new things about the world and universe. Often they seek solutions to problems that affect the lives of us all.

Scientists work in four major areas of study. Life scientists, or biologists, study living things. Chemists investigate the make-up, structure, properties, and reactions of matter. Earth and space scientists study the earth and the objects in space. Physicists explore the interactions between matter and energy. Each area of study includes several specialties. For example, life science includes ecology, which is the study of the interactions between living things and their environment.

(*Allyn and Bacon General Science*,
Carolyn Sheets Brockway, Robert Gardner, and Samuel F. Howe)

5

Some time in the 1970s, magazine editor Norman Cousins returned home exhausted from a stressful overseas trip. He had great difficulty staying on his feet, and checked himself into a hospital. His physicians' diagnosis: a stress-induced, painful arthritis-type disease that was breaking down the connective tissue in his spine. Their prognosis: further deterioration of the spine, leading to paralysis and complete disability, with little chance of survival.

Thinking about his grim future, Cousins reasoned that if negative emotional experiences could cause physical harm, then positive emotions—most notably "hope, faith, laughter, confidence, and the will to live"—might improve health. With his doctor's approval, he checked in a hotel room, where for weeks he watched funny movies (Marx Brothers, Buster Keaton) and had someone read him funny stories.

In the early weeks, Cousins was in such pain that he was hardly able to sleep. Gradually, however, he found that ten minutes of "genuine belly laughter" would relax him enough to give him two hours of pain-free sleep. Eventually, he gained complete recovery and went on to write about his experience in a medical journal, which led to more serious scientific study of the relationship between emotions and healing.

(*Healthy for Life*)

6

Jack Campbell is a nervous type. Although he boasts about his reading of magazines and newspapers, the truth is that he's a "skimmer" where advertisements are concerned. Unless advertisers can catch his attention with headlines and subheads, they can scratch our Mr. Campbell as a prospect. A quick flick of his gaze is all they get for their carefully prepared advertisements.

Mrs. Campbell, although she runs the household and works at a parttime job, spends much more time on advertising than does her husband. But with her double duties, she has no time to waste. The advertiser's task is to get busy Mrs. Campbell, and others like her, to hesitate before going on to the next advertisement.

In either situation, the advertiser relies on headlines to flag the reader and to create enough interest to force that pausing over the advertisement. The headline doesn't *convince* the reader, that comes later. It says in effect, "Here's something interesting," "Here's news," "Here's a useful item," "Here's something profitable for you," or "Here's an easy way to do something."

When you've written your headline, you've taken your first step toward the sale. It's a vital step because if you fail to attract Mr. or Mrs. Campbell to your advertisement or your message, you're out of the action completely. You must get that initial attention and that initial sparking of interest.

(*Advertising Copywriting*)

7

Psychological abnormalities come in many forms. Some are difficult to recognize, because "abnormal" behaviors are just exaggerations of normal ones. Students in medical school often contract what is known as "medical students' disease." Imagine that you are just beginning your training in medicine. One of your textbooks describes "Cryptic Ruminating Umbilicus Disorder":

"The symptoms are very minor until the condition becomes hopeless. The first symptom is a pale tongue." (You go to the mirror. You can't remember what your tongue is supposed to look like, but it *does* look a little pale.) "Later a hard spot forms in the neck." (You feel your neck. "Wait! I never felt *this* before! I think it's something hard!") "Just before the arms and legs fall off, there is shortness of breath, increased heart rate, and sweating." (Already distressed, you *do* have shortness of breath, your heart *is* racing, and you *are* sweating profusely.)

Sooner or later, most medical students decide they have some dreaded illness. The problem is imaginary; they merely confuse the description of some disease with their own normal condition. When my brother was in medical school, he diagnosed himself as having a rare, fatal illness, checked himself into a hospital, and wrote a will. (Today he is a successful physician.)

"Medical students' disease" is even more common among students of psychological disorders. As you read this chapter and the next, you may decide that you are suffering from some such disorder: "That sounds exactly like me! I must have Deteriorating Raving Odd Omnivorous Lycanthropy!"

Well, maybe you do. But more likely you do not. Psychological disorders are just exaggerations of tendencies that nearly all of us have; we simply recognize ourselves in the descriptions of the disorders. The difference between "normal" and "psychologically disordered" is a matter of degree.

(*Introduction to Psychology*)

8

You are sitting at home doing your homework when your mom comes home early from her job at the factory. "Is anything wrong?" you ask here. "I just lost my job to a robot," she says sadly.

Does this sound far-fetched? Already many thousands of robots are being used in factories all across the country. More are being installed each day. Some new factories are completely automated. All of the production is done by machines.

One result of this trend towards automation is increased unemployment in industrial areas. Factory workers in these regions are concerned. They are demanding a slowdown in the pace of the "robot revolution."

Even when jobs are kept, workers complain that robots change the nature of the work. They say their jobs become much less interesting and creative. Skilled machinists, for example, complain that now they only "baby-sit" for the new machines.

Other people think that robots will benefit both factory owners and the work force. Company spokespersons are quick to point out that robots often perform jobs that people would rather not do, jobs that can be boring or dangerous. For example, a robot may paint thousands of automobiles without being affected by fumes that might be hazardous to humans. So the use of robots for "dirty work" can improve the working conditions for humans.

For many factory tasks, robots are simply cheaper to operate and more efficient than humans. Many factory owners think that they must either use robots or lose business to companies that do. As one business analyst put it, "Are you going to reduce your work force by 25 percent by putting in robots, or by 100 percent by going out of business?"

Some industry experts feel that robots will create many new jobs. After all, people will have to build, maintain, and fix the machines. But other experts point out that although using robots may create more jobs in the long run, they certainly cause job losses in the short run. Such large-scale unemployment may offset the benefits of automation for the economy and society.

(*Allyn and Bacon General Science*)

9

Medical science is now capable of prolonging the functioning of bodily systems long after the systems would normally have failed. It is not unusual to see patients in institutions living as near vegetables for months and even years. Such individuals create a definite problem for family members and physicians: Would it not be better to put these patients out of their misery?

On the question of this sort of "mercy killing," or *euthanasia,* Americans are divided into three groups. One group consists of the people who insist that all possible efforts be made to prolong the life of seriously ill patients. Those who take this stance maintain that any tampering with human life is a form of playing God and that the result is either murder or, if the patient concurs, murder combined with suicide.

A majority of Americans, on the other hand, admit to belief in *indirect euthanasia,* sometimes referred to as negative euthanasia. In forms of indirect euthanasia, death is not directly caused or induced; rather, it is allowed to take place through the withdrawal of specific treatments. Such indirect euthanasia is not uncommon in medical practice, though it is rarely acknowledged by doctors for fear of legal complications. This position has considerable authoritative backing, including that of the late Pope Pius XII, who declared that no extraordinary means need be taken to prolong human life.

The third—and smallest—group consists of those who believe in *direct euthanasia.* The number of people who actually practice direct euthanasia is difficult to ascertain. Some physicians admit in private to having done so—either directly, by administering a lethal drug, or indirectly, by allowing the patient, the family, or the support staff to cause the death.

(*Essentials of Life and Health*)

10

Many psychologists have described their concepts of the emotionally mature person. Although these theories differ in several ways, there are a few qualities that seem to appear again and again.

The ability to be *intimate* is one important attribute of the emotionally mature person. The only way to gain a true perspective on one's place in the world is through intimacy with others. Being able to give and accept love and affection, opening oneself to the rich and sometimes confusing "otherness" of a separate person, is an experience that adds immeasurably to one's understanding.

Also important is the ability to be *sociable*—to maintain amicable and sustained relations with a circle of friends. There is a difference between intimacy and sociability. In order to be sociable, one needn't reveal oneself to the core. Yet the emotionally mature person does exhibit qualities of loyalty, devotion, and interest with his or her friends. But it is also necessary to develop a degree of independence. Having friends is important—but not so important that one should be willing to sacrifice all else simply to be "one of the group."

A *sense of self* is another important attribute of the emotionally mature person. In order to function effectively, it is necessary for a person to have a clear and vivid sense of himself or herself as a separate, distinct personality. A sense of self is particularly important in terms of a person's behavior because behavior is primarily determined by how people see a situation with reference to themselves. Rewarding emotional development and health depends on each of us finding our own identity as an individual.

Part of a person's sense of self is the *value system* which he or she lives by. A value system is a set of beliefs, ideas, and guidelines on which a person relies to bring him or her through life's perplexities. Value systems may vary greatly. The emotionally mature person, however, will select values that are capable of modification as new experiences arise.

Finally, an emotionally mature person has an interest in and an ability to do *productive work*. He or she is not satisfied with mere self-gratification, but demands some project or occupation that is engaging at the highest level and that is interesting and fulfilling beyond the monetary rewards it may bring.

(*Essentials of Life and Health*)

Exercise 8

You may refer to selections in Part 3 for a change of pace.

In your notebook summarize and paraphrase any three paragraphs or passages you find in your textbooks. Once again, if you currently are not using additional textbooks, substitute any books or periodicals you choose.

CHAPTER 9

Using Inference

Chapter Objectives: To introduce inference as a critical reading skill and to highlight the importance of reading with a questioning mind.

Reading between the Lines

Look carefully at the two pictures on page 242 and read the words printed with them. You see that the same person is in both pictures, but the descriptions differ significantly. The message in the first picture is that the man's career has advanced from clerk to vice-president, while the words used with the second one indicate that his career progressed to executive administrative assistant but then ended abruptly in unemployment. Furthermore, we are led to conclude that his unemployment was a direct result of the use of crack in 1994. The overall message implied in the second case is that "crack destroys careers." The words do not say that explicitly nor do the pictures illustrate it, but the clues point clearly in that direction.

Now let's look at another picture (*see Photo 9.3 on page 243*).

Can you determine the overall message of the final picture? If you guessed "smoking kills," you are probably right. Although words do not say that, you still are able to make the connection between the boy lighting the cigarette and the skeleton. You used the clues in the picture along with your knowledge and/or experience regarding the dangers of smoking to lead you to that logical conclusion. We draw inferences like these every day of our lives, sometimes without even realizing it!

When we read, we often are required to read between the lines to come to conclusions because writers do not always provide information in an explicit manner. In these instances, we use the clues that are

Ask students to present additional examples of everyday inferences that they have used and discuss them in class.

241

- Clerk, 1990
- Administrative Assistant, 1992
- Executive Administrative Assistant, 1993
- Assistant Manager, 1995
- Manager, 1996
- Vice-President, 1998

Photo 9.1

- Clerk, 1990
- Administrative Assistant, 1992
- Executive Administrative Assistant, 1993
- Crack, 1994
- Unemployed, 1995

Photo 9.2

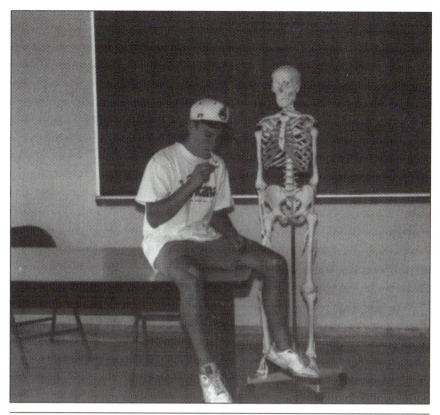

Photo 9.3

present in addition to depending upon our knowledge and experience to help us. To this point you have been encouraged to use various reading skills, such as finding stated main ideas and patterns of organization, to pick out information stated clearly in a given passage. However, you also have been asked to recognize main ideas and uncover certain word meanings in context even though they were not stated in so many words. There will be many other occasions in college when you will have to read with a questioning mind in order to draw inferences regarding the messages authors want you to take away from their writing. For example, read the following passage and think about its overall message.

> My psychology professor warned the class that is was going to be a hard examination because so much material was involved and the questions were very difficult. However, I did not heed her advice and spent the weekend

At this point, you may want to distinguish between literal comprehension and critical reading. Emphasize that students have already used inference when they read to uncover unstated main ideas and the context clue definitions of certain words.

skiing in Vermont with my friends. Furthermore my notes were incomplete, and I made no effort to fill in the gaps. In the end I had only an hour to review my notes and skim the chapter material. You can imagine the grade I found on my paper when I got it back.

A logical conclusion that can be inferred from the clues presented is that the writer did not do well on the psychology examination. He does not come right out and say that, but the evidence points clearly in that direction. Although we cannot be a hundred percent sure of that conclusion, it is a solid, educated guess based on the facts—the exam was difficult and the student did not prepare enough for it. In other words, the more clues available the more secure we can be about our inferences!

The same thing can be said with regard to inferences based on our knowledge and/or experience. For instance, read the following paragraph and try to determine what person is being described.

> He was 41 years old, a skilled sailor, and he had a plan. By plotting a new nautical trade route, he could bring back wealth in the form of gold, gems, drugs, and spices. He would also be honored for the rest of his life. But the axiom "it takes money to make money" applied to his plan, and he would need at least $14,000 to finance the venture. His own meager savings were totally inadequate, and no commercial lender would provide the funds. A formal request for funding from the Portuguese government was rejected.
> (*Contemporary Business*)

If your knowledge and/or experience regarding the subject matter of the paragraph are limited, then the clues may not give you the help that you need to make an educated guess. If that is the case, it is probably better not to draw the inference because you have a greater chance of being wrong.

Now look at the next paragraph to see if that helps. (We are still looking for the same person.)

> Finally, almost in desperation, he dispatched his brother Bartholomew to London and Paris to seek financing from the English and French governments. He decided to handle personally the presentation of his proposal to the Spanish government. It took five years, but finally the leaders of the Spanish government accepted his ideas and agreed to back the venture. The government agreed to provide the necessary funds for the implementation of the plan, to grant him a percentage in any ensuing trade that might develop, to award him the title of Admiral, and to make him governor of any new lands he might discover. (*Contemporary Business*)

This passage should illustrate for students how knowledge of a particular subject will vary from person to person. Students should be reminded that this is quite normal and nothing to be ashamed of!

Perhaps you are now in a better position to identify the person: you know that his brother's name was Bartholomew, that he presented his proposal to the Spanish government and that it was eventually accepted, and that he was given the title of admiral. If you need more clues to be on solid ground with your inference, read the following and last paragraph.

> He invested the $14,000 in hiring a crew, purchasing the necessary provisions, and preparing a fleet of three ships that would subsequently become famous: the flagship, Santa Maria, and the two smaller vessels, the Nina and the Pinta. Although the venture did not prove to be a financial success for _____, his voyages to the West Indies rank among the most important events in history. And finance made them possible. (*Contemporary Business*)

You may be aware of the names of the three vessels that finally gives you the clues you needed to conclude that the person is Christopher Columbus.

The extent of our knowledge and experience in a given area varies from person to person and that affects our ability to use clues to draw inferences. Obviously the more we know about a topic, such as Christopher Columbus, the easier it will be to arrive at logical conclusions. Also, there will be a much better chance that those conclusions will be correct, which is very important if we are to recognize hidden messages and understand completely what we are reading. So when you read, approach the material with a questioning mind and use your knowledge, experience, and the clues provided by the author to help you to draw solid inferences.

Highlight the need to read with a questioning mind and the importance of basing inferences on clues, experiences, and knowledge. When clues, experiences, and/or knowledge are lacking with regard to a given topic, then students must be very careful about drawing inferences.

Exercise 1   Making "Educated Guesses"

Use your knowledge, experience, and the available clues to help you answer the questions that follow each of the passages. Remember that sometimes knowledge and/or experience with a given topic may be limited, and under those circumstances, the clues may not provide enough help to draw logical conclusions that we can feel confident about. Although we are never one hundred percent sure that our inferences are correct, we want to increase our chances of being right by basing them on as much information as possible. Do the very best job that you can with each of your "educated guesses."

For this exercise, you may want to divide the class into small groups in order to promote classroom discussion.

See Instructor's Manual, Chapter 9 Answers.

1

A sign painter was just 31 years old when he found out he had AIDS; the diagnosis led to an emotional tidal wave that left depression in its wake.

Soon after he learned of the diagnosis, and well before he experienced any debilitating symptoms, he confided to his therapist that he was stockpiling Seconal, a powerful sedative, and he added that he knew the fatal dose.

(*The New York Times,* 12/4/91)

1. What does the sign painter intend to do?

   _____

   _____

2. On what clues did you base your inference?

   _____

   _____

   _____

   _____

2

He was the symbol of peace to many Americans of all colors, who looked to him as, perhaps, the last hope for progress and justice. His speeches were not only eloquent, but they also moved people to take action at great risk to themselves. In 1964, he won the Nobel Peace Prize for his accomplishments and for the great effect he had on this country and, for that matter, on the entire world. Although his dream was that all people would be judged equally, that dream died for him when an assassin's bullet took his life. However, what he stood for will live on forever!

1. What person is being discussed in the paragraph?

   _____

   _____

2. On what clues did you base your inference?

   _____

   _____

   _____

3

You notice your memory is off a little. You pause in a conversation, unable to find the right word. It is harder to keep track of things. When asked about something you have just read, the answer escapes you. You cannot remember someone's name. Sometimes you even forget where you are. After shopping, you do not remember where you parked. You misplace the keys. You forget to meet your spouse at the bank as planned. At tennis, you sometimes serve to the wrong court.

No one comments on the memory lapses, but as they get worse and worse family members know that something is wrong.

(*The New York Times*, 4/7/92)

1. The person described in the paragraph is quite possibly suffering from the early stages of what disease?

   _____

   _____

2. On what clues did you base your inference?

   _____

   _____

   _____

   _____

4

Remember those childhood days when time passed without a care? Remember how all those childhood activities, playing house or going fishing, were seldom calculated in terms of time? True, our parents were constantly reminding us of time: "Be home for supper." "Be in by 10:00." "You have to have your homework done by 6:00 or you can't watch TV." No matter. When we were engrossed in pursuits of the imagination, time did not seem to matter.

If anything, time hung heavy. School days could wear on and on. Waiting to become an adult seemed like a trip down the long road of eternity itself. And being an adult meant being on your own and being able to do with your time what you wanted.

(*Stress and Health*)

1. What is the writer implying about what happens to time as we age?

   _____

   _____

2. On what clues did you base your inference?

   _____

   _____

   _____

   _____

5

It was approximately 8 P.M., and I was working late at the office when the pain started. My chest felt like it was going to explode with the pressure that seemed to radiate to my shoulders. I broke into a cold sweat and had great difficulty breathing. My day had been long and stressful, so I attributed the episode to tension and overwork. Although the pain would not subside, the fact that I was also experiencing a burning sensation in my abdomen accompanied by nausea convinced me that I was having a severe case of indigestion. When I arrived at the hospital, however, I had a rude awakening!

1. What was this person *really* experiencing?

   _____

   _____

2. On what clues did you base your inference?

   _____

   _____

   _____

   _____

6

A group of young people are deciding what to take with them on a backpacking trip through the mountains. They decide not to take a Swiss army knife: "After all, how often do we use a Swiss army knife?" They also decide against taking a map and a compass: "We'll probably never need them." They leave behind a book on how to identify edible mushrooms: "Why should we take that? We hardly ever eat mushrooms." They also decide against taking a snake-bite kit: "Why carry that around? We'll probably never get bitten by a snake." They end up taking only their tent and a portable stereo, which is set to a decibel level that warrants an environmental impact statement.

(*Introduction to Psychology*)

1. What is the writer implying about how the group is preparing for the trip?

   _____

   _____

2. What does the writer mean when he states that the portable stereo ". . . is set to a decibel level that warrants an environmental impact statement"?

   _____

   _____

3. On what clues did you base your inferences?

   _____

   _____

   _____

   _____

7

"So I'm sitting here with the most recognizable face in the history of the world. I'm the only man in history to become famous under two different names. And I feel like I should be doing more with what I've got to help people. My main goal now is helping people and preparing for the hereafter. I'm working harder now than I ever worked in boxing. When I was in boxing, I used to get up at six o'clock in the morning to run. Now I'm up at five o'clock, praying, signing pamphlets, and reading the Qur'an. I'm not looking to be idolized. Maybe I was great in the ring, but outside boxing, I'm just a brother like other people. I want to live a good life, serve God, help everybody I can. And one more thing. I'm still gonna find out who stole my bike when I was twelve years old in Louisville, and I'm still gonna whup him. That was a good bike."

1. What person is being quoted in the paragraph above?

   _____

   _____

2. On what clues did you base your inference?

   _____

   _____

   _____

   _____

Reading between the Lines 253

8

The intruder swims silently in the murky waters off the Salem nuclear power plant in South Jersey, moving dangerously close to the cooling water intakes and the churn of more than 2 million gallons being sucked in every minute.

Under the water, the shadowy, mottled-brown form is well camouflaged, coming up to the surface for a quick gulp of air before sinking back down, unseen for the moment.

Its progress, however, is being carefully tracked on a glowing computer screen as the sea creature slowly drifts past the big nuclear generating station. Trailing an electronic satellite transponder attached to its shell with a short tether, the young _____ dives for food.

(*The Sunday Star-Ledger*, 8/16/92)

1. What creature is described?

   _____

   _____

2. On what clues did you base your inference?

   _____

   _____

   _____

   _____

9

We soon became aware of his genius for comedy as one after another of his record albums climbed the charts, providing us with welcome relief from the intense struggles of the civil rights movement. It was clear that he was one of the most talented performers of our age, but I didn't fully appreciate his extraordinary personal decency until my husband was assassinated in 1968 and Bill and his *I Spy* costar, Robert Culp, came to my home to pay their respects. Many of those who visited during those difficult days offered their help, but it was the *I Spy* team who provided the support that I needed most, comforting my children, while I met with an endless stream of visitors who came to express their condolences.

(*TV Guide*, 4/25/92)

1. Who wrote this paragraph?

   _____

   _____

2. Who is the person with a "genius for comedy"?

   _____

   _____

3. On what clues did you base your inference?

   _____

   _____

   _____

   _____

10

Studies have shown that nearly one hundred percent of all criminals drank milk as children. This is even true of those who have committed violent crimes. The occasional drinking of milk by street gang members has been estimated at over 96 percent. Nearly 97.3 percent of hard-core gamblers have confessed to bouts of milk drinking. Moreover, the evil effects of milk not only warp people's attitudes and sap their moral fiber but also lead to inevitable physical debilitation. Professional athletes who have continued their milk-drinking past the age of forty have found their reflexes slower, their speed reduced, their strength diminished. Most importantly, the effects of milk drinking are not reversible. Exhaustive research has failed to discover even one milk-drinker born prior to 1880 who is still alive. All the rest have perished. We must take action against this scourge today.

(*Developing Creative and Critical Thinking*)

1. Is this paragraph believable?

   _____

   _____

2. On what clues did you base your inference?

   _____

   _____

   _____

   _____

11

Here is an experience one of the authors had as a student in college on a Friday night: I had gone to bed early and lay in bed tossing and turning. I was behind in my studies in a course I felt I was not good at, with an exam coming up on Monday. I had invited a friend I was interested in to go to a party on Saturday and was hesitant to cancel. My parents had called to say that a family member was seriously ill and hinted I should come home for the weekend.

In the next room, my two roommates were drinking and talking. It's difficult to say whether they were being unusually loud. Nonetheless, at about 11:30, I'd finally had it. I stormed out into the living room. *"Shut up! Shut up! Shut up!",* I screamed at the top of my lungs.

They looked at me aghast. Immediately I felt embarrassed. Maybe I had overreacted, I thought. "Got to get up early tomorrow," I mumbled, and left the room.

(*Healthy for Life*)

1. What was the *real reason* for the author's anger?

   _____

   _____

2. On what clues did you base your inference?

   _____

   _____

   _____

   _____

12

A parent's nightmare: The mother turns from her shopping cart for an instant. Her toddler disappears. Store security locks the doors. In the washroom, officers recover the missing boy, his clothes already changed, his head shaved.

A women's nightmare: Emerging from the grocery at dusk, she spots two men converging across the parking lot. She jumps into her car and locks the door as the men knock on her window.

A man's nightmare: Confident of his physical strength, he scans the office lot around his car. All seems safe. He slips the key into the door. A baseball bat swings from beneath the vehicle, knocking his legs out from under him. In a flash, a knife is at his throat.

(*The New York Times*, 5/29/92)

1. What point is being illustrated by the examples?

   _____

   _____

2. On what clues did you base your inference?

   _____

   _____

   _____

   _____

13

At seven feet two inches, 275 pounds, Chamberlain would have been the most imposing figure in ring history, but the bout never happened. As to why not, there are differing views. Chamberlain says the deal fell apart because "the people controlling the fight weren't willing to relinquish a fair share of the ancillary rights." And certainly, it's true that most failed negotiations in boxing do break down over money. However, Bob Arum maintains that the stumbling block wasn't economic at all. "Chamberlain agreed to the fight," says Arum. "Everything had been negotiated; all we needed were the signatures. I was sitting in the Astrodome with Ali and Fred Hofheinz, waiting for Wilt and his lawyer so we could do a press conference announcing the fight. And I said to Ali, 'Ali, shut your mouth. Let's get him signed to the contract before you start riding him.' Ali told me, 'Don't worry.' Then Chamberlain comes in, and Ali shouts, 'Timber!' Chamberlain turns white, goes into the next room with his lawyer, comes out, and says he's not fighting. I think Ali intimidated him; that's all it was. At the moment of truth, Wilt realized that fighting Ali was a totally ridiculous concept."

(*Muhammad Ali: His Life and Times*)

1. What was Ali implying when he shouted "Timber!"?

   _____

   _____

2. On what clues did you base your inference?

   _____

   _____

   _____

14

Y ou are 16, 17, maybe 18 years old. You are given the job of your dreams but told that in order to fill it, you must move to a foreign land where hardly anyone will speak your language or understand your valiant attempt to converse in theirs.

Laws and traditions are not readily provided. Nor are full-time interpreters. If you are lucky, perhaps one or two of your peers might have time to help you sift through your obvious struggles. To keep you going as far as your new employers need you to go, you are taught a few essential phrases, such as how to say the equivalent words for "cheeseburger" or "taxi" or "hotel."

Other than that, you're on your own.

Now, if that all seems ludicrous, unreasonable and unworkable, add such phrases as "cutoff man," "hit-and-run" and "take sign" to that rudimentary vocabulary lesson and you have an apt description of the lonely, and often frightening, life of the _____ .

(*The New York Times,* 5/29/92)

1. What words would you use to complete the last sentence in the passage? (What kind of person is being described? What is his career?)

    _____

    _____

    _____

    _____

2. On what clues did you base your inference?

    _____

    _____

    _____

    _____

15

This girl is taking an important test. First she went through the test and answered all the items she knew well. Now she is trying to remember the answer to one of the more difficult questions. She gazes off into the distance, trying to remember everything she has read about this topic. She finally remembers, writes down the correct answer, and gets a perfect score. Later she goes on to college, becomes a Rhodes scholar, and eventually becomes a famous inventor.

Contrast that story with this one:

This girl is sitting through a very boring class. She is gazing off into the distance, thinking about the party she went to last weekend. As soon as class is over, she goes out and has a good time with her friends.

(*Introduction to Psychology*)

1. What is the writer implying about the future of the second girl?

   _____

   _____

2. On what clues did you base your inference?

   _____

   _____

   _____

   _____

16

Americans are living longer but the later years are often not so golden! They are filled with unhealthy days characterized by continual battles with various ailments and illnesses. The health care required to fight those battles costs money, and insurance does not always cover all of the medical expenses. In fact, speaking of money, there often are not enough funds to provide for the necessities of life—to say nothing of the frills. Regarding psychological well-being, the later years can be depressing because of the diminished quality of life, the general deterioration of the body, and the inevitable loss of loved ones. In the end, "the alternative" to the so-called golden years may be better!

1. What is the writer's general opinion of the "golden years"?

   _____

   _____

2. What does the writer mean by "the alternative"?

   _____

   _____

3. On what clues did you base your inferences?

   _____

   _____

   _____

17

The night was very dark, and the street was virtually deserted. There was barely any sound, with the exception of the faint hum of a factory in the distance and the wind blowing through the branches of the trees. Richard and Jonathan walked softly in the darkness to the corner store. Even though they had planned this for days, the fear and tension was almost unbearable. With eyes wide open, they kept looking from side to side as their breathing became more pronounced. Carefully they reached for the rocks, staring nervously at the window.

1. What time was it?

   _____

   _____

2. How old are Richard and Jonathan?

   _____

   _____

3. What were Richard and Jonathan going to do?

   _____

   _____

   _____

   _____

4. Why were they going to do it?

   _____

   _____

5. On what clues did you base your inferences?

18

Some time ago, a television program about the alleged dangers of playing the game Dungeons and Dragons reported 28 known cases of D&D players who had committed suicide. Alarming, right?

Not necessarily. At least 3 million young people play the game regularly. The reported suicide rate among D&D players—28 per 3 million—is considerably *less* than the suicide rate among teenagers in general.

So do the results mean that playing D&D *prevents* suicide? Hardly. The 28 reported cases are probably not a complete count of all suicides by D&D players. Besides, the correlation between playing D&D and committing suicide, regardless of its direction and magnitude, could not possibly tell us about cause and effect.

(Introduction to Psychology)

1. What conclusions can be drawn from the data?

2. On what clues did you base your inferences?

19

The story horrified racially tense Boston. A young white couple were shot driving to their suburban home through a racially mixed neighborhood after attending a birthing class at Brigham and Women's Hospital. Carol Stuart died soon after the incident. Eight-week premature Christopher Stuart was taken from his mother's dying body, but died seventeen days later. Chuck Stuart suffered a gunshot wound. Later he told police that while stopped at an intersection in the racially mixed Mission Hill district, a black man in a jogging suit shot him and his wife, suspecting that they were police undercover agents.

The mayor ordered every available cop into the hunt for the man Stuart had described. Hundreds of black men were stopped and frisked. The search continued for two months until William Bennett was arrested on the basis of information from three teenagers that Bennett's nephew had boasted that his uncle had shot the Stuarts. Bennett insisted that he was innocent, but his long rap sheet did not serve him well; still, the police held off filing formal charges. Meanwhile, the Boston news media were having a field day. Portrayed as a Willie Horton, Bennett seemed to confirm for many Bostonians the link between African-Americans, drugs, and violence. It was not until January 3, when Chuck Stuart's brother went to the Boston Police, that the story began to unravel. Matthew Stuart said that the night of the shooting he had driven to a prearranged spot in Mission Hill where his brother had given him a bag and told him to "Take this to Revere" [a Boston suburb]. Matthew said he saw something on the front seat of Chuck's car, but couldn't identify it. On opening the bag he discovered a gun and woman's jewelry. He threw the gun and bag into a river. It was not until two months later that he went to the police. Chuck Stuart committed suicide the next day.

(*The American System of Criminal Justice*)

1. Who killed Carol Stuart?

_____

_____

_____

2. On what clues did you base your inference?

20

Jim Rourke stood in front of Desk Sergeant Jack Sweeney at the Redwoods City Police Station. Rourke was handcuffed and waiting to be booked. He had been caught by Officers Davis and Thatcher outside of a building in a prestigious neighborhood soon after the police had received a frantic 911 call from a resident who reported that someone had entered her apartment. Rourke was seen loitering in the alley with a flashlight in his back pocket. He was known to the police because of his prior arrests for entering at night. As Thatcher held Rourke, Davis went around behind the desk and spoke to Sergeant Sweeney in a soft voice.

"I know we don't have much on this guy, but he's a bad egg, and I bet he was the one who was in that apartment. The least we can do is set the bail high enough so that he'll know we are on to him."

"Davis, you know I can't do that. You've got nothing on him," said Sweeney.

"But how's it going to look in the press if we just let him go? You know the type of people who live in Littleton Manor. There will be hell to pay if it gets out that this guy just walks."

"Well, he did have the flashlight . . . I suppose that's enough to indicate that he's a suspect. Let's make the bail $1,000. I know he can't make that."

(*The American System of Criminal Justice*)

1. Was Rourke guilty of burglarizing the apartment?

   _____

   _____

2. Would the case have been handled differently if the call had come from a poorer section of town?

   _____

   _____

3. On what clues did you base your inferences?

_____

_____

_____

_____

_____

_____

_____

_____

21

Lately, nearly everything seems to be going wrong for Herman, a 48-year-old college professor. Two years ago, after a stormy marriage, he and his first wife separated. Last year he was divorced, remarried, and demoted from dean to professor. He filed for bankruptcy and lost his home. Moreover, his relationship with his second wife, Michele, has not gone smoothly. They frequently quarrel over money problems, his two stepdaughters, his wife's demands for more "breathing room," and a variety of minor matters.

Each of these events has increased Herman's level of stress, and their unfortunate accumulation in such a relatively short period of time has left him bewildered, angry, and depressed. His divorce from his first wife surprised him because he was barely aware of her dissatisfaction. He had recently purchased an expensive home and had spent money lavishly, buying his wife jewelry, clothes, and tropical island vacations. He was stunned, therefore, when his wife decided to leave and take the children with her. Herman made a gallant gesture, insisting that Rose and the girls remain at home while he moved into an apartment.

Quickly, Herman became involved with another woman, and soon they were married. He moved to a new home with his second wife, his youngest daughter from his first marriage, and his two stepdaughters. Herman enjoyed this new family, but his happiness was short-lived. Before long Herman and Michele were quarreling, and the stability of their marriage was threatened. Herman found it impossible to make mortgage payments on two houses. At about the same time, his daughter moved back to her mother's home, and Herman was left with a feeling of living in enemy territory.

Herman's demotion hit hard too. He had no notion that he was doing anything but a superb job. The discovery that his department heads and faculty were displeased with him came as a complete shock. His disappointment over the demotion was magnified by his expectation that he would become a vice-president within a few years. Herman was angry, but he wasn't sure at whom he should direct his wrath. He blamed the president and the academic vice-president for demoting him, but at the same time he felt betrayed by his faculty members. One department head in particular became the target of his resentment because Herman suspected her of undermining his position to enhance her own chances of becoming dean. Herman's problems at work have added fuel to his domestic disputes. His constant preoccupation with his own concerns has earned Michele's bitterness instead of her sympathy or support.

As a result of his stress at work and at home, Herman has been sleeping less and smoking more. In addition, his diet, which never included many vegetables, has become even less balanced. For breakfast he has three cups of coffee and an occasional doughnut or Danish. Lunch is a quick sandwich and a soft drink. His evening meal usually consists of fast-food hamburgers or fried chicken, along with another soft drink.

(*Health Psychology*)

1. What is the writer implying about Herman's future?

_____

_____

_____

_____

_____

2. On what clues did you base your inference?

_____

_____

_____

_____

_____

22

The five members of the parole board questioned Jim Allen, an offender with a long history of sex offenses involving teenage boys. Now approaching forty-five and having met the eligibility requirement for a hearing, Allen respectfully answered the board members.

Toward the end of the hearing, Richard Edwards, a dentist who had recently been appointed to the board, spoke up:

"Your institutional record is good, you have a parole plan, a job has been promised, and your sister says she will help you. All of that looks good, but I just can't vote for your parole. You haven't attended the behavior modification program for sex offenders. I think you're going to repeat your crime. I have a thirteen-year-old son, and I don't want him or other boys to run the risk of meeting your kind."

Allen looked shocked. The other members had seemed ready to grant his release.

"But I'm ready for parole. I won't do that stuff again. I didn't go to that program because electroshock to my private area is not going to help me. I've been here five years of the seven year max and have stayed out of trouble. The judge didn't say I was to be further punished in prison by therapy."

After Jim Allen left the room, the board discussed his case. "You know, Rich, he has a point. He has been a model prisoner and has served a good portion of his sentence," said Brian Lynch, a long-term board member. "Besides, we don't know if Dr. Hankin's program works."

"I know, but can we really let someone like that out on the streets?"

(*The American System of Criminal Justice*)

1. Is Richard Edwards punishing Jim Allen for what he did or for what he might do in the future?

2. How would you vote? Why?

3. On what clues did you base your inferences?

Exercise 2 Developing Inference Questions

See Instructor's Manual, Chapter 9 Answers. As with Exercise 1, you may want to have students work in groups.

In Exercise 1 you were asked to answer the questions provided for you. However, when you read, you most often have to ask and answer your own questions. For practice read the following passages with a questioning mind, develop your own inference questions, and then answer them.

1

Through the years, he became my very best friend—always by my side. From the time he was very tiny, we spent many happy hours together. When we walked through the woods, we played games with each other. For instance, I would hide from him behind trees or sometimes throw sticks that he chased and quickly retrieved. How very quickly the years went by, and with their passing, his youth slipped away. The sparkle eventually disappeared from his eyes, and he slowly lost his energy. In fact, when the final hour came, he could not walk nor even recognize his loyal friend. I feel so very empty and alone.

1. Your inference questions

   _____

   _____

   _____

   _____

   _____

2. Answers to your inference questions

   _____

   _____

   _____

   _____

   _____

3. On what clues did you base your answers?

___

___

___

___

___

___

2

Margarita finished typing just before lunch, and she was able to file the remaining papers even though she was late for her appointment. Passing thoughts of her two sons, José and Hector, brought a smile to her pretty face. They were growing up so quickly and would be entering high school next year. Where have all the years gone? It seemed like only yesterday that they were little babies in her arms. Suddenly her smile disappeared as thoughts of Maria crossed her mind. Has it really been ten years? Margarita's eyes filled with tears as she began to sob uncontrollably. It was obvious that she would never experience complete tranquillity in her life.

1. Your inference questions

___

___

___

___

2. Answers to your inference questions

3. On what clues did you base your answers?

3

Assistant Prosecutor Debra McCoy looked at the case file. The police had arrested Leslie Wiggins, a prominent local businessman, for drunken driving. It seemed that Wiggins had been stopped after weaving on the highway at a high rate of speed. From the moment Officer Tompkins asked Wiggins to get out of the car, he knew he was very drunk. A breathalizer test revealed that he was well above the limit for sobriety. There was no question that this was an open-and-shut case. McCoy noted that Wiggins had been previously arrested, but the DWI charge had been dropped by her chief, Prosecutor Marc Gould.

"I don't know what happened last time," she thought, "but there is no question now." She recorded the charge of "driving while intoxicated" in the case file and forwarded it for review.

When the file had not yet returned for arraignment several days later, McCoy went to Gould's office.

"What happened to the Wiggins case?" she asked.

"Wiggins? Oh, that. Seems that the breathalizer wasn't reading right that night."

"Gee, I'm surprised. Tompkins didn't say anything about that when I talked with him yesterday. In fact, he was wondering when the case was coming up."

"Well, let's just not worry about this. I'm sure that Tompkins had other things to concern him. Don't think anything more about Wiggins."

McCoy left the office and wondered, "What's going on here?"

(*The American System of Criminal Justice*)

1. Your inference questions

_____

_____

_____

_____

2. Answers to your inference questions

   _____

   _____

   _____

   _____

   _____

   _____

3. On what clues did you base your answers?

   _____

   _____

   _____

   _____

   _____

   _____

   _____

4

Ethics in the business world creates a dilemma for people. What makes a practice unethical? An action that is simply shrewd to one manager may be unethical to another. Practices in an organization that managers might condemn in profitable times might not seem so offensive when a firm is battling for its financial survival, with thousands of jobs and the welfare of supplier firms hanging in the balance. The following are some situations governed by ethics. What are your reactions to each situation?

- The company allows twenty-minute coffee breaks. All the members of Department A take thirty minutes or more. What would you do?
- The head buyer for the company has been receiving gifts from vendors, a practice frowned on by the company. What would you do?
- As a potential major supplier to an electronics corporation, you have been assured that shipments can be made if the "right arrangements are made" (kickbacks). What would you do?
- A business acquaintance who has personally guaranteed business loans states that he will "file personal bankruptcy before he will pay off the loans." What do you think?
- A person in a land development company who sees company plans to purchase large undeveloped farm lands immediately purchases some. What do you think?
- A loan officer in a bank grants a friend a loan at 0.5 percent less than other loans are made. What do you think?

(*Introduction to Business*)

1. Your inference questions

   _____

   _____

   _____

   _____

   _____

2. Answers to your inference questions

3. On what clues did you base your answers?

5

The short, muscular black man strode through the Los Angeles International Airport carrying an attaché case and a small piece of luggage. He abruptly set down the bag and walked to a row of pay phones. His telephone conversation was interrupted by two Drug Enforcement Administration (DEA) agents, who grabbed the phone and started asking the man a series of questions. When the suspected "drug smuggler" did not respond, he fell or was thrown to the floor and was then handcuffed and led off for questioning. Only after his protestation that they had stopped the wrong person was Joe Morgan—a broadcaster for ESPN, former Cincinnati Reds second baseman, and National Baseball Hall of Fame member—released.

Los Angeles narcotics detective Clayton Searle and DEA agent Bill Woessner have claimed that they did nothing wrong; they merely responded to a DEA-developed profile of the characteristics of persons likely to be drug couriers. The fact that race is a major element of this profile has been justified as conforming to reality. Blacks and Hispanics, it is argued, are more likely to be involved in this aspect of the drug trade. Others have said that this is merely an expression of institutional racism—the darker your skin, the more likely that you will be stopped for questioning.

(*The American System of Criminal Justice*)

1. Your inference questions

2. Answers to your inference questions

   _____

   _____

   _____

   _____

   _____

   _____

   _____

3. On what clues did you base your answers?

   _____

   _____

   _____

   _____

   _____

   _____

   _____

CHAPTER 10

Five Steps to Effective Textbook Reading

Chapter Objective: To introduce the five-step approach to effective textbook reading, emphasizing that this approach incorporates all of the reading skills presented in this textbook.

Throughout this chapter, emphasize the importance of an organized, disciplined approach to textbooks. Also, reiterate that the five-step approach brings together all of the reading skills that have been introduced this semester.

Besides your instructors, your textbooks are the most valuable learning tools you have in college. With your limited time, you need an organized, disciplined approach to them that enables you to understand fully the material presented. This chapter introduces you to such an approach—one that incorporates all of the reading skills you have learned in this textbook.

The five-step approach presented here begins as soon as you purchase your textbooks at the start of the term and ends after you have completed your final examinations. It requires that you get acquainted with your textbooks immediately, guides you through them as chapters are assigned, and helps you to focus on the most important information in preparation for tests. Although we discuss each of the steps separately, remember that they should *all* be used in sequence for best results.

Step 1: Overview the Textbook

To get acquainted with your textbooks, overview them immediately after you purchase them. Overviewing involves skimming through the front and back matter of the textbook to find out what it is about, how it is organized, and what learning aids are present to help you to understand it better. Learning aids include such things as appendixes, bibliographies, glossaries, graphic aids, indexes, objectives, outlines, prefaces, questions, reference sources, tables of contents, vocabulary lists, or anything else designed to help you to comprehend the textbook material.

The front matter of a textbook usually includes the title page, table of contents, and preface. The title page includes the title, author(s), edition, publishing company, and place of publication. The date of publication, which indicates how current the book is, is on the copyright page, on the back of the title page. The table of contents provides a very clear picture of how the textbook material is organized. It shows you whether there are just chapters or whether the chapters are divided into various parts as well. In addition, it lists most of the headings within each of the chapters. Next comes the preface, which is sometimes called the introduction or foreword. It gives valuable information regarding the author's purpose and sometimes discusses the textbook's content, organization, and learning aids.

Textbooks vary in what they include in their back matter, but there is almost always an alphabetically arranged index that gives page locations for very specific information. To make it easier, sometimes an index is divided into name and subject sections. We have already discussed the usefulness of a glossary, which is also often found in the back matter. As you recall, it provides meanings for the specialized terms used frequently in the subject matter under discussion. Sometimes an alphabetized bibliography of the sources used by the author to write the textbook and/or a list of general reference sources is included at the back of the book. Either comes in handy if you are required to write a research paper, or if you have to read further on any given topic. Occasionally texts contain an appendix that includes maps, charts, diagrams, or other information that you can use to increase your understanding and for additional study or research purposes.

As you can see, just a few minutes of overviewing tells you a great deal about your textbooks. The sooner you get to know them, the better for you in terms of understanding what is in them, which is why this should be done before your first assignment. Speaking of assignments, let us move on to the remaining steps.

Reinforce the necessity of overviewing immediately after a textbook is purchased and before the first assignment is read. In short, the sooner students become familiar with their textbooks the better!

Step 2: Preview Each Chapter before Reading

The remaining steps give you an approach to use with the chapter material as it is assigned. When your instructors ask you to read one or more chapters for the next class, preview each chapter before you

> Make the point that previewing, like overviewing, takes little time and is worth the effort. Compare reading a textbook chapter to taking a trip to an unknown destination: emphasize the importance of first getting directions and determining the length of the trip before starting out. The resulting familiarity will save much time and money. Similarly, previewing also saves time in the long run by acquainting the reader with the material, thus enabling him or her to read faster and with more understanding.

read it. Previewing is a way of getting acquainted with a chapter by skimming through it to find out: (1) what it is about; (2) how it is organized; (3) what learning aids are provided; (4) and how long it will take you to read the assignment. Getting even a little familiar with a chapter enables you to read more quickly and with better understanding because you are much more organized in your approach. In addition previewing helps you to make connections between the new material and what you already know, which also aids comprehension.

When previewing, use this procedure.

1. Look at the chapter title to get a general idea of the subject matter.
2. Check the length and general difficulty of the chapter so that you can determine approximately how much time it will take you to read. You want to prepare yourself psychologically for the assignment and plan your study schedule accordingly. There is a big difference between a one-hour and a three-hour assignment!
3. Read or skim the first few paragraphs, which often serve as a general introduction to the material.
4. Read or skim the last few paragraphs to see if there is a summary of the most important information covered. If there is one, use it to focus on the major points when you read the chapter later on.
5. Skim the headings so that you can become acquainted with the major and minor topics.
6. Take a look at all of the charts, graphs, maps, pictures, and tables. These graphic aids can help you to understand the written material, so do not ignore them. Make sure that you understand what they are about, how they are organized, and the most important information that they illustrate.
7. Check to see if there are questions at the end of the chapter that you can try to answer as you read. They usually deal with the most important information and can serve as guides as you make your way through the chapter.
8. Familiarize yourself with other learning aids provided by the writer including exercises, objectives, vocabulary lists, or anything else that will assist you with your reading.
9. Finally, after you have completed your preview, take a moment to think about what you have learned from it and how that is going to help you to read the chapter with much more understanding.

Step 3: Construct a Broad Topic Outline of the Chapter

This step is really a logical continuation of previewing that, among other things, had you skim the headings. As you remember, Chapter 8 dealt with outlining using topics, main ideas, major details, and minor details. It was designed to show you the relationship among the various sentences in a given paragraph or passage. The purpose of broad topic outlining is different in that it helps you to see the connections between all of the headings and gives you a clear picture of the chapter's organization. In fact sometimes your text provides such an outline at the beginning of each chapter.

Writing out a broad topic outline is neither difficult nor time consuming. It simply involves indenting and placing the minor and smaller headings under the major ones. Major headings are easily distinguished either by print size or print color. For example, take a look at the following broad topic outline of the chapter headings taken from a health psychology textbook.

Make sure students understand how broad topic outlining differs from detailed outlining, particularly with regard to purpose and technique. Emphasize that broad topic outlining shows the relationship among the various headings in a chapter, while detailed outlining shows the relationship among the various sentences in a given passage.

Exercising (chapter title)

I. Types of Exercise (major heading)
    A. Isometric Exercise (minor heading)
    B. Isotonic Exercise (minor heading)
    C. Isokinetic Exercise (minor heading)
    D. Anaerobic Exercise (minor heading)
    E. Aerobic Exercise (minor heading)

II. Reasons for Exercising (major heading)
    A. Physical Fitness (minor heading)
        1. Muscle Strength (smaller heading)
        2. Muscle Endurance (smaller heading)
        3. Flexibility (smaller heading)
        4. Aerobic (Cardiorespiratory) Fitness (smaller heading)
    B. Weight Control (minor heading)

III. Psychological Effects of Exercise (major heading)
    A. Decreased Depression (minor heading)
        1. Normal Subjects (smaller heading)
        2. Clinically Depressed Subjects (smaller heading)
    B. Reduced Anxiety (minor heading)

- C. Buffer Against Stress (minor heading)
  - D. Increased Self-Esteem (minor heading)
- IV. Cardiovascular Effects of Exercise (major heading)
  - A. Early Studies (minor heading)
  - B. The San Francisco Longshoreman Study (minor heading)
  - C. The Harvard Alumni Study (minor heading)
  - D. The Framingham Heart Study (minor heading)
  - E. Exercise and Cholesterol Levels (minor heading)
  - F. How Much Is Enough? (minor heading)
- V. Other Health Benefits of Exercise (major heading)
  - A. Protection Against Colon Cancer (minor heading)
  - B. Prevention of Osteoporosis (minor heading)
- VI. Summary of Exercise Benefits (major heading)
- VII. Hazards of Exercise (major heading)
  - A. Exercise Addiction (minor heading)
  - B. Injuries from Exercise (minor heading)
  - C. Other Health Risks (minor heading)
  - D. Death During Exercise (minor heading)
- VIII. Exercise Dropouts (major heading)
  - A. Predicting Dropouts (minor heading)
  - B. Reducing Dropout Rates (minor heading)

(Health Psychology)

In this textbook major, minor, and smaller headings are printed in three different sizes, so distinguishing among them is not difficult. The numbering used in the outline is not important as long as the minor and smaller headings are indented clearly so that you can see the relationship among the topics. For instance, when you look at the outline, it is obvious that the types of exercise discussed are isometric, isotonic, isokinetic, anaerobic, and aerobic. Furthermore, according to this chapter, the reasons for exercising include physical fitness and weight control, and the former involves muscle strength, muscle endurance, flexibility, and aerobic fitness. At this point, we certainly do not know everything we need to know about these topics, but we are well on our way. The outline has given us a definite picture of how the entire chapter is organized, and it has helped us to see clearly how the topics are related to each other. That improves comprehension when you read and helps you remember the material at test time.

If you want to you can leave space between the various headings in the broad topic outline so that you can fill in detailed information as you read the chapter. Doing this makes the broad outline into a more specific study outline that you can use for review when you prepare for tests. Either way, this step is a valuable aid to understanding that will not require a great deal of your time. However, if you are so pressed for time that you cannot write out a broad topic outline, make absolutely sure that you at least study all of the chapter headings so that you have a good feel for how they are related to each other.

Step 4: Turn Chapter Headings into Questions and Read to Find the Answers

Chapter 9 on using inference emphasized the importance of approaching reading material with a questioning mind. When you do so it helps to focus your attention, thereby improving concentration, and forces you to think, which aids comprehension. As you know, the headings are the major topics in a chapter that you are expected to master. In fact, they are often used by instructors to develop their test questions. For instance, if a given chapter had a heading titled "Purposes of Communication," it is reasonable to expect on your next test a question like: "What are the purposes of communication?"

Reiterate the importance of approaching reading with a questioning mind.

Turning headings into questions is not difficult because, for the most part, it simply involves using the words "what," "when," "where," "who," "why," or "how" to form the question. For example, take a look at the possible questions that can be made out of the headings from the broad topic outline used in Step 3.

Exercising

I. Types of Exercise *(What are the types of exercise?)*
   A. Isometric Exercise *(What is isometric exercise?)*
   B. Isotonic Exercise *(What is isotonic exercise?)*
   C. Isokinetic Exercise *(What is isokinetic exercise?)*
   D. Anaerobic Exercise *(What is anaerobic exercise?)*
   E. Aerobic Exercise *(What is aerobic exercise?)*

II. Reasons for Exercising *(What are the reasons for exercising?)*
   A. Physical Fitness *(Why is physical fitness a reason for exercising?)*
      1. Muscle Strength *(What is muscle strength?)*
      2. Muscle Endurance *(What is muscle endurance?)*

3. Flexibility *(What is flexibility?)*
4. Aerobic (Cardiorespiratory) Fitness *(What is aerobic fitness?)*

B. Weight Control *(Why is weight control a reason for exercising?)*

III. Psychological Effects of Exercise *(What are the psychological effects of exercise?)*
  A. Decreased Depression *(How does exercise decrease depression?)*
    1. Normal Subjects *(How does exercise decrease depression in normal subjects?)*
    2. Clinically Depressed Subjects *(How does exercise decrease depression in clinically depressed subjects?)*
  B. Reduced Anxiety *(How does exercise reduce anxiety?)*
  C. Buffer Against Stress *(How does exercise serve as a buffer against stress?)*
  D. Increased Self-Esteem *(How does exercise increase self-esteem?)*

IV. Cardiovascular Effects of Exercise *(What are the cardiovascular effects of exercise?)*
  A. Early Studies *(What do the early studies say about the cardiovascular effects of exercise?)*
  B. The San Francisco Longshoreman Study *(What does the San Francisco Longshoremen Study say about the cardiovascular effects of exercise?)*
  C. The Harvard Alumni Study *(What does the Harvard Alumni Study say about the cardiovascular effects of exercise?)*
  D. The Framingham Heart Study *(What does the Framingham Heart Study say about the cardiovascular effects of exercise?)*
  E. Exercise and Cholesterol Levels *(How does exercise affect cholesterol levels?)*
  F. How Much Is Enough? *(How much exercise is enough?)*

V. Other Health Benefits of Exercise *(What are the other health benefits of exercise?)*
  A. Protection Against Colon Cancer *(How does exercise protect against colon cancer?)*

> Make sure that students understand the necessity sometimes of making up questions that connect major and minor headings.

      B.   Prevention of Osteoporosis *(How does exercise prevent osteoporosis?)*
VI. Summary of Exercise Benefits *(What does the author think are the most important benefits of exercise?)*
VII. Hazards of Exercise *(What are the hazards of exercise?)*
      A.   Exercise Addiction *(What is exercise addiction?)*
      B.   Injuries from Exercise *(What are the possible injuries from exercise?)*
      C.   Other Health Risks *(What are the other health risks of exercise?)*
      D.   Death During Exercise *(Why is their death during exercise?)*
VIII. Exercise Dropouts *(What are exercise dropouts?)*
      A.   Predicting Dropouts *(How can we predict exercise dropouts?)*
      B.   Reducing Dropout Rates *(How can exercise dropout rates be reduced?)*

Notice that although all of the questions for these particular headings use either the words "what," "why," or "how," sometimes it is necessary to make the connection between major and minor headings with a question. For example, "Why is physical fitness a reason for exercising?" This is also the case for some of the minor and smaller headings, as seen in the question "How does exercise decrease depression in normal subjects?" Although these kinds of questions are a little more difficult to make up, do try because they show the relationship among the various headings. Having completed a broad topic outline helps particularly in making up those more involved questions. In the beginning you may be uncertain about whether you are asking the right questions, but with experience you will become much more confident.

After you turn each chapter heading into a question, read the relevant section to find the answer. This makes your reading very focused by giving it a distinct purpose, thereby improving your understanding of the material. Remember that Chapter 1 stressed the importance of setting specific goals every time you study or do assignments because it improves concentration and builds self-confidence. These questions serve very nicely as your specific study goals that are to be answered (accomplished) by the time you finish each study session.

When answering your questions look for main ideas, patterns of organization, and context definitions because they often provide the information you need. As already mentioned in Chapter 4, textbooks sometimes use boldface type or italics for key words when they are first defined in context, which helps you to locate or recognize them. Also remember that graphic aids are usually very helpful, and be prepared to draw inferences when necessary. At this point, then, you are using all of the reading skills that you have learned and practiced in this textbook.

It is a good idea to underline, or even write out, the answers to your questions because that helps you to concentrate, learn, and remember by getting you actively involved in your reading. Furthermore it makes it easier to review later and eliminates having to reread entire chapters. As you recall, the technique and benefits of underlining were discussed in Chapter 8.

If you decide to write your answers, you may wish to summarize and/or paraphrase. As you know, summarizing—if done correctly—reduces material and makes it more manageable without missing any of the important information. Paraphrasing involves using your own words rather than the writer's to make the material more understandable to you.

Whether you decide to underline or write out the answers, remember to pay attention to additional important information that goes beyond the answers to your questions. Sometimes your questions and answers do not cover *all* of the points a writer makes in a given section of a textbook. Therefore you need to focus on those points as well. They cannot be ignored!

For purposes of illustration, let us read one section taken from a business textbook.

Advantages of Corporate Organization

Corporations, too, have their advantages and disadvantages. One of the key drawbacks of sole proprietorships and partnerships—unlimited liability—is avoided under the corporate form of organization. Owners of a corporation enjoy **limited liability,** which is *a feature inherent in corporations;* it means that *stockholders' responsibility for debts is restricted to the amount of their investment in the corporation.* One practical point should be mentioned here. A corporation that decides to borrow money may have trouble doing so if its assets are inadequate security for the loan. A lender may then require one or more stockholders with substantial personal assets to cosign the loan agreement with the corporation. The stockholders who agree to such an arrangement voluntarily relinquish their limited liability for their company to borrow funds.

A second advantage is ease of expansion. Corporations can raise funds by selling stock, a financing device that does not exist for sole proprietorships or partnerships. Corporations also can borrow against the value of their assets by selling bonds. Both of these corporate securities will be explored in detail in Chapter 14.

Emphasize that questions will serve nicely as study goals, and that main ideas, patterns, and context definitions will often provide the information to answer the questions. Also, review the importance of and techniques involved in underlining, summarizing, and paraphrasing.

Step 4: Turn Chapter Headings into Questions and Read to Find the Answers

A third advantage of corporations is the ease of transferring ownership. Stockholders can transfer their shares to someone else merely by endorsing the stock certificate in the space provided on the back.

Relatively long life is a fourth advantage. Corporations, unlike sole proprietorships and partnerships, can be chartered for perpetual existence. They do not terminate with the death or incapacitation of the stockholders-owners. In fact, approximately twenty American corporations can trace their roots to before the Revolutionary War.

A fifth advantage of incorporation is the greater ability to hire specialized management. As we said earlier, most sole proprietorships and partnerships are managed by the owners. One reason is that these people are often entrepreneurs who want to run their own business. Another reason is that these businesses are usually smaller and cannot afford to bring in sought-after managers. Corporations, on the other hand, have the facilities and money necessary to attract top talent to management jobs in critical business areas such as labor-management relations, finance, marketing, manufacturing, and personnel. Unlike sole proprietorships and partnerships, corporations can replace top managers if their performance is unsatisfactory. *(Introduction to Business)*

We easily can turn the heading into the question: "What are the advantages of corporate organization?" Our reading, then, will focus on finding the advantages, and that is not a difficult task because of the presence of the simple listing of fact pattern of organization. Also notice how the context definition of "limited liability" helps us to locate the first advantage on the list:

Question:
What are the advantages of corporate organization?

Answer:
- Owners of a corporation enjoy **limited liability,** which is *a feature inherent in corporations*; it means that *stockholders' responsibility for debts is restricted to the amount of their investment in the corporation.*
- A second advantage is ease of expansion.
- A third advantage of corporations is the ease of transferring ownership.
- Relatively long life is a fourth advantage.
- A fifth advantage of incorporation is the greater ability to hire specialized management.

Even though we have answered the question, there is much additional important information that should be taken note of.

Additional Important Information:
- A corporation that decides to borrow money may have trouble doing so if its assets are inadequate security for the loan. A lender may then require one or more stockholders with substantial personal assets to cosign the loan agreement with the corporation. The stockholders who agree to such an arrangement voluntarily relinquish their limited liability for their company to borrow funds.
- Corporations can raise funds by selling stock, a financing device that does not exist for sole proprietorships or partnerships. Corporations also can borrow against the value of their assets by selling bonds.
- Stockholders can transfer their shares to someone else merely by endorsing the stock certificate in the space provided on the back.
- Corporations, unlike sole proprietorships and partnerships, can be chartered for perpetual existence. They do not terminate with the death or incorporation of the stockholders.

Keep in mind that this information can be condensed, and perhaps simplified, by summarizing and/or paraphrasing it.

To illustrate further, let us read one last section, this time taken from the same chapter on "Exercising" for which the headings already have been outlined and turned into questions.

PREDICTING DROPOUTS

What factors predict the exercise dropouts? Martin and Dubbert (1985) reviewed the research on this question and divided the relevant factors into subject variables, social-environmental variables, and exercise program variables.

Subject variables include preexisting psychological, behavioral, and biological factors. Interestingly, one subject variable that does not appear to relate to adherence is the person's attitude toward physical activity. Sedentary people, it seems, often report favorable attitudes toward exercise. Subject variables found to be related to dropout included low self-motivation, depression, denial of the seriousness of one's heart disease, and low self-efficacy for maintaining an exercise program. Also, smokers, blue-collar workers, obese patients, people with the Type A behavior pattern, and those with inactive jobs and inactive leisure-time pursuits were most likely to drop out of prescribed exercise programs.

Among the social-environmental factors found to relate to dropout were lack of social support from spouses and others, family problems, change of job or residence, and job-related duties that conflicted with exercise.

Reinforce the necessity of paying attention to additional information that may not be included in the answers to the questions.

Martin and Dubbert reported that, among the exercise program factors, lack of support from other exercise participants was positively related to noncompliance. In other words, group exercise programs usually have lower dropout rates than individual programs. Convenience, or location of the exercise center, was another important program variable, as was the intensity of the exercise itself. As one might expect, more distant centers and more vigorous workouts were both associated with increased dropout rates. (*Health Psychology*)

As you recall the question developed from the heading was: "How can we predict exercise dropouts?" The answer to it is not difficult to find.

Question:
How can we predict exercise dropouts?

Answer:
- Martin and Dubbert (1985) reviewed the research on this question and divided the relevant factors into subject variables, social-environmental variables, and exercise program variables.

- Subject variables include preexisting psychological, behavioral, and biological factors. Subject variables found to be related to dropout included low self-motivation, depression, denial of the seriousness of one's heart disease, and low self-efficacy for maintaining an exercise program. Also, smokers, blue-collar workers, obese patients, people with the type A behavior pattern, and those with inactive jobs and inactive leisure-time pursuits were most likely to drop out of prescribed exercise programs.

- Among the social-environmental factors found to relate to dropout were lack of social support from spouses and others, family problems, change of job or residence, and job-related duties that conflicted with exercise.

- Martin and Dubbert reported that, among the exercise program factors, lack of support from other exercise participants was positively related to noncompliance. In other words, group exercise programs usually have lower dropout rates than individual programs. Convenience, or location of the exercise center, was another important program variable, as was the intensity of the exercise itself. As one might expect, more distant centers and more vigorous workouts were both associated with increased dropout rates.

Additional Important Information:
Interestingly, one subject variable that does not appear to relate to adherence is the person's attitude toward physical activity. Sedentary people, it seems, often report favorable attitudes toward exercise.

We have now focused our attention on the major points made in both sample sections and would follow this procedure for every other one in a given chapter. As you have seen, Step 4 is not difficult to accomplish, but it does take some time. The result, however, is well worth the effort for it leads to a much better understanding of textual material.

Step 5: Review Answers to Questions Continually

You will have a great deal of information to learn when you complete Step 4. If you have not underlined or written out the answers to your questions, you have to reread, or at least skim, the chapter. This takes quite a bit of time because it requires that you find the answers all over again. Obviously, it is much easier to locate the important information when it has been underlined or written down.

Emphasize the importance of continuous review and of reciting answers aloud to help in retaining information.

The first few chapters in this textbook stressed the importance of continuous review. There is simply too much information in your notes and textbooks to try to learn it at the last minute. In fact, most tests cover more than one chapter, so as soon as you complete Step 4 with an assigned chapter, start reviewing your answers immediately and do so every time that you sit down to study. Part of each study block should be devoted to review. Read all of your questions and answers over and over again until you have learned—even memorized—them. *Recite your answers aloud to help you remember them.* It takes this kind of commitment to master textbook material, but in the end your hard work will pay off!

Exercise 1

Now you have the opportunity to apply Step 1 by overviewing the front matter from a college textbook. When you are done with your overview of the front matter, beginning on page 295, fill in the information requested on the following pages. The information on the back matter can often be obtained from the table of contents of a textbook, as is the case with the book featured in this exercise. When overviewing an actual textbook, however, you should overview the material at the end of the book.

TOOLS FOR TECHNICAL AND PROFESSIONAL COMMUNICATION

ARTHUR H. BELL
McLAREN SCHOOL OF BUSINESS
UNIVERSITY OF SAN FRANCISCO

NTC Publishing Group
Lincolnwood, Illinois USA

Executive Editor: John T. Nolan
Developmental Editor: Marisa L. L'Heureux
Cover and interior design: Ophelia M. Chambliss
Interior art: Paula Weber
Production Manager: Rosemary Dolinski

Credits
p. 22: Courtesy of Sears, Inc.
p. 94: Courtesy of Instructional Technology Program, College of Education, Wayne State University.
p. 96: Courtesy of Ryobi American Corporation.
p. 144: Courtesy of BellSouth, Inc.
pp. 171, 172, 173, 174, 176: Courtesy of Western Economic Association International.
pp. 237, 238, 239, 254, 255, 257, 262, and 314: From *The Complete Business Writer's Manual*, Arthur H. Bell. © 1992. Reprinted by permission of Prentice Hall.

Published by NTC Publishing Group.
© 1995 by NTC Publishing Group, 4255 West Touhy Avenue,
Lincolnwood (Chicago), Illinois 60646-1975 U.S.A.
All rights reserved. No part of this book may be reproduced, stored in a retrieval system, or transmitted in any form or by any means, electronic, mechanical, photocopying, recording or otherwise, without the prior permission of NTC Publishing Group.
Manufactured in the United States of America.
Library of Congress Catalog Number: 94-66703

4 5 6 7 8 9 ML 9 8 7 6 5 4 3 2 1

Contents

Preface xiii

Part One
An Overview of Technical and Professional Communication 1

CHAPTER ONE
Communication Activities in Science,
Business, and Government..3

What Is Technical Writing? 4
Technical Writing and College Writing 5
Style 5
Audience 6
Diction 6
Format 7
Correctness 8
Revision 8
Time Pressure 9
What Does a Technical Writer Do? 9
The Technical Writer as a Team Player 12
Ethical and Legal Principles for Technical Communication 15
    Ethics Codified into Law: Three Areas of Concern 14
Intercultural Issues in Technical Communication 15
    Recognizing Five Areas of Cultural Difference 16
A Sampler of Common Technical Documents 18

CHAPTER TWO
Principles of Communication 27

Technical Writers Distinguish Between Words and Things 28
Technical Writers Know Denotative and Connotative Meanings 30
Technical Writers Eliminate Static in Communication 31
    The Static of Poorly Selected Diction 33
    The Static of Communication Overload 33
    The Static of Preconceptions..34
    The Static of Environmental Influences...34
    The Static of Attention Span 39
Technical Writers Value Feedback..39
Technical Writers Recognize that the Medium Is the Message 40

Part Two
The Process of Technical and Professional Communication 45

CHAPTER THREE
Generating and Analyzing Ideas..47

Task Analysis...48
Goal Analysis...48
Audience Analysis 49
Resource Analysis..53
Why Analysis Matters 53
Getting Ideas..53
    The Idea Circle 55
    Classic Questions 55
    Clustering 56
What to Do with Ideas..57
    Ideas Used to Define 57
    Ideas Used to Analyze...59
    Ideas Used to Evaluate 60
    Ideas Used to Describe 61
    Ideas Used to Compare and Contrast 61
    Ideas Used to Show Cause and Effect 62
    Ideas Used to Summarize 63

Organizing Ideas for Logic and Impact 64
Forms of Organization 64
    Intrinsic Organization 65
    Extrinsic or Imposed Patterns of Organization 65
    Logical Organization 66

CHAPTER FOUR
Developing and Researching Documents 71

Ten Patterns of Organization 72
The Effects of Organization 75
    Effect 1: A Sense of Orientation 75
    Effect 2: Information 76
    Effect 3: Persuasion 77
    Effect 4: Unity 77
    Effect 5: Emphasis 78
Outlining 78
Supporting Your Points with Details, Examples, and Statistics 81
Directed Details, Examples, and Statistics 81
The Research Process for Technical Writing 82
    The Research Hypothesis 82
    Secondary Research via Reader Guides and Card Catalogs 83
    Secondary Research via Computer Search 84
    Useful Data Bases for Technical Writers 85
    What to Look for in Secondary Research 86
    How to Record Pertinent Portions of Secondary Research 87
    Notes on Cards 87
    Highlighted Photocopies 88
    Computer-assisted Note-taking 88
    Primary Research 90
Looking Toward the Future 91

CHAPTER FIVE
Drafting Documents 99

How to Use a Working Outline 100
Drafting by Hop, Skip, and Jump 103

Drafting at a Word Processor	104
Building Blocks for Effective Drafting	105
Words	105
Sentences	107
Paragraphs	110
A Naturally Professional Style	114
Voice	115
Tone	116
Other Stylistic Techniques	116
Final Thoughts about Your Technical Style	118

CHAPTER SIX
Editing and Revising 121

Revising for Clarity	122
Keys to Clear Writing	124
Revising for Efficiency	126
Revising for Unity	127
Revising for Coherence	130
Revising for Readability	131
Revising for Accuracy	133
The Art of Proofreading	133
Revising for Attractiveness	136
Making a Commitment to Revise Your Work	136

CHAPTER SEVEN
Word Processing and Desktop Publishing............................139

Technical Writing before Word Processing	140
Word Processing to the Rescue	140
Six Common Word-processing Capabilities	141
Learning More about Word Processing	142
The Relationship between Word Processing and Desktop Publishing	142
Walking through Desktop Publishing	143
Getting to Know a Desktop Publishing System	146
Word-processing Technologies: Looking toward the Future	146

CHAPTER EIGHT
Collaborative Writing..149

The Hazards of Team Writing 150
The Advantages of Team Writing 151
How to Avoid the Pitfalls of Team Writing 151
How to Participate as a Member of a Writing Team 154
How to Lead a Writing Team 155
Team Writing in Your Future 157

CHAPTER NINE
Graphics 161

Working with a Graphics Specialist 162
The Rationale for Visual Aids 163
The Placement of Visual Aids 163
Misinformation and Visual Aids 164
Ethics and Technical Communication 164
    Finding Your Own Answers to Ethical Dilemmas 166
    Handling Ethical Conflicts on the Job 166
Types of Visual Aids 167
    Line Drawings 167
    Cutaway or Exploded Drawings 167
    Line Graphs 168
    Multi-line Graphs 168
    Bar Graphs 170
    Segmented Bar Graphs 170
    Line-Bar Graphs 171
    Time Graphs 172
    Pie Charts 173
    Pictograms 174
    Flowcharts 177
    Organizational Charts 177
    Maps 177
    Tables 177
    Photographs 177

Visual Aids for Oral Technical Presentations 180
    Handouts 180
    Slides 182
    Overhead Transparencies 182
    Films 182
    Flipcharts 182
    Storyboards 182
The Growing Importance of Graphics 184

Part Three
The Products of Technical and Professional Communication 187

CHAPTER TEN
Memos 189

General Guidelines in Writing Technical Memos 190
    Memo Headings 190
    Memo Bodies 194
Memos and Electronic Mail 195
Memos and Confidentiality 197
Routine Technical Memos 197
    The Inquiry Memo 197
    The Order Memo 199
    The Response Memo 199
    The Cover Memo 203
    The Memo to File 203
    Other Technical Memos 206

CHAPTER ELEVEN
Letters 209

The Two Levels of Communication through Technical Letters 210
A Professional Look for Technical Letters 210
    Elements of Block Style 212
    Envelope Conventions 217
The Tone of Technical Letters 217
    Keys to a Natural Style 219

Five Common Types of Technical Letters 220
    The Technical Inquiry Letter 220
    Guidelines for the Technical Inquiry Letter 220
    The Technical Response Letter 222
    Guidelines for the Technical Response Letter 222
    The Technical Explanation Letter 222
    Guidelines for the Technical Explanation Letter 225
    The Technical Claim Letter 225
    Guidelines for the Technical Claim Letter 225
    The Technical Sales Letter 227
    Guidelines for the Technical Sales Letter 227
Technical Letters Sent by Fax 229
    To Fax or to Mail? 229

CHAPTER TWELVE
Short Reports 233

Reports within Companies 234
The Functions of Technical Reports 235
The Parts of a Short Technical Report 236
    Title Page 236
    Executive Summary or Abstract 236
    Table of Contents 236
    The Body Text 241
    Supplements and Appendixes 241
    Footnotes, Endnotes, and Bibliography 241
Formats for Short Technical Reports 242
    Headings 242
    Margins 243
    Spacing 243
    Pagination of the Short Technical Report 243
Types of Short Technical Reports 243
    The Progress Report 244
    Guidelines for Writing the Progress Report 244
    The Periodic Report 247
    Guidelines for Writing the Periodic Report 247
    The Project Completion Report 247

Guidelines for Writing the Project Completion Report 247
The Trip Report 253
Guidelines for Writing the Trip Report 253
The Test/Investigation Report 253
Guidelines for Writing the Test/Investigation Report 253
The Feasibility Report 253
Guidelines for Writing the Feasibility Report 253
The Status Report 261
Guidelines for Writing the Status Report 261
The Continuing Importance of Technical Reports 261

CHAPTER THIRTEEN
Formal Reports 267

The Parts of a Formal Report 269
    The Cover 269
    The Flysheet 270
    The Title Page 270
    The Table of Contents 271
    The Letter (or Memo) of Authorization 271
    The Letter (or Memo) of Transmittal 271
    The Executive Summary or Abstract 273
    The Report Body 273
    The Stages of Argument 275
    The Conclusion and Recommendations 275
    Appendixes 275
    Endnotes 276
    The Bibliography 276
    The Index 276
Pagination in a Formal Report 276

CHAPTER FOURTEEN
Proposals and Business Plans 291

Proposal Writing Strategies 292
    Step One: Determine the Requirements for Your Proposal 293
    Step Two: Develop an Outline for Your Proposal 293

Common Proposal Mistakes 295
    General Assurances vs. Specific Answers 295
    Sound Ideas vs. High Expenses 296
    Sufficient Information vs. Data Overload 296
Model Technical Proposals 296
The Technical Business Plan 296
    A Sample Business Plan 312

CHAPTER FIFTEEN
Articles for Publication 321

The Process of Professional Publication 323
    Shaping Your Idea 323
    Writing the Query Letter 323
    Learning from Rejection 324
    Writing for Information 327
Different Articles for Different Audiences 328
Learning to Write Articles by Reading 329

CHAPTER SIXTEEN
Speaking and Listening 331

Better Listening 332
    Barriers to Effective Listening 332
    Stages of Effective Listening 333
Interpersonal Communication 334
    Defensive Communication 335
    Exploratory Communication 335
Telephone Communication 336
    Telephone Techniques 337
    Eight Hints for Speaking and Listening on the Telephone 337
Conducting Technical Interviews 339
Leading and Participating in Meetings 340
    Leading Technical Meetings 341
    Participating in Technical Meetings 343
Making Technical Presentations 344
    Presentation Outline 1 345

Presentation Outline 2 345
Beginning the Technical Presentation 346
Speaker's Nerves 349
Keys to Effective Delivery 351
Eye Contact 351
Gestures 351
Posture 352
Voice 352
Reading from a Script or Speaking from Notes 353
The Continuing Importance of Speaking Skills 353

CHAPTER SEVENTEEN
Employment Communication 357

Sources of Job Leads 359
Placement Services and Agencies 359
Professional Associations and Trade Journals 359
Friends and Instructors 360
Writing Your Résumé 360
A Step-by-step Guide to Constructing the Technical Résumé 364
Writing a Cover Letter 368
Surviving the Interview Process 369
The Hard Work and Substantial Payoff of the Job Search 375

Cases for Technical and Professional Communication 377

Appendix A: Brief Guide to Grammar, Mechanics, Usage, and Spelling 393

Appendix B: Guide to Documentation 407

Index 417

Preface

Let's not waste words.

You want to learn up-to-date communication skills used by engineers, computer scientists, government analysts, biologists, and other professionals. *Tools for Technical and Professional Communication* focuses on the communication skills you will need from day one on the job. These skills include the ability to communicate effectively in a wide range of written documents and in oral presentations.

Technical writing classes in the U.S. and Canada attracted more than 1.7 million students in 1993. Some students in such courses require rather narrow technical writing instruction, such as writing catalog descriptions of mechanical parts or filling out technical forms for regulatory agencies.

Most students in such courses, however, require a different kind of curriculum and text—one that bridges the traditional concerns of technical communication and the broader, emerging requirements of what is sometimes called "professional" communication. This text is written for and dedicated to these students. It envisions writers and speakers who in their daily work use a wide variety of communication skills: learning to generate and organize ideas quickly and well; writing effective memos, letters, reports, proposals, and business plans; contributing to collaborative writing and presentation teams; devising graphics to aid communication; leading or participating in worthwhile meetings; producing articles for publication; employing the listening skills and interviewing strategies so crucial to career success.

How *Tools for Technical and Professional Communication* Is Organized

Part One, "An Overview of Technical and Professional Communication," describes the *what, why,* and *how* of communication in science, business, and government: *What* communication skills will you be expected to display? *Why* does communication matter so much in achieving the mission of your organization? *How* does communication function in various companies and government agencies?

Part Two, "The Process of Technical and Professional Communication," takes you step-by-step through the stages of developing effective documents. You will learn practical ways to break through writer's block, generate your best ideas, and then develop and organize those ideas to suit your audience, purpose, and resources. You will learn state-of-the-art techniques for researching, organizing, drafting, revising, and editing, including the revolutionary advances made possible by word processing and desktop publishing. You will also learn how to produce and position meaningful graphics using the latest technologies.

Part Three, "The Products of Technical and Professional Communication," explains in close detail how to produce the dozens of documents required in a technical or professional career. You will see actual examples of company communications, meet practicing communicators, and learn time-saving approaches to written and oral communication, whether you are working by yourself or as part of a team. You will also read about crucial presentation skills, including self-presentation in résumés and interviews, as well as oral presentation skills for meetings, briefings, and speeches.

Finally, you will find three important supplements at the end of the book. "Cases for Technical and Professional Communication" present real-life scenarios posing dilemmas that require critical analysis and carefully constructed communications. Appendix A, "Brief Guide to Grammar, Mechanics, Usage, and Spelling," answers the most common questions about punctuation, word form, and word choice as they relate to technical and professional communication. Appendix B, "Guide to Documentation," provides rules and examples for constructing accurate notes and bibliographies in both MLA and APA formats.

Simply stated, *Tools for Technical and Professional Communication* will help you master the communication concepts and skills necessary for your professional future.

Acknowledgments

This book is dedicated to my colleagues at the McLaren School of Business, University of San Francisco.

Art Bell

Exercise 1: Overviewing a Textbook

Front Matter

Textbook title: _____

_____

See Instructor's Manual, Chapter 10 Answers.

Author(s): _____

_____

Edition: _____

Publishing company: _____

Place of publication: _____

Date of publication: _____

Number of parts: _____

Number of chapters: _____

Author(s) purpose: _____

_____

Learning aids provided: _____

_____

_____

_____

Additional important information mentioned in the preface or introduction:

_____

_____

_____

_____

_____

_____

_____

_____

Back Matter

Check List (Refer to the table of contents for this exercise.)

Index:	Yes _____	No _____
Name:	Yes _____	No _____
Subject:	Yes _____	No _____
Combined:	Yes _____	No _____
Glossary:	Yes _____	No _____
Bibliography:	Yes _____	No _____
General Reference Sources:	Yes _____	No _____
Appendix(es)	Yes _____	No _____

Exercise 2

Now you apply Step 2 by previewing a chapter from the textbook that you just overviewed. When you have completed your preview, fill in the information requested at the end of this chapter, and then think about what you have learned.

CHAPTER EIGHT

Collaborative Writing

"I was surprised," says technical writer Jill Edwards, "to discover how often I worked with others on writing projects when I began my career. College prepared me to write alone, not as a member of a team." By some recent estimates, team writing accounts for as much as 60 percent of all technical writing done in science, business, industry, and the professions, including law and medicine.

Collaborative writing—team writing—involves sharing writing responsibilities with at least one other person. You may work in dyads (pairs) or as a member of a larger project team. All collaborative writing, however, requires that you understand:

- what can go wrong when groups write together;
- what advantages accrue from the team approach to writing;
- how group problems can be avoided;
- how to participate as a member of a writing team; and
- how to lead a writing team.

The Hazards of Team Writing

"A camel is a horse designed by committee," goes the old corporate joke. Many workers at all levels have a deep distrust for shared responsibility and shared decision-making. They have seen delays, compromises, and shoddy work on projects all because of personality squabbles or lack of direction among group members. (Many college students have had equally negative experiences in trying to produce a group presentation or paper.) This ambivalence about group work applies especially to documents written by committee. Four complaints are heard loud and clear across industries:

1. *"One person ends up doing all the work."* Many teams quickly divide into spectators and a single gladiator doing battle in the ring. Of course, those watching usually have plenty of advice for the person doing the work—and plenty of criticism for the person if the project isn't well received.
2. *"We can't keep things moving forward."* Each team member often has a different idea of how the project should develop. Planning meetings turn into exercises in frustration.
3. *"We each have a different style."* When team planning begins to break down, group members each grab their preferred piece of the project to work on. The result is unsatisfactory: they bring back fragments of writing that can't be unified into a single, organized document.

4. *"We're wasting time by trying to work together."* The time misspent on chaotic meetings and misdirected writing leads group members to despair of the team approach to writing. They urge management to assign writing tasks to individuals, never to teams.

These negative judgments are often deserved—team writing can and does go astray. But why shouldn't it? Technical writers have spent their school and college years perfecting the art of *working alone*. Most college papers are written alone, with severe penalties for "cheating" by working with someone else. Students typically show their work to no one but the instructor. Writing, in short, is learned as an individual sport, not a team activity.

The Advantages of Team Writing

The practical world of technical writing, however, can't afford to keep each writer in a private ivory tower. Real-world problems in science and industry usually require a team approach to writing for three reasons:

1. *One writer can't do it all.* Documents dealing with large problems often demand the shared skills and insights of several writers working in close coordination.
2. *Time is money.* Even when one writer could accomplish a major writing task over an extended time, few companies have the luxury of providing that time. Deadlines loom, and only a writing team can produce the required volume of work.
3. *The team provides a safety net.* What happens to an important writing project when an employee falls ill or quits? Nothing disastrous, if the project has been assigned to a team instead of to an individual. Companies ensure continuity and reliability by using the team approach to producing major documents.

How to Avoid the Pitfalls of Team Writing

If team writing at its best is both necessary and desirable, how can technical writers prepare to work effectively as collaborative writers? Let's return to provide constructive responses to the four complaints cited above:

1. *"One person ends up doing all the work."* Divide work fairly among team members. Each member of a well-selected writing team has particular strengths. Discover those strengths and assign writing

tasks accordingly. Here's how one writing team divided initial writing responsibilities for an extended report on total quality (TQ) procedures for their company:

Pablo: Determine which data bases will be most useful for a computer search for relevant books and articles. Gather key descriptor terms [essential words and phrases relevant to the writing project] from team members. Make arrangements with the company to conduct the computer search.

John: Interview senior managers [the primary audience for the writing project] to determine their recommendations for length, format, and style. Obtain examples, when possible, to illustrate their expectations. Distribute these examples and a summary of your interviews to all team members.

Susan: Work with a company graphics specialist and our budget liaison to determine the kinds of graphics that are within our financial means. Distribute samples of such graphics to all team members along with your cost analysis.

Maria: Make sure that all team members are trained in the use of For Comment [the groupware used for this writing project]. Provide training for team members who need it.

Chin: Obtain a copy of *The Chicago Manual of Style* (14th ed.) for each team member and distribute. Determine company deadlines for draft approval and for final publication. Determine production time and costs from word processing and duplication. Distribute a summary of your findings to all team members.

2. *"We can't keep things moving forward."* Keep the project moving forward by developing a shared game plan. The writing team must decide in its initial meetings on target dates for completion of work stages and on the review process that will take place when work is handed in. One writing team agreed on the following schedule. Their shared commitment to these dates exerted peer pressure on all team members to meet or beat the target dates:

Sept. 1 Completion of idea generation (brainstorming)

Sept. 5 Completion of initial idea selection and organization

Sept. 10 Completion of computer search #1 (data gathering)

Sept. 17 Completion of working outline

Sept. 22 Completion of computer search #2 (additional data gathering)

Sept. 25 Completion of final working outline and assignment of writing tasks

Oct. 2 Completion of first drafts of assigned sections
Oct. 7 Completion of initial graphics (rough)
Oct. 12 Completion of revised drafts and final graphics
Oct. 15 Completion of final editing/revision
Oct. 20 Completion of document, including presentation plan

3. *"We each have a different style."* Decide upon issues of style and organization *before* team members begin to write, not after. Team members should decide on matters of voice, tone, and support techniques (as discussed in Chapter 4). Each writer needs to know, for example, whether "I" and "you" will be used; to what degree statistics will be used to support assertions; to what extent footnotes will be added; and so forth. Team members also should agree in advance upon a master outline.

   One technical writing team summed up their mutual agreement on style and organization in this written planning statement:

   As a writing team, we have agreed to avoid the bureaucratic style commonly found in this company's prior formal reports. Instead, we will emulate the direct, concrete, and appropriately conversational style found in such business publications as *Fortune, Business Week,* and *Forbes*. Specifically, we will strive for short sentences and paragraphs, common diction, active voice, and frequent headings. Because our work will be read by a wide audience, we will avoid jargon and unnecessarily complicated charts and graphs.

4. *"We're wasting time by trying to work together."* Value the time spent in comparing ideas and coordinating effort. The time devoted to the *process* of team writing is as important as the individual time given to the *product* of putting words on paper. The company wants the eventual document to speak for a consensus in the company, not just an individual. That consensus can be forged only by patient, active participation by team members in sharing insights, resolving conflicts, and coordinating work activities.

   Consider the experience of one writer on a team:

   I'll admit that I wasn't happy at first to be assigned to a writing team for an important report. As a veteran engineer in the company, I'm more comfortable working on my own projects, where I have more personal control and accountability. But after a few meetings with the team, I began to see one of the advantages of group writing. Even though our specific work was writing a document, our more general work was getting to know and trust one another. Until I worked with this team, I had little to do with employees outside of Engineering. Now I know how other people from other departments think and work. When our document is eventually published in the company, I'll be in a position to explain or even defend it to the people I work with in Engineering.

How to Participate as a Member of a Writing Team

Getting ready to work effectively in a writing team involves, first, a shift in attitude. A technical writer fresh from college writing experiences must be prepared to *listen* at the organizing meeting of the writing team. When each team member shows sincere interest in the opinions of other members, an environment of trust quickly develops. Team members aren't tempted into prima donna roles or competitive rivalries. It's "one for all, and all for one."

Second, team members should express ideas and reactions candidly and provisionally, not in an absolute way. All team members have to speak up if the project is to take shape. It does little good for one team member to tell another, "Your idea is completely worthless." Absolute judgments drive team members apart. If negative judgments need to be expressed, they should be phrased constructively: "I want to understand how your idea fits this project."

Third, team members have to avoid sole ownership of ideas. Once a suggestion is made to the group, it becomes the property of the group—for better or for worse. Ideas should not automatically be labelled as "Cal's opinion" or "Barbara's notion." That kind of ownership limits discussion to little more than interpersonal politics; Cal's idea can't be discussed without challenging Cal's expertise or integrity. The team should agree that there's "nothing personal" about positive or negative comments about ideas. The goal is simply to come up with the best writing plan possible, no matter whose ideas won or whose lost.

Finally, team members must respect one another's differences. It's not uncommon for each member of a writing team to look at the work of others and say, silently, "I could have done it better." In other words, the final document reflecting the work of the team will probably not be completely pleasing to any one team member. There will always be a turn of phrase, an elaboration here, or condensation there that will raise an eyebrow of someone on the writing team.

Such differences are inevitable and should be expected. They don't prove that team writing is mediocre writing; instead, these differences demonstrate that we each have our own opinions of what makes good writing. A major writing project shouldn't be held captive to any one vision of writing style. The strength of team writing lies precisely in its ability to harmonize somewhat different voices into a shared chorus.

How to Lead a Writing Team

Some technical writers have risen to modest fame within their organizations for their ability to lead writing teams. I asked Robert Underwood, a technical writer at Lockheed, to explain in detail how he assembles, organizes, and guides a writing team:

> As senior technical writer in my division, I'm usually the first to hear about a major writing project. I get the news by phone call or memo from an upper-level manager. The next step is a meeting with him or her to learn as much as I can about the project: what's expected of me, what resources are available, when the project must be completed, who will review our work, and so forth. I take careful notes at this meeting; the information gathered there must be shared accurately with the writing team I'll be putting together.
>
> I'm usually given some freedom in selecting members for the writing team. After eleven years with the company, I think I know the strengths and weaknesses of our various staff writers. Some are known for their thoroughness and attention to detail, others for their speed in drafting, and others for content knowledge or organizational abilities. My goal is to shape a team that includes all these strengths.
>
> I try to determine approximately how many writers I'll need on the team, then add one more. Too large a team can't work in a coordinated way and too small a team gets swamped by the workload. I don't put the same people together on the same teams time after time. That approach leads to an "A Team," "B Team" mentality that hurts morale. Whenever possible, I try to involve at least one new writer on major projects. Hands-on experience is the only way to grow.
>
> Once I've selected team members and notified them of our first meeting, I put together a folder of project information for each participant. The more information we can share from the beginning, the more productive our initial meetings. The first meeting is a bit more social than later meetings. It's important that we all get to know one another and to trust one another. If we're going to speak frankly about what we like and don't like in each other's writing, we have to establish a bond of good fellow-feeling from the beginning. Otherwise, the work of the group will break down because of personality conflicts and petty disagreements.
>
> I try not to dominate the first meeting of the team. I've learned that the more I talk at the first meeting, the more of the project I'll have to do on my own. My goal is to present what I know about the project as concisely as possible, then to open up discussion for the

opinions, questions, and suggestions of team members. I explain why we're doing the project, who will read it, and how much time and money the company wants to spend on it.

By the end of the meeting, our discussion will hopefully lead to at least three initial decisions on the part of the team: (1) when to meet again; (2) what each member will bring to that meeting; and (3) what additional information we need as a group to proceed with our work. I don't try to come up with a working outline or document design at the first meeting. These decisions, made too early or by only one person, can discourage fresh thinking by the group.

At the second meeting, I listen for interest areas. By this time, each team member has had a chance to think through the project and to decide, in a tentative way, where he or she can make a contribution. Team members will tell me what they *want* to do if I listen well enough. I've learned that they do their best work in their areas of special interest. Once we've settled upon areas of responsibility, we make plans for drawing up a tentative outline. This master agenda for our document will change many times during the writing process. But it's important to make a start—to get some kind of orderly thoughts on paper. We also set approximate milestones for our work. Although these may change, we have to consider the resource of time from the very beginning of the project.

At following meetings, we will refine our master outline, then move on to the document design, drafting, review, and revision stages. Our work in these areas has been made much easier in the last few years by groupware, a form of word-processing software designed specifically for team writing. Using groupware, we can each work at our computers on our assigned portions of the document while having the work of other team members always accessible at the same computer. Here's a list of some of the capabilities of our groupware:

1. All team members see document changes suggested by others.
2. Changes can be discussed on screen before becoming part of the document draft.
3. Team members can send comments, questions, and data to one another during the writing process.
4. Team members can develop, and switch back and forth to, alternative patterns of organization, types of graphics, and tentative drafts.

During the outlining and drafting stages, I keep in close touch with upper management to make sure the team is heading in the right direction. Too often in this company, as in others, a writing team has completed a major project without consultation with management along the way. The result can be wasted effort, squandered resources, and sometimes even terminations.

We formalize the review process by management when the team has compiled its first edited draft. This prototype is circulated among upper managers for their sign-off and suggestions. We revise accordingly.

The team usually settles upon one or two members to act as final editors for the last draft. It's important that each page of the document read as if it were written by one person, although in fact many team members contributed. We achieve this sense of a single voice "speaking" in the document by limiting the number of final editors. The completed document is then given to each team member for a painstaking final reading. We want to eliminate all errors in form, content, grammar, mechanics, style, usage, and spelling.

I usually invite a senior manager to our final team meeting to receive the completed document. It's important that all team members share in the sense of accomplishment that comes with the presentation of the document to management. Managers have a chance to ask questions about the document at the meeting, and to thank those who worked on it. Although I probably shouldn't say it, we writers value this last meeting as a chance to tell senior managers what's in the document. Often their reading of our work isn't as thorough as it should be.

Team Writing in Your Future

Because team writing is so widely established in business and government, you should take every opportunity in your college experience or career to practice collaborative writing skills. In working together on a group project, remember to consider the process of your interaction, not just the eventual product of your efforts. Discuss how to organize your mutual activities and how to avoid conflict or isolation among group members. In so doing, you will be practicing skills that may well determine your effectiveness in your eventual career.

Discussion Questions

1. Why is collaborative or team writing so prevalent in science, government, and business? What kind of projects are particularly suited to the collaborative approach?

2. Discuss the pitfalls of collaborative writing.
3. Discuss how the pitfalls of collaborative writing can be avoided.
4. Discuss effective ways to participate as a member of a writing team.
5. Discuss roles and responsibilities for the leader of a writing team.
6. Discuss a typical series of meetings for collaborative writing teams.
7. What is groupware? What are its uses for the writing team?
8. If collaborative writing is so common in careers, why is it practiced so little in secondary and college education? Discuss changes that you feel should be made to the writing curriculum in this regard.

Exercises

1. Meet with a group of your classmates to write a collaborative document describing problems you have individually experienced as participants in group writing projects in the past.
2. In a collaborative writing group, discuss ways in which collaborative writing could be emphasized across disciplines in the college curriculum. Report on your discussion in written form.
3. In a collaborative writing group, discuss an assignment you have previously completed individually for your class. How would that assignment have been approached differently if it had been written collaboratively. In what ways might the results have differed from the individual papers handed in? Report on your discussion in writing.
4. In this assignment, you will work with a writing team on the initial planning stages of a collaborative project. You will not actually complete the project, unless asked to do so by your instructor. Meet with your writing group to undertake a long report on the topic, "Homelessness in America." Follow the planning stages described in the chapter to distribute work assignments to each participant. Report in writing on your successes and difficulties working through the initial planning stages of a document.
5. Meet with your writing group to discuss the challenges of leading a writing team. Each member of the team should write several paragraphs describing his or her approaches to such leadership responsibilities.

6. Interview a person in a business, technical, or scientific career. Determine the degree to which that person participates in or leads collaborative writing teams. Report on your findings in writing.

7. Investigate commercially available groupware packages at your college computer center or local computer store. If possible, experiment with such software. Report on your investigation in writing.

8. Meet with your writing group to discuss and define the kind of software your group would find helpful to its work. The group will, in effect, "invent" the specifications for a computer system ideally suited to the group's needs. Write up the description of that computer system.

Chapter title: _____

_____

See Instructor's Manual,
Chapter 10 Answers.

Number of pages: _____

Introduction: Yes _____   No _____
    Important information mentioned:

_____

_____

_____

_____

_____

_____

_____

_____

_____

Summary: Yes _____   No _____
    Important information mentioned:

_____

_____

_____

_____

_____

_____

_____

_____

_____

Graphic Aids: Yes _____   No _____
   Titles:

_____

_____

_____

_____

_____

_____

_____

_____

Questions: Yes _____   No _____
   Other learning aids provided:

_____

_____

_____

_____

_____

Exercise 3

In your notebook apply Step 3 to the same chapter by writing out a broad topic outline that lists all of the headings. Remember to indent the minor headings under the appropriate major ones and to indent the smaller headings under the appropriate minor ones.

Exercise 4

Now apply Step 4 to the same chapter by turning all of the headings into questions and reading each section to find the answers. Try to use the reading skills you have learned from this textbook to help you to locate the answers. Underline the answers in the chapter or write them in your notebook. Also remember that you can summarize and/or paraphrase your answers if that makes it easier for you.

Exercise 5

Your instructor may decide to test you on the chapter "Collaborative Writing," so apply Step 5 to it by reviewing the answers to your questions. Because there is much information to learn, make sure that you review it immediately and on a continuous basis. Recite your answers aloud so that they stick in your mind.

Exercise 6

Your instructor may ask you to apply the five-step approach to another textbook. Now that you have used this approach, you know that it is well worth the time and effort. Remember to use the five steps with all of your textbooks.

For Exercise 3, See the Instructor's Manual, Chapter 10 Answers.

When doing Exercise 4, emphasize how patterns of organization enable a reader to find some of the answers to the questions developed from the headings. For instance, simple listing of facts and chronological order patterns help to provide the answers to the respective questions: How should you participate as a member of a writing team? How should you lead one?

For Exercise 5, you may choose to test students on the chapter "Collaborative Writing," so that they gain experience using the five-step approach. See Instructor's Manual, Chapter 10 Answers, for further suggestions on assessment.

Exercise 6: If feasible, have students apply the five-step approach to a textbook for another class or provide alternate textbook material. Students using the same textbook or textbook material can, of course, be grouped for purposes of instruction and class discussion.

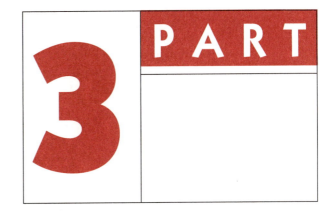

Change-of-Pace Readings

On the following pages you will find reading selections and comprehension questions. These readings are a change of pace from the other material presented in this book. They serve as practice exercises to help you improve test-taking and comprehension skills. As you read these selections, apply the skills that you have learned.

Part 3 Objectives: To provide ten reading selections that offer a change from purely textbook material, while giving students additional practice with comprehension and test-taking skills.

These ten selections, which vary in difficulty and subject matter, should prove interesting for students and provide an opportunity for stimulating class discussions. Thus, they can be assigned periodically throughout the semester as a diversion from textbook material.

See Instructor's Manual, Part 3 Answers, for further suggestions on using these selections.

SELECTION 1: "The Dark Menace"

I will never forget my first encounter with a bat; it is an experience that will live in my memory forever. It all started at 3:00 A.M. on a muggy summer morning in late July when I got out of my bed to use the bathroom. As I left the bedroom, in what can best be described as a near comatose state, something went whizzing by my head. With half-closed eyes, I looked up and saw what I thought was a large moth flying around in circles. It made several more sweeps around the periphery of the room before I realized that this was no moth.

Never at a loss as to what to do in a potentially dangerous situation, I did what any intelligent, if not courageous, person would do: I ran back into the bedroom, quickly slamming the door behind me. At that point, my wife woke to ask why I was exercising so early in the morning. I explained what was happening and suggested that she investigate immediately. My offer was rejected promptly with a look of utter disappointment at my obvious lack of courage.

My last hope was our big, bad 115-pound golden retriever, who was fast asleep on his back on our bedroom floor. After much prodding he managed to get up, although he had a look about him of total annoyance. Ignoring his reaction, I pushed him out of the bedroom into the living room and quickly slammed the door shut behind him. Now, I gloated, the bat was finished!

I listened intently by the door for the sound of what surely would be a fierce struggle, but there was total silence. After a few more impatient moments, I opened the door a crack and peered into the living room. To my shock, our great protector was waiting anxiously to return to the bedroom, which he did with great speed nearly knocking me down in the process. It was only a matter of minutes before he was—like my wife—again fast asleep. What a disappointment!

With no clear remedy to the situation, I became increasingly upset and disillusioned. Through the years I had heard several unpleasant "bat stories," which only contributed to my apprehension: bats fly into people's hair; bats attack; bats drink people's blood; bats can have rabies. After much thought and soul-searching, it became clear to me that I was going to have to be the saviour of the household. Armed with nothing, but dressed like a soldier ready for combat, I made my way into the living room to confront the dark menace.

The bat was not at all impressed with my presence as she whisked by my head several times while circling the room. Although her body was relatively small, her wing span was wide, much the way an airplane is proportioned. I marveled at her exceptional grace as she flew within the confines of the darkened room never once hitting a wall or anything else. She made no sound as she glided through the air. It was only later that I learned that bats do emit high-frequency sounds as they fly, which after striking various objects, bounce back as echoes. Using these echoes that cannot be heard by the human ear, bats navigate in total darkness without running into anything. This explains why bats function so well as nocturnal beings and can sleep away virtually all of their days. Although they are able to see, they do not have to depend on their eyes to fly. In short, they are extraordinary flying machines.

Eventually I put my admiration for the bat aside and returned to the immediate problem of ridding the premises of her company. I theorized that if I could entice her to fly into the front hall, the inside door could be closed quickly trapping her in that small area. If I then ran out the back door and came around to the front of the house, I could open that door and send her on her merry way. In case you are wondering why the front door would be open at 3:00 a.m., the answer is simple. I always leave my keys in it, which is very convenient for me as well as for any uninvited guests who decide to visit. Needless to say, the rest of the family is not particularly impressed with my hospitality.

By the way, the plan worked perfectly for both the bat and me. In the years since this episode, I have learned much about bats through extensive reading. Although bats can be rabid, they are basically peaceful creatures who generally do not attack humans unless provoked. They are not particularly interested in human hair, which in my case is irrelevant because I have so little. Finally, some bats, who live mainly in South and Central America, are indeed called vampire bats, but they *usually* enjoy the blood of animals of the nonhuman variety and do not spend much time biting people's necks. When they do take blood, they drink very little, and the unsuspecting victim is in fairly good shape when they leave.

With my expanding knowledge, I have come to appreciate these strange creatures of the night with their magnificent flying abilities. They may not be beautiful, but they sure are fascinating to watch. Unlike many people, I am not nearly as terrified of them as was once the case. Nevertheless, I would just as soon meet my next bat in the zoo!

Part 3 Change-of-Pace Readings

Comprehension Questions

Regarding question 1, you may wish to ascertain if your students know what is meant by tone. Discuss as needed.

See the Instructor's Manual, Part 3 Answers.

1. The tone of this selection can best be described as which of the following?
   a. Humorous
   b. Serious
   c. Matter-of-fact
   d. Sad
   e. Both a and b
   f. Both b and d
   g. None of the above

2. What does the word *comatose* mean in the sentence: "As I left the bedroom, in what can best be described as a near comatose state. . . ."?

   _____

   _____

3. What does the word *periphery* mean in the sentence: "It made several more sweeps around the periphery of the room. . . ."?

   _____

   _____

4. What does the word *prodding* mean in the sentence: "After much prodding he managed to get up. . . ."?

   _____

   _____

5. What does the word *emit* mean in the sentence: "It was only later that I learned that bats do emit high-frequency sounds. . . ."?

   _____

   _____

Selection 1: "The Dark Menace" 331

6. What does the word *nocturnal* mean in the sentence: "This explains why bats function so well as nocturnal beings. . . ."?

7. *True or False:* From this selection we can conclude that the phrase "blind as a bat" is an accurate way to describe someone who doesn't see well?

8. List five facts about bats that are mentioned in the selection.

9. What does the author mean when he talks about uninvited guests visiting his house in the middle of the night?

10. In this particular situation, the author can best be described as which of the following?
    a. Courageous
    b. Intelligent
    c. Resourceful
    d. All of the above
    e. None of the above

11. Can we assume that the author at first intended to destroy the bat? Why? Why not?

12. Which of the "bat stories" turned out to be not true?

13. What is the overall message of the selection?

SELECTION 2: "The Experience of a Lifetime"

There is scarcely a person alive who has not thought about death at one time or another. Our interest in the subject is aroused because it is an experience that we all must confront sooner or—hopefully—much later. Add to this the fact that, as far as I know, no one has ever returned from the other side to tell us what it is like, and you can understand why death is so fascinating. It is precisely the ultimate mystery of it all that both intrigues and frightens us. In fact, fear helps explain why we even hesitate to use the word "died" opting instead for euphemisms like "passed away" or "passed on."

We have all heard or read about people who have had near death or out-of-body experiences, which they generally describe as somewhat pleasant and/or peaceful. To say the least, I was skeptical about those stories—that is, until that wintry morning in 1990 when my view changed dramatically. It was a Sunday, and I was sleeping off the effects of a very late Saturday night. In my supine position, with arms and legs fully extended and the back of my head resting comfortably on two pillows, I did not have a care in the world. My wife had gotten up much earlier, so the bed was mine exclusively.

As I started to make my way back to consciousness, I became aware of a rather loud swishing sound in my ears. At the same time, I felt a sensation that was similar to moving through a tunnel at top speed. The ride can best be described as very thrilling without being scary at all. My body seemed to be levitating toward the ceiling and yet I could picture it still on the bed. Later I concluded that this must have been my spirit taking leave of its bodily home. Nevertheless, I was clearly heading toward what I perceived to be a bright light located in the corner where the wall meets the ceiling. At that exact point, there was a large opening through which I could see shadows and hear voices far off in the distance. As my spirit tried to proceed a gentle, soothing voice said, "Not now, it is not time." It was precisely at that moment that my body and spirit came together again, and I awakened to the normal sounds of my surroundings.

Surprisingly, I recalled immediately what had happened and was touched deeply by how pleasant and peaceful it had been. There had been absolutely no fear, just a feeling of great tranquility and complete relaxation. In a way, I was sorry that it had ended so abruptly, and to this day, I really hope to go on that trip again some time soon. When I told others about the experience, they expressed genuine envy as if they had been deprived of something very special. Indeed, they had been deprived!

Although I am still not in any hurry to die, the thought is not as frightening as it once was. The utter peacefulness of that Sunday morning has stayed with me through the years. I had begun what I think was my final journey, only to be forced to turn back because of a poor sense of timing. Someday that journey will have to be continued to its inevitable conclusion. In the meantime, I yearn to have that experience one more time with the hope that the gatekeeper once again turns me away.

Comprehension Questions

1. In your own words, what is the overall message of this selection?

2. Why does the author believe that we are so interested in death?

See Instructor's Manual, Part 3 Answers.

Selection 2: "The Experience of a Lifetime"

3. In the sentence: "Add to this the fact that, as far as I know, no one has ever returned from the other side. . . ." *the other side* refers to:

   _____

   _____

4. Using the context, find the meanings of the following words.

   euphemisms _____

   skeptical _____

   tranquility _____

5. Provide some examples of other euphemisms.

   _____

   _____

   _____

   _____

   _____

6. A person who is in a *supine* position is lying on his/her

   _____ .

7. What does the word *levitating* mean in the sentence: "My body seemed to be levitating. . . ."?

   _____

   _____

8. To whom does the voice that said, "Not now, it is not time." belong?

9. Contrast the author's opinion of near death or out-of-body experiences before and after his own experience.

10. Contrast the author's feelings about death before and after his experience.

11. In your own words describe in detail what happened to the author.

_____

_____

_____

_____

12. In one or two paragraphs in your notebook, discuss your views on near death or out-of-body experiences.

SELECTION 3: "The Trajectories of Genius: Work echoing the man: many Conceits—and edges"

He was thought to be dead at birth in Málaga on October 25, 1881. Then his uncle Salvador Ruiz, a celebrated Spanish physician who had delivered the boy, calmly puffed cigar smoke up the baby's nose, provoking howls of protest. Thus did Picasso embark on 91 years of rugged life.

Pablo Ruiz Picasso (he adopted Picasso,* his mother's maiden name, a not uncommon practice in Hispanic societies) was not only the youngest nicotine inhaler in Spain. He was to prove extraordinarily precocious in every other respect. By the age of 14, the pug-nosed, stocky, black-haired Pablo was a familiar figure in the Barrio Chino, the redlight district of *fin de siècle*** Barcelona, the city to which the family had moved when he was five. Some of his earliest work was inspired by the *putas**** and dancers of that wicked cosmopolitan seaport. Though he later won admission to Madrid's esteemed Academy of San Fernando, an art school, he did not take his studies seriously, preferring to spend his time in the Prado and other museums—and in the demimonde with other young artists and poets.

Then, in late 1900, Picasso decided to go to Paris. His departure was, for the world of art, the equivalent of Paul's journey to Damascus. He spent his working life in France, but he remained a Spaniard to his elegant fingertips. His piercing, unblinking deep-chestnut eyes spoke of the Spanish soul's passion. Even after he began to prosper, he was content to dress and live like a Spanish peasant, eating beans and drinking coarse red wine, in loud cafés and private rooms of indescribable clutter. And though it was in France that he found fame and fortune, he remained curiously indifferent to that nation's life struggles in two world wars and a depression. To the outside world, it seemed that the only external event that seared Picasso's imagination and conscience was the Spanish Civil War, the fratricidal bloodletting that inspired *Guernica*. A fervent supporter of the Republic against Franco, he contributed many paintings to raise funds for the war's victims.

Copyright 1980 TIME Inc. Reprinted by permission.

---

*He also may have chosen the name because of a 17th century Genoese painter named Matteo Picasso, though he always denied this.
**(Spanish) turn-of-the-century.
***(Spanish) prostitutes.

For much of his life, he kept his liquid capital in a locked suitcase. (His real capital, of course, lay in Picasso's Picassos and a huge store of works by other artists that he accumulated over the years.) He did not lightly dispense those bank notes. He preferred to give a delivery boy an instant drawing rather than a five-franc tip. Fernande Olivier, with whom Picasso had his first lasting love affair, a liaison that lasted seven years, died of pneumonia in 1958, 46 years after their breakup. She received no financial help from her old lover. Picasso died worth at least $400 million. In the more realistic values of today's market-place, his legacies are worth much more.

He bestowed little love on his children after they passed the age of cherubic portraiture. Born over a span of 28 years, they were: Paulo, his only legitimate child, by Dancer Olga Koklova (he died in 1975); Maya, by Marie-Thérèse Walter; and Claude and Paloma, by Françoise Gilot. One of the few paramours or wives with any pretension to intellectuality, Gilot (now married to famed U.S. Scientist Dr. Jonas Salk) was co-author of a bitter book, *Life with Picasso,* in which she calls him a manipulator of human beings: "He loved only one thing—his painting. Not his women, not his children." Gilot broke with Picasso in 1953. Jacqueline Roque, the aspiring poet he married in 1961, was described by one acquaintance as "the only woman who ever was able to lead him around by the nose."

That nose was, for a while, ringed by the French Communist Party. He joined in 1944 and painted for it the famed *Dove of Peace,* which the Soviets happily substituted for the hammer and sickle as their symbol of peace on earth. No political sophisticate and certainly no ideologue, Picasso eventually distanced himself from the party after the Soviet invasion of Hungary in 1956. As Salvador Dali quipped: "Picasso is a Spaniard—so am I. Picasso is a genius—so am I. Picasso is a Communist—nor am I."

After World War II, despite sporadic explosions of artist energy, usually fired by some new love, the once gregarious Picasso gradually became more than ever a recluse. He sustained many old feuds and started new ones with fellow artists, critics, and dealers, but welcomed the obsequities of a faithful coterie. In 1958 he purchased a medieval château near Aix-en-Provence called Vauvenargues. "I've bought Cézanne's view!" he said. He spent most of his final years, however, at Notre-Dame-de-Vie, a hilltop villa at Mougins on the Riviera, named after a chapel that once stood on the site. He worked until dawn on the last day of his life, April 8, 1973.

Comprehension Questions

1. How many children did Picasso have?
   a. One
   b. Two
   c. Three
   d. Four
   e. Five

2. In 1958, Picasso purchased a chateau called _____ .

3. What is the Prado?
   a. An art school
   b. A city in Spain
   c. A museum
   d. A painting
   e. A seaport

4. List all of Picasso's mistresses or wives mentioned in the reading.

   _____

   _____

   _____

   _____

   _____

   _____

   _____

5. What is *Guernica*?

   a. A city in France
   b. One of Picasso's paintings
   c. A Spanish term for "republic"
   d. The Spanish Civil War
   e. All of the above
   f. None of the above

6. Where is Málaga located?

   a. Cuba
   b. Spain
   c. Puerto Rico
   d. Portugal
   e. Italy

7. The redlight district of Barcelona was called _____.

8. Which is Picasso's only legitimate child?

   a. Claude
   b. Paloma
   c. Maya
   d. Paulo
   e. Olga

9. Where did Picasso work most of his life?

   a. Damascus
   b. Spain
   c. France
   d. Italy
   e. Barcelona

10. Which of the following describe Picasso?

    a. Politically sophisticated
    b. Loving to women and children
    c. Generous with his money
    d. A supporter of Franco
    e. All of the above
    f. None of the above

11. Place the letter of the correct year in the space next to each of the following events.

____ Birth of Picasso

____ Picasso goes to Paris

____ Picasso marries Jacqueline Roque

____ Death of Picasso

____ Picasso's family moves to Barcelona

____ Picasso joins the French Communist Party

a. 1973
b. 1886
c. 1944
d. 1881
e. 1900
f. 1961
g. 1974
h. 1956
i. 1958

SELECTION 4: "Why Run?"

By Marlene Cimons

Los Angeles—More than a decade ago, the evening before I was to run my first marathon, I went to a runners' party in a Manhattan restaurant where a mutual friend introduced me to Frank Shorter, the 1972 Olympic marathon gold medalist.

"Frank," my friend said, "she's running her first marathon tomorrow. Give her the word."

Shorter smiled.

"Why?" he asked.

Why, indeed.

Why would anyone deliberately set out to run 26 miles, 385 yards? It is a grueling and humbling event that can take a monumental toll on body and spirit.

But the reality is hundreds of marathons are held each year in cities and small towns all over the world. Tens of thousands of people run in them annually, and there is no evidence that the marathon's popularity is diminishing.

Marathoning is one of the few athletic events in which some of the world's best-conditioned athletes, who are chasing records and lucrative prize money, brush shoulders with middle-of-the-packers such as myself, who seek only to meet a personal challenge.

When you ask people why they run marathons, they will almost always say they want to improve their health. But there is more to it than that.

Regular running certainly provides numerous health benefits. It strengthens the heart, lungs, and the immune system, lowers blood pressure, thins the blood, elevates the level of the good cholesterol and reduces the bad. It also increases energy, relieves stress, and improves the mood. It is a good way to burn calories and fight obesity. Many former smokers say running helped them stop. Also, many people say they are able to solve problems while running.

But all of this can be had with moderate mileage, without the heavy and often time-consuming training logged by the serious marathoner. Further, marathoners who overtain can also run the risk of injury.

So why do it?

"Most people run marathons for reasons they themselves don't understand," says Bob Sevene, who coached Joan Benoit Samuelson to

Copyright 1992 Los Angeles Times Syndicate. Reprinted by permission.

a gold medal in the marathon at the 1984 Los Angeles Olympic Games. "I think the marathon has come to represent the ultimate challenge, the measuring stick of whether you're an athlete or not."

The marathon can mean different things to different people. It can be a race against other athletes. It can also be a contest against the clock, the course, and the elements, as well as the distance. And it can also be a confrontation with yourself.

"Life has become tough, with the economy and with all the other stresses we have to deal with in our daily lives," Sevene says. "It has become very hard for many of us to find something to give us a lift. The marathon gives us something to focus on, a chance to step outside our normal lives and succeed at something. It also gives us a chance to fail."

For those who train wisely marathoning is a safe sport. To be sure, there are occasional stories of runners who have collapsed and died while running marathons. But such tragedies are like airplane crashes: They make news simply because they happen so rarely.

In fact, Dr. Paul D. Thompson, a cardiologist and associate professor of medicine at Brown University, in 1982 collected data on deaths from running during a six-year period and found only one death for every 15,000 healthy runners per year.

The greatest danger from marathoning is overdoing it. There are overzealous people who are driven to running dozens of marathons every year. "I think people who go out and run them every weekend, as some do, are a little bit touched," says Amby Burfoot, who won the Boston Marathon in 1968 and is now executive editor of *Runner's World* magazine. "They have agendas other than their own health when they do that. For most of us, the act of training sensibly for marathons and running one or two a year is part of a lifelong fitness regimen."

Cardiologist Thompson agrees. "I liken it to buying stock. Exercise long term has a benefit. I don't care whether someone ran a marathon two weeks ago. I care that he's running 20 years from now."

High mileage accumulated slowly over a reasonable period enables the body to adjust. Those who increase their mileage rapidly will be prone to muscular-skeletal problems, Says Dr. David Brody, a Norwalk, Conn., orthopedic surgeon and medical consultant to Washington's Marine Corps Marathon.

Stress fractures are the most common result of injudicious training or of running too many marathons. These small breaks in the bone are caused by cumulative stress and often require six to eight weeks to heal. Other problems include the usual array of minor muscle strains and sprains, blisters, and cramping. Women whose high-mileage training has resulted in extremely low body fat, which is believed to be tied to estrogen production, can also experience the temporary loss of menstrual periods.

Brody says there has never been evidence that marathons or marathon training produce arthritis. However, "individuals with pre-existing conditions, such as early arthritis in the knee or the hip, or a disc problem in the back, may aggravate them through training," he says.

While moderate running appears to strengthen the immune system, there is some evidence that running marathons may temporarily weaken it.

David C. Nieman, associate professor in the department of health, leisure and exercise science at Appalachian State University in North Carolina, studied 2,300 runners who competed in the 1987 Los Angeles Marathon. He found that 13 percent became sick with a cold or the flu during the week after the race, compared with 2 percent of those who trained for the marathon but didn't run it.

Neiman believes that marathoners are more vulnerable to bacterial or viral attacks during the six post-race hours.

I happen to know this is true. In the fall of 1990, when I ran the Marine Corps Marathon, I felt drained and couldn't understand why. I had trained well. I was rested. But the morning after the race, I woke up with one of the worst colds I have ever had. Apparently, I had been fighting an infection in the days before the event. By running the marathon, I'd given the virus the advantage.

That marathon was my first since 1985; in previous years I had finished six. I had been running regularly, but the demands of work and new motherhood had forced me to put my marathon training on hold. During the summer of 1990, I decided that it was now or never. If I didn't run another marathon soon, I might never run one again.

Secretly, I was hoping to run a personal best—anything faster than 3:44. But I told people I wanted only to break 3:55, a time that would qualify me to run in the Boston Marathon, a long-time dream.

But race day turned out to be warm and sunny—in the 70s—terrible for a marathon. The aforementioned cold was brewing. And if all that wasn't enough, I developed blood blisters on both feet after only six miles. The weather had already eliminated the possibility of a personal best. By the time I reached the 16th mile, with both feet screaming, I knew that Boston was also out of the question. I would be lucky to finish.

I have never dropped out of a marathon. And I swore that I would not on this day either.

I crossed the finish line in a rather disappointing 4:14, having walked much of the last 10 kilometers. Not a performance to boast about.

I tried again last fall. This time the weather was perfect—sunny and in the mid-40s at the start—and I was healthy. And I was well-trained, or so I thought.

But the one predictable thing that can be said about marathons is that they are unpredictable. I clocked exactly what I had the year before: 4:14. I don't know what went wrong.

But I don't intend to give up.

Despite two discouraging performances, the overwhelming feeling that washed over me as I crossed the finish line each time was not disappointment—but elation. I had finished another marathon; I was back in marathoning again.

Bob Sevene is right. The marathon does give you the opportunity to fail.

Comprehension Questions

1. Small breaks in bones are called _____

2. Name the four marathons mentioned in this article.

   _____

   _____

   _____

   _____

3. What is the length of a typical marathon?

   _____

   _____

4. High-mileage training among women can lead to the loss of

   _____.

5. A marathon can be a race against which of the following?
    a. Yourself
    b. The distance
    c. The elements
    d. The course
    e. The clock
    f. Other athletes
    g. All of the above
    h. None of the above

6. What does the word *injudicious* mean in the sentence: "Stress fractures are the most common result of injudicious training or of running too many marathons."?

_____

_____

_____

_____

7. What is the number one reason given by people when they are asked why they run marathons?

_____

_____

_____

_____

8. What is a "middle-of-the-packer?"

_____

_____

_____

_____

9. Name five health benefits of regular running.

   _____

   _____

   _____

   _____

   _____

10. The one predictable thing that can be said about marathons is that they are _____ .

11. Identify the following by placing the correct letter next to each name.

    ____ Amby Burfoot   a. 1972 Olympic Gold Medal winner
    ____ Joan Benoit Samuelson b. 1968 Boston Marathon winner
    ____ Frank Shorter   c. 1984 Olympic Gold Medal winner

12. Would a finishing time of 3 hours 43 minutes have been a "personal best" for the author?

    _____

    _____

13. Is the author likely to continue to run marathons? Why? Why not?

    _____

    _____

14. In what city did the author run her first marathon?

   _____

   _____

15. In your opinion, is marathon running a good idea? Why? Why not? (Write a couple of paragraphs in your notebook.)

SELECTION 5: "With No Parents, Ladeeta, 18, Presses On"

By Felicia R. Lee

It was 3:30 on a Monday morning and Ladeeta Smith could not sleep. Just hours earlier she had visited her mother in a Bronx nursing home, and she was haunted by the image of her emaciated body covered with sores. At 41, Patricia Bobo Smith was dying of AIDS and no longer recognized her daughter.

Later that day, Ladeeta would walk into Boys and Girls High School in Bedford-Stuyvesant, Brooklyn, where its signs proclaim, "We Are Survivors." The 18-year-old senior would turn in final semester reports, lead an English class discussion, and put finishing touches on the college applications that she hoped would take her far away from this tattered neighborhood.

"I know that if I don't get my education I won't have anything—and I want everything," said Ladeeta, a tall, thin girl who wears her hair in long braids swept to one side of her face and a tiny ring through her left nostril.

"I want family and love and money," she said, waving in the direction of Brooklyn streets lined with garbage. "I know I can do better than this."

"I know Mommy would want me to go on, she would not want me to sit around and cry," Ladeeta said. "If I get down and start doing poorly, who knows how long it would take me to get back up?"

Ladeeta Gaynell Smith has survived almost every plague of adolescence in neighborhoods defined by hopeless girls with babies and angry boys with guns. Not long ago, isolated in the projects without relatives or support, she was losing herself to the same despair that had driven her mother to crack houses and her father to drink himself to death.

She ran with a gang of girls who beat and robbed other girls of their jewelry and cash. She struggled alone to take care of her two younger sisters, Lakisha, now 13, and Latreece, 5. She was more often absent from school than not. Her first job was holding drugs and cash for a major neighborhood crack dealer.

"It was all I knew," she said.

Ladeeta's story shows how much darker childhood can be in an age of AIDS and crack. Like a shattered mirror, her life reflects fragments of the experience of many.

"I think a lot of kids know they're not going anywhere," Ladeeta said. "People aren't motivated because they see people who aren't educated who are surviving."

Copyright © 1993 by the New York Times Company. Reprinted by permission.

Ladeeta was able to envision another life only after her grandmother plucked her from the chaos of her mother's home and enrolled her in a school where she found teachers who are convincing her that she can have a future.

"Sometimes I think, how far am I going to be able to go being female and black—two things against me," she said.

Although she no longer sees most of her friends from the projects and has been accepted to three colleges, Ladeeta worries. That her two younger sisters do not succumb to the same pressures that tempted her. That she will be able to navigate the world of college as easily as she could the streets of Brooklyn. That the trauma of those years of watching friends die and watching her mother waste her life will come back to haunt her.

Changes

New Drug, New Violence

It was 1984 and there was a new drug in the Cypress Hills housing project called crack. Ladeeta, who was 9, did not quite understand what was happening in her East New York neighborhood. The boys who used to be her friends now stood somberly on street corners crowded with people looking for a high. They would warn her if they expected trouble and shoo her into the apartment. The older guys had new jobs where they carried guns about the vacant lots and abandoned buildings and shot at boys from other projects.

"More people started getting high because it was right there," she said. "Older people I respected started smoking and fighting and stealing right in the streets. They would have shoot-outs."

Ladeeta said that there was still a sense that everyone who lived in the project was family. When the shoot-outs came, though, she learned to duck for cover. One girlfriend was shot in the arm. Another died from a gunshot in the back.

That was later. The first ones to die were the boys: friends like Butch and Pig and Charles who became caught up in what seemed to be the easy money and adventure of street life. In all, she has seen eight friends die.

At the end of 1986, Ladeeta's father died. Elbert Smith was an alcoholic who had a convulsion that Ladeeta believes was related to pills and liquor. No one in the family would talk about it, she said, although his death changed their lives completely.

Ladeeta's older sister, Lavelle, had gone off to Clark Atlanta University in Georgia. Her mother, who had lost the man she had been with since she was 14, fell heavily into drugs.

Ladeeta was 12 when her mother—who was three months' pregnant—began staying away from home for days at a time. When she did come home, she was often high.

"I saw her high plenty of times," she said. "They start singing and dancing and acting all jolly. I was disgusted with her. I would walk past her like I didn't know her on the streets."

That left Ladeeta to take care of the house. "I had to cook and clean and go shopping," she said. "I thought everybody was talking about me and my sisters and how my mother was a crackhead."

'Never Did Teen-Age Stuff.' In June 1987 Ladeeta went to Kings County Hospital to pick up her mother and the new baby, Latreece. They came home on the bus. When they got there, her mother went out to look for drugs.

Left at home with her two sisters, with little money and no telephone, Ladeeta's only diversion was a group of girls who rode the subways and robbed other girls. She saw it as an escape.

"I never did teenage stuff like go to the movies, to dinner," Ladeeta said.

Hanging out was all she knew. "I didn't see people going to school," she said. "If you were too smart, you were a nerd. I thought girls having babies at 15, 16, 17 was normal. I thought selling drugs was normal."

Between her subway excursions and caring for her sisters, she missed months of school at a time. She was held back a year.

Lavelle, down in Atlanta, wrote constantly, promising that life would improve if Ladeeta would just stay in school and try to get their mother into a drug-rehabilitation program.

But privately, she said, she wondered if she should come home.

"I wish I could have eased her from going through that," said Lavelle, who works for an insurance company in Chicago. "DeDe came out good. She's a lot tougher than I am emotionally."

The Business

Crack and Cash in a Closet Safe

Unknown to Lavelle, Ladeeta began working for a big crack dealer in the projects. There was a safe in their apartment where wads of cash from crack sales and $200 packets of the drug were kept. Ladeeta's job was to give the dealer downstairs a new packet when he needed one, and—with her mother's tacit approval—to tuck the money in the safe in her mother's bedroom closet.

The dealer made thousands of dollars a week, Ladeeta said. She made $400 a week, money she spent on gold jewelry and clothes. She was 14 or 15 years old.

"It was there and I just couldn't say no, I guess," she said. "They were in my house constantly. It was just there."

Almost all of her friends were involved in the drug trade at some point, Ladeeta said. There were many jobs: selling, cutting it up, putting it in little vials, picking it up.

Ladeeta said she no longer associated with many people from that period of her life. "I stopped because I wanted more," she said. "I knew what drugs had done to my mother."

It was a lonely time. Other than Lavelle, Ladeeta said she had no one to help her sort out her feelings. She had never really gotten to know Thelma Simmons, her maternal grandmother who lived in Crown Heights, Brooklyn. When her grandmother called to chat, Ladeeta told her that things were O.K. Then, in 1990, her mother was arrested for drug use and Mrs. Simmons took charge.

Thelma Simmons, at age 66, had already raised eight children of her own and was caring for her 19-year-old grandson. She said she took in her three granddaughters because she felt she had to.

"I pray," Mrs. Simmons said. "Otherwise I would have cracked up a long time ago. It is a terrible thing to lose a child, but I have to be there for these young ones coming up."

The Past

2-Parent Family Teaches Values

Years ago, Ladeeta remembers, she had a real life in Cypress Hills. Her parents, Patricia and Elbert Smith, Ladeeta, and her three sisters lived in apartment 6D—three bedrooms, brightly decorated. Lavelle, now 24, was the oldest. When she was a teenager, her parents sent her to Connecticut to get away from the projects. Lisa, now 22, had always lived with an aunt because her parents were homeless when she was born. Lakisha was the baby.

Every evening the family had dinner together. The rule was no television until homework was done. Although both her parents were high school dropouts who later earned G.E.D.s, they always taught the girls that education was the way to make it, Ladeeta recalled. The family mostly relied on welfare, although Ladeeta remembers her mother sometimes had a factory job.

The Smiths stood out, because they were the only two-parent family in their building.

"Everybody I knew, it was just their mother," Ladeeta said. "I didn't think about it. Except, maybe, I used to think we could get along without my father because my father upset me so much. He was drunk a lot."

The kids in the project used to call Mr. Smith "Mr. Peanut" because he was thin. When drunk, he preached self-reliance. The most embarrassing time Ladeeta remembers is the winter he ran outside naked.

"My father couldn't make an example of himself," Ladeeta said. "All he could do is tell us."

After Crack, Shame. Still, those were good times, Ladeeta said. No one in the projects had much, so the family never considered themselves poor. Ladeeta recalls that it was safe enough that in the summers they played until 3 A.M.

It was only when crack took over that Ladeeta said she became ashamed to live in the projects. It became a place associated with losers. The whole family was proud when she passed a test to enter a junior high school for gifted students. But Ladeeta said she felt uncomfortable around the middle-class blacks there who spoke and dressed differently, even though she knew she was just as smart as they were.

Even now, with Clark Atlanta University her first choice for school, she wonders if she can make an easy transition.

"I am concerned that I won't fit it—that people will prejudge me because I'm from New York, from Brooklyn," Ladeeta said. "I'm afraid people will think that I'm no good, that I can't do anything."

The Present

Finding Stability in Crown Heights

Life in Crown Heights with her grandmother offered Ladeeta a chance to be a real teenager. On the block where they live in the lively, racially turbulent neighborhood of Caribbean immigrants, middle-class blacks and Hasidic Jews, home life grew more stable.

Her grandmother was there, and there were no longer nights of strange people drifting in and out of the apartment.

In February 1991, Mrs. Simmons got Frank Mickens, the principal of Boys and Girls High School, to admit Ladeeta. Mr. Mickens reluctantly agreed, knowing that she had family support and a role model in Lavelle.

Mrs. Simmons said she knew that Boys and Girls had a reputation for turning around students like Ladeeta. Mr. Mickens, a mock-gruff bear of a man with a penchant for bow ties, had a student dress code and a low tolerance for troublemakers. He has become a surrogate father and role model to Ladeeta, who quickly excelled once she left her Cypress Hills gang behind.

Ladeeta is something of a loner these days, but her friends reflect a range of possibilities. The student she probably admires most is Paul Allen, a bright, bespectacled, well-spoken junior. She says she sometimes laughs at how strict his parents are; they don't let him watch television during the week.

Then there are friends like Sandra Wigfall, who at 21 still lives in Cypress Hills and braids hair for a living. Sandra's mother is mentally ill, and her brother is a drug addict. She dropped out of high school after she was beaten up by a gang of girls.

"Old Men and Women." Cathie Wright-Lewis, an English teacher to whom Ladeeta has become close, said she had seen many young people like Sandra with broken spirits. But Ladeeta is unusual, she said, "an old soul with a whole lot of strength and she refuses to go out without a fight."

That fight in Ladeeta's soul was challenged last year when she learned that her mother's H.I.V.—diagnosed in 1991—had become AIDS. Ladeeta helplessly watched her mother deteriorate. She would stare into space, forget to take her medication and mumble incoherently. She lost weight and her hair began falling out.

"I couldn't believe it," Ladeeta said. "It was not my mother."

Ladeeta said the only thing that kept her going was her belief that the years ahead would be brighter.

There was still January to get through, though, filled with cold and sickness and her mother's death.

The funeral for Patricia Bobo Smith at the Evening Star Baptist Church in Brooklyn was simple. Ladeeta wore a jaunty black hat and did not cry, even when Lavelle began wailing: "Mommy! Mommy!" The white coffin covered with red and white carnations.

Mr. Mickens sat in the back of the church with his head bowed. He had been to too many of these funerals, for students and their parents and their friends. When Ladeeta came to hug him, he told her, "Be strong."

Ladeeta says she is feeling strong these days, keeping the ghosts of the past at bay. The bad thing about ghosts, Ladeeta knows, is that they can reappear. One of her biggest worries now is that her sisters can find mentors to keep them safe from the crime, the drugs, the smooth-talking men.

"I'm O.K.," Ladeeta said, her eyes focused somewhere only she could see. "As drastic as my mother's death was, I know I have to go on. I proved I could make it and now a lot of people are depending on me. I don't want to let anyone down."

Comprehension Questions

1. What is the name of the housing project where Ladeeta was introduced to the world of crack?

   _____

   _____

2. What does the word *surrogate* mean in the sentence: "He has become a surrogate father and role model to Ladeeta. . . ."?

   _____

   _____

3. What does the word *emaciated* mean in the sentence: "Just hours earlier, she had visited her mother in a Bronx nursing home, and she was haunted by the image of her emaciated body covered with sores."?

   _____

   _____

Selection 5: *"With No Parents, Ladeeta, 18, Presses On"*

4. Why did Ladeeta give up her involvement in the drug trade?

   _____

   _____

   _____

   _____

5. How many friends has Ladeeta seen die?

   _____

   _____

6. Name three of Ladeeta's friends who have died.

   _____

   _____

   _____

   _____

   _____

7. Why did the project kids refer to Elbert Smith as "Mr. Peanut"?

   _____

   _____

   _____

   _____

   _____

   _____

8. Why did Ladeeta feel uncomfortable at the junior high school for gifted students?

_____

_____

_____

_____

_____

_____

9. Name Ladeeta's sisters.

_____

_____

_____

_____

_____

10. Identify the following by placing the correct letter from the second column on the line in the first one.

    ____ Elbert Smith   a. Broken spirit
    ____ DeDe   b. "We Are Survivors"
    ____ Thelma Simmons   c. Clark Atlanta University
    ____ Cathie Wright-Lewis   d. AIDS
    ____ Frank Mickens   e. Ladeeta
    ____ Paul Allen   f. Patricia's mother
    ____ Sandra Wigfall   g. Alcoholic
    ____ Boys and Girls High School h. English teacher
    ____ Lavelle   i. Principal
    ____ Patricia Bobo Smith   j. Admiration

Essay Questions (Use your notebook.)

11. Based upon your reading of the selection, will Ladeeta Smith overcome her difficult background and succeed in life? Provide specific reasons for your answer.

12. Discuss the problems that Ladeeta may face in the future because she is African American and a woman.

SELECTION 6: "The Stono River Rebellion and its Impact on the South Carolina Slave Code"

By John E. Fleming*

Unlike other North American colonies, South Carolina was settled with the express purpose of establishing perpetual Negro slavery patterned after slavery in the island of Barbados. Many early settlers of South Carolina came from Barbados and borrowed liberally from the island's mature slave code. A rigid control of the slave population coupled with the development of the rice plantation made slavery in this province the most depraved of all the English colonies.[1]

During the 1730s a surge of rebellions arose in the province to protest human bondage. Aside from the inherent horror of the form of slavery practiced in South Carolina, there were other factors which contributed to these rebellions, especially the Stono River Rebellion of 1739. In the year 1737 a general famine occurred throughout the southern colonies, striking South Carolina with extraordinary severity and causing a number of blacks to die of starvation. Two disastrous epidemics swept the province in 1738 and 1739, creating further misery for those held in bondage. One of the prime contributors to unrest in the province was the importation of 16,000 slaves directly from Africa between 1729 and 1737.[2] Unlike the slaves who had been "seasoned" in the islands or those who were born on the plantation, the new recruits were unaccustomed to bondage and consequently infused their ideas of freedom into the slave country. One author described them as being not only far from docile, but, in fact, "turbulent" with "unruly tempers." Although special laws were passed to regulate the slaves, whites were forced to maintain vigilance against any possible outburst of violence. Yet, the frequency of violent disorders was such that, in 1734, St. Phillip's Parish was forced to establish a slave patrol.

"The Stono River Rebellion and Its Impact on the South Carolina Slave Code," John E. Fleming, *Negro History Bulletin*. Copyrighted and reprinted with permission from the Association for the Study of Afro-American Life and History.

---

*Senior Fellow, Institute for the Study of Educational Policy, Howard University.
[1] Winthrop T. Jordon, *White Over Black, American Attitudes Toward the Negro, 1550–1812* (Baltimore: Penguin Books, Inc., 1968), pp. 84–85; A South Carolinian, "South Carolina Society," *The Atlantic Monthly* XXXIX (June 1877), pp. 670–71.
[2] Herbert Aptheker, *American Negro Slave Revolts* (New York: International Publishers, 1969 [1943]), p. 185.

The patrol consisted of two mounted squads of eight men and a captain; each squad rode alternately on weekends and holidays.[3]

As for the new African slaves, they were not prepared to submit voluntarily to slavery. They were also unprepared for the ordeal of being shackled and placed in a ship's hold for the midpassage, an experience which no doubt caused many of them to develop a burning desire for revenge. This was evidenced in efforts to mutiny and kill their white captors by some of the slaves, while others sought to escape through suicide.[4] Once face to face with the grim reality of the harsh treatment perpetual slavery held in store, many slaves covertly rebelled by running away.[5] There were also those who could not tolerate the ordeal of slavery after suffering the barbaric ocean crossing and the indignity of the slave auction. One authority has suggested that some of these desperate human beings readily destroyed themselves with fervent hopes that after death "they will return to their beloved friends and native country."[6] This view is reflected in the slaves' songs with their recurring theme of escape to "heaven"—Africa.[7]

The whites of South Carolina lived in constant fear from both internal and external threats. Because the province was on the frontier of conflicting international land claims, and coupled with the numerical superiority of blacks, there was the serious possibility that the province would not be able to defend itself if attacked. In 1734, there were three times as many slaves as whites in the colony. By 1737, blacks increased to 22,000 as opposed to 5,000 white fighting men. Within two years the ratio of black to white was 39,000 to 9,000. For an unexplained reason, one author suggests that whites declined to 5,000 in 1740 while blacks increased to 40,000.[8] No doubt the earlier epidemics and famines killed many whites and spurred others to leave the area. New immigrants migrating into the state were too few to offset those who

---

[3]Carl Bridenbaugh, *Cities in the Wilderness, The First Century of Urban Life in America, 1625–1742* (New York: The Ronald Press Company, 1938), pp. 201, 377.

[4]John W. Blassingame, *The Slave Community, Plantation Life in the Antebellum South* (New York: Oxford University Press, 1972), pp. 5–9.

[5]Bridenbaugh, *op. cit.*, p. 380.

[6]Alexander Hewatt, *An Historical Account of the Rise and Progress of the Colonies of South Carolina and Georgia.* Vol. 2 (London: Alexander Donaldson, 1779 [reprint, 1962]), p. 93.

[7]Miles Mark Fisher, *Negro Slave Songs in the United States* (New York: Citadel Press, 1963), p. viii.

[8]Ruth Scarborough, *The Opposition to Slavery in Georgia Prior to 1860* (Nashville: George Peabody College for Teachers, 1933), pp. 4, 12–13.

either died or left. The threat posed by the blacks probably played no small part in the Carolinians' decision to depart from the area.

The external threat to the province was posed by the Spanish in Florida. For 60 years after South Carolina was settled, there were no settlements south of the Savannah River, an area claimed by both Spain and England. To the consternation of South Carolinians, the Spaniards had for a number of years harbored runaway slaves.[9] The colonists were exposed to attacks from the Indians, the French from Mobile and the Spanish from St. Augustine who encouraged the slaves to rebel.[10] In an attempt to meet the threat posed by St. Augustine, Georgia was settled as an English colony which increased antagonism with Spain.[11] James Oglethorpe, major-general of the forces in the two provinces, was commissioned to protect the Southern frontier of the British territory.[12]

In 1733, the King of Spain issued an edict which promised liberty and protection to all slaves that deserted the English colonies. Conspiracies were formed and attempts made by slaves to desert to St. Augustine, but as everyone was by that time alarmed with apprehensions of that nature, by great vigilance they were prevented from succeeding.[13]

On a number of occasions, South Carolinians discovered Spaniards encouraging slaves to escape to Florida. Blacks were so successful in escaping to the Spanish colony that the Governor of Florida formed a regiment composed entirely of ex-slaves with their own officers appointed from among their ranks. These black soldiers were given the same pay and clothing allowance as the regular Spanish soldiers. One author has suggested that the more "sensible" slaves not only knew of the ebony regiment, but when they ran away, they proceeded in the direction of St. Augustine to join their comrades in arms.[14]

---

[9] *Ibid.*, p. 4.
[10] Edward McCrady, *The History of South Carolina Under the Proprietary Government, 1670–1719* (New York: Paladin Press, 1969 [1897]), p. 5.
[11] Robert L. Meriwether, *The Expansion of South Carolina 1729–1765* (Kingsport, Tennessee: Southern Publishers, Inc. 1940), p. 26.
[12] Hewatt, *op. cit.*, p. 67.
[13] *The St. Augustine Expedition of 1740, A Report to the South Carolina General Assembly.* Reprinted from the Colonial Records of South Carolina with an introduction by John Tale Lanning (Columbus: South Carolina Archives Department, 1954), p. 8.
[14] Hewatt, *op. cit.*, pp. 71–72.

As if the dangers from rural slaves were not enough, urban blacks presented an even greater threat to the peace and security of the province. The slaves who lived in and around urban areas generally were tradesmen, mechanics, domestics, etc., who were in close proximity to firearms and, when mistreated, often took revenge by killing or poisoning their owners. Although slaves were severely punished for such crimes, many crimes were frequently undiscovered.[15]

The early settlers made few attempts to convert their slaves. One author concludes that, except for a few, blacks "are to this day so great strangers to Christianity, and as much under the influence of Pagan darkness, idolatry and superstition, as they were at their arrival from Africa."[16] Africans, even though enslaved, were able to retain their cosmology or world view. This linkage to their African past enabled them to retain their own self-identity and overcome the psychological brutalities of slavery.[17]

The Rebellion

Stono is the name given to the inland-like area bound by the Stono River southwest of Charleston,[18] the scene of the slave rebellion of September 9–10, 1739. The rebellion was planned by slaves and led by one named Jemmy. The group of blacks assembled at Stono for the purpose of breaking into an arms warehouse to gain weapons for their journey to Florida.[19] No evidence has been uncovered concerning just who this Jemmy was. From the records of the rebellion itself, one can conclude that he was a slave who was familiar with the area and knew that sufficient arms for his purposes were obtainable from the Hutchenson warehouse. He was a leader and had gained the confidence of upwards of 80 men. After considering the fundamental role that the conjurer played on the plantation and in other rebellions, it is

---

[15] *Ibid.*, p. 97.
[16] *Ibid.*, p. 100.
[17] Blassingame, *op. cit.*, p.25.
[18] McCrady, *op. cit.*, 1715 map of the colony of South Carolina. The author was unable to find a town or large settlement on any map of the period which listed Stono. His conclusion is that it was the name given to a general area of settlement.
[19] Hewatt, *op. cit.*, p. 72. Aptheker, *op. cit.*, pp. 187–8.

entirely possible that Jemmy was a conjurer. It must be remembered that most slaves were first and second generations from Africa with strong African beliefs prevalent.

The perceived invincibility of a conjurer's portion could explain why the slaves tarried after capturing the warehouse.[20] One source provides a further account of the rebellion:

> [O]ur slaves ... masacred twenty-three whites after the most cruel and barbarous manner to be conceived and having got arms and ammunition out of a Store they bent their Course to the southward burning all the Houses on the Road. But they marched so slow, in full Confidence of their own strength from the first Success, that they gave time to a Party of our Militia to come up with them. The Number was in a manner equal on both Sides and an Engagement ensued such as may be supposed in such case where one fought for Liberty and Life, the other for their Country and every thing that was dear to them.[21]

Prior to the battle, the group had killed two warehouse guards, a Mr. Bathurst and Mr. Gibbs, before proceeding toward the Province of Florida. Every white person they encountered was killed with the exception of an innkeeper named Wallace who was considered a "kind" slave master. Approximately six or seven buildings were burned. Other blacks joined the band swelling their ranks to about eighty, as they marched "like a discipline company." The rebels were actually first spotted by Lieutenant-Governor William Bull, on his way from Charleston, who immediately spread the alarm. At the time, a church service was being conducted by the Reverend Archibald Stobo in the

---

[20] See Blassingame, *op. cit.,* pp. 32–33, 45–46, for a discussion of the significance of the conjurer. Also note "A. Ranger's Report of Travels with General Oglethorpe, 1939–1942" cited in Newton D. Mereness, ed., *Travels in the American Colonies* (New York: The Macmillan Company, 1916), pp. 222–23. "What was said of the Negroes Rising in Carolina was True and that they had marched to Stono Bridge where they murdered two Storekeepers [,] Cut their Heads off and Set them on the Stairs [,] Robbed the stores of what they wanted and went on killing what men, women and children they met. . . ." He relates the following account of the battle, ". . .One Negro fellow who came up to his Master [,] his Master asked him if he wanted to kill him [and] the Negroe answered he did at the same time Snapping a Pistol at him but it mist fired and his Master shot him thro' the Head. . . ." Was there a ritualistic purpose in removing the men's heads? What possessed the slave to walk boldly up to his master and attempt to kill him? This evidence further suggests that the slaves thought themselves invincible.

[21] *The St. Augustine Expedition of 1740,* p. 8

Presbyterian Church at Wiltown. The men attending the service had come with their arms as required by a provincial law. They joined the militia while their women remained in church trembling with fear. When the militia reached the rebels, they were singing and dancing, supposedly from the influence of rum. During the encounter with the militia, fourteen freedom fighters were killed on the spot; and within ten days, about twenty more, with a total of forty brought down altogether. Although some surrendered, the search continued months later for the others.[22]

There are certain inconsistencies in these accounts of the rebellion. At one point it appears clear the white residents of the province thought that blacks were incapable of engineering a rebellion on their own; hence the overemphasis on the role played by the Spaniards of Florida. For example, B. R. Carroll notes that the "forty thousand Negroes in the province" were "a fierce, hardy and strong race . . . who could scarcely be supposed to be contented with that oppressive yoke under which they groaned." Further on he writes that "the Spaniards were deeply concerned in promoting the mischief, and by their secret influence and intrigues with slaves had instigated them to this massacre."[23] Although wanting to deny that the slaves had the ability and ingenuity to raise an insurrection by claiming that white men instigated the episode, they nevertheless could not escape the slave's pervasive hostility to slavery and great desire for freedom.

Spaniards could not be everywhere in the province stirring up trouble in the slaves' quarters to justify the fact that ". . . Carolina was kept in a state of constant fear and agitation from this quarter [i.e., slaves]." After the rebellion, one author continues, "All Carolina was struck with terror and consternation by this insurrection . . ."[24] It is clear that the

---

[22]*Ibid.*, p. 8. This source indicates that all but two or three were captured; Hewatt, *op. cit.*, pp. 72–73. McCrady states that it was a Mr. Golightly who warned the Presbyterian congregation to warn the Charlestonians. He also indicates that 21 whites and 44 blacks were killed; since, he further states, that a number of slaves had been forced to join the band, they were later pardoned. See Edward McCrady, *The History of South Carolina Under the Royal Government 1719–1776* (New York: The Macmillan Co., 1899), pp. 185–86: B. R. Carroll, Compiler, *Historical Collections of South Carolina; Embracing Many Rare and Valuable Pamphlets and Other Documents, Relating to the History of that State, From Its First Discovery to its Independence in the Year 1776.* Vol 1 (New York: Harper and Brothers, 1836), pp. 332–33. Aptheker, *op. cit.*, pp. 188–89.
[23]Carroll, *op. cit.*, pp. 331–33.
[24]Hewatt, *op. cit.*, pp. 72–73.

Spaniards posed a menace to the province, yet, the real threat was harbored within the state, within the slave quarter itself.

The Aftermath

Shortly after the rebellion, the Twelfth General Assembly met September 12, 1739–August 3, 1742. The slave code adopted during this session was so comprehensive that it remained in effect, substantially unchanged from 1740 until the Civil War.[25] The legislators were eager to debate the question of Negro slavery. They soon concluded that more whites were needed in the state because blacks vastly outnumbered whites and because of the continued fear of slave insurrections. Planters were obliged by the Assembly to provide white men for militia duty in proportion to the amount of land possessed by the planters, a measure disregarded by the Council. The Committee on methods of defense felt pressured by circumstances to force planters to employ white servants on their plantations as a means of increasing the number of whites in the province. This bill too was rejected by the Council. A reversal of strategy was then tried. The bill, which placed a duty on the importation of slaves (1731 Act), was reenacted; the duty was set at 14 pounds for those slaves over four feet two inches tall, which in effect nearly prohibited the importation of slaves for a period of three years.[26]

After months of discussion and debate, "An Act for the better Ordering and Governing Negroes and other Slaves in this Province" was passed on May 10, 1740.[27] The Act was divided into two parts: restrictive measures designed to protect the white residents of the province and protective measures designed to provide the slaves a measure of protection or at least to protect the master's investment in his chattel.

In the preamble of the Act, "Negroes, Indians, mulatos and Mestigos" were deemed "absolute slaves."[28] Contrary to English law,

---

[25] W. Roy Smith, *South Carolina as a Royal Province, 1719–1776* (New York: The Macmillan Company, 1903), pp. 144–409.
[26] *Ibid.*, pp. 50–171, Meriwether, *op. cit.*, pp. 27–28.
[27] The following discussion of the Act is based upon the statute itself found in *The Public Laws of the State of South Carolina From Its First Establishment as a British Province Down to the Year 1790.* (Philadelphia: R. Aitken and Son, compiled by John F. Grimke), pp. 163–74.
[28] Negroes, Indians, mulattoes and mestizos, who were free when the Act was passed, were exempted from its provisions.

the slaves assumed the status of their mother to prevent the extension of freedom to slaves fathered by white males. Aimed directly at preventing circumstances which led to the Stono rebellion, travel and assembly restrictions were imposed on the slaves. A slave was required to carry in his possession a ticket which indicated that he had permission from his master to be away and where he was going. Any white man was given the right to examine a "suspicious" slave and the right to kill him without fear of punishment if the slave refused. No slave could travel in a group of more than seven persons on the highways. Assemblies which disturbed the public peace were prohibited.

The Stono River Rebellion is only one among many which occurred during the ante-bellum period. Other acts of rebellion and protest against slavery assumed a variety of forms, all of which attest to the fact that blacks did not willingly accept slavery and their loss of freedom.

See Instructor's Manual, Part 3 Answers.

Comprehension Questions

1. Which of the following were included in the South Carolina slave code?
    a. Provided for protection of whites
    b. Prohibited slaves from traveling in groups of more than 25
    c. Imposed travel restrictions
    d. Imposed assembly restrictions
    e. a, b, and c
    f. a, c, and d
    g. b, c, and d

2. Why did the South Carolina whites live in constant fear?
    a. They were outnumbered by blacks
    b. External threats
    c. The English harbored runaway slaves
    d. The importation of slaves directly from Africa
    e. Both a and b
    f. Both c and d
    g. All of the above

3. Most slaves arriving in South Carolina could be described by the following.
   a. Over 50 inches tall
   b. Under 14 pounds in weight
   c. Over 80 inches tall
   d. Under 50 inches tall
   e. Under 40 inches tall

4. South Carolinian slavery was patterned after slavery in which of the following?
   a. Africa
   b. Barbados
   c. Florida
   d. Spain
   e. England

5. Slaves escaping from South Carolina usually went to which of the following?
   a. Mobile
   b. Barbados
   c. Africa
   d. Charleston
   e. Both a and d
   f. None of the above

6. Identify the following by placing the correct letter or letters next to each name.

   _____ Jemmy   a. Reverend

   _____ Bathurst   b. Leader of the rebellion

   _____ Gibbs   c. Kind slave master

   _____ Wallace   d. Warehouse guard

   _____ Bull   e. Lieutenant-Governor

   _____ Stobo   f. Warehouse

   _____ Hutchenson   g. Major-General

Selection 6: "The Stono River Rebellion"

7. The external threat to South Carolina was posed by which of the following?
   a. The Spanish
   b. The French
   c. The Indians
   d. The slaves
   e. a, b, and c
   f. b, c, and d
   g. a, c, and d
   h. a, b, and d

8. What was the name of the regiment of ex-slaves formed in Florida?

   _____

   _____

9. Under the slave code, slaves were made to assume the status of their mothers for which of the following reasons?
   a. To gain freedom for those with white fathers
   b. To increase the number of slaves
   c. To decrease the number of slaves
   d. To prevent freedom for those with white fathers
   e. To provide protection for ex-slaves

10. The rebellions that arose in South Carolina in the 1730s were caused by which of the following?
    a. Famine
    b. Epidemics
    c. The importation of slaves directly from Africa
    d. Harsh slavery practices
    e. All of the above
    f. None of the above

11. *True or False:* Rural slaves presented an even greater threat than urban blacks to the peace and security of South Carolina.

    _____

    _____

12. *Cosmology* refers to which of the following?
    a. Slavery
    b. Christianity
    c. A view of the universe
    d. Superstition
    e. Idolatry

13. List the following events in chronological order
    a. Adoption of slave code
    b. General famine
    c. King of Spain issues edict granting liberty to ex-slaves
    d. Epidemic
    e. Beginning of importation of African slaves
    f. Stono River rebellion
    g. End of the Twelfth General Assembly
    h. Establishment of slave patrol
    1. ____
    2. ____
    3. ____
    4. ____
    5. ____
    6. ____
    7. ____
    8. ____

14. State the major conclusion of this selection.

    _____

    _____

    _____

    _____

    _____

SELECTION 7: "The Decline and Fall"

The inadequate term Watergate has come to encompass all the wrongdoing of which Richard Nixon and other members of his Administration stand accused—and in many cases convicted—including the politicization of federal agencies, misuse of federal funds for private purposes, attempted bribery by milk producers, misprision of felony, subornation of perjury, obstruction of justice. This catalogue of crimes and misdeeds did not begin with the break-in at the Democratic National Committee headquarters, but were it not for that bungled burglary and the subsequent cover-up, most or all of the offenses might have gone unnoticed and unpunished. Why the President allowed himself to become entrapped in the web of events that followed the crime is a puzzle. Indeed, there is a great deal about Watergate that will only be sorted out after much time has passed. But much is already known. Here is a recapitulation of the critical events that destroyed Nixon's presidency.

I The Break-In

Planning for the Watergate operation begins in January 1972. In his office, Attorney General John Mitchell, along with Presidential Counsel John Dean and Acting Director of the Committee for the Re-Election of the President (C.R.P.) Jeb Stuart Magruder, listens as G. Gordon Liddy, general counsel to C.R.P., spells out a $1 million intelligence plan: electronic surveillance, abduction of radical leaders, muggings, the use of call girls to obtain information from leading Democrats. According to Magruder, Mitchell tells Liddy to come up with something more "realistic." On March 30, Mitchell, now director of C.R.P., meets with Magruder to discuss a $250,000 proposal. Magruder later says that Mitchell approved the plan: Fred LaRue, a special assistant to Mitchell who was present at the meeting, says it was tabled for future discussion; Mitchell denies ever giving his approval. Two crucial questions remain: Who gave final O.K. for the burglary? What were they seeking that would justify so bizarre a crime?

An intelligence-gathering operation is set into motion. Checks worth $89,000, illegal corporate contributions, are laundered through a Mexican bank and transmitted to Bernard Barker, who deposits them in his Miami bank. He also deposits a $25,000 check given to C.R.P.

Copyright 1974 TIME Inc. Reprinted by permission

by Kenneth Dahlberg, Republican finance chairman in the Midwest. This money will help uncover the C.R.P. involvement in Watergate.

Liddy takes charge of the operation, aided by former CIA agent E. Howard Hunt and C.R.P. Security Coordinator James McCord. Several Cuban refugees are recruited: Barker, Eugenio Martinez, Virgilio Gonzalez, and Frank Sturgis. The stage is set.

After two botched attempts, the burglars on May 27 get into the D.N.C. offices. McCord places wiretaps on the phones of Democratic National Chairman Lawrence O'Brien and Executive Director of Democratic State Chairmen R. Spencer Oliver Jr. Soon transcripts of Oliver's conversations are being passed to Magruder and through him to Mitchell. As Magruder later testifies, Mitchell orders Liddy to get better information.

Another break-in is arranged for June 17. But shortly after 1 A.M., private security guard Frank Wills spots a door in the Watergate with its lock taped open. He summons the police, who catch McCord, Barker, Sturgis, Gonzalez, and Martinez in the D.N.C. The police confiscate surveillance equipment and find thirty-two sequentially numbered $100 bills, which Barker has withdrawn from the $89,000 in Miami.

II The Cover-Up Begins

Two days after the arrest, White House Press Secretary Ronald Ziegler dismisses the affair as "a third-rate burglary attempt," adding that "certain elements may try to stretch this beyond what it is." But others are less blasé. Within hours of the break-in, FBI agents find Hunt's name in the address books of Barker and Martinez. Administration officials are also worried because Hunt and Liddy were involved in another secret operation, the White House plumbers, set up in mid-1971 to stop security leaks and investigate other sensitive security matters.

The cover-up begins. On June 20, Dean cleans out Hunt's safe, discovering files on the Pentagon papers case and a forged diplomatic cable that implicates the Kennedy Administration in the assassination in 1963 of South Vietnamese President Ngo Dinh Diem. Dean later testifies that Nixon's chief domestic adviser John Ehrlichman subsequently tells him to "deep six" a briefcase full of surveillance equipment and other evidence.

On June 23, Nixon orders Haldeman to have the CIA block the FBI's investigation into the source of Watergate funding. That day Haldeman and Ehrlichman meet with CIA Director Richard Helms and Deputy Director Vernon Walters. Helms says that no CIA operations will be endangered by the FBI probe. Haldeman insists that it is the "President's wish" that Walters ask the FBI not to pursue the investigation into Mexico. A tape transcript of a conversation with Haldeman (released last week in the move that finally forces Nixon's resignation) shows that Nixon hopes to hide White House and C.R.P. involvement in the break-in by getting the CIA to limit the FBI's activities. Nixon's personal attorney Herbert Kalmbach gets $75,000 from Maurice Stans, chairman of the Finance Committee to Re-Elect the President—the first of more than $400,000 distributed to the Watergate defendants and their lawyers.

The cover-up holds through the summer. On August 29, Nixon tells a news conference that Dean has conducted a thorough investigation and "I can say categorically that . . . no one in the White House staff, no one in this Administration, presently employed, was involved in this very bizarre incident." Dean never made such an investigation, according to his testimony months later. On September 15, in a recorded Oval Office conversation, Nixon congratulates Dean: "The way you, you've handled it, it seems to me, has been very skillful, because you—putting your fingers in the dikes every time that leaks have sprung here and sprung there."

On November 7, Nixon and Vice-President Spiro Agnew are re-elected by a landslide. Watergate is all but forgotten. Early the next year, as the Watergate trial of the five burglars plus Liddy and Hunt gets under way with Judge John J. Sirica presiding, there is no hint that anybody else will be implicated. On January 11, Hunt pleads guilty to all counts against him, and four days later the four Cuban Americans follow suit. Despite pressure from Sirica to get the burglars to tell the whole story, Hunt tells reporters that no "higher-ups" are involved.

III Cracks in the Stonewall

Still, there have already been some damaging disclosures. *The Washington Post,* relying partly on a still secret source known to outsiders as "Deep Throat," reports that Dahlberg's $25,000 check found its way into Barker's bank account, and that Watergate was part of a massive program of political sabotage. TIME discloses that Donald Segretti had been hired by White House Aides Dwight Chapin and Gordon Strachan and paid out of C.R.P. funds by Kalmbach to sabotage the Democratic presidential campaign.

Sirica, meanwhile, continues to push aggressively for the truth. On February 2 he says he is "not satisfied" that the trial disclosed the full story. On February 7, the Senate votes 77–0 to establish a select committee to investigate Watergate. Sam Ervin is named its chairman the next day.

Within a few weeks, the engineers of the cover-up begin to lose control. On February 28, the Senate Judiciary Committee begins hearings on L. Patrick Gray's confirmation as FBI director. Gray discloses that he gave Dean FBI reports on the Watergate and that Chapin and Kalmbach have been involved in Republican espionage activities. These revelations precipitate a frantic scramble in the White House.

March 13: Nixon learns that Gordon Strachan has reportedly lied to federal investigators. The President explicitly rejects "the hang-out road," the White House term for full disclosure. March 17: Nixon later tells Ziegler that on this day, he has ordered Dean "to cut off any disclosures that might implicate him in Watergate." Worried that Magruder could implicate Haldeman in the affair, Nixon says: "We've got to cut that back. That ought to be cut out." March 21: Talking about Hunt's demands for money, the President says: "For Christ's sake, get it!"

At this point, Sirica's efforts pay off. On March 23 he reads the court a letter from McCord charging that perjury has been committed in the Watergate trial and that defendants have been pressured to remain silent. Pouring on the pressure, Sirica gives Hunt and the Cubans harsh provisional sentences of up to forty years in an effort to make them talk.

IV The Gathering Storm

Maintaining a "stonewall" policy on Nixon's instructions, Ehrlichman on March 28 informs Attorney General Richard Kleindienst that nobody in the White House had prior knowledge of the burglary. Two days later he has Ziegler tell the press that "no one in the White House had any involvement or prior knowledge of the Watergate event."

But on April 13, Magruder tells U.S. attorneys that he perjured himself during the burglars' trial. He implicates Dean and Mitchell in Watergate crimes. On April 15, according to his testimony, Dean tells Nixon that he has been cooperating with the U.S. attorneys.

On April 15, prosecutors tell Nixon that Haldeman, Ehrlichman, Dean, and other White House officials are implicated in the cover-up.

Faced with the evidence against his top aides, knowing that Dean and Magruder are talking, and concerned that the upcoming Senate hearings will cast even more suspicion on the White House, Nixon makes the first of a series of strategic retreats.

April 30: He announces the resignations of Haldeman and Ehrlichman, calling them "two of the finest public servants it has been my privilege to know," and of Dean and Kleindienst. Nixon grants the new Attorney General the authority to appoint a special prosecutor.

May 18: Attorney General-Designate Elliot Richardson names Archibald Cox to the promised new position. In the days following, McCord tells his story to the nationally televised Senate Watergate committee hearings, which open May 17. Faced with a flood of revelations, Nixon issues a statement admitting that there was a cover-up within the White House, though he denies participating in it. Nixon says that after the break-in he had restricted certain aspects of the investigation on the grounds of "national security."

Nixon's speech is designed to end suspicions of his own involvement, but the televised Senate hearings provide a flood of incriminating new revelations. From June 25 to 29, Dean tells the committee that Nixon knew about aspects of the cover-up as early as September 15, 1972. Equally embarrassing: Dean discloses White House efforts to hound political "enemies."

The White House retaliates on June 27 by calling Dean the "mastermind" of the cover-up and Mitchell his "patron." But the President's position is weakened by the release the same day of the "enemies list" by the Senate committee.

V The Telltale Tapes

A far more devastating blow comes on July 16. Former White House Aide Alexander Butterfield tells the Watergate committee that Nixon secretly taped his own conversations.

Why Nixon allowed his participation in the cover-up to be recorded is one of the affair's greatest mysteries. Cox and Ervin request that Nixon turn over key tapes. On July 23, he rejects the requests on the ground of executive privilege. Ervin and Cox issue subpoenas.

On August 15, the President maintains: "Not only was I unaware of any cover-up. I was unaware there was anything to cover up." Earlier, Ehrlichman and Haldeman tell the Senate committee that Dean was responsible for the cover-up, and that they and the President are innocent. August 22: Nixon terms Watergate "water under the bridge."

But on August 29, Sirica orders that he turn over tapes of the nine conversations subpoenaed by Cox.

Meanwhile other developments further tarnish the image of the White House. In early September, a Los Angeles grand jury indicts Ehrlichman, Liddy, and Plumbers Co-Directors Egil Krogh and David Young in connection with the break-in at the office of the psychiatrist of Daniel Ellsberg, the man who claimed to have given the Pentagon papers to the press. October 12: Nixon nominates Gerald Ford as the new Vice-President. On the same day, the U.S. Court of Appeals rules that Nixon must turn the subpoenaed tapes over to Judge Sirica. A week later the President publicly offers a compromise: he will issue summaries of the tapes that will be checked by Senator John Stennis for accuracy. Cox rejects this. Cox is already probing other embarrassing situations, including the mysterious disposition of a $100,000 contribution from Howard Hughes to Nixon Pal Charles ("Bebe") Rebozo. The following evening, in the "Saturday Night Massacre," Nixon fires Cox; Richardson and his deputy, William Ruckelshaus, resign. There follows what White House Chief of Staff Alexander Haig calls "a fire storm" of protest, leading to calls from TIME (in its first editorial in 50 years), the New York *Times,* the Detroit *News* and *National Review* for the President's resignation.

Angered by Cox's dismissal, Democratic House leaders agree to have the Judiciary Committee begin an investigation into impeaching the President. On October 23, Nixon agrees to hand over the subpoenaed tapes. Three days later he promises that there will be a new special prosecutor with "total cooperation from the executive branch."

Texas lawyer Leon Jaworski is appointed to the post on November 1, in the midst of new disclosures. The day before, Presidential Lawyer J. Fred Buzhardt revealed that two of the subpoenaed conversations did not exist on tape. Three weeks later, the White House discloses that there is an $18\frac{1}{2}$-minute buzz obliterating a crucial taped discussion between Haldeman and the President on June 20, 1972. January 15: electronics experts report that the gap was the result of at least five separate erasures.

March 1: the Watergate grand jury indicts seven former Nixon aides or re-election officials—Mitchell, Haldeman, Ehrlichman, Strachan, former Special Counsel to the President Charles Colson, former Political Coordinator for Nixon's Re-Election Committee Robert C. Mardian, Washington attorney Kenneth W. Parkinson—for conspiring to obstruct justice. In a secret report to Sirica, Nixon is named an unindicted co-conspirator in the case. Jaworski on April 18 subpoenas sixty-four more taped conversations for use in the Watergate prosecution. April 11: the Judiciary Committee subpoenas forty-two conversations.

On April 30, one year after the departure of his top aides and his announcement that he would appoint a special Watergate prosecutor, the President says he is making public edited transcripts of certain subpoenaed conversations. Republican Senator Hugh Scott declares that they reveal "deplorable, disgusting, shabby, and immoral performances." Worse for the President, the 1,254 pages of conversation seem to corroborate some of Dean's allegations: that Nixon was aware of aspects of the cover-up before March 21; that he seems to have wanted to pay hush money to Hunt.

VI The Final Debacle

On May 9, the Judiciary Committee begins its inquiry into Nixon's conduct in office. Over the next two months, nineteen volumes of evidence are accumulated. During that time, several top Nixon aides either plead guilty or are convicted of crimes: Kleindienst on May 16, Colson June 3, Ehrlichman July 12.

July 24: the Supreme Court rules 8–0 that Nixon must turn over the tapes subpoenaed by Jaworski, rejecting Nixon's claim of absolute executive privilege. On the 27th, the Judiciary Committee votes 27–11 to recommend the impeachment of Nixon for obstruction of justice. Two more articles are passed in the next three days.

On August 5, in the most sensational revelation of the entire two years of Watergate, Nixon admits that by June 23, 1972, six days after the break-in, he did indeed know of the involvement of C.R.P. and White House officials and tried to cover it up. The apparent reason for his admission: pressure from Presidential Counsel James St. Clair, who is stunned by the contents of the July 23 tape and strongly suggests that he will resign unless the President makes his statement. Whether Nixon had prior knowledge of the break-in or the intelligence-gathering plan is still unanswered, but the August 5 revelation gives the lie to all his past assertions that he was not involved in the cover-up. In the wake of Nixon's disclosures, all the Republicans on the Judiciary Committee who voted against impeachment say they will change their votes when the issue comes before the full House. Republican Senators say that Nixon has almost no chance of acquittal.

Faced with impeachment and conviction, Nixon goes before a nationwide TV audience and announces that he is resigning.

Part 3 Change-of-Pace Readings

Comprehension Questions

See Instructor's Manual, Part 3 Answers.

1. *True or False:* Nixon finally admitted that he knew of the Watergate break-in six days before it occurred.

2. *True or False:* This article states that Nixon had prior knowledge of the Watergate break-in.

3. Nixon referred to _____ and _____ as "two of the finest public servants it has been my privilege to know."

4. The firing of Cox and resignation of Richardson and Ruckelshaus is called the _____.

5. The second special Watergate prosecutor was _____.

6. Who was the person who supposedly gave the Pentagon Papers to the press?
    a. Egil Krogh
    b. David Young
    c. Daniel Ellsberg
    d. John Stennis
    e. Alexander Butterfield

7. What does the term "Watergate" refer to?
    a. The break-in at the Democratic National Committee headquarters
    b. The attempted cover-up of the Watergate affair
    c. All the wrongdoing of which Richard Nixon and members of his administration were accused.
    d. Both a and b
    e. None of the above

8. Who of the following were caught inside the Democratic National Committee headquarters?
    a. Jeb Stuart Magruder
    b. G. Gordon Liddy
    c. E. Howard Hunt
    d. Lawrence O'Brien
    e. All of the above
    f. None of the above

9. Who was the leader of the Watergate operation?
   a. G. Gordon Liddy
   b. E. Howard Hunt
   c. James McCord
   d. Virgilio Gonzalez
   e. Jeb Stuart Magruder

10. The name given to the secret source who provided information to *The Washington Post* is which of the following?
    a. Plumber
    b. Deep Throat
    c. Deep six
    d. The source
    e. None of the above

11. Who was the chairman of the Senate Watergate Committee?
    a. Sam Ervin
    b. John Sirica
    c. Richard Kleindienst
    d. L. Patrick Gray
    e. Archibald Cox

12. The break-in at the Democratic National Committee headquarters would probably have gone unnoticed had it not been for:
    a. James McCord
    b. Bernard Barker
    c. Frank Sturgis
    d. Frank Wills
    e. Eugenio Martinez

13. What were the White House plumbers given the responsibility for?
    a. Stopping security leaks and investigating other sensitive security matters
    b. Organizing the Watergate break-in
    c. Organizing the coverup of the Watergate affair
    d. Both b and c
    e. None of the above

14. Explain what Ehrlichman meant when he told Dean to "deep six" a briefcase full of evidence.

    _____

    _____

    _____

    _____

15. Explain what Nixon meant by "the hang-out road."

    _____

    _____

    _____

    _____

16. Match the date in the second column to the event in the first.

_____ The Saturday-night massacre	a.	August 5, 1974
_____ Judiciary Committee begins the inquiry into Nixon's conduct in office	b.	October, 20, 1973
_____ Nixon nominates Ford as the new vice-president	c.	July 16, 1973
_____ Nixon admits that six days after the break-in he knew of the White House involvement and tried to cover it up	d.	July 27, 1974
_____ Butterfield tells the Senate Watergate Committee that Nixon secretly taped his own conversations	e.	October 12, 1973
_____ Nixon orders Haldeman to have the CIA block the FBI investigation into the source of Watergate funding	f.	January 1972
_____ Planning for the Watergate operation begins	g.	June 20, 1972

_____ Nixon announces the resignations of Haldeman, Ehrlichman, Dean, and Kleindienst

h. June 17, 1972

_____ Prosecutors tell Nixon that Haldeman, Dean and other White House officials are implicated in the coverup

i. April 30, 1973

_____ The coverup of the White House involvement begins

j. June 23, 1972

_____ The burglars break into Democratic National Committee headquarters for the second time and are caught by the police

k. April 15, 1973

_____ The Judiciary Committee recommends the impeachment of Nixon for obstruction of justice

l. May 9, 1974

_____ The Supreme Court rules that Nixon must turn over the subpoenaed tapes

m. May 18, 1973

_____ Nixon and Agnew are reelected by a landslide

n. May 27, 1972

_____ The Senate votes to establish a select committee to investigate Watergate

o. November 7, 1972

_____ Cox is named special Watergate prosecutor

p. July 24, 1974

_____ The burglars break into Democratic National Committee headquarters for the first time

q. February 7, 1973

SELECTION 8: "Young Cassius Clay"

Cassius Clay was cruising west on Walnut Street, through the black part of Louisville known as the West End, consorting with the world from behind the wheel of a Cadillac convertible. It was the autumn of 1960. Clay was only 18, a few days away from his first professional fight and just beginning to yank the clapper in the national bell tower, the one he would use forever after to announce his arrival. Almost standing in the car, the youngster yelled over and over, to everyone he passed, "I'm Cassius Clay! I am the greatest!"

The girl sitting next to him, the one sinking shyly in her seat, trying to look as inconspicuous as possible in a pink Cadillac in the middle of black Louisville, was Wilma Rudolph, a 20-year-old college student who was visiting Clay from Tennessee State. They were a matched pair, two links on the fresh cuffs of history, as they drove that October afternoon. Clay was, by consensus, the finest amateur boxer in the world. Only two months before, at the Olympic Games in Rome, the 178-pound youth had won the gold medal in the light heavyweight division by whipping Zbigniew Pietrzykowski, a portly coffeehouse keeper from Poland. The white trunks Clay showed off to West End neighbors on his return were stained a candy pink by the Polish fighter's blood. Rudolph was the fastest woman on earth. Her victories in three sprints—the 100 and 200 meters and the 4 × 100-meter relay—had made her the first American woman to win three gold medals in a single Olympics.

The two athletes had become friends in the days they spent together in Rome. Clay was sweet on Rudolph, but he was too shy to tell her how he felt. His diffidence with girls was painful. He had fainted dead away the first time he kissed one, two years earlier, and it took a cold washcloth to bring him to. So he concealed his shyness in bravura.

"I can still see him strutting around the village with his gold medal on," recalls Rudolph. "He slept with it. He went to the cafeteria with it. He never took it off. No one else cherished it the way he did. His peers loved him. Everybody wanted to see him. Everybody wanted to be near him. Everybody wanted to talk to him. And he talked all the time. I always hung in the background, not knowing what he was going to say."

His six-year amateur career had taken him to many American cities, from San Francisco to New York, but the journey to Italy had been his

Reprinted courtesy of *Sports Illustrated* from the 1/13/92 issue. Copyright 1992, TIME Inc., All Rights Reserved.

first outside his native land, and gold medal and all, it had been a turning experience in his life. Clay's triumphant return to River City, with police sirens leading the 25-car motorcade through the streets, raised a clamor usually reserved in those latitudes for the Kentucky Derby winner. Not since 1905, when cumbersome Marvin Hart whipped Jack Root to win the heavyweight championship of the world, had Louisville produced a fighter of such celebrity.

Now there he was, driving up Walnut Street, waving at the crowds and stopping at an intersection and rising to announce himself. "And this," he yelled, "this is Wilma Rudolph. *She* is the greatest!"

"Sit down," she said.

"Come on, Wilma. Stand up!"

Crowds were stopping on the street and craning to look inside the car. "No, I can't do that," she said.

"Yes, you can," said Clay. "Stand up, Wilma! Come on."

Wary of crowds, she began sinking lower, covering her face with her hands, trying to crawl inside the glove compartment, slowly disappearing in the cracks of the seat. It was no use. "Look!" Clay said, pointing down to her. "Here she is, down here! It's Wilma Rudolph. She is the greatest! And I'm Cassius Clay. I am the greatest! Come on, Wilma, stand up!"

There was no place to hide with Cassius Clay on Walnut Street. So she rose, reluctantly, for the gaping crowds. What would be the longest running circus in American sport was pushing off. "I saw him at the very beginning," says Rudolph. "It was bedlam. I always told him, 'You should be on stage.'"

On Walnut Street, of course, he already was. This was more than 31 years ago—in a different incarnation, as Muhammad Ali, he turns 50 on January 17—and that rarest of all careers, spanning two decades and part of a third, was only beginning. On October 29, 1960, in his first pro fight, he won a six-round decision from heavyweight Tunney Hunsaker, the police chief of Fayetteville, West Virginia. Clay emerged unscathed and promptly crowned himself king. One of his cornermen for that fight was George King, a former amateur bantamweight from Louisville who first met the 12-year-old Clay when the youngster began hanging around trainer Fred Stoner's all-black boxing team at the Grace Community Center. With Rome and Hunsaker behind him, Clay was not a boy anymore.

"Where'd you get that name?" he asked King one day. "You ain't big enough to be a king. They ought to call you Johnson or somethin'. There's only one king."

"Who's that?" asked George.

"You're lookin' at him," Clay said.

Clay's days in Louisville were numbered. By the end of the year he had moved to Florida and was fighting out of Angelo Dundee's Fifth Street Gym in Miami Beach. Increasingly the town of his birth and boyhood became a place more of memory than of moment. Gone were the days when he skipped down the halls of Central High between classes, shadowboxing as he danced past knots of tittering students, stopping to throw a flurry that would fall just short of an incoming freshman's outgoing nose, then ducking into a washroom to box himself silly in front of a mirror. Gone was the laughter in the classrooms when Central's tall, scholarly principal, Atwood Wilson, would flip on the school intercom and, tugging on his suspenders, gravely intone his warning: "You act up, and I'm going to turn Cassius Clay on you." Gone were all those early mornings when young Clay raced the school bus for 20 blocks east down Chestnut Street, waving and grinning at the faces in the windows as he bounded past pedestrians scurrying to work.

"Why doesn't he ride to school like everybody else?" a sleepy-eyed young Socrates asked on the bus one day.

"He's crazy," replied one of Clay's classmates, Shirlee Lewis Smith. "He's as nutty as he can be."

Young Clay was an original, sui generis, a salad of improvisations—unpredictable, witty, mischievous, comical. An indifferent student, he lived within his own world during class, day-dreaming by the hour. "Most of the time, when he wasn't paying attention, which was often, he'd be drawing," recalls his senior English teacher, Thelma Lauderdale. "But he never gave me any trouble. Shy and quiet in my class. Meditative."

She never met the other Clay. Beyond her doors, flitting here and over there, he was forever a cutup. "He was a jolly-go-happy guy," says Jimmy Ellis, a boyhood friend who also went on to become heavyweight champion of the world.

"He was just a playful person," says Indra Leavell Brown, a friend of Clay's since childhood. "He had a lot of friends. We'd eat in the cafeteria, and he'd come in and crack his jokes and say little silly things and have all the table laughing."

"He always used to tell me he was in love with me," says Dorothy McIntyre Kennedy, who knew Clay from the time he was 12. "But he always made a joke out of everything. I *never* took him seriously. It was like he never wanted to grow up. He always wanted to be this *person*—the class clown."

Clay was different, all right, as elusive as the butterfly he would soon proclaim himself to be, inventing and reinventing himself as he went along. He dated Mildred Davis for a spell his senior year, and she remembers the Monday after he won the Golden Gloves championship in Chicago, when he showed up at school bearing in his hands, like an offering, a golden pendant. "A little gold glove, with a diamond embedded in it, on a gold chain," says Davis. "And he put it around my neck and said, 'I don't ever want you to take this off. I want you to wear this all the time.' And I said, 'Fine.' That was about 8:30 in the morning. At about 11, he came back and said, 'Someone else wants to wear it.' So he took it off and let someone else have it the rest of the day. And the next day, some other girl wore it. I never questioned him about it because he was always so silly. *So* silly. He wanted me to wear it forever, and I had it for about two-and-a-half hours."

Every day with Clay was an adventure, and Davis never quite knew what to expect from him. She hardly knew what to make of the bottle he was sipping from all the time. "He carried a bottle of water with fresh garlic in it," says Davis. "He would drink it, and he reeked of garlic. I remember asking him why he put the garlic in the water, and he said, 'I do that to keep my blood pressure down.' And he would do some of the craziest things with his eyes. He would come up to guys, make his eyes big, press his lips together and say, 'I'm gonna knock you out!' He always carried his money all folded up in a small change purse, like a little old lady. If you met him, there were things about him that you could never forget. Even in high school, he would always say, 'I'm not gonna let anyone hit me, as pretty as my face is. I'm almost as pretty as you.' He did have beautiful skin. And I'll never forget the night he said to me, 'Come on, I'll run you home.'"

That was the night of the variety show at Central High, a takeoff on *The Jackie Gleason Show* on television. "The girls would come out to announce the acts and I was the last one, and I'd say, 'And away we go!'" says Davis. "Cassius was on the show that night. He was shadowboxing, as usual. That was his act. After the show he said, 'Come on, I'll run you home.' And I was thinking, He doesn't drive. How is he going to run me home?"

They left the school and starting walking west on Chestnut. Pretty soon Clay began to jog in place next to her as she felt her way along the sidewalk in her high heels. "It was dark," says Davis. "He would run up ahead a block or two and jog back. He trotted beside me most of the way. That's what he meant by running me home. So I walked 13 blocks in my high heels. How *crazy* he was."

Davis and Clay took long walks together around Chickasaw Park that spring, watched television at the Clay house on Grand Avenue, sat together at her mother's dinner table over meat loaf and corn bread and cabbage. He was, at all times, unfailingly polite. "Would you like something to eat?" Mildred's mother, Mary, would ask. "Yes, ma'am," Cassius would say. Indeed, there was something old-fashioned about the way he viewed things.

"You know," he once told Mildred, "when we get married, you'll have to wear longer skirts."

"Why would I have to do that?" she asked.

"To look like a lady," he said.

That was not the only time he spoke of marriage to Davis. Clay always built models in his mind, including a make-believe world with a large, happy family of which he was the benevolent father. "We watched a lot of TV at his mother's house," recalls Davis, "and little kids would come over. He loved kids—he always liked to have five or six around him—and I remember one time, it was around Easter, and my mother wouldn't let me go to one of his fights. He came by after the fight, and we sat together on the front porch. At one point he said, 'Pretty soon we're gonna get married, and we're gonna get a real big house with a swimming pool. All the kids in the neighborhood are gonna come over—we're gonna have a lot of kids—and they'll all swim in the pool.'"

Clay was his mother's son. Odessa Grady Clay was a sweet, pillowy, light-skinned black woman with a freckled face, a gentle demeanor, and an easy laugh. Everyone who knew the family in those days saw the kindness of the mother in the boy. In his sophomore year, when he was still 15, Cassius began working after school in the Nazareth College library, across town, for 60 cents an hour. He carried books from floor to floor, dusted the volumes and the shelves, waxed the tables and dry-mopped the brown linoleum floors. The first day he walked into the library, Sister James Ellen Huff, the librarian, was struck by his shy, gentle manner.

"Do they call you Cash?" Sister Huff asked.

"No ma'am," he said. "I'm Cassius Marcellus Clay."

"He had his mother's sweetness," says Sister Huff.

In fact, when Clay talked about his parents at all, it was of his mother. "Everything related to his mom," says Indra Brown. "He would say, 'My mother comes first, before anybody. My mom will be treated right.'"

Of course, all the diversionary commotion he created in his life—the incessant shadowboxing and grandstanding, the flights of fantasy into becalmed worlds of aqua pools and frolicking children—mirrored and masked the chaos of his life at home, where violence and turmoil often came and went with his father, Cassius Sr., a gifted religious muralist and commercial sign painter. The old man, chesty and fast-talking, had always cut a popular figure around town. "Everybody around Louisville knew Mr. Clay," says Yates Thomas, a boyhood pal of young Cassius's. "Up on his ladder painting signs."

And down along the streets, he moved from saloon to saloon, his rich singing voice belting out his favorite songs for the audiences bellying up to the bar. The elder Clay was a wild, free-roaming drunk and womanizer whose peregrinations around town made him a legend along the river's shore. "I just loved him," says West End liquor store owner John (Junior Pal) Powell, a longtime friend of Cassius Jr. "A fun-loving type of guy. But he did drink a lot. One time some lady stabbed him in the chest, and he came up to my apartment. I tried to get him to let me take him to the hospital, but he said, and he always talked real fast, 'Hey, Junior Pal, best thing you can do for me is do what the cowboys do. You know, give me a little drink and pour a little bit on the chest, and I'll be all right.'"

By the time he died, in 1990—of a heart attack, in his car, in a Louisville parking lot—Cassius Sr. had embroidered a long police rap sheet with his troubled history, most of it fueled by alcohol. Thomas Hauser, the author of *Muhammad Ali: His Life and Times,* an oral history of the fighter, says that an FBI investigation into Ali—initiated in 1966, the year before he refused induction into the armed forces—revealed that the elder Clay had been arrested nine times on charges that included reckless driving, disorderly conduct, and assault and battery. According to the file, Odessa thrice summoned the police seeking protection from her husband. The last file on him, obtained from the Louisville police department, showed he was arrested five times for drunken driving since 1975. Ali declines to talk about violence in the Clay household, but Hauser says he could imagine, in something that Ali once told him, a young Clay fleeing the early-morning chaos at home.

"I don't know what it was," Hauser recalls Ali saying, "but I always felt I was born to do something for my people. Eight years old, 10 years old; I'd walk out of my house at two in the morning, and look at the sky for an angel or a revelation or God telling me what to do. I never got an answer. I'd look at the stars and wait for a voice, but I never heard nothing."

The bars in Louisville closed at 2 A.M. Regardless of what things that go bump in the night drove the boy from his home at two in the morning, he would soon find his calling outside the thin walls of the bungalow on Grand Avenue. And when he did, predictably, he created another world for himself, floated through it, escaped into it until, at last, he used it to express himself like no other man of his time.

Clay was six pounds, seven ounces at birth, but by age three he had grown as big as a calf. One day, when he was still an infant, he jarred loose one of Odessa's front teeth. "We were lying in bed," she says, "and he stretched his arm out and hit me in the mouth. He just loosened the tooth. They couldn't straighten it. Finally it had to come out."

Cassius and his brother, Rudy, 18 months younger, would visit their uncle William Clay, and neighbors would bolt the doors. "One day they broke the birdbath in Mrs. Wheatley's yard," says William. "We called them the Wrecking Crew."

The sea change in his life occurred when, at age 12, he was attending a fair downtown and a rascal stole his new bike. Told a cop was downstairs in the Columbia Gym, Cassius went there to complain. In tears, he told his tale to the policeman, Joe Martin, who was training an amateur boxing team. "I'm gonna whip him if I can find him," said Cassius of the thief.

Martin remembers asking the boy if he could fight. "You better learn to fight before you start fightin'," Martin said.

Cassius looked around the gym at all the wondrous activity—the snap of the punching bags and the skipping of rope and the sparring in the ring. Finally, he said, "I didn't know this was here. Can I come?"

He was back the next day. "He didn't know a left hook from a kick in the ass," says Martin. "But he developed quite rapidly. I'd tell him what to do—how to stand, how to keep his arms and hands, how to punch. He'd be hitting the heavy bag, and I'd tell him, 'Cassius, there's a fly on that bag. I want you to hit him, but I don't want you to kill him. You got to turn the hand over. Snap punches. *Phew! Phew!*'"

Cassius loved to fire and turn the jab. Even at 12, when he was an 89-pound novice, he had a beguiling cocksureness that played well with the older amateurs in Louisville. George King first met Cassius during an intracity tournament at the Columbia Gym. Cassius was boxing for Martin's team, but he drifted over to Fred Stoner's team in the locker room and stood next to King, who was 21 years old and already married with a child. "I'm taller than you," Cassius said. "Do you think you could beat me?"

Soft laughter lifted among the older Stoner fighters. King smiled.

"Think you could stop this jab?" Cassius asked, throwing out two quickies. King pushed a jab toward Clay.

"My jab's quicker than yours," the boy said.

Rudell Stitch, then age 21, turned a thumb down. Fixing Stitch with a smirk, Cassius said, "Come on, I'll give you some of it, too."

All these years later, King's voice lilts at the memory. "We were down there, grown men, and he didn't give a damn," says King. "That's just the way he was. He'd pick at you, mess with your head, tease you to death. I kind of liked him. He was a neat lookin' kid, and he had all that personality. Everybody just took to him."

Over the next six years Cassius grew into a surpassing amateur boxer: 100 victories in 108 bouts; two consecutive national AAU championships, in 1959 and '60, both times as a light heavyweight; two straight national Golden Gloves titles, in '59 as a light heavy and the next year as a heavyweight; and, of course, an Olympic gold medal. "His secret was his unusual eye speed," says Martin. "It was blinding. The only other athlete I ever saw who had that kind of eye speed was Ted Williams. When he started fighting, Cassius was so fast with his eyes that you could give a guy a screen door and he wouldn't hit Cassius 15 times with it in 15 rounds. He was *different*. Quick as lightning for a big man, the quickest I ever saw."

He was born with phenomenal physical gifts, but unlike so many others, he nurtured them and squandered nothing. Indeed it was as if, in Martin's gym, Cassius had found the message in the silence of the stars. In high school he lived as ascetic an existence as possible for a teenager. Yates Thomas remembers Cassius showing up at school in the morning after buying two raw eggs and a quart of milk.

"He would break the eggs into the milk, shake it up and drink it," says Thomas. "He'd say, 'Now I'm ready to go to school. I'm the baaaaddest man in Looville!' All he thought of was fight-fight-fight. We used to go to a teenage place at night, and he'd stay till 10 o'clock, even on a Saturday night, and then he'd say, 'I'll see ya. I'm goin' home to bed.' He didn't smoke. He'd say, 'Ain't gonna put that stuff in my lungs.'"

At some point in his senior year Clay began to eschew pork, and for the same reason that he reeked of garlic. "Pork's not good for you," he warned Davis. "It raises your blood pressure." When Junior Pal offered him a grape soda early one morning as Clay was working out, Cassius waved him away. "The sugar and acid ain't good for you," he said.

Despite what was happening at home—or, more likely, because of it—he shunned alcohol. It was as if he were studying, high on his own

Himalayan peak, the evanescent secrets of the butterfly. "He didn't chase women," Martin says. "And I never heard him say a curse word in my life. We used to go to a lot of towns, and he used to sit down and read a few pages of the Bible before he went to bed."

Clay's dalliances with women had far less to do with romance than with fantasy—his flirtations had the fizz life of a soft drink—and, according to Indra Brown, he was a virgin when he graduated from high school. "I know that for a fact, because he confided in me on things like that," she says. "He used to say to me, 'I will always have money. I'm not going to be a Joe Louis. Women are not going to drag me down. They are not going to be my downfall!'"

Late in his junior year he began doing experiments in the technique of kissing, and on his first try he nearly blew up the lab. Areatha Swint had first met Clay after a high school variety show, when she needed someone to walk her home. They dated for three weeks before he got around to asking her for a kiss goodnight. "On the night he did, it was late," Swint would recall in a newspaper memoir. "It must have been around 12:30 or one. We were being quiet because my mother had said there was no company after 12, and he didn't have any business being up that late because he was in training.

"I was the first girl he had ever kissed, and he didn't know how. So, I had to teach him.... When I did, he fainted. Really, he just did. He was always joking, so I thought he was playing, but he fell so hard. I ran upstairs to get a cold cloth. Well, when you live in the projects, a lot of times mother would wash and lay the towels on the radiator to dry. So I looked for one and got some cold water on it and ran back down the stairs."

She doused him with it. When he finally came to, Swint asked, "Are you O.K.?"

"I'm fine, but nobody will ever believe this," he said.

His shyness was such that at times the mere presence of girls struck him dumb. In 1959, recalls Wilbert (Skeeter) McClure, who was another young boxer, he and Clay were in Chicago for the Golden Gloves when Cassius began pestering him and a few other fighters to don their Golden Gloves jackets and head over to Marshall High, a largely black school, to meet some girls. McClure was in college and had no interest in high school girls, but Clay kept bugging him to go. McClure finally agreed, and so they visited the school for lunch. Girls were all over the place, eyeing this team of young gladiators with the new jackets. After Clay got his tray of food, he sat down, said nothing and never looked up.

McClure turned the needle. "You wanted to get us here," he said to Clay. "Come on. Do your thing."

Cassius sat frozen. Recalls McClure: "He was silent, staring at his plate and eating his food."

By this time, Clay was a minor celebrity back home. He had often been featured on *Tomorrow's Champions,* a local Saturday afternoon television program featuring young boxers, and his name had begun appearing in the Louisville *Courier-Journal* as far back as 1957, when he was 15 and he stopped a tough named Donnie Hall. The headline read: CLAY SCORES T.K.O. OVER HALL IN 4TH.

When Jimmy Ellis, a 17-year-old untutored roughneck from Louisville, saw that bout on *Tomorrow's Champions,* he went to the Columbia Gym to learn how to box. Says Ellis, "Hall was a friend of mine, and I figured, I can beat that other guy." So Ellis started fighting. History would soon be up to its old tricks, for it was Ellis, eleven years later, who would win the vacant heavyweight championship after Ali was stripped of it for having refused to serve in the military during the Vietnam War. Ellis traveled frequently with Clay in their amateur years, and what he remembers most vividly about Clay was his almost boundless capacity for work in the gym.

"I don't know where he got the energy," says Ellis, who now works for the Louisville parks system. "He'd box and box. He'd box three or four rounds with one guy. Then he'd sit down. Then another guy would come into the gym, and he'd go three or four rounds with him. Then he'd come out and hit the heavy bag. And then he'd go three or four rounds with another guy."

And anytime a professional fighter came to town, says Ellis, Clay would train where the pro was. Dundee brought light heavyweight Willie Pastrano to Louisville in 1957, and they were sitting in their hotel room one day when the phone rang. Dundee took the receiver and heard this: "My name's Cassius Marcellus Clay. I'm the Golden Gloves champion of Louisville, Kentucky. I'm gonna win the Golden Gloves, and I'm gonna win the Olympics in 1960, and I want to talk to you."

Dundee invited him up. For the next three hours, recalls Dundee, Clay picked and probed and prodded his brain, asking him how his fighters trained, what they ate, how far they ran, how much they hit the bags. "He was a student of boxing," Dundee says. "He was so inquisitive. A very interesting young man."

Two years later Dundee and Pastrano were back again—Pastrano was only four years away from winning the light heavyweight crown—

training for a fight in Louisville against Alonzo Johnson. There was young Clay again, this time hustling Dundee for a chance to spar with Pastrano. Dundee turned him down—he did not believe in matching amateurs against pros—but the kid persisted: "Come on, come on. Let me work with him."

So Dundee finally yielded. Pastrano sparred one round with Clay, and the boy danced around him. "In and out, side-side, in and out," says Dundee. "Stick-stick-stick. Move-move-move. He was so quick, so agile, Willie couldn't do nothing with him."

Dundee called it off, saying, "Willie, baby, you ain't gonna spar no more. You're too fine, baby."

Pastrano wasn't buying. "——!" he said. "The kid kicked the hell out of me."

So much of what came to characterize Ali as a fighter—his tactics in and out of the ring—he began cultivating as an amateur. Ellis recalls Clay working on opponents' minds as deftly as he would soon work on their chins. Says Ellis, "We'd be fighting in the wintertime, in Chicago, and there'd be his opponent sitting there sniffling or blowing his nose. Cassius would say, 'Man, you got a cold? I'm gonna knock you out—cold! You can't beat me if you got a cold. I'm gonna knock you out!'"

Martin says that long before Clay went berserk at the weigh-in before his first bout with Sonny Liston, in 1964, he had become a performer—even an artist—at the scales. He was being weighed on March 9, 1960, only hours before facing Jimmy Jones, the defending heavyweight titleholder in Chicago's Tournament of Champions, when he turned to his trainer. "Mr. Martin," Clay said, "are you in a hurry to get away from here tonight?"

"Not really," said Martin. "Why?"

Clay pointed to Jones and said, "This guy over here, I can get rid of him in one round *if* you're in a hurry. Or, if you're in no hurry, if you want me to box, I can carry him for three rounds."

"I'm in no hurry," said Martin.

"I'll let him go three," Clay said.

The kid spun Jones like a top. Clay slipped the champion's heavy artillery in the first round, and then, according to the *Louisville Times,* he "deftly outboxed him the final two rounds."

Clay was on a path to glory, only six months away from the Rome Olympics, and by then he was rising at four in the morning, before first light, to climb into his sweats and strap on his work boots with the steel toes. At that hour John Powell was usually done sweeping out the liquor dispensary where he worked, and he would listen to the wind blow outside. Recalls Powell: "I'd be sitting on the counter, and I could see his shadow coming around the corner from Grand Avenue. Clay was on his way to Chickasaw Park. Cold, dark winter mornings. You could see that shadow coming. Then here he comes, running by, with those big old Army brogans. He'd be the onliest person in the early morning. And I'd walk outside, and he'd stop and shadowbox. He once said to me, 'Someday you'll own this liquor store, and I'll be the heavyweight champion of the world.' Both of those came true, too."

Clay ran all over Louisville in those steel-toed boots—west to Chickasaw Park in the early morning, east down Chestnut racing the school bus, up and down Walnut Street, downtown and back again, the brogans clomping on the pavement, the fists flying, the litany always the same: "I'm gonna be the next world champion. You're gonna read about me. I'm the greatest!" At 10th and Walnut crowds of men used to gather around a peanut vendor, crack nuts and talk sports.

"Cassius Clay used to come up the street acting like he was hitting people," says Lawrence McKinley. "Shadowboxing and throwing punches in his heavy shoes. Nobody ever dreamed he'd be world champ."

One day one of the street-corner habitués, Gene Pearson, got tired of hearing the litany and vowed to put Clay in his place. "He ain't gonna be no champion," Pearson said. The next time Clay passed the corner, Pearson stepped out from behind a post and hit him with a straight right.

"Pow!" says McKinley. "As hard as he could. Clay liked to go all the way down. He went to his knees, just like he was gonna fall, and he stopped himself and looked up at Gene, and he stretched his eyes real wide and he came up and—whew!—he must have hit Gene 15 or 20 times, so fast you could hardly see the punches, and Gene started saying, 'Get him off me! Get him off me! Yeah, you're gonna be the champ.' And Cassius went right on running up the street. Never said nothin'. The next time Cassius came by, one of the guys said, 'Are you gonna hit him again?' And Gene said, 'Hey, champ!'"

Clay was never a street fighter, and classmates can recall only one occasion when he was goaded into fighting. According to Indra Brown, the episode nearly brought Clay to tears. They were at a delicatessen across from the school when two kids began baiting Cassius, pushing him around and saying, "Come on, let's fight. You can fight." Clay kept backing off. "Leave me alone," he kept saying. "I don't want to do this. Leave me alone."

The boys pushed too far. "Cassius finally went after one of them," Brown says. "He floored him. A right hand. To the jaw. Cassius almost cried. I could tell by his voice. But that was the end of that. They never bothered him again."

He avoided all confrontations, including the civil rights demonstrations downtown in which blacks were involved during the late 1950s. Clay was born in a town where most of the public facilities were segregated. Until the barriers starting coming down in the '50s, Chickasaw was the only park that blacks could use, and most of the libraries, restaurants, and movie theaters were for whites only. Central was the all-black high school. When Clay was at Central, one of the teachers, Lyman Johnson, regularly led students on picket lines and lunch-counter sit-ins. Clay never participated, says Yates Thomas, except the one time that Thomas talked him into joining him on a picket line at a downtown restaurant.

Clay was standing on the sidewalk, says Thomas, when an eighth-floor window opened and a white woman emptied a bucket of water on the marchers below. "She emptied it right on his head," says Thomas. "She got him exactly. Water spilled all over him. He was just standing there."

That ended his career as an activist in Louisville. "He said he would never demonstrate again," says Thomas. "He never did." For years it was believed that Clay's activism began for real upon his return from the Olympics, when a Louisville restaurant refused to serve him and a white motorcycle gang threatened him. According to long-accepted Ali lore, Clay threw his gold medal into the Ohio River. In fact, says Hauser, "he lost it." And while Clay was turned away from restaurants on many occasions, the biker incident never happened.

His life had become so consumed by the rigors of boxing—aside from all the roadwork, he trained in two gyms, with both Martin and Stoner—it was something of a wonder that he made it through Central at all. But in his junior and senior years, Clay had as his ally the most powerful man at Central, the principal. Atwood Wilson adored the young man. At assemblies Wilson would embrace him onstage and announce, "Here he is, ladies and gentlemen: Cassius Clay! The next heavyweight champion of the world. This guy is going to make a million dollars!"

Academically Clay paddled in the doldrums—he ended up ranked 376th in a class of 391 students—but his failure at scholarship did not trouble the principal with the master's degree in education from the University of Chicago. What Wilson admired most of all was excellence, says Bettie Johnson, a counselor at Central, and no one at the school excelled at his job in life more than young Clay did. So the grades be damned. Clint Lovely, a Central student at the time, recalls Wilson saying, "Cassius doesn't need to know anything but how to fill out his income tax. And *I'm* gonna teach him that."

With graduation drawing near, there was a powerful sentiment among some teachers not to permit Clay to graduate because, says Johnson, he wasn't going to pass English. Thelma Lauderdale required a term paper from her English students, and Clay had not done his. "He wanted to do it on the Black Muslims," recalls Johnson, "and the teacher did not feel that was acceptable. The subject was controversial at the time. You have to understand what was going on in black thinking prior to the militancy of the sixties. Black Muslims were considered by blacks as very, very questionable people. Cassius was not a militant, outspoken guy. He always had this mischievous twinkle in his eye, like he had a private joke he was telling himself. He just had this interest in the Muslims."

Before a faculty meeting in the music room, Wilson rose and delivered his Claim to Fame speech: "One day our greatest claim to fame is going to be that we knew Cassius Clay, or taught him." At this point, says the former school librarian, Minnie Alta Broaddus, "I thought, maybe he knows something I don't know."

Wilson argued that Clay had a unique set of gifts, that he was going to be the heavyweight champion of the world and that he should not be held to the rules governing the average student. No one in the room was more of a scholar than the eloquent Wilson—he was ruthless with any teacher he perceived as mediocre—but here he argued that Clay was so exceptional that he should not be denied a diploma simply because he could not parse a sentence or quote from *Macbeth*. "The coaches all thought it was great because they were always trying to play guys who were ineligible scholastically," says Johnson. "The academic people were outraged because they thought we were letting our standards down."

Wilson was unmoved. "Do you think I'm going to be the principal of a school that Cassius Clay didn't finish?" he said. "Why, in one night, he'll make more money than the principal and all you teachers make in one year. If every teacher here fails him, he's still not going to fail. He's not going to fail in my school. I'm going to say, *I taught him!*"

The Claim to Fame speech carried the day. Clay fulfilled his term paper requirements when Lauderdale permitted him to give an oral presentation to her class, a travelogue on his adventures touring various American cities as an amateur boxer. He passed. At the graduation ceremonies on June 11, 1960, Clay received a standing ovation as he strode to get his diploma. It was, in a sense, a classic final performance for the clown who would be king.

"I remember when he graduated," says Davis. "All the guys had white shirts and ties under their caps and gowns. And dress shoes. He had on a T-shirt, and he walked down the aisle in his brogan work boots. With the steel toes."

It is more than three decades later, the autumn of 1991, and Muhammad Ali is sitting with his head back and his eyes closed in the high-backed leather chair in the office behind his house on a farm in Berrien Springs, Michigan. His 50th birthday is two months away. Out back, a horse in a pasture is galloping along a fence. Dusk, in orange silks, approaches from the west. Ali rises slowly from his chair and begins moving sideways across the room, dancing, sliding in and out, shooting out the jab, shadowboxing, daydreaming.

"I'll win the heavyweight championship back when I'm 50 years old!" he says. "Isn't that somethin'? Is that powerful? They can pay $20 million or $50 million to whoever I fight. Holyfield or Tyson. This is gonna shake 'em up. It's like a miracle, a dream. Muhammad Ali is back! Can you picture this?"

Ali sweeps left and right across the rug, stops in front of the hall door and sets his feet. He throws a flurry, snaps a jab, crosses with an overhand right—*Phew! Phew! Phew!*—comes back to his toes. slips back into the chair. He is breathing heavily as he leans back and closes his eyes again. His left hand, resting on his chest, is trembling. The grin is childlike, mischievous.

"Can you believe it?" he says. "Dancin' at 50! . . . Ooooohhh. . . . Dancin' at 50. Maaannnn. It'll be bigger than the moon shot! I'm dedicatin' the fight to the baby boomers, the people who were six years old when I beat Sonny Liston. Now they're thirty-four. I'll do the Ali shuffle!"

Back on his feet, he rolls to the left, stops, stutter-steps a shuffle, dances left and pulls back his head, dodging punches here and sliding there. Ali is inventing himself again, dreaming again, picking and messing with all of the old ghosts in new fantasies.

"I get a hundred million," he says. "Did you hear me say that? A hundred million dollars! In the first 25 seats there'll be 25 presidents. President of Egypt. President of Syria. Gaddafi. Mobutu. Kings. Can you imagine the security? Maaaannnn. A hundred million dollars for architects and builders to build a big school. If you had a chance to build a school, wouldn't you? Imagine: the Muhammad Ali School of Technology or whatever. Seventy-five classrooms. Big kitchen.

Auditorium. My dream is to make lectures in the school, to 300 kids! Take them off dope. In the school that I built. Can you imagine that?"

Yes, of course. Three hundred kids, a big, happy family at last. And they can all go swimming in the pool.

Comprehension Questions

See Instructor's Manual, Part 3 Answers.

1. In what year was Cassius Clay born?

   _____

   _____

2. How old was Cassius Clay when he graduated from high school?

   _____

   _____

3. How old was Clay when he won the Olympic gold medal?

   _____

   _____

4. What happened to Clay's Olympic gold medal?

   _____

   _____

5. What was the "Claim to Fame" speech?

   _____

   _____

   _____

   _____

6. Where did young Clay first learn how to box?

7. Why did Clay drink garlic water and also decide not to eat pork?

8. Louisville is known as _____ City.
9. Cassius and Rudy were called the _____ _____ .

10. What happened to Clay when he kissed a girl for the first time?

11. a. What is the meaning of the Latin phrase *sui generis,* as used to describe Clay?

    b. What does the word *eschew* mean in the sentence "At some point in his senior year Clay began to eschew pork. . . ."?

12. What are army brogans, and how did Clay use them?

Selection 8: "Young Cassius Clay"

13. Where was Clay ranked when he graduated from high school?
    a. First quarter of his class
    b. Second quarter of his class
    c. Third quarter of his class
    d. Last quarter of his class
    e. None of the above

14. *True or False:* Cassius Clay was militant during his early years.

15. a. How did Clay fulfill his high school term paper requirement?

    b. Was this fair to the other students? Why? Why not?

16. How would you describe Odessa Grady Clay?

17. How would you describe Cassius Clay Sr.?

18. How would you describe young Cassius Clay?

19. Identify the following by placing the correct letter next to each name.

   ____ Atwood Wilson
   ____ Joe Martin
   ____ Chickasaw Park
   ____ *Tomorrow's Champions*
   ____ Areatha Swint
   ____ Wilma Rudolph
   ____ Zbigniew Pietrzykowski
   ____ Black Muslims
   ____ Tunney Hunsaker
   ____ Angelo Dundee
   ____ Gene Pearson
   ____ Jimmy Jones
   ____ Cassius Sr.
   ____ Jimmy Ellis
   ____ Thelma Lauderdale

   a. First American woman to win three gold medals in a single Olympics
   b. Commercial sign painter
   c. Fifth Street Gym
   d. First pro fight
   e. Olympic gold medal
   f. Principal of Central High School
   g. English teacher
   h. Street-corner
   i. Introduced Clay to boxing
   j. Heavyweight champion
   k. "I'll let him go three"
   l. Segregation
   m. Term paper
   n. Television program
   o. First kiss

20. If Cassius Clay's new bike had never been stolen, would he have still become a boxer? Why? Why not?

   _____
   _____
   _____
   _____
   _____
   _____
   _____

SELECTION 9: "'A Generation of Clumsy Feeble-Minded Millions' Starved Brains"

By Roger Lewin

We know the picture well: the bloated bellies, stick-thin arms, and sad listless eyes that mark severe malnutrition. Countries sapped by chronic food shortages or thrown into despair by sudden devastating famines and war have burned those images into our conscience. But less dramatic, and therefore more insidious, are the effects of long-term under-nutrition, which more than 300 million children already suffer.

Although these children may escape the worst rigors of starvation, there is now mounting and inescapable evidence that their intellectual development suffers damage from which there is no chance of complete recovery.

The beautifully complex architecture of the human brain follows an innate blueprint, but factors in the environment of the growing infant partly influence its final form, and therefore its final performance. One major factor during the early stages of brain development, we now realize, is an adequate supply of food. Without the necessary flow of nutrients the brain simply cannot create the structures—the cells, the wiring, and the complex circuits—that fuse to form the functioning human mind.

Researchers in Europe, Africa, and South America are also learning of a delicate but crucial interplay between adequate diet and environmental stimulation in the first two years of life. During this critical period the brain's potential has to be reached, or it is too late. There is no second chance. An infant deprived of nutrition or stimulation will never develop to full mental capacity. The implications of this situation are frightening: cycles of poor nutrition and environmental poverty enhance each other, leading to personal suffering and chronic social malaise. Today 70 percent of the world's population seriously risks permanent brain damage.

The critical period of development of the human brain results from its peculiar pattern of growth. At birth an infant's brain has already reached 25 percent of its adult weight, and by six months it is half way to the final target. In comparison, total body weight at birth is a mere 5 percent of its adult maximum, and reaches the 50 percent mark only at age ten.

Reprinted With Permission From *Psychology Today* September 1975 issue. Copyright © 1992 (Sussex Publishers, Inc.).

Selection 9: "'A Generation of Clumsy Feeble-Minded Millions' Starved Brains"

Until recently we had no clear picture of the stages and timing of human brain growth. Now, John Dobbing and Jean Sands of the University of Manchester, England, have examined the composition of almost 150 human brains ranging in age from ten weeks of gestation to seven years. What they found helps us understand the effects of malnutrition in children.

Progress of the Brain

Basically, the brain grows in two stages. First, between weeks 10 and 18 of pregnancy, the adult number of nerve cells develops. Second, beginning about 20 weeks, the brain's packing cells (the oligodendroglia) begin to appear, followed by the production of the insulating material (myelin) that coats the long fibers along which the nerve cells send their messages. This second stage continues for at least two years after birth; myelination progresses at a lower rate until the age of four years. The second stage, known as the brain-growth spurt, represents the most vulnerable period of brain development. It is the critical period when inadequate nutrition and lack of stimulation inflict the most lasting damage.

Before Dobbing and Sands laid out clearly the timing of the human brain's growth spurt, we assumed that most of the brain's important development took place prenatally and was more or less complete by birth. But their demonstration that about five-sixths of the growth spurt comes *after* birth forced an awareness of the hazards of prolonged malnutrition in the early years of life.

There are several ways of exploring what happens to an infant nurtured in an impoverished womb and born into a world where he or she is deprived of food. One can study what physically happens to the brain or one can examine the physical and behavioral consequences of malnutrition in animals. Or one may observe children born under deprived circumstances and determine the effect of environmental factors in improving or worsening their condition.

One thing that is more or less safe from nutritional insult in the growing human brain is the number of nerve cells it contains. Because this number is established very early in pregnancy, at a time when outside nutritional factors fail to impinge on the developing fetus, the brain's basic nerve-cell complement escapes unscathed. There is, however, a major exception. The cerebellum, a wrinkled structure at the back of the brain that coordinates movement of the arms and legs, is vulnerable to nutritional deprivation because its nerve-cell generation and growth spurt are delayed. A starving brain risks delayed creation of the oligodendroglia and the later myelination of the nerve fibers.

Post-mortem examinations of human beings can't answer questions about these early developmental phases, so we have to rely on animal experiments. This approach is justified, because although the *timing* of the growth spurt in human and other animal brains differs, the *stages* are identical. Dobbing and his colleagues find that rats with malnutrition have significantly smaller brains than healthy rats, with the cell deficit concentrated in the oligodendroglia. Starved rats also show reduced myelination, and some enigmatic enzyme imbalances too. The cerebellum, compared with the rest of the brain, suffers more: it weighs less and doesn't have the adult complement of nerve cells, due to its delayed growth spurt. The particular vulnerability of the cerebellum is important because damage to this structure goes a long way toward explaining the reported clumsiness and reduced manual skills of malnourished children.

Malnourished Neurons

One thing that brain researchers readily admit is that they have measured what is easiest to measure. The feature of brain development that is probably most difficult to quantify, but is almost certainly the most important, is the lacework of connections between the nerve cells (neurons). Reliable reports show that the major part of the nerve fibers, the axons, shrink in diameter in malnourished animals. But the really crucial area of interneuron communication centers on the end of the axon, where it branches into literally thousands of tiny fingers that make contact with the neighboring neurons. B. G. Cragg from Monash University, Australia, has had a crack at this problem, and what he finds is most disturbing.

Cragg did some microscopic investigations of the cerebral cortex in rats malnourished early in life. In what must have been a crashingly tedious experiment, he counted the number of minute nerve endings (the synapses) in the cortex of undernourished animals. He found a 40 percent reduction, compared to normal rats. Cragg suspects too that some of the synapses may have been unable to function because of molecular breaks. The creation of the interneural network is one of the brain's major construction projects during the first two years of life, so Cragg's result is crucial and needs to be confirmed. If the undernourished cerebral cortex really lacks almost half of its interconnections (or even a tenth), the consequences for brain function are frightening. The planet may be raising a generation of clumsy, feeble-minded millions.

A crucial point about all these experiments is that moderate degrees of malnutrition—of the sort that 300 million children experience daily—can produce these physical side effects and deficiencies. More important, we cannot repair these physical deficiencies by normal feeding once the brain growth spurt has passed.

The typical undernourished child is shorter and lighter than his counterpart in affluent countries. He is about 70 percent of his correct weight, and the brain weight and head diameter are marginally smaller as well. The next step we've taken is to find out what this means for intellectual and social activity.

In the attempt to find the consequences of chronic undernutrition, most research groups have used the longitudinal study, observing the progress of a group of children over a period of years. For example, Joaquín Cravioto and Elsa DeLicardie studied a group of infants born in 1966 in a small rural village in southwest Mexico. They have been observing the children ever since. The village has a "normal" background of undernutrition, but the researchers concentrated on 22 children who at times had had almost no food and thus had been severely malnourished.

Food and Language

Cravioto and DeLicardie studied nutrition and mental development against the background of social and economic factors. Their outstanding discovery was the effect of malnutrition on language development and verbal-concept formation. As a group, the severely malnourished children began to lag behind in language at about six months. At the age of one year the matched control group had language development equivalent to 334 days, compared with 289 days for the hunger group. By three years the gap was 947 days to 657.

Because verbal concepts are a basic area of human intelligence, the researchers gave children tests to measure their understanding of 23 pairs of opposites (such as big-little, long-short, in-out). At 31 months of age the control group of normals understood an average of 5.46 concepts, compared with 3.92 for the malnourished children; by 46 weeks their scores were 16.92 and 12.16; and at 58 weeks the controls knew 20 of the concepts, three ahead of the malnourished group. Even after 40 months the children who had suffered malnutrition in infancy were behind the control children in language development and concept formation. Although the worst physical symptoms of their malnutrition were gone, and although they did make up some of the lost ground, they didn't catch up with their healthier playmates. The trend line suggests they never will.

Because the poverty that produces severe malnutrition also produces deprived environments, Cravioto and DeLicardie compared the home lives of the children. They used the Caldwell Inventory of Home Stimulation to measure factors such as frequency and stability of adult contacts, the number of voices the child hears, availability of toys and games, whether the child's needs are met, and how many restrictions there are on the child's activity. The researchers found that the malnourished infants came from homes that were significantly impoverished in activity that brings the human mind alive.

Although this poor environment of the malnourished children contributes to their slowed intellectual development, Cravioto claims that it is not the sole explanation. This conclusion is supported by Stephen Richardson and his colleagues, who studied a community of children in Jamaica, and found that malnutrition is as damaging as an impoverished social life. Richardson measured the physical and intellectual status of a group of boys, aged seven to 11 years, who had during the first two years of their lives suffered severe malnutrition. These children were smaller in stature, lighter in weight, and had smaller heads than normal children. Behaviorally, they were disadvantaged too: they did less well in formal tests of reading, writing and arithmetic; teachers found their school performance to be poorer, with more special problems in classwork (see table).

Further, the previously malnourished children were less popular among their schoolmates. When Richardson asked all the children to pick the three peers in their class with whom they most preferred to spend their time, they named the malnourished children much less frequently. This is a tricky result to untangle, but the cause may have some parallels with the observation that malnourished animals are socially disturbed and more irritable. Perhaps the children were too.

Teacher's overall evaluation	*Malnourished Children*	*Comparison*
outstanding/ above average	11	27
below average	18	20
poor or severely retarded	32	18
Special problems in classwork		
yes	50	40
no	12	25

Poor Nutrition Vs. Poor Environment

The researchers also measured the children's home environments, and this time found that not all of the malnourished children came from impoverished homes. So they were able to compare four groups: malnourished children from rich environments, malnourished children from deprived environments, healthy children from rich environments, and healthy children from deprived environments.

The results showed clearly how a home that is poor in stimulation and opportunity for a child will impair his or her intellectual development, regardless of the extent of malnutrition. Among healthy children, those from stimulating environments averaged 71.4 on an intelligence test, while those from deprived environments averaged 60.5. Malnourished children from enriched homes scored 62.7. But the combination of malnutrition *and* a poor environment produced the deadliest deficit in learning of all, averages of only 52.9.

One report that seemed to counter the evidence for the prolonged effects of malnutrition comes from the Columbia University School of Public Health and Administrative Medicine, which detailed the intellectual performance of 19-year-old Dutch youths entering the army. These men had either been born or were young infants during the famine the Nazis imposed on their country during World War II. These young men showed normal intelligence, which suggested that malnutrition has no lasting effect on mental development. The crucial fallacy in such a conclusion is that the Dutch famine was very short, only six months, and before and immediately after the famine there was no severe food shortage. Any brain-growth deficit inflicted by this brief famine would therefore be made up for by enhanced development within the two-and-one-quarter-year brain-growth period. The Dutch infants, who went hungry for a brief period but otherwise were well-nourished in infancy and childhood, are thus not comparable to the Mexican and Jamaican children, who live in a state of chronic malnutrition.

Curing Deprived Children

Now researchers are beginning to ask what can be done to help children who do not get adequate food and environmental enrichment. Leonardo Sinisterra and his colleagues in Cali, Colombia, are giving malnourished children food and supplemental schooling from the age of three-and-a-half on. Compared with their fellows, the children in his program have a marvelously rich environment indeed. They build with wooden blocks and even make large-scale structures with poles and planks; they paint pictures of their environment, make up stories, and even act out adult situations; and they get an expanded view of the world by going on trips into the country, all of which are outside the experience of most of the poor children of Cali. These children are now five years old, and have made remarkable strides toward catching up with the intellectual ability of more affluent children, both in verbal reasoning and general intelligence.

Sinisterra gave a second group of formerly malnourished children one part of the treatment but not the other: they got good food, but no extra schooling. So far, it looks as though they are doing no better than malnourished children who have had no supplementary program. The reason seems to be that the children did not get the additional food until they were three-and-a-half, well after the critical brain-growth period had passed.

One aspect of intellectual performance remains resistant to repair in malnourished children, regardless of whether or not they get additional food and special schooling—short-term memory. So far no program has been able to help deprived children gain a normal ability to remember what they just learned.

Another compensation study is underway in a poor agricultural village in Mexico, Tezonteopan. Few families in Tezonteopan show signs of severe and clinical malnutrition, but almost all are chronically underfed, barely managing to survive. Passive children and tired mothers barely communicate, rarely play. Adolfo Chavez is studying the long-term effects of supplementary food on both parents and children. He began his food supplements with pregnant women and continued them throughout the brain growth spurt, i.e. until the children were over two years old.

For a start, the supplemented mothers produced babies that were roughly eight percent heavier than normal in the village, and this weight advantage continued and expanded. But behavioral differences appeared rapidly too. The test children showed superior language development within the first year, and in simple physical activity they far outshone their underfed fellows. On a measure of movement, they were three times as active by age one year, and four times as active by age two.

Further, the well-fed children spent less time in their cots, walked at a younger age, were more vigorous in play, and were more likely to take the lead in play, and were generally much more independent. And because of their greater activity and exploratory behavior, their parents and siblings took a greater interest in them, which in turn was strengthened by the infants' tendency to smile more. The whole family dynamics gained a higher level.

Some Tezonteopan fathers even took an active part in child care, something they almost never do. They were enthused by having a vigorous, alert child. Several were so impressed with their "special" children that they declared to Chavez, "This child will not be a farmer like me."

Chavez's work reveals the tragedy and the promise. Millions of people today accept deep, grinding hunger and poverty as normal and inevitable, and pay the price with lowered intellect and activity. We know that if the brain is not well fed during its critical period of growth, it will never develop to the full and rich potential that is our heritage. We also know that massive doses of good diet, fun and games, teaching and stimulation can help to overcome the intelligence gap that malnutrition leaves in its wake.

Ultimately, the efforts to untangle the effects of malnutrition and a poor environment may make little difference in the real world, where the two exist in a vicious circle. Poverty inflicts a double insult—its victims condemned to a dearth of food and a sterile environment. The combination is at work daily, eroding the mental capacity of 300 million children.

Comprehension Questions

1. One aspect of intellectual performance that is resistant to repair in malnourished children, regardless of whether or not they get additional food and special schooling, is _____ .

2. The brain-growth spurt is which of the following?
   a. Is the first stage of brain growth
   b. Occurs between the tenth and eighteenth weeks of pregnancy
   c. Is responsible for the development of nerve cells
   d. Is dependent upon nutrition and stimulation
   e. Continues for one year after birth

3. *True or False:* The stages of brain growth are identical in humans and animals.

4. The number of nerve cells in the brain is which of the following?
   a. Is affected by nutritional factors
   b. Is not really affected by nutritional factors
   c. Is affected by stimulation
   d. Is established during the first five years of life
   e. Both a and c

5. *True or False:* Most of the brain's important development takes place prenatally and is complete by birth.

6. The author believes that an infant will not develop to full mental capacity if the child is deprived of which of the following?
   a. Nutrition
   b. Stimulation
   c. Proper rest
   d. Love
   e. Both a and b
   f. Both c and d

7. The cerebellum is which of the following?
   a. Is located in the back of the brain
   b. Coordinates movement of the arms
   c. Coordinates movement of the legs
   d. If affected by nutritional deprivation
   e. All of the above
   f. None of the above

8. For the study of early brain development, we must rely on which of the following?
   a. Postmortem examinations
   b. Human experiments
   c. Brain surgery
   d. Brain scans
   e. Animal experiments

Selection 9: "'A Generation of Clumsy Feeble-Minded Millions' Starved Brains"

9. Where is Cali located?
   a. Mexico
   b. Colombia
   c. Jamaica
   d. Holland
   e. Tezonteopan

10. *True or False:* According to the author, 70 percent of the U.S. population seriously risks permanent brain damage.

11. Nerve endings are called _____.

12. The insulating material of the brain is called which of the following?
    a. Oligodendroglia
    b. Packing cells
    c. Synapses
    d. Myelin
    e. Neurons

13. The effect of malnutrition on language development and verbal concept formation was studied by _____ and _____.

14. The brain's packing cells are called which of the following?
    a. Myelin
    b. Neurons
    c. Oligodendroglia
    d. Synapses
    e. None of the above

15. Once the growth spurt has passed, physical deficiencies of the brain can be repaired with which of the following?
    a. Normal feeding
    b. Normal stimulation
    c. Both normal feeding and normal stimulation
    d. Brain surgery
    e. None of the above

16. At birth an infant's brain has already reached which of the following?
    a. 20 percent of its adult weight
    b. 15 percent of its adult weight
    c. 35 percent of its adult weight
    d. 22 percent of its adult weight
    e. None of the above

17. *True or False:* Regardless of the extent of malnutrition, a home that is poor in stimulation will impair a child's intellectual development.

18. The most important feature of brain development involves which of the following?
    a. Neurons
    b. Oligodendroglia
    c. Myelin
    d. Cerebellum
    e. Lacework of connections between the nerve cells

19. The first stage of brain growth occurs when?
    a. Between the tenth and eighteenth weeks of life
    b. At about the twentieth week of life
    c. During the first two years of life
    d. Between the tenth and eighteenth weeks of pregnancy
    e. During the first six months of life

20. Nerve cells are called _____.

21. In your notebook, write a few paragraphs in which you discuss what you have learned about nutrition and stimulation from this article and how you can best put it to use.

> SELECTION 10: "A Historical Overview of the African American Literary Tradition"

Slavery (1700s to 1865)

The Africans who were brought to the United States of America as slaves were faced first with the ordeal of surviving the middle passage—the voyage across the Atlantic Ocean—and then surviving within the institution of slavery. As slaves, they were denied the right to retain their languages and religions. Instead, they were forced to learn a new language, English, and a new form of religion, Christianity.

The fact that there is any evidence of African American literature written before 1865, when the Civil War ended, is remarkable. In many areas it was against the law to educate a slave. Thus, the majority of slaves were illiterate. Some slaves tricked their owners' children into teaching them to read and write. A few slaves were lucky; their owners believed in educating slaves.

We should not confuse illiteracy, however, with a lack of literature or culture. The African literary tradition that the slaves carried with them was an oral tradition. The customs, values, traditions, and history of a people were embodied in their oral literature. The earliest survivors of the African oral tradition were the work songs and field hollers that slaves called to each other as they worked in the fields. Another literary survivor was the folktale. Early African Americans shared folktales that explained the unexplainable, expressed values, and identified acceptable and unacceptable behavior. Folktales such as "How Buck Won His Freedom" and "People Who Could Fly" provided the slaves with hope and entertainment.

In the late 1700s, a limited amount of African American literature had been written or published. Early African American poetry, such as that of Phillis Wheatley and Jupiter Hammon, reflects the strong religious influences of the time. Revolutionary War-era writers like Benjamin Banneker, mathematician and astronomer, and Olaudah Equiano (Gustavus Vassa) spoke out for the equality of all people, especially African Americans.

By the early 1800s, African American literature appeared in a number of forms. White abolitionists encouraged the writing and publication of slave narratives, such as *Incidents in the Life of a Slave Girl* by Harriet

From *African American Literature,* Demetrice A. Worley and Jesse Perry, Jr. National Textbook Company, 1993.

A. Jacobs. Often, illiterate African American slaves were encouraged to tell their life stories to white writers who wrote them down. African American abolitionists produced nonfiction, such as Nat Turner's pamphlet *The Confessions of Nat Turner* (1831), and drama, such as William Wells Brown's *The Escape, or A Leap for Freedom* (1858), the first African American play. In 1859 Harriet E. Wilson published *Our Nig; or, Sketches from the Life of a Free Black,* the first novel published in the United States by an African American. Poets such as Frances Watkins Harper captured the horror of the institution of slavery. Other black writers, such as Frederick Douglass and Davis Walker, used the podium and essays to promote the right of African Americans to freedom and equality. Educated African Americans, such as Charlotte Forten Grimké, kept journals of their daily lives.

From its beginnings to the Civil War, the African American literary tradition was built and focused on a quest for freedom and equality. This quest has continued to serve as a foundation for much of the African American literary effort to this day.

Post Civil War, Reconstruction, and Reaction (1865 to 1920)

After the Civil War, the Reconstruction Act of March 1867 provided federal protection to African Americans in the South. For the first time, education—even though segregated—became a legal reality for all African Americans. However, many blacks still received little beyond a rudimentary education because of their financial need to work. By 1880 the economic and political gains that African Americans had made after the Civil War were eroded by the Ku Klux Klan, lynchings, increased unemployment, and legalized segregation of public accommodations and facilities (Jim Crow laws).

The African American literature produced between 1865 and 1920 reflects the disappointments, fears, and frustrations produced by America's failure to fulfill its promises of freedom and equality after the Civil War. Biographies and autobiographies, such as Frederick Douglass' *Narrative of the Life of Frederick Douglass, an American Slave* (1845) and Booker T. Washington's *Up from Slavery* (1901), were created. Charles W. Chesnutt became the first published short story writer and one of the first African American novelists. Paul Laurence Dunbar, whose dialect poetry was well received by whites, wrote novels such as *The Uncalled* (1898). Another excellent writer, James Weldon Johnson, author of *The Autobiography of an Ex-Coloured Man* (1912), published novels, as well as sermons in verse. This growing body of literature, however, was often ignored by white literary critics.

As the number of educated African Americans increased, so did the number of African American writers. At the beginning of the 1920s, this growing number of black writers were seeing their work published, and—more importantly—a growing number of educated African Americans were reading it.

Harlem Renaissance (Early 1920s to the Early 1930s)

Between 1915 and 1918 two events—the Great Migration and the end of World War I—contributed to the beginning of the Harlem Renaissance, a very creative literary period for African Americans. In 1915 African Americans began moving from the rural South to the urban North in search of jobs and a better life. Lured by the promise of employment, hundreds of thousands of African Americans migrated to large cities such as Chicago, Detroit, New York, and Philadelphia. After fighting in World War I to make the world safe for democracy, African Americans returned home to be confronted with racism, unemployment, and poverty. However, their racial identity had been solidified by their participation in the war. Blacks' experiences in Europe had made them more aware of this country's prejudices against them. After World War I, African Americans began to fully recognize something that racism and poverty in the United States could not take from them—their culture.

The Harlem Renaissance was a celebration of African American culture at a time in America's history when the restraints of the Victorian era were giving way to the boldness of the Roaring Twenties. The word *renaissance,* literally, means rebirth. Instead of a rebirth, however, the Harlem Renaissance was actually the first opportunity African Americans had to give birth to—and to celebrate—the uniqueness of African American culture. Both black and white readers were eager to experience a slice of African American life. The literature of the time provided that experience.

Young, educated African Americans traveled to New York City—in particular to Harlem, the cultural and artistic center of African Americans—to make a place for themselves in the literary scene. Harlem was *the* gathering place for what black leader, sociologist, and historian W. E. B. Du Bois had labeled the talented tenth: the 10 percent of African American intellectuals and artists who would lead African Americans in the United States. In Harlem these intellectuals and artists argued about the future of African Americans. Some conservative African American critics believed that the literature written by blacks should "uplift" the race—show African Americans in a positive light.

Younger, more radical African Americans believed that a "realistic" view of African American life had to be presented because it was art.

During the Harlem Renaissance, New York City provided a wide variety of publishing opportunities. Major publishing companies began soliciting and publishing literary works by black writers. Several agencies had magazines that published work by young black writers and sponsored writing contests. Two such periodicals were *The Crisis*, published by the National Association for the Advancement of Colored People (NAACP) and edited by W. E. B. Du Bois, and *Opportunity*, published by the Urban League and edited by Charles S. Johnson. Independent magazines, such as *The Messenger*—a militant socialist journal edited by A. Philip Randolph and Chandler Owen—published up-and-coming African American writers. Some writers, such as Wallace Thurman, Langston Hughes, Zora Neale Hurston, Aaron Douglas, John P. Davis, Bruce Nugent, and Gwendolyn Bennett, even tried to start their own literary journal—*Fire!!*—which lasted only one issue.

Many young African American writers came into prominence during the Harlem Renaissance. Four in particular were recognized as the premier writers of the time: Claude McKay, Jean Toomer, Countee Cullen, and Langston Hughes. Many others, including James Weldon Johnson, Zora Neale Hurston, Nella Larson, Sterling Brown, Georgia Douglas Johnson, Jessie Fausett, and Rudolph Fisher, received recognition for their poetry, short stories, drama, and novels. Continuing work he had begun at the beginning of the century, Du Bois produced books and essays on the position of African Americans in this country and on the steps African Americans needed to take to achieve equality.

The Harlem Renaissance writers reflected both the "uplifting" theme of the conservative African American critics and the "realistic" artist movement of the younger, more radical African American critics. Both sides succeeded in showing African Americans and the world that their culture was a worthy literary topic, that it was "beautiful"—a theme that would reemerge during the Black Power movement of the mid-1960s and early 1970s.

Social Change and Civil Rights (Mid-1930s to the Mid-1960s)

The stock market crash in 1929 signaled the beginning of the Great Depression. African Americans, who were typically the last to be hired and the first to be fired, suffered even more extreme economic and political hardships during the 1930s. Thousands of already poor African Americans joined the soup lines that formed across the country.

Franklin D. Roosevelt, elected President of the United States in 1932, promised the country a New Deal. The Federal Writers' Project, supervised by the Works Progress Administration, was one part of President Roosevelt's New Deal. Established African American writers like Langston Hughes, Zora Neale Hurston, and Arna Bontemps participated in the Federal Writers' Project in order to earn a living while they continued their writing. New African American literary voices emerged as well, including those of Richard Wright, Robert Hayden, Frank Yerby, and Margaret Walker.

Wright is considered the major writer of the late 1930s and the 1940s. His novel *Native Son* (1940) protested the conditions under which African Americans lived in the urban North. Like Wright, novelists Chester Himes, author of *If He Hollers, Let Him Go* (1945), and Ann Petry, author of *The Street* (1946), wrote strong novels about the effect of environment on the individual.

After World War II, many African Americans were more disillusioned than ever with the state of equality in the United States. Black soldiers who had risked their lives fighting fascism in Europe were denied rights upon their return home—rights that were guaranteed to all citizens under the U.S. Constitution. Some African Americans saw the end of World War II as a sign that they could and should assimilate into the dominant culture. In the 1940s a number of African American literary critics believed that black writers should emerge into the mainstream of American literature and deny that the African American experience in this country had any influence on their work.

The publication of Ralph Ellison's *Invisible Man* (1952), winner of a National Book Award, established that black authors could write social protest literature about the condition of African Americans in this country and, at the same time, write about the universal concerns of humanity. James Baldwin's first novel, *Go Tell It on the Mountain* (1953), further stressed black writers' abilities to present a uniquely African American viewpoint and the universal concern for personal identity. These works, and others by black writers such as dramatist Alice Childress, showed that African American literature did not have to fit within this country's literary mainstream to qualify as literature.

Rosa Parks' refusal in 1955 to move to the back of the bus in Montgomery, Alabama, signaled the birth of the civil rights movement. Led by the Reverend Dr. Martin Luther King, Jr., African Americans began to protest the denial of their rights as U.S. citizens. By the late 1950s and the early 1960s, black writers were responding to the fight for civil rights. Such poets as Gwendolyn Brooks, who won a Pulitzer

Prize in 1950 for *Annie Allen* (1949), Robert Hayden, Melvin Tolson, Margaret Danner, Langston Hughes, Mary Elizabeth Vroman, and Sterling Brown registered their awareness of that fight in their poetry. Other writers, such as Lorraine Hansberry, Mari Evans, Paule Marshall, William Melvin Kelley, and Ernest Gaines, expressed their views in plays, short stories, and novels.

Black Power Movement (Early 1960s to the Early 1970s)

During the 1960s, the African American fight for civil rights was in full force—from the peaceful demonstrations led by Dr. King to the more militant call for action in the early works of Malcolm X. Major battles were won in the middle and late 1960s. The Civil Rights Acts of 1964 and 1968 prohibited discrimination in public accommodations, schools, and employment. The Voting Rights Act of 1965 prohibited discrimination in voting because of color, religion, or national origin. A new wind was blowing across the country. In this wind, African Americans heard "Black Is Beautiful" and "Black Power."

For the first time since the Harlem Renaissance, a movement was underway that emphasized the beauty and uniqueness of the African American culture. Unlike the Harlem Renaissance, which took place primarily in New York City, the Black Power movement took place throughout the country. African Americans openly celebrated and incorporated into their lives the songs, stories, and customs of their African ancestors.

After the riots in the urban ghettos in the mid-1960s, African American poetry became a political weapon. Such poets as Amiri Baraka (LeRoi Jones), Nikki Giovanni, Haki Madhubuti (Don L. Lee), Sonia Sanchez, Dudley Randall, Lucille Clifton, and Etheridge Knight used their poetry to speak not for themselves as individuals, but in a dramatic voice for all African Americans. The Black Power movement made an impact also on African American novelists, such as William Melvin Kelley (*dem*, 1967). Powerful autobiographies and biographies appeared, including *The Autobiography of Malcolm X* (1964) by Malcolm X with Alex Haley, *Soul on Ice* (1968) by Eldridge Cleaver, and *I Know Why the Caged Bird Sings* (1970) by Maya Angelou. Playwrights, such as Amiri Baraka (*Dutchman*, 1964), Douglas Turner Ward (*Day of Absence*, 1965), and Charles Gordone (*No Place to Be Somebody*, 1967) brought the new awareness to the stage. The movement was expressed in the short stories of Paule Marshall and Ernest Gaines and in the books by Julius Lester.

Selection 10: "A Historical Overview of the African American Literary Tradition"

In 1968 Amiri Baraka and Larry Neal published *Black Fire, An Anthology of Afro-American Writing.* In the foreword, the editors explained that a new day had arrived for African American art. Their anthology served as the birthplace of the Black Arts movement. Larry Neal explained that this movement was opposed to any concept that separated African American artists from their community. He felt that African American art was directly related to the quest of African Americans for self-determination. Many African American writers and critics embraced the ideas of the Black Arts movement. Other more conservative African American critics argued against it. The Black Arts movement attracted much attention to African American literature. More and more, independent African American and white publishers began to seek out and publish literature by black writers. The increased availability of this literature allowed the number of readers, both African American and white, to grow.

Building on the Tradition (Mid-1970s to the Present)

In the early and mid-1970s, the civil rights movement began to wane. Attention shifted from gaining equal rights for African Americans as a whole to achieving individual rights. Blacks had made some economic and political gains through the civil rights and Black Power movements; across the country—however—unemployment, poverty, and discrimination still plagued African Americans.

The literary texts of African American writers in the middle and late 1970s reflected this shift in national focus. Writers like Nikki Giovanni and Haki Madhubuti moved from writing only black power poetry to writing poetry about the political and economic conditions of people of color throughout the world. Ishmael Reed's "Hoo Doo" fiction satirized America's culture. Throughout all of these works runs a theme that continues to be prominent in African American literature in the 1980s and 1990s: the importance of African Americans' knowledge of their history. August Wilson's dramas *Fences* (1987, Pulitzer Prizewinner) and *Piano Lesson* (1990) and Charles Johnson's National Book Awardwinner, *Middle Passage* (1990), illustrate the power of one's history.

The civil rights movement increased awareness of the inequality of women. America's growing interest in women's issues has helped female African American writers gain prominence. The literature produced by African American women often stresses the interconnectedness of family, home, and community as well as a black woman's ability to survive. In these works, characters name themselves and the world in which they live. This "specifying" of the African American women's experience can be seen in such works as Ntozake Shange's choreographed poem *For Colored Girls Who Have Considered Suicide/When the Rainbow is Enuf* (1977) and in novels by Alice Walker (*The Color Purple,* 1982), Gloria Naylor (*The Women of Brewster Place,* 1983), and Paule Marshall (*Praisesong for the Widow,* 1984). Rita Dove's Pulitzer Prize-winning book of poetry *Thomas and Beulah* (1986) and Toni Morrison's Pulitzer Prize-winning novel *Beloved* (1989) are powerful examples of women's literary voices. Fiction writers and poets such as Terry McMillan, Paulette Childress White, and Ai have firmly established themselves in the African American literary tradition.

At the close of the twentieth century, African American literature continues to build on the foundation established in the eighteenth century: the quest for freedom and equality. This quest has taken African Americans from the chains of slavery through war and peace, prosperity and poverty. African American literature has recorded the defeats and the triumphs. It contains the fears and the dreams. Its strength lies in its ability to present the truth, whether ugly or beautiful. The validity of African American literature, like the rights of African Americans as individuals and as citizens of this country, cannot be denied.

Comprehension Questions

See Instructor's Manual, Part 3 Answers.

1. Explain what the Harlem Renaissance was.

   _____

   _____

   _____

   _____

   _____

Selection 10: "A Historical Overview of the African American Literary Tradition" 421

2. Education became a legal reality for all African Americans as a result of the _____ Act.

3. What was the *middle passage*?
   _____
   _____

4. What two events between 1915 and 1918 contributed to the beginning of the Harlem Renaissance?
   _____
   _____
   _____
   _____

5. What new language and religion were slaves forced to learn upon their arrival here?
   _____
   _____

6. African Americans began to fully recognize their _____ after World War I.

7. What does the word *illiterate* mean?
   _____
   _____

8. Legalized segregation of public accommodations and facilities was provided for in _____ laws.

9. What does the word *renaissance* mean?

　

10. Name three of the earliest literary survivors of the African oral tradition.

　

11. Why was the Harlem Renaissance not really a rebirth?

　

12. Name the first play written by an African American.

　

13. Who was the first African American to publish short stories?

　

14. Name the first novel published in the United States by an African American. Who was its author?

Selection 10: "A Historical Overview of the African American Literary Tradition"

15. What does the talented tenth refer to and who coined this label?

16. From its beginnings, through the Civil War and right up to the present time, the African American literary tradition was built and focused on a quest for _____ and _____ .

17. How did the conservative and radical African Americans differ in their view of how black literature should be written?

18. Name the premiere African American writers during the Harlem Renaissance, according to the selection.

_____

_____

_____

_____

_____

_____

_____

19. Who was *the* major African American writer of the late 1930s and the 1940s?

_____

_____

20. What event signaled the birth of the civil rights movement?

_____

_____

21. What is the title of James Baldwin's first novel?

_____

_____

22. What poet won a Pulitzer Prize in 1950?

_____

Selection 10: "A Historical Overview of the African American Literary Tradition"

23. What does the literature produced by African American women often stress?

_____

_____

24. Identify the following.

   a. Voting Rights Act

   _____

   _____

   b. *Fences*

   _____

   _____

   c. Civil Rights Acts

   _____

   _____

   d. *Beloved*

   _____

   _____

   e. Gloria Naylor

   _____

   _____

   f. Black Arts Movement

   _____

   _____

25. What was the difference in location between the Harlem Renaissance and the Black Power movement?

INDEX

A
Abbreviations, use of, in note taking, 16
Antonyms, in showing context, 63–64

C
Cause and effect, 166–68
Change-of-pace readings, 327–426
Chapter headings, turning into questions, 287–94
Chronological order, 160–62
Colons, in showing context, 61–62
Commas, in showing context, 62
Comparison and contrast, 163–65
Concentration, improving, 8–9
Context
    antonyms in, 63–64
    commas in, 62
    dashes in, 62
    examples in, 64
    parentheses in, 62–63
    punctuation in showing, 61–63
    sentence clues in, 64
    synonyms in, 63
    word parts in, 82–85

D
Dashes, in showing context, 62
Details
    identifying, 126–54
    major, 126, 128
    minor, 126, 128–29
Diagrams, 216–26
Dictionary, 92–94. *See also* Glossary
Directions, following, 11–12, 47

E
Educated guesses, making, 245–72
Effect. *See* Cause and effect

Essay questions, 48–49, 57
Examples, in showing context, 64

F
Facts, simple listing of, 155–60
Fill-in questions, 48

G
Glossary, 85–91. *See also* Dictionary
Goal-setting, 2–3

I
Inference
    developing questions for, 272–81
    reading between lines, 241–81

L
Listening, in note taking, 15–17
Long-range goals, setting your, 2–3

M
Main ideas, 96–125
    between first and last sentences, 98–99
    as first sentence, 97
    importance of, 96
    as last sentence, 98
    that covers more than one paragraph, 100–1
    as two sentences, 99–100
    unstated, 101–2
Mapping, 216–26
Matching questions, 48
Multiple-choice questions, 47

N
Note taking, 14–44
    correcting and/or rewriting in, 17
    listening and taking notes, 15–17
    preparation for lecture, 15
    reviewing, on continuous basis, 17

O

Objective questions, 47–48, 50–57
Outlining, 203–16
    in textbook reading, 285–87
    in writing answers to essay questions, 49
Overviewing, in textbook reading, 282–83, 309–10

P

Paraphrasing, 227–40
Parentheses, in showing context, 62–63
Patterns of organization
    cause and effect, 166–68
    chronological order, 160–62
    comparison and contrast, 163–65
    simple listing of facts, 155–60
Previewing, in textbook reading, 283–84
Punctuation, in showing context, 61–63

Q

Questions
    continual review of answers to, 294
    inference, 272–81
    turning chapter headings into, 287–94

R

Reading between lines, 241–81
Reciting notes, 17

S

Sentence clues, in showing context, 64
Signal words, 155, 157, 159
Stress management, 10–11
Study goals, setting specific, 8–9
Study location, finding, 9–10
Summarizing, 227–40
Support, getting, at home and at school, 6–7
Synonyms, in showing context, 63

T

Terminology, in essay questions, 48–49
Test taking, 45–57
    posttest, 49–50
    preparing, 46
    taking, 47–49
Textbook material
    making diagrams (mapping), 216–26
    organizing, 203–16
    outlining, 203–16
    summarizing and paraphrasing, 227–40
Textbook reading, 282–326
    construct broad topic outline of chapter, 285–87
    overview of, 282–83, 309–10
    preview each chapter before, 283–84
    reviewing answers to questions continually, 294
    turning chapter headings into questions and reading to find answers, 287–94
Time management, 4–6
Topic, finding, 96–125
True-false test, 47

U

Underlining, 227–28
Unstated main ideas, 101–2

V

Vocabulary, 60–95
    learning and reviewing words, 95
    using context, 61–82
    using dictionary, 92–94
    using glossary, 85–91
    using word parts, 82–85

W

Word parts, in learning vocabulary, 82–85

CREDITS

Grateful acknowledgment is made to the following sources for their permission to reprint copyrighted material:

From *Advertising Copywriting,* Sixth Edition, by Philip Ward Burton. Copyright © 1990 by NTC Business Books. Reprinted by permission of the publisher.

From *African American Literature* by Demetrice A. Worley and Jesse Perry, Jr. Copyright © 1993 by National Textbook Company. Reprinted by permission of the publisher.

From *Allyn and Bacon General Science,* Second Edition, by Carolyn Sheets Brockway, Robert Gardner, and Samuel F. Howe. Copyright © 1989 Prentice-Hall. Reprinted by permission of Prentice-Hall, Inc., Englewood Cliffs, N.J.

From the *American System of Criminal Justice,* Sixth Edition, by George F. Cole. Copyright 1992 by Wadsworth, Inc. Reprinted by permission.

From *Biology: Concepts and Applications* by Cecie Starr. Copyright © 1991 by Wadsworth, Inc. Reprinted by permission of Brooks/Cole Publishing Company.

From *Body Structures and Functions,* Seventh Edition, by Elizabeth Fong, Elvira B. Ferris, and Esther G. Skelley. Copyright © 1984 by Delmar Publishers, Inc.

From *Business Communications,* Tenth Edition, by William C. Himstreet, Wayne Murlin Baty, and Carol M. Lehman. Copyright © 1993 by Wadsworth, Inc. Reprinted by permission of Brooks/Cole Publishing Company.

From *Business: Its Nature and Environment,* Eighth Edition, by Raymond E. Glos, Richard D. Steade, and James R. Lowry. Copyright © 1976 by South-Western Publishing Company.

From *Business Law,* alt. ed., by Rate A. Howell, John R. Allison, and N. T. Henley. Copyright © 1978 by The Dryden Press, reprinted by permission of the publisher.

From *Contemporary Business,* Second Edition, by Louis E. Boone and David L. Kurtz. Copyright © 1979 by The Dryden Press, reprinted by permission of the publisher.

From *Crime and Justice In Two Societies: Japan and the United States* by Ted D. Westermann and James W. Burfeind. Copyright © 1991 by Brooks/Cole Publishing Company.

From *Cultural Anthropology,* Third Edition, by William A. Haviland. Copyright © 1981 by Holt, Rinehart and Winston, Inc., reprinted by permission of the publisher.

"Dark Menace" and "The Experience of a Lifetime" by Richard Pirozzi. Reprinted by permission.

From "The Decline and Fall" from TIME, August 19, 1994 issue. Copyright © 1974 Time Inc. Reprinted by permission.

From *Developing Creative and Critical Thinking* by Robert Boostrom. Copyright © 1992 by National Textbook Company. Reprinted by permission of the publisher.

From *Elements of Biological Science,* Second Edition, by William T. Keeton, by permission of W. W. Norton & Company, Inc. Copyright © 1973, 1972, 1969, 1967 by W. W. Norton & Company, Inc.

From *Essentials of Business Communication,* Second Edition, by Mary Ellen Guffey. Copyright © 1991 by PWS-Kent Publishing Company.

From *Essentials of Life and Health,* Second and Fifth Editions, by M. Levy et al. Copyright © 1977 and 1988 by McGraw-Hill, Inc. Reprinted by permission of the publisher.

From *Exploring Biology* by Pamela S. Camp and Karen Arms. Copyright © 1981 by Saunders College Publishing.

From *Family Science* by Wesley R. Burr, Randal D. Day, and Kathleen S. Bahr. Copyright © 1993 by Wadsworth, Inc. This and all other quotes from the same source are reprinted by permission of Brooks/Cole Publishing Company, Pacific Grove, California 93950.

From *Four Software Tools Plus* by Tim Duffy. Copyright © 1989 by Wadsworth, Inc. Reprinted by permission of Brooks/Cole Publishing Company.

From *Fundamentals of Computer Education,* Second Edition, by Janice L. Flake, C. Edwin McClintock, and Sandra Turner. Copyright © 1990 by Wadsworth, Inc. Reprinted by permission.

"'A Generation of Clumsy Feeble-Minded Millions' Starved Brains" by Roger Lewin, reprinted with permission from *Psychology Today,* September 1975 issue. Copyright © 1992 (Sussex Publishers, Inc.).

From "Goodbye, Bill" by Coretta Scott King. *TV Guide,* April 25, 1992.

From *Handbook for Public Relations Writing,* Second Edition, by Thomas Bivins. Copyright © 1992 by NTC Business Books. Reprinted by permission of the publisher.

From *Health Psychology: An Introduction to Behavior and Health,* Second Edition, by Linda Brannon and Jess Feist. Copyright © 1988, 1992 by Wadsworth, Inc. This and all other quotes from the same source are reprinted by permission of Brooks/Cole Publishing Company, Pacific Grove, California 93950.

From *Healthy for Life* by Brian K. Williams and Sharon M. Knight. Copyright © 1994 by Wadsworth, Inc. This and all other quotes from the same source are reprinted by permission of Brooks/Cole Publishing Company, Pacific Grove, California 93950.

From *A History of Art and Music,* by H. W. Janson and Joseph Kerman. Copyright © 1968 by Prentice-Hall.

From *A History of the Modern World,* Fifth Edition, by R. R. Palmer and Joel Colton. Copyright © 1978 by Alfred A. Knopf, Inc.

From "How Much Violence?" by Neil Hickey. *TV Guide,* August 22, 1992.

From "I Fight For Our Future" by Hank Whittemore. *Parade* Magazine, April 12, 1992.

From *I Never Knew I Had a Choice,* Fifth Edition, by Gerald Corey and Marianne Schneider Corey. Copyright © 1978, 1983, 1986, 1990, 1993 by Wadsworth, Inc. This and all other quotes from the same source are reprinted by permission of Brooks/Cole Publishing Company, Pacific Grove, California 93950.

From *Introduction to Advertising Media* by Jim Surmanek. Copyright © 1993 by NTC Business Books. Reprinted by permission of the publisher.

From *Introduction to Business,* Fourth Edition, by Joseph T. Straub and Raymond F. Attner. Copyright © 1991 by PWS-Kent Publishing Company.

From *Introduction to Patient Care,* Third Edition, by Beverly W. DuGas. Copyright © 1977 by Saunders College Publishing.

From *Introduction to Psychology,* Third Edition, by James W. Kalat. Copyright © 1986, 1990, 1993, by Wadsworth, Inc. This and all other quotes from the same source are reprinted by permission of Brooks/Cole Publishing Company, Pacific Grove, California 93950.

From *Introductory Chemistry,* Second Edition, by Robert J. Ouellette. Copyright © 1975 by Robert J. Ouellette. Reprinted by permission of HarperCollins Publishers, Inc.

From *The Irony of Democracy,* Ninth Edition, by Thomas R. Dye and Harmon Zeigler. Copyright © 1993 by Wadsworth, Inc. Reprinted by permission of Brooks/Cole Publishing Company.

From *The Language of Learning,* Second Edition, by Jane N. Hopper and Jo Ann Carter-Wells. Copyright © 1994 by Wadsworth, Inc. Reprinted by permission of Brooks/Cole Publishing Company.

From *Looking Out/Looking In: Interpersonal Communication,* Third Edition, by Ronald B. Adler and Neil Towne, copyright © 1981 by Holt, Rinehart and Winston, Inc. Reprinted by permission of the publisher.

From *Marketing* by David L. Kurtz and Louis E. Boone. Copyright © 1981 by The Dryden Press.

From *Marriage and the Family,* Third Edition, by Marcia Lasswell and Thomas Lasswell. Copyright © 1991 by Wadsworth, Inc. Reprinted by permission of Brooks/Cole Publishing Company.

From *The Middle East: A History,* Second Edition, by Sydney Nettleton Fisher. Copyright © 1969 by Alfred A. Knopf.

From *The Middle East Today,* Third Edition, by Don Peretz. Copyright © 1978 by Holt, Rinehart and Winston.

From *Muhammad Ali: His Life and Times,* Copyright © 1991 by Thomas Hauser and Muhammad Ali. Reprinted by permission of Simon and Schuster, Inc.

From *The National Experience,* Fourth Edition, by John M. Blum et al. Copyright © 1977 by Harcourt Brace Jovanovich, Inc.

From "New Promise for Nicodemus" by Angela Bates. *National Parks,* July/August 1992.

From *Patterns of Civilization: Africa.* Copyright © 1975 by Cambridge Book Company.

From *Political Science: An Introduction* by Richard L. Cord, James A. Medeiros, and Walter S. Jones. Copyright © 1974 by Prentice-Hall.

From *Principles and Practice of Respiratory Therapy,* Second Edition, by J. A. Young and Dean Crocker. Copyright © 1976 by Yearbook Medical Publishers.

From *Principles of Anatomy and Physiology* by Gerard J. Tortora and Nicholas P. Anagnostakos. Copyright © 1976 by Burgess.

From *Principles of Finance,* Fourth Edition, by Carl A. Dauten and Merle T. Welshans. Copyright © 1975 by South-Western Publishing Company.

From *Psychology* by Spencer A. Rathus. Copyright © 1981 by Holt, Rinehart and Winston.

From *Race and Slavery in the Middle East* by Bernard Lewis. Copyright © 1990 by Oxford University Press.

From *Society: A Brief Introduction* by Ian Robertson. Copyright © 1989 by Worth Publishers, Inc.

From *Sociological Ideas,* Fourth Edition, by William C. Levin. Copyright © 1994 by Wadsworth, Inc. Reprinted by permission of Brooks/Cole Publishing Company.

From *Sociology,* Fourth Edition, by Rodney Stark. Copyright © 1992 by Wadsworth, Inc. Reprinted by permission of Brooks/Cole Publishing Company.

"The Stono River Rebellion and Its Impact on the South Carolina Slave Code" by John E. Fleming, from the *Negro History Bulletin* Volume 42, issue 3. Copyrighted and reprinted with permission from the Association for the Study of Afro-American Life and History, Inc.

From the *Strategic Plan For The Cooperative Education Program,* Passaic County Community College, Paterson, New Jersey.

From *Stress and Health: Principles and Practice for Coping and Wellness,* Second Edition, by Phillip L. Rice. Copyright © 1992 by Wadsworth, Inc. This and all other quotes from the same source are reprinted by permission of Brooks/Cole Publishing Company, Pacific Grove, California 93950.

From *Textbook of Medical-Surgical Nursing,* Third Edition, by Lillian S. Brunner and Doris S. Suddarth. Copyright © 1975 by Lippincott.

From *Tools for Technical and Professional Communication* by Arthur H. Bell. Copyright © 1995 by NTC Publishing Group. Reprinted by permission of the publisher.

"The Trajectories of Genius" from TIME, May 26, 1980 issue. Copyright © 1980 Time Inc. Reprinted by permission.

From *Understanding American Government* by Robert Weissberg. Copyright © 1980 by Holt, Rinehart and Winston.

"Why Run?" by Marlene Cimons. Copyright © April 12, 1992, *Los Angeles Times.* Reprinted by permission of the *Los Angeles Times* Syndicate.

From "With No Parents, Ladeeta, 18, Presses On" by Felicia R. Lee. Copyright © April 6, 1993 by The New York Times Company. Reprinted by permission.

From *World History* by Joseph Reither. Copyright © 1973 by McGraw-Hill Inc.

"Young Cassius Clay" by William Nack. Reprinted courtesy of SPORTS ILLUSTRATED from the 1/13/92 issue. Copyright © 1992, Time, Inc. All Rights Reserved.

Photos and Illustrations
Reprinted by permission of Richard Pirozzi.

STRATEGIES FOR READING AND STUDY SKILLS

INSTRUCTOR'S MANUAL

CONTENTS

About This Instructor's Manual   IM-4

Chapter 1   Getting Started   IM-5

Chapter 2   Effective Classroom Note Taking   IM-5

Chapter 3   Effective Test Taking   IM-7

Chapter 4   Vocabulary   IM-10

Chapter 5   Finding Topics and Main Ideas   IM-18

Chapter 6   Finding Major and Minor Details   IM-21

Chapter 7   Recognizing Patterns of Organization   IM-28

Chapter 8   Organizing Textbook Material   IM-35

Chapter 9   Using Inference   IM-43

Chapter 10   Five Steps to Effective Textbook Reading   IM-49

Change-of-Pace Readings   IM-50

About This Instructor's Manual

This manual provides answers and examples—chapter by chapter—for the exercises in *Strategies for Reading and Study Skills*. Included for each chapter are suggestions for assessment or evaluation.

Chapter 1: Getting Started

Exercise on "Following Directions": Suggestions

1. Read written directions at least twice.
2. Underline key words in written directions.
3. For oral directions, give the person who is talking your undivided attention by stopping whatever you are doing, controlling excessive anxiety, and looking directly at him or her.
4. If confused, ask the instructor questions.

Assessment

It is very early in the semester, and although Chapter 1 is an introductory chapter that does not call for formal testing, it does address many important points that students should understand. You can gauge their understanding through class discussions and perhaps by collecting and reviewing each student's list of the most important suggestions mentioned in the chapter. Make sure that every student participates in class discussions.

Chapter 2: Effective Classroom Note Taking

Answers to questions on "Practice Lecture 2: Introduction to the Middle East"

1. *Arab*   *Non-Arab*
   Egypt   Israel
   Iraq   Turkey
   Jordan   Iran
   Lebanon
   Syria
   Saudi Arabia

2. Israel   — Jerusalem and Tel Aviv
   Iran   — Teheran
   Turkey   — Ankara
   Syria   — Damascus
   Saudi Arabia   — Riyadh
   Iraq   — Baghdad

3. June 1967
4. (1) Religious—The three great monotheistic religions were born in the Middle East: Judaism, Christianity, and Islam.
   (2) Historical—Many world events have taken place there, and it has been a part of many great civilizations in world history.
   (3) Strategic-Geographic—The region is a part of Asia, Africa, and Europe, and it is located at the very crossroads of these three great continents.
   (4) Economic—Substantial oil resources.
5. False
6. Belief that there is only one God
7. Judaism, Christianity, and Islam
8. Persian, Roman, Arab, Turkish
9. Asia, Africa, Europe
10. False
11. Saudi Arabia, Iran, Iraq
12. Egypt, Syria, Turkey
13. Wheat
14. Cotton
15. Semites, Turks, Iranians
16. Semites
17. One whose native language and culture are Arabic, and who identifies with Arab problems or ways of life.
18. A follower of the Jewish religion who identifies with Jewish problems and life.
19. Arabic and Hebrew
20. Hebrew
21. Persian
22. 75; 20; 5
23. Wanderer
24. False
25. Cities
26. Bedouins
27. Sheikhs
28. False

29. Near East or Southwest Asia
30. True

Answers to questions on "The Nursing Process"

1. c	11. d
2. c	12. d
3. d	13. a
4. c	14. c
5. c	15. c
6. c	16. d
7. d	17. d
8. b or d	18. b
9. a	19. d
10. b	20. d

Assessment

In order to assess understanding of the most important note taking suggestions in Chapter 2, collect student lists for Exercise 2, or have each student read his or her list aloud. An alternative is to summarize the most important suggestions and give a short quiz on them during the next class period.

Chapter 3: Effective Test Taking

Answers to Objective Questions: "Effective Test Taking" (Lecture)

1. nonstop
2. e
3. not following directions; foolish errors
4. confusion; anxiety
5. d
6. false

7. questions; the answers
8. true
9. positive
10. f
11. It may help your confidence and lower your anxiety level if you see that you know many of the answers.
12. false
13. ask the instructor for clarification
14. c
15. Some questions may be worth more points than others and, if that is the case, you should spend more time on those that are worth the most.
16. false
17. d
18. all; always; every; never; none; only
19. false
20. d
21. Study both lists carefully so that you know exactly what you are matching; Use the list containing items with the most information as your base, and try to match them with the shorter items on the other list; Cross out items as you match them; Make sure that you find out whether you can use an item more than once.
22–34. h
         i
         f
         k
         c
         b
         g
         a
         e
         l
         d
         m
         j

35. Determine how many words are needed for each blank; If you can't think of the exact word or words to complete a statement, then use similar ones; When you have finished a question, read it over very carefully to see that it makes sense.
36. false
37. true
38. answer
39. knowledge; the ability to get your ideas down on paper in a neat, coherent fashion
40. 1) Read each question carefully and make sure you know exactly what the instructor wants.
    2) Outline or make a list of all the points that you have learned.
    3) Write out your answer in complete sentences by referring back to your outline or list.
41. false
42. d
43. objective questions
44. use your outline or list as your answer
45. true
46. to see whether you may have missed any questions
47. objective; answers; careless mistakes; essay; clear; legible
48. to learn from your mistakes so that you do not make them a second time
49. make a notation in your notebook and textbook indicating what information was covered by the questions so that you can refer back to it.
50. Answers will vary.

Assessment

After going over the questions, use some to quiz the students during the next class period in order to determine how well they understood the test taking suggestions.

When you have completed Chapter 3, invite a guest speaker to lecture and then quiz the students on the lecture material.

Chapter 4: Vocabulary

Answers to Exercise 1 (Passages 1–44)

1. urethritis: inflammation of the urethra
2. Bedouins: desert Arabs
3. inspiration: inhalation or breathing in
4. Chicano: Mexican-American or Hispano
5. laissez-faire: the noninterference of government in the business sector
6. abolitionists: people who opposed slavery

    advocates: people who supported slavery
7. scripts: the rules governing who will do what and when
8. sphere of influence: the area whose inhabitants depend on the central city for jobs, recreation, newspapers, television, and a sense of common community
9. range: the difference between the lowest and highest values
10. philanthropic: charitable
11. recidivists: habitual criminals
12. malocclusion: crooked teeth
13. mortgage: a means of securing a loan to finance the purchase of real estate; a lien against that property in order to secure the loan

    mortgagor: the borrower in a loan transaction

    mortgagee: the lender in a loan transaction
14. delirium tremens: a condition induced by alcohol withdrawal and characterized by excessive trembling, sweating, anxiety, and hallucinations
15. parallel play: two or more infants play at the same time, in the same place, but almost independently
16. stress: any stimulus that creates an imbalance in the internal environment

    homeostasis: internal balance
17. real wages: what the wage earner's income would actually buy
18. incongruence: mismatch

19. ecology: the study of the interactions between organisms and their environment

    environment: all those things extrinsic to the organism that in any way impinge on it; anything not an integral part of a particular organism

    extrinsic: external

20. condiments: seasonings

21. constituent: part; component; ingredient

    excreted: let out; eliminated

    diuretic: stimulate formation of urine

22. mediation: the process of bringing in a third party, called a mediator, to make recommendations for the settlement of differences between union and management.

    arbitration: the final step in settling union-management differences; the process of bringing in an impartial third party, called an arbitrator, who renders a binding decision

23. enveloped: surrounded

24. converted: changed

25. loquacious: talkative

    taciturn: quiet

26. adversaries: enemies

    Ghazis: warriors for the Islamic faith

27. hyperthermia: excessively high body temperature

28. piece wage: wages paid to employees based on the amount of output produced

    time wage: wages paid to employees based on the amount of time spent on the job

    incentive: reward for exceptional performance

29. aneurysm: a bubble in an artery

30. deglutition: swallowing

31. learning disability: a disorder of one or more of the basic psychological processes used in spoken or written communication

    discrepancy: difference; disagreement

32. palliation: to relieve pain without curing

33. class action: suits initiated by interest groups directly on behalf of a group or class of people whose interests they represent

    amicus curiae: brief filed by an interest group as a "friend of the court" in support of a person whose suit seeks to achieve goals that the interest group is also seeking

34. triage: the process of sorting the sick and wounded on the basis of urgency and type of condition presented so that the patient can be properly routed to the appropriate medical area

35. association: the linking of sensations or ideas

36. vacillated: shifted back and forth

37. Nicodemus: a town named for an African prince who became the first slave in the U.S. to buy his freedom

38. shaman: a medicine man

    pharmacy: plants from the forest that are used as drugs

39. epidermis: outer layer of skin

    sebaceous: oil

40. gastroenteritis: inflammation of the stomach and intestine

41. euphemisms: the substitution of a word, phrase, or expression that sounds less harsh or offensive

42. intimacy: how well you can talk with and confide in your partner

    passion: erotic attraction and the feeling of being in love

    commitment: an intention to continue in the relationship

43. facsimile transmission: a fax machine reads a document that has been inserted into the machine and transmits the document over telephone lines to another fax machine that receives the message and prepares a printed copy of the document

    transmits: sends

44. borgo: borough, a major section of a city

    borghetto: little borough

    diminutive: small

    ghetto: shortened version of *borghetto,* which originated in Venice in late medieval times as a section of the city in which Jews were required to live; today applied to any neighborhood occupied by an ethnic or racial minority

Answers to Exercise 3 (Student examples will vary.)

Roots

aquatic: living or growing in water
audible: capable of being heard
autobiography: the story of a person's life written by that person
benign: of a kind disposition; not malignant
biography: the story of a person's life written by someone else
synchronize: to occur at the same time; to operate in unison
credible: believable
culprit: a person charged with an offense or crime
dermatology: the medical study of the skin
geology: the study of the origin, history, and structure of the earth
polygraph: an instrument used for lie detection
dialog: a conversation between two or more people
microbiology: the science that deals with microorganisms
mortal: subject to death
pedicure: care or treatment of the feet or toenails
claustrophobia: fear of confined spaces
phonics: pertaining to sound
polygamy: having more than one wife, husband, or mate at a single time
transport: to carry from one place to another
pseudonym: fictitious or false name assumed by an author; pen name
psychology: the science of the human mind
Scripture: a sacred writing or book, such as the Holy Scripture
spectacles: a pair of eyeglasses
hyperthermia: unusually high fever

Prefixes

atheist: one who denies the existence of God
anterior: placed in front; located on or near the front

antiseptic: free from germs
bilingual: able to speak two languages
circumference: the boundary line of a circle
congregate: to come together in a crowd
contraception: the prevention of conception or impregnation
extraterrestrial: outside the limits of the earth
hyperactive: excessively active
hypodermic: introduced under the skin
illegitimate: illegal; born out of wedlock
immobile: unable to move
inoperative: not working
interstate: connecting two or more states
intrastate: within the boundaries of a state
irrational: without the faculty of reason; lacking sound judgment
malignant: causing harm
misadvise: to advise wrongly
monologue: a long speech or talk by one person
nonprofit: not seeking profit
posterior: situated behind or at the rear
prejudice: an unfavorable opinion formed beforehand or without knowledge
proponent: one who argues in support of something
recede: to move back or away
retroactive: effective as of a past date
semiconscious: half-conscious
subservient: submissive; serving to promote some end
supernatural: existence outside the natural world
transfer: to shift from one person or place to another
tripod: a three-legged stool or stand
uncivil: impolite or rude

Suffixes

readable: capable of being read easily
solar: derived from the sun

golden: made of gold

adviser: one who gives advice

plentiful: great quantity or supply

pacify: to calm or bring to a state of peace

bachelorhood: condition of being an unmarried man

edible: fit to be eaten as food

sterilize: to make sterile or free from bacteria or other microorganisms

penniless: without any money

sociology: the study of human social behavior or human society

harassment: the state of being disturbed or irritated

conductor: a person who conducts or leads

westward: toward the west

Exercise 4 (Sentences will vary.)

Exercise 5 (Sentences will vary.)

Answers to Exercise 6 (Glossary Definitions)

Exaggeration principle: under stress, a family has a natural tendency toward exaggerating its own special character.

Anticipatory socialization principle: the enhancement of development—through disclosure of information, advice, and experience—for persons involved in a transition.

Coping strategies: processes, behaviors, or patterns of behaviors that families use to adapt to stress: getting help from others, trying to be adaptable, and learning to accept new realities.

Double bind paradox: in family communication, the situation where two conflicting demands are transmitted to a family member, followed by a third demand for family closeness.

Allocation principle for resources: on Foa's model, the closer resources and goals are, the greater the likelihood that the resources can be used to attain the desired goals.

Deviation amplifying feedback is sometimes called: positive feedback loops or variety feedback loops

Concrete-symbolic dimension: refers to whether a resource is tangible or intangible.

Aftermath phase of violence: the time when tension is released, and the batterer is contrite and seeks forgiveness.

Cognitive coping strategies: things families can do mentally to help them cope with stress.

Deviation dampening feedback: sometimes called negative feedback loops or constancy feedback loops

Answers to Exercise 7 (Dictionary Questions—Answers may vary.)

1. narrow, nativism, nasalize, narthex, narrator, nationwide, nascent, natty
2. nationalize, primrose, envision, salamander, slouch, brassiere
3. illustrations will vary
4. confluence: noun
   insolvable: adjective
   within: preposition
   deposit: verb
   truly: adverb
   an: article
5. terrapin: from Eastern Algonquian *toolepeiwa* (unattested)
   voodoo: Louisiana French *voudou*, from Ewe *vodu*
   tapioca: Portuguese and Spanish, from Tupi *tipioca*, "residue"
   laudable: Latin *laudare*, to praise
   geriatrics: Greek *geras*, old age
6. demolish: -ished, -ishing, -ishes
   vibrate: -brated, -brating, -brates
   obfuscate: -cated, -cating, -cates, -tion
   asphyxiate: -ated, -ating, -ates, -tion, -tor
   condense: -densed, -densing, -denses
   sage: -er, -est, -ly, -ness

7. apathy: lack of emotion, feeling, or interest

   bourgeois: member of the middle class of society

   conservative: inclined to keep things as they are; opposed to change

   entrepreneur: person who establishes a business enterprise or a series of them

   heterogeneous: made up of different and varied parts or members

   homogeneous: similar or identical; alike

   liberal: favoring social progress and democratic reform; tolerant

   metabolism: the sum of all the chemical processes that occur in living organisms

   neurosis: any of various emotional disorders marked by anxiety, depression, or other abnormal behavior symptoms

   physiological: having to do with the study of processes and functions in living things

   psychosis: severe mental disorder in which a person's sense of reality is impaired or lost

   prognosis: in medicine, the probable course and outcome of a disease

   verbose: using more words than necessary; wordy

   whimsical: playful, capricious

   zealous: eager; enthusiastic

Exercise 8 (Words will vary.)

Assessment

Using the Context

Be certain that students can tell you the various ways that context can be used to find word meanings. Because Exercise 1 is extensive, you could have students complete items 36–45 as a quiz to illustrate their mastery of the use of context, or you could use examples from other textbooks.

Using Word Parts

Drill students regularly to make sure they know the meanings of the word parts. In addition, give students a list of words and have them apply their knowledge of word parts to determine their meanings.

Using a Glossary

Ask students to find definitions and other information from glossary pages that you have selected from various content textbooks, or use the glossary pages provided in this textbook to make up additional questions.

Using the Dictionary

Write additional questions that students may use their dictionaries to answer.

Chapter 5: Finding Topics and Main Ideas

Exercise 1 (Passages 1–25)

1. Word processing in the classroom

   Using word processing in the classroom is not without its problems.

2. Teachers and the instructional process

   Teachers spend considerable time managing the instructional process.

3. Environment and energy conservation

   As indicated by these few examples, a realistic program of environment and energy conservation should be adopted by every business.

4. Men's efforts to get along

   Fundamentally, history is the story of men's efforts to get along with one another. But men have not found the problem of getting along together a simple one.

5. The arts

   Architecture, sculpture, and painting are the most permanent of the arts. Music and dance are the most perishable.

6. Stress and physical well-being

   Stress can have a negative effect on the physical well-being of the body.

7. What makes people happy?

   Common sense tells us that people are happy when more good things than bad things happen to them. However, such events make people happy only for a little while. Most people do not become permanently depressed because of a single tragic event, and hardly anyone becomes permanently happy because of a single good event.

8. Defining problems

   The accurate definition of a problem affects all the steps that follow.

9. Olympic champions

   There is a reason the Olympics are held every four years. It takes time to develop champions worthy of the ideal.

10. The responsibilities of college students

    College students have many responsibilities.

11. Analogies

    In short, an analogy can be a trap if you think that it sums up all the relationships between two objects. You can, however, open up your thinking if you use analogies imaginatively to help you find and think about relationships.

12. Love

    None of this advice seemed very helpful. Even so, we all knew that whatever love was, it was very serious; or, for preteens or early teenagers, the topic of love can sometimes be confusing.

13. Respiratory therapy

    The departments of anesthesiology and internal medicine usually assume the medical direction of the respiratory therapy department; or, historically, many respiratory therapy departments have been organized under the direction of anesthesiologists.

14. Peas

    Peas have one great advantage for genetic experiments: they can be cross-fertilized or self-fertilized, as the experimenter wishes.

15. Student opinions and learning

    You are most certainly entitled to your opinions, and as a student, you are often expected to evaluate what you read. However, you must be careful not to let your beliefs interfere with learning; or, your viewpoint, preferences, and experiences are very important, but you must try to keep an open mind when reading textbooks.

16. Buying instructional computer software

    You are going to be very thorough and selective when choosing instructional computer software for purchase.

17. Police officers and danger

    The danger of their work makes police officers especially attentive to signs of potential violence and lawbreaking; or, with these as examples, it is not hard to understand how police officers become suspicious of everyone and all situations.

18. Socialization experiences

    People, like monkeys, are influenced by early socialization experiences—messages and experiences provided for us by other people to direct our growth in particular directions.

19. The meaning of Islam

    The word "Islam" is used with at least three different meanings, and much misunderstanding can arise from the failure to distinguish among them; or, in discussing Muslim attitudes or ethnicity, race, and color, I shall try to deal to some extent at least with all three but to make clear the distinction among them.

20. Mental hospital patients and pills

    Mental hospital patients take pills for different reasons.

21. Fear and caution

    It is normal to have a certain amount of fear and to avoid situations that might provoke fear. But excessive fear and caution are linked to some of the most common psychological disorders.

22. Crime in the United States

    What is striking about crime in the United States is that the problem is so much greater than it is in other industrialized countries.

23. Anatomy and physiology

    Whereas anatomy and its branches deal with structures of the body, physiology deals with functions of the body parts—that is, how the body parts work. As you will see in later chapters, physiology cannot be completely separated from anatomy.

24. Geographic features of the Middle East

    Two geographic features of the Middle East have been significant in all periods of history.

25. Nonreporting of crime

    Many reasons have been advanced to account for nonreporting of crime; or as these examples suggest, multitudes of people feel that it is rational not to report criminal incidents because the costs outweigh the gains.

Exercise 2 (Examples will vary.)

Assessment

Using paragraphs from this textbook or copied paragraphs from other sources, have students find the topics and main ideas. Also, you can use some of the passages from Exercise 1 in Chapter 6 to quiz students on finding the topic and main idea.

In addition, it would be useful to have students create their own paragraphs that illustrate the various locations for main ideas.

Chapter 6: Finding Major and Minor Details

Exercise 1 (Passages 1–25)

1. Topic: Ann's reaction

   Main Idea: Ann's first reaction to being told that she had only about a year to live was shock and denial.

   Major Details: She refused to believe that the diagnosis was correct, and even after obtaining several other medical opinions she still refused to accept that she was dying.

   Minor Details: None

2. Topic: Words

   Main Idea: In addition to borrowing words from other languages, we create words as we need them.

   Major Details: For example, we "blend" breakfast and lunch to form *brunch* and smoke and fog to form *smog*. We "compound" words by putting them together to label new concepts like *downtime* and *spinout,* and we make new words from the first letters of other words, as in the acronyms *scuba* (self-contained underwater breathing apparatus) and *radar* (radio detecting and ranging). Business creates trademark words such as *Xerox* and *Kleenex,* and we use them in a much more general way.

   Minor Details: Words, words, everywhere! You can see why the language is so rich!

3. Topic: Law of sales

   Main Idea: Thus we can hardly question the relevance of studying the law of sales.

   Major Details: All of the above have at least two things in common. First, they are quite ordinary transactions, occurring countless numbers of times. Second, they involve sales of goods.

   Minor Details: (Remaining sentence)

4. Topic: Commercials and prominent personalities

   Main Idea: Commercials in which screen stars, sports heroes, and prominent figures from all walks of life are used as salespeople are a proven type of commercial. The main concern in this type of commercial is to avoid staginess and artificiality.

   Major Details: A viewer is all too ready to disbelieve the words of your prominent personality unless you phrase the message in comfortable, conversational language that fits your star salesperson. Keep the testimonial brief, natural, and believable, for even professional actors are not always capable of adjusting to selling roles.

   Minor Details: None

5. Topic: Animal behavior studies

   Main Idea: Questions of this sort lead us into the world of animal behavior studies.

Chapter 6: Finding Major and Minor Details   IM-23

Major Details: (Remaining sentences)
Minor Details: None

6. Topic: Cable TV

   Main Idea: About six out of ten homes in the United States have cable TV through which they receive all televisions programs. Although there is an abundance of programs and stations that can be viewed, there is currently no defined and accepted geographic area which can be called a Cable TV Market.

   Major Details: (Remaining sentences)
   Minor Details: None

7. Topic: Normal vs abnormal behavior

   Main Idea: Our point: what is considered psychologically healthy or unhealthy, or normal or abnormal behavior, can vary according to culture and according to situations within a culture.

   Major Details: (Remaining sentences)
   Minor Details: None

8. Topic: Relationships and conflict

   Main Idea: We'll start by saying that without exception every relationship of any depth at all has conflict.

   Major Details: No matter how close, how understanding, how compatible you are, there will be times when your ideas or actions or needs or goals won't match those of others around you. There's no end to the number or kinds of disagreements that are possible.

   Minor Details: (Remaining sentences)

9. Topic: Quitting smoking

   Main Idea: If you are a smoker now, and have been smoking for some time, you may feel that you're just too far along to give it up. In fact, however, it is almost never too late to quit.

   Major Details: A study of elderly smokers—people in their 60s, 70s, and beyond—contradicts the widely held belief that by the time smokers reach old age the habit has either already taken its toll or those who survive that long have somehow become immune to the dangers of cigarettes.

   Minor Details: (Remaining sentences)

10. Topic: Broadcast writing

    Main Idea: Simplification is the key to broadcast writing.

Major Details: Because it is harder to absorb the spoken word than the written word, concepts need to be pared down to the bare bones. Even so, you must learn to write as though your audience will only hear or see your message one time.

Minor Details: Radio is meant to be heard and television is made to be seen and heard. That means you have to write for the ear or for the ear and eye. Sentences must be shorter, speech more colloquial, and complex issues distilled to their essence.

Main Idea: One of the major advantages of using broadcast media is its repeatability.

Major Details: Listeners may hear or see a message many times in the course of a single day or a single week.

11. Topic: Graduate education

    Main Idea: There is a great irony about graduate education.

    Major Details: People get into graduate schools by having been good students. They succeed in graduate school by learning to cease being students.

    Minor Details: (Remaining sentences)

12. Topic: Business

    Main Idea: Business is a major force in American life. As a result of the dominant role business plays in our lives, people have a natural curiosity to learn more about it.

    Major Details: (Remaining sentences)

    Minor Details: None

13. Topic: Televised violence

    Main Idea: More televised violence than at any time in the medium's history is flowing into American homes. The overwhelming weight of scientific opinion now holds that televised violence is indeed responsible for a percentage of the real violence in our society.

    Major Details: (Remaining sentences)

    Minor Details: None

14. Topic: Use of context clues

    Main Idea: To use context clues effectively, you must try to understand the writer's point of view and his style as well as considering the subject matter of the written work. Your use of the context clues will be influenced by your knowledge of the subject matter and your understanding of just how the author is trying to transmit his message to you.

Major Details: For example, the mournful tone of Edgar Allan Poe is unlike the brisk tone set by Rudyard Kipling. The vocabulary and sentence patterns used by Charles Dickens are different from those used by Ernest Hemingway. But the importance of style and vocabulary extend beyond literature. If you are reading a biology book and come to an unknown word, your guess about its meaning would be different from the guess you would make if you were reading an auto repair manual.

Minor Detail: (Remaining sentence)

15. Topic: Individuality

    Main Idea: All of us are individuals. Looking at today's workforce brings the concept of individuality into sharp focus.

    Major Details: (Remaining sentences)

    Minor Details: Being liked may be important to us today; a year from now it may be more important to us to be recognized for what we have accomplished.

16. Topic: Robert Morris

    Main Idea: Robert Morris was perhaps the foremost business and financial leader in the nation in 1787. Later in life, his financial empire collapsed, probably because of overspeculation, and he died in debt.

    Major Details: (Remaining sentences)

    Minor Details: None

17. Topic: College students and intimate relationships

    Main Idea: Although many college students encounter difficulties in keeping intimate relationships alive, you can make choices that will increase your chances of developing lasting friendships.

    Major Details: (Remaining sentences)

    Minor Details: None

18. Topic: The nomination of Geraldine Ferraro

    Main Idea: The nomination of Geraldine Ferraro for vice president of the United States in 1984 brought out many conflicting points of view.

Major Details: There seemed to be widespread agreement among Americans that it was a welcome step toward the full participation of women in positions of power and influence. Still, there was a lot of disagreement over the net effects of Representative Ferraro's candidacy on voters.

Minor Details: (Remaining sentences)

19. Topic: Touching

    Main Idea: Some people are very comfortable with touching themselves, with touching others, and with being touched by others. Other people show a great deal of discomfort in touching themselves or allowing others to be physical with them.

    Major Details: They require a degree of touching to maintain a sense of physical and emotional well-being. They may bristle and quickly move away if they are touched accidentally. If such people are embraced by another, they are likely to become rigid and unresponsive.

    Minor Details: (Remaining sentences)

20. Topic: The Founding Fathers

    Main Idea: The Founding Fathers—those fifty-five men who wrote the Constitution of the United States and founded a new nation—were a truly exceptional elite, not only "rich and well-born" but also educated, talented, and resourceful.

    Major Details: (Remaining sentences)

    Minor Details: Jefferson and Adams were among the nation's very few notables who were not at the Constitutional Convention.

21. Topic: Sexuality

    Main Idea: Many people express some very real fears as they begin to recognize and accept their sexuality. It's important to learn that we can accept the full range of our sexual feelings yet decide for ourselves what we will do about them.

    Major Details: (Remaining sentences)

    Minor Details: None

22. Topic: Inferences and inductive reasoning

    Main Idea: When you make an inference, you go beyond the facts at hand to reach a conclusion. Anytime you draw a new idea out of the facts at hand, you're making an inference.

These three examples are not only inferences but also examples of inductive reasoning. When you reason inductively, you draw a conclusion that seems likely or probable, but it isn't necessarily so.

Major Details: (Remaining sentences)

Minor Details: None

23. Topic: My grandfather's pocket watch

    Main Idea: When I was nine years old, I pulled apart my grandfather's pocket watch to investigate its operation. My mother still displays the more attractive parts because I never got the watch back together again.

    Major Details: (Remaining sentences)

    Minor Details: None

24. Topic: Dread diseases of the past and new diseases

    Main Idea: A mere decade or so ago, we might have thought medical science was well on its way to wrapping up some of the dread diseases of the past. Then, almost as punishment for our complacency, *new* diseases began to appear.

    Major Details: (Remaining sentences)

    Minor Details: None

25. Topic: Reflecting

    Main Idea: Reflecting is a special kind of thinking.

    Major Details: In the first place, it's both active and controlled. The second way that reflecting is different from other kinds of thinking is that it's persistent. The third way that reflecting is different from some other kinds of thinking is that it's careful.

    Minor Details: (Remaining sentences)

Assessment

You can use Exercise 2 in this chapter to quiz students on their skill at finding major and minor details.

Chapter 7: Recognizing Patterns

Exercise 1 (Passages 1–23)

1. Topic: The retro craze
   Main Idea: Analysts can find endless reasons for the retro craze.
   Pattern: Cause and effect
   Major Details: (Remaining sentences)
2. Topic: Products
   Main Idea: Products you buy are created by the work of many businesses.
   Pattern: Chronological order
   Major Details: (Remaining sentences)
3. Topic: Stress
   Main Idea: When most people talk about stress, it is usually in terms of pressure they are feeling from something happening around them or to them.
   Pattern: Simple listing of facts
   Major Details: (Remaining sentences)
4. Topic: Barbara and Marvin
   Main Idea: After years of marriage, Barbara and Marvin have grown apart.
   Pattern: Cause and effect
   Major Details: As the years passed, Marvin was consumed by his job. At another level, Barbara perceived her husband as rejecting, cold, and insensitive to the changes that were occurring in her life. She reports arising one morning and realizing that in fact it did not matter.
5. Topic: Crack cocaine
   Main Idea: In the middle of the 1980s, crack cocaine quickly became a national problem in the United States.
   Pattern: Chronological order
   Major Details: (Entire paragraph)

6. Topic: Michelle and Kim

   Main Idea: Michelle and Kim have much in common even though they really are not close friends.

   Pattern: Comparison and contrast

   Major Details: (Remaining sentences)

7. Topic: Effects of overcrowding on animals

   Main Idea: The effects of overcrowding on animals have been extensively studied by social and natural scientists.

   Pattern: Cause and effect

   Major Details: (Remaining sentences)

8. Topic: People and the fear of crime

   Main Idea: People take certain actions as a result of their fear of crime.

   Pattern: Cause and effect or simple listing of facts

   Major Details: (Remaining sentences)

9. Topic: Sexual motivation vs. hunger

   Main Idea: Sexual motivation and hunger have similarities and differences.

   Pattern: Comparison and contrast

   Major Details: Sexual motivation, like hunger, depends on both a physiological drive and available incentives. Again as with hunger, the sex drive increases during a time of deprivation, at least up to a point, and it can be inhibited for social and symbolic reasons including religious vows. Many people experience little sex drive in the absence of such incentives as a loving partner or erotic stimuli. Moreover, people differ greatly in the incentives that arouse them sexually.

10. Topic: Love Canal

    Main Idea: The dumping of chemicals in Love Canal by the Hooker Chemical Company has forced many families to be relocated and left many other families to worry about their safety and their fate.

    Pattern: Chronological order or cause and effect

    Major Details: (All sentences except the first and last)

11. Topic: Managers and poor morale

    Main Idea: Managers can do several things to uncover clues to poor morale.

    Pattern: Simple listing of facts

    Major Details: One approach is to check company records on tardiness, absences, quality rejects, and comments received during exit interviews. Another approach is to observe and listen: employees' comments to each other, direct remarks to their supervisors, and informal communications through body language are all clues to work attitudes. A more formal way to check on morale is by conducting an employee attitude or opinion survey.

12. Topic: Corrupt police officers

    Main Idea: Corrupt police officers have been described as falling into two categories: "grass eaters" and "meat eaters."

    Pattern: Comparison and contrast

    Major Details: (Remaining sentences)

13. Topic: Learning the craft of writing

    Main Idea: Good writers learn the craft of writing in four stages.

    Pattern: Chronological order

    Major Details: The first stage involves learning how to use the *tools of the trade*. In the second stage the writer learns the *proper techniques* for efficient and coherent combination of these basic tools. After learning these techniques, the writer needs a *plan of action*. The third stage, then, involves learning and applying strategies for producing the desired result. Finally, in the fourth stage, the writer practices *applying the tools, techniques, and strategies* in varying situations.

14. Topic: Why women become anorexic

    Main Idea: Women become anorexic for several reasons.

    Pattern: Simple listing of facts or cause and effect

    Major Details: First, many women who become anorexic have always prized self-control. Second, by becoming so thin that they lose their secondary sexual characteristics, including breast development, they stop being attractive to men. Third, maintaining a dangerously low weight is a way of rebelling quietly and of attracting attention. There are probably other reasons behind anorexia.

15. Topic: Different viewpoints on human nature

    Main Idea: Throughout history there has been a debate between the different viewpoints on human nature and on what makes humans tick.

    Pattern: Comparison and contrast

    Major Details: (Remaining sentences)

16. Topic: Reasons for drinking alcohol

    Main Idea: People drink alcohol for different reasons.

    Pattern: Cause and effect or simple listing of facts

    Major Details: Many people in our society drink alcohol because it serves as a *social lubricant.* Alcohol serves a similar social function when it is used for *celebration.* Some people use alcohol or other drugs not only to celebrate the good times but also to escape the bad times. Young people, especially males, sometimes use drugs or alcohol to *attract attention,* to demonstrate to their friends how completely stoned or drunk they can get. A less common motivation for using alcohol or other drugs is *self-handicapping*—putting oneself at a disadvantage in order to have an excuse for failure.

17. Topic: Promotional strategy

    Main Idea: A promotional strategy is composed of the four elements of the promotional mix: personal selling, advertising, publicity, and sales promotion.

    Pattern: Simple listing of facts

    Major Details: The first element of the promotional mix is personal selling. It is a personal attempt to persuade the prospective customer to buy a product. The second element of the promotional mix is advertising. Advertising is any nonpersonal message paid for by an identifiable sponsor for the purpose of promoting products, services, or ideas. The third element of the promotional mix is publicity. It is nonpaid, nonpersonal communication to promote the products, services, or image of the company. Sales promotion is the fourth element of the promotional mix. It involves marketing activities, other than personal selling and advertising, that stimulate consumer purchasing and dealer effectiveness.

18. Topic: Gases vs. liquids and solids

    Main Idea: Gases are easily distinguished from liquids and solids.

    Pattern: Comparison and contrast

    Major Details: They have no characteristic shape or volume and can be contained in any size or shape vessel. The volumes of solids and liquids have clearly visible boundaries. A gas, on the other hand, completely fills any container in which it is placed and is bounded only by the walls of the container. Gases are highly compressible. Gases undergo considerable expansion when heated under constant pressure.

19. Topic: The human circulatory system

    Main Idea: Let us trace the movement of blood through the human circulatory system, beginning with that returning to the heart from the legs or arms.

    Pattern: Chronological order

    Major Details: Such blood enters the upper right chamber of the heart, called the *right atrium* (or auricle). This chamber then contracts, forcing the blood through a valve (the tricuspid valve) into the *right ventricle,* the lower right chamber of the heart. Instead, contraction of the *right ventricle* sends the blood through a valve (the pulmonary semilunar valve) into the *pulmonary artery,* which soon divides into two branches, one going to each lung. In the lungs, the pulmonary arteries branch into many small arteries, called arterioles, which connect with dense beds of capillaries lying in the walls of the alveoli. From the capillaries, the blood passes into small veins, which soon join to form large pulmonary veins running back toward the heart from the lungs. The four pulmonary veins (two from each lung) empty into the upper left chamber of the heart, called the *left atrium* (or auricle). When the left atrium contracts, it forces the blood through a valve (the bicuspid or mitral valve) into the *left ventricle,* which is the lower left chamber of the heart. When it contracts, it pushes the blood through a valve (the aortic semilunar valve) into a very large artery called the *aorta.* Numerous branch arteries arise from the aorta along its length, and these arteries carry blood to all parts of the body. Each of these arteries, in turn, branches into smaller arteries, until eventually the smallest arterioles connect with the numerous tiny capillaries embedded in the tissues. From the capillary beds the blood runs into tiny veins, which fuse to form larger and larger veins, until eventually one or more large veins exit from the organ in question. These veins, in turn, empty into one of two very large veins that empty into the right atrium of the heart: the *anterior vena cava* (sometimes called the superior vena cava), which drains the head, neck, and arms, and the *posterior vena cava* (or inferior vena cava), which drains the rest of the body.

20. Topic: The 1960s

    Main Idea: The decade that had begun in exhilaration and hope was dissolving into bitterness and hate.

    Pattern: Cause and effect

    Major Details: Some Americans began to lose faith in a society that destroyed the three men (John F. Kennedy, Robert F. Kennedy, and Martin Luther King) of the decade who seemed most to embody American idealism. Frustrated minorities, feeling the "system" hopelessly rigged against them, turned to violence, if only because they could see no other way to get a hearing for just grievances.

21. Topic: Computers

    Main Idea: Today's computers can be roughly divided into microcomputers, minicomputers, mainframes, and supercomputers, with each group characterized by size, price, speed of operation, and memory/processing capabilities.

    Pattern: Simple listing of facts or comparison and contrast

    Major Details: (Simple listing of facts) Microcomputers are the smallest, least costly, and most popular computers on the market. Minicomputers were first developed during the 1960s to perform specialized tasks such as handling data communications. Mainframe computers are large, fast systems capable of supporting several hundred input and output devices such as keyboards and monitor screens. Supercomputers are the fastest, most expensive computers manufactured. (Comparison and contrast pattern includes virtually the entire passage by organizing many differences between the various computers.)

22. Topic: The Rosa Parks affair

    Main Idea: Rosa Parks's refusal to give up her seat for a white person on a Montgomery, Alabama bus started what was to become one of the most important events in the history of the civil rights movement.

    Pattern: Chronological order

    Major Details: The entire passage is part of the pattern with the exceptions of the leaflet excerpt and the sentence: "Robinson was a leader of the newly organized political affairs committee at the Dexter Avenue Baptist Church."

23. Topic: Learning

    Main Idea: Before we examine some commonly recognized categories of learning, we should mention several factors that complicate its study.

    Pattern: Simple listing of facts

    Major Details: First, it is often difficult to determine whether improvement in the performance of a behavior pattern is due to experience or simply to greater maturity or to a different physiological condition. A second complication in studying the learning ability of animals is that an animal may readily learn something in one context and be completely incapable of learning it in some other context. Another difficulty in determining what an animal can learn is that a particular behavior can often be learned only during a rather limited critical period in its life. Still another difficulty is that one cannot always tell immediately whether or not learning has occurred. Much caution is needed in any attempt to compare the learning capabilities of different species.

Exercise 2 (Examples will vary.)

Assessment

Some of the passages from Exercise 1 in both Chapters 5 and 6 can be used to quiz students on their ability to identify the pattern of organization. Make sure that students can determine the purpose of the pattern in each case.

Chapter 8: Organizing Textbook Material

Exercise 1 (Passages 1 and 2—Model Outlines)

Topic: Preventing Accidents

I. There are several approaches . . .
   A) *Persuasion* and *education* are . . .
      1) Driver-education classes, campaigns . . .
   B) *Laws* are generally more . . .
      1) We have laws for . . .
   C) Historically, the most successful . . .
      1) That is, they do . . .
      2) For example, milk is . . .
      3) Let's take a look . . .

Topic: Learning How To Drive

I. Learning how to drive can be . . .
   A) This is because there . . .
      1) Two hands, two feet . . .
II. Learning how to drive can also be . . .
   A) Cars seem to come . . .
      1) They blow their horns . . .
      2) Their behavior makes one . . .

Exercise 2 (Passages 1–6—Model Outlines)

Topic: Lipids

I. Lipids are found in many living organisms, and they are categorized into three groups: simple lipids, compound lipids, and derived lipids.
   A) Simple lipids contain the elements carbon, hydrogen, and oxygen.
      1) Examples are fats and oils such as butter, margarine, and corn, olive, peanut, and safflower oils.
      2) Other simple lipids are waxes such as beeswax and lanolin.

- B) Compound lipids are composed of carbon, hydrogen, oxygen, nitrogen, and phosphorus.
    1) They include the phospholids, which are found in cell membranes, and the glycolipids in brain and nerve cells.
- C) Finally, there are the derived lipids containing only carbon, hydrogen, and oxygen.
    1) These include the steroids found in the male and female sex hormones and cholesterol and the fat-soluble vitamins A, D, E, and K.

Topic: Cars

I. Cars can be deadly weapons.
   - A) Every year, half of all the people who die from injuries and half of those with permanent spinal cord injuries are hurt in car accidents.

II. Cars are especially dangerous in the hands of people who are drunk.
   - A) As we saw in Chapter 5, a blood alcohol level of 0.10 percent or higher means that a person is legally drunk and should not drive.
   - B) Nevertheless, half of all drivers killed are drunk, and of these, nearly one-quarter were convicted of a moving violation within the previous three years.
       1) In other words, many drunk drivers have a history of dangerous driving.

Topic: U.S. Law

I. U.S. law is usually divided into two basic types: criminal and civil.
   - A) A criminal law defines an action as a crime and specifies a penalty.
       1) Serious crimes are called felonies and less serious ones are labeled misdemeanors (the precise line between these varies from state to state).
       2) In principle, all criminal actions are against the public order.
       3) If Smith assaults Jones, the government (not Jones) will prosecute Smith

B) In contrast, under civil law, the government provides a code regulating conduct for settling disputes between private persons.
   1) For example, if Jones buys a car from Smith and the car suddenly falls apart, Jones may sue Smith for damages under provisions of state civil law regulating contracts and liability.
   2) Because civil law sanctions are less severe than criminal law punishments, civil law standards of proof are less demanding.

Topic: Americans, Food, and Nutrition

I. As these examples suggest, Americans are now more interested in food and nutrition than they ever have been.
   A) An item on the television news connects the use of saccharin with cancer.
   B) A diet book that recommends eating large amounts of pineapple becomes a best seller.
   C) A suburban supermarket begins to offer alfalfa sprouts and cakes of tofu to its customers.
   D) We are concerned about whether certain foods may be hazardous to our health, and many Americans have initiated changes in their eating habits to maintain their health.
   E) The federal government, aware of the growing public concern about nutrition and health, has released a number of health-promotion pamphlets, including "Objectives for the Nation," a list of seventeen nutritional goals.
   F) As a nation, we seem to be obsessed with keeping our weight down, and we are more likely than ever to choose "diet" soft drinks—and even "sugarless" chocolates and chewing gum.
   G) Our changing tastes in food have led some of us to sample new foods—yogurt, for example.
   H) Whatever we eat, we probably wonder whether we're eating the right thing.
   I) Increasingly, we are concerned about nutrition.

Topic: The Amish and American Indian Subcultures

I. The experience of the Amish is one example of the way a subculture is tolerated by the larger culture within which it functions.
   A) As different as they are, the Amish actually practice many values that our nation respects in the abstract: thrift, hard work, independence, a close family life.
   B) The degree of tolerance accorded to them may also be due in part to the fact that Amish are white Europeans, of the same race as the dominant culture.

II. American Indian subcultures have been treated differently by whites.
   A) There was a racial difference: the whites came as conquerors, and Indian values were not as easily understood or sympathized with by the larger culture.
      1) The nation was less willing to tolerate the differences of the Indians, with results that are both a matter of history, as well as very much a current concern.

Topic: Forms of Prostitution

I. The occupation of prostitute takes several basic forms.
   A) Most female prostitutes work as streetwalkers, soliciting clients in public places such as streets and hotel lobbies.
      1) These women are generally poorly educated and include a high proportion of minority-group members, teenage runaways, and older prostitutes who are nearing the end of their careers.
   B) Other women work in brothels, which are today disguised as "massage parlors" or "clubs"; these prostitutes have higher status and better earnings than the streetwalker and they face less danger from their clients or the police.
   C) Still others work as call girls, operating out of hotel rooms or apartments, either on their own or through an "escort agency."
      1) These are usually the better-educated prostitutes, who may regard the occupation as a potential avenue to higher social status as the mistress or even the wife of a wealthy man.

D) Male prostitutes catering to homosexuals solicit clients on certain streets, in some gay bars, and occasionally through "escort agencies."

E) Male prostitutes catering to women generally work through private introductions and try to establish regular relationships with a small number of clients rather than transient relationships with many women.

Exercise 3 (Paragraphs will vary.)

Exercise 4 (Information in diagrams will vary.)

Model Diagram

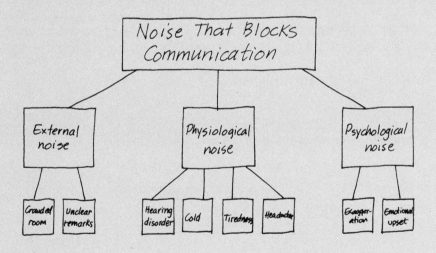

Model Diagram

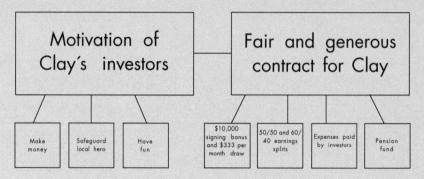

Exercise 5 (Diagrams will vary.)

Exercise 6 (Diagrams will vary.)

Exercise 7 (Passages 1–10)

Summaries and paraphrased passages will vary. The following can be used as models.

1

Whereas almost all children acquire language skills, chimpanzees do not, even though they are related genetically. Researchers have studied chimpanzees and human language in an effort to better understand language in general.

2

Few people changed their attitudes toward candidates Jimmy Carter and Ronald Reagan after watching one of their presidential debates in 1980. Persuading people to change their attitudes depends on who says what, how he or she says it, and to whom.

3

People change from moment to moment, situation to situation, and over longer stretches of time.

4

Scientists always ask questions and try to find answers to problems that often affect our lives. They work in four major areas of study: biology, chemistry, earth and space, and physics. Each of these includes several specialties. Biologists study living things, chemists investigate matter, earth and space scientists study the earth and objects in space, and physicists explore the interactions between matter and energy.

5

Magazine editor and writer Norman Cousins used positive emotions like hope, faith, laughter, confidence, and the will to live to improve his physical health. This led to increased scientific study of the relationship between emotions and healing.

6

Advertisers must rely on headlines to catch busy people's attention and persuade them to pause over an advertisement. That initial interest is a crucial first step to making a sale.

7

Psychological abnormalities, which are exaggerations of normal behaviors, come in many forms. Most medical students decide wrongly that they have some dreaded illness. Medical students' disease is even more common among students of psychological disorders. They are also usually wrong! Psychological disorders are an extreme version of tendencies that most of us already have.

8

Many robots are being used in factories in this country, and this trend toward automation is either causing unemployment in the industrial areas, or making workers' jobs less interesting and creative. However, robots are also beneficial because they often perform boring or dangerous jobs that people would rather not do. Also, robots are cheaper to operate and more efficient than humans for certain factory tasks making them a necessity for competing factory owners. Finally, some experts believe that robots will create new jobs because people will have to build, maintain, and fix the machines. Other experts feel, however, that although robots may create jobs in the long run, they cause job losses in the short run which offsets their benefits for the economy and society.

9

Medical science now can keep people alive even after their bodily systems have failed, which brings up the question of mercy killing or euthanasia. Americans are divided into three opinion groups regarding euthanasia. One group does not believe in it at all. They feel that every effort should be made to prolong life, otherwise it is murder, or murder combined with suicide. The majority of Americans believe in indirect euthanasia which involves the withdrawal of specific treatments, resulting in death. This is not an uncommon medical practice, and it has been given authoritative support. The smallest group of Americans believes in direct euthanasia which involves taking an action that causes death. It is difficult to determine how many people have actually practiced direct euthanasia.

10

The emotionally mature person has certain qualities including the abilities to be both intimate and sociable, having a sense of self, and having an interest in and an ability to do productive work. Intimacy involves giving and accepting love and affection from another person. To be sociable is to have friendly and long lasting relations with a group of friends by showing loyalty, devotion, and interest while developing a degree of independence at the same time. A sense of self involves seeing yourself clearly as a separate, distinct personality with your own identity, which is particularly important in terms of your behavior. Part of this includes a value system which is a set of beliefs, ideas, and guidelines that one lives by, but that can be changed for new experiences. Finally, the emotionally mature person seeks a highly interesting occupation or project that is very satisfying beyond its monetary rewards.

Assessment

Reproduce four relatively simple passages from content textbooks and have students outline the first, diagram the second, summarize the third, and paraphrase the fourth. Be certain that students follow the proper outlining format, but be flexible with their diagrams, summaries, and paraphrasing. These are higher-level skills that will take students time to develop, so be lenient in grading.

Chapter 9: Using Inference

Exercise 1—Making Educated Guesses (Passages 1–22)

1

1. Commit suicide
2. Depression; the sign painter mentioned that he was stockpiling Seconal and that he knew the fatal dose.

2

1. Martin Luther King
2. Symbol of peace; eloquent and moving speeches; won Nobel Peace Prize in 1964; his dream; assassinated

3

1. Alzheimer's disease or dementia
2. Memory is off; hard to keep track of things; cannot remember what has been read or someone's name; forget where you are or where you parked; misplace keys; forget appointments; serve to the wrong tennis court

4

1. It goes by very quickly.
2. She talks nostalgically of how time went by slowly and did not seem to matter during childhood.

5

1. A heart attack
2. Chest pressure radiating to the shoulders; cold sweat; difficulty breathing; long and stressful day; burning sensation in abdomen and nausea; rude awakening at hospital

6

1. They are not properly prepared.
2. It is very loud.
3. They do not take a Swiss army knife, map, compass, book that identifies edible mushrooms, or a snake-bit kit.

Decibels are units that measure intensity of sound. If an environmental impact statement is warranted, then that must mean that the sound is loud enough to have a negative impact on the environment.

7

1. Muhammad Ali
2. Two different names; boxer; reading the Qur´an; bike stolen in Louisville when he was twelve years old

8

1. Turtle
2. Swims; mottled-brown form; coming up to surface for a quick gulp of air; sea creature; its shell

9

1. Coretta Scott King
2. Bill Cosby
3. Civil rights movement; husband assassinated in 1968; genius for comedy; talented performer; Bill and his *I Spy* costar, Robert Culp

10

1. No
2. No scientific studies cited for percentages; usually after forty one's reflexes are slower, speed is reduced, and strength is diminished anyway; people born prior to 1880 would be well over 100 years old and not likely to be still alive whether or not they drank milk

11

1. He was under stress because of the upcoming test and outside pressures, as well.
2. Tossing and turning in bed; behind in a course that he was not good at with an exam scheduled for Monday; had a date for Saturday that he was reluctant to cancel; family member seriously ill with pressure from parents to come home for the weekend

12
1. Crime is everywhere and everyone can be a victim.
2. These criminal acts were committed against a typical man, woman, and child involved in ordinary, everyday activities.

13
1. He was going to knock him out.
2. Chamberlain was very tall; "timber" is a word used to warn of a falling tree; Chamberlain turns white and refuses to fight

14
1. Baseball player from another country
2. You must move to a foreign land where hardly anyone will speak your language or understand your valiant attempt to converse in theirs; laws, traditions, and full-time interpreters are not provided; taught a few essential phrases; "cutoff man," "hit-and-run," and "take sign" are baseball terms

15
1. She will probably not succeed in school nor be well-prepared for a career.
2. The second girl is not conscientious or interested in school, particularly when compared to the first girl who is very successful in school and later in her career.

16
1. They are not very pleasant.
2. death
3. Unhealthy days; health care costs; not enough funds; depressing; diminished quality of life; general deterioration of the body; loss of loved ones
   The *only* alternative to the later years is, by necessity, death.

17
1. Late at night
2. Difficult to be sure, but probably in the teens
3. Break the window

4. Because there are not enough clues or information to answer this question, it is safer not to draw an inference.
5. Very dark; street deserted; barely any sound; reached for rocks while staring nervously at the window. Little children probably would not be out that late, and the boys were not behaving the way adults do.

18

1. In general, we must be very careful how we interpret data. The data are not sufficient to tell us about the relationship between Dungeons and Dragons and suicide.
2. The reported suicide rate among D&D players—28 per 3 million—is considerably *less* than the suicide rate among teenagers in general. The 28 reported cases are probably not a complete count of all suicides by D&D players. Besides, the correlation between playing D&D and committing suicide, regardless of its direction and magnitude, could not possibly tell us about cause and effect.

19

1. Chuck Stuart
2. The story began to unravel after Chuck's brother went to the police. On the night of the shooting, Matthew claimed what he met Chuck at a prearranged spot and was given a bag containing a gun and women's jewelry. After Matthew went to the police, Chuck committed suicide.

20

1. There are not enough clues present to answer the question with any degree of certainty (loitering with flashlight; prior arrests). Under the circumstances, it is probably better not to draw an inference.
2. Yes, he probably would have been released.
3. "But how's it going to look in the press if we just let him go? You know the type of people who live in Littleton Manor. There will be hell to pay if it gets out that this guy just walks."

21

1. He could suffer a heart attack or some other health problem.
2. Herman is living under tremendous stress at work and at home, and his eating and sleeping habits are poor. He also has been smoking more.

22

1. Both
2. Answers will vary.
3. "You haven't attended the behavior modification program for sex offenders. I think you're going to repeat your crime." Edwards believes that because Allen has not made the effort to try to change his behavior, he will commit the same offenses as in the past.

Exercise 2—Developing Inference Questions (Passages 1–5)

1

1. Who was this person's friend?
   What happened to his friend?
   What is the mood of this person?
2. A dog
   He died
   Sad
3. He chased sticks and quickly retrieved them.

   How quickly the years went by and with their passing his youth slipped away. The sparkle eventually disappeared from his eyes, and he slowly lost his energy. In fact, when the final hour came, he could not walk nor could he recognize his loyal friend. I feel so very empty and alone.

2

1. What kind of job does Margarita have?
   How old are Jose and Hector?
   Who was Maria and what happened to her?
2. Probably a secretary
   Thirteen or fourteen
   Her daughter, and she probably died
3. Margarita finished typing just before lunch, and she was able to file the remaining papers.

   They were growing up so quickly and would be entering high school next year.

Margarita had been thinking about her other children when thoughts of Maria crossed her mind. Margarita's eyes now filled with tears as she began to sob uncontrollably. It was obvious that she would never experience complete tranquillity in her life.

3

1. Why was the previous DWI charge against Wiggins dropped?

   Why is McCoy's chief not pursuing the current charge against Wiggins?

2. Because Wiggins is a prominent local businessman who probably has much political muscle.

3. Charges against Wiggins were dropped twice for no apparent reason. In the second instance, Tompkins did not say anything about the breathalizer not reading right, and Wiggins was obviously very drunk. The passage hints that Wiggins is an important person in the community and that there is a coverup taking place, at the very least, on the prosecutor's level and maybe even higher.

4

1. Students can develop questions such as: What is the productivity of Department A? or, If you become the major supplier to the electronics corporation, will that prevent your company from going bankrupt or will it result in substantial profits?

2. There are not enough clues or information available to draw any valid inferences. In addition, students may have a difficult time answering the questions posed in the passage without more information. Nevertheless, the passage is of value because it should make for some interesting class discussion on ethics, while demonstrating to students the importance of reading with a questioning mind but not jumping to conclusions when there is a lack of information.

5

1. If Joe Morgan were white, would he have been stopped for questioning? Was this an expression of institutional racism? If it was institutional racism, is there a way to correct this situation?

2. No

   Yes

   Maybe

3. The profile indicates that blacks and Hispanics are more likely to be involved in this aspect of the drug trade, so the agents probably would not have stopped a white person unless he were doing something characteristic of what drug dealers do

   The profile by its very nature singles out all blacks and Hispanics for suspicion, which leads law enforcement agents to focus on them as a group and view them negatively.

   Perhaps, by making sure that a particular profile is correct and based on valid statistics and by having law enforcement agents become more sensitive to the spirit—and not necessarily the letter—of the profile. Also, they must show some flexibility by judging people as individuals. In a general sense, we cannot say that all members of any group are likely to do something unless we know every member of that group.

Assessment

Provide additional passages in class so students can practice their inference skills. It is important that students read with questioning minds as demonstrated by the asking and answering of their *own* inference questions. Have students justify both their questions and their answers, and pay particular attention to the clues they use to support their responses.

Chapter 10: Five Steps to Effective Textbook Reading

Exercise 1 (Model Overview of Front Matter)

Front Matter

Textbook Title: *Tools for Technical and Professional Communication*
Author: Arthur H. Bell
Edition: First
Publishing Company: NTC Publishing Group
Place of Publication: Illinois

Date of Publication: 1995

Number of Parts: 3

Number of Chapters: 17

Author's Purpose: To serve students and others preparing for careers in science, business, and government; the book serves as a bridge between technical and professional communication; to expand the boundaries of traditional technical communication to meet the full range of communication skills needed by professionals in science, business, and government; to meet the career needs of students in the present and the future; to develop skills to help students communicate effectively in a wide range of written documents and in oral presentations

Learning aids provided: Three supplements are provided: "Cases for Technical and Professional Communication" present real-life scenarios posing dilemmas that require critical analysis and carefully constructed communications for solution. The "Brief Guide to Grammar, Mechanics, Usage, and Spelling" answers the most common questions about punctuation, word form, and word choice in technical and professional communication. The "Documentation" guide provides rules and examples for constructing accurate notes and bibliographies.

Additional important information mentioned in the preface or introduction: Summaries of the major topics covered in the three parts of the textbook are provided.

Back Matter

Index: yes (Subject)

Glossary: no

Bibliography: no

General Reference Sources (Cases): yes

Appendixes: yes

Exercise 2 (Model Preview of Chapter)

Chapter title: "Collaborative Writing"

Number of pages: 11

Introduction: yes

College prepares students to write alone. Team writing accounts for as much as 60 percent of all technical writing done in science, business, industry, and the professions, in-cluding law and medicine. Collaborative writing—team writ-ing—involves sharing writing responsibilities with at least one other person. You may work in dyads (pairs) or as a member of a larger project team. Collaborative writing requires that you understand: what can go wrong when groups write to-gether, how group problems can be avoided, what advantages accrue from the team approach to writing, how to participate as a member of a writing team, and how to lead a writing team.

Summary: yes

Because team writing is widely established in business and government, every opportunity should be taken to practice collaborative writing skills in college and career. In working together on a group project, remember to consider the process as well as the eventual product. Discuss how to organize your mutual activities and how to avoid conflict or isolation among group members.

Graphic Aids: no

Questions: yes

Other learning aids provided: Exercises provided at end of chap-ter; some real-life experiences of technical writers are related.

Exercise 3 (Model Broad Topic Outline of Chapter—"Collaborative Writing")

I. The Hazards of Team Writing
   A. One person ends up doing all the work.
   B. We can't keep things moving forward.
   C. We each have a different style.
   D. We're wasting time by trying to work together.

II. The Advantages of Team Writing
   A. One writer can't do it all.
   B. Time is money.
   C. The team provides a safety net.

III. How to Avoid the Pitfalls of Team Writing
       A. One person ends up doing all the work.
       B. We can't keep things moving forward.
       C. We each have a different style.
       D. We're wasting time by trying to work together.
   IV. How to Participate as a Member of a Writing Team
    V. How to Lead a Writing Team
   VI. Team Writing in Your Future

Exercise 4 (Turning Headings Into Questions and Finding the Answers)

I. What are the hazards of team writing?

   One person ends up doing all the work; We can't keep things moving forward; We each have a different style; We're wasting time by trying to work together.

Additional Important Information: Many workers and students have a deep distrust for shared responsibility and shared decision-making which they see as causing delays, compromises, and shoddy work. Team writing does go astray because colleges do not prepare students to write in groups. In short, students are taught to work alone.

A. How or why does one person end up doing all the work?

   Many teams end up with mostly spectators and only one person carrying the load.

B. Why can't we keep things moving forward?

   Each team member often has a different idea of how the project should develop.

C. How or why are different styles hazardous to team writing?

   Because group members each take their preferred piece of the project to work on, it results in fragments of writing that can't be unified into a single, organized document.

D. How or why do we waste time by working together?

   Chaotic meetings and misdirected writing leads group members to lose faith in the team approach to writing.

II. What are the advantages of team writing?

   One writer can't do it all; Time is money; The team provides a safety net.

A. Why can't one writer do it all?

Documents dealing with large problems often demand the shared skills and insights of several writers working in close coordination.

B. How or why is time money?

Few companies have the luxury of providing the time for one person to accomplish a major writing task over an extended time. Only a writing team can produce the required volume of work to meet deadlines.

C. How does the team provide a safety net?

Nothing will happen to a writing project when an employee is ill or quits provided that the project has been assigned to a team. The team approach to producing major documents ensures continuity and reliability.

III. How do you avoid the pitfalls of team writing?

By responding constructively to the four complaints cited above.

A. How do you avoid one person doing all the work?

Divide work fairly among team members by discovering the strengths of each member and assigning writing tasks accordingly.

B. How can we keep things moving forward?

Develop a shared game plan. During initial meetings, decide on target dates for completion of work stages and on the review process that will take place when work is handed in. Shared commitment to target dates exerts peer pressure on all team members to meet or beat the dates.

C. How can we prevent different styles from becoming a pitfall of team writing?

Decide upon issues of style and organization before team members begin to write, including such matters as voice, tone, support techniques, and a master outline.

D. How can we avoid wasting time when we work together?

The time devoted to the process of team writing is as important as the individual time given to the product of putting words on paper. The eventual document must speak for a consensus in the company which should be based on the patient, active participation of the team members sharing insights, resolving conflicts, and coordinating work activities.

IV. How should you participate as a member of a writing team?

First, there should be a shift in attitude. You must be prepared to listen at the organizing meeting and show interest in the opinions of other team members in order to develop an environment of trust. Second, team members should express ideas and reactions candidly and provisionally, not in an absolute way. All team members have to speak up, but avoid absolute judgments. Negative judgments should be phrased and expressed constructively. Third, team members have to avoid sole ownership of ideas. Once a suggestion is made to the group, it becomes the property of the group. The team should agree that there's nothing personal about positive or negative comments about ideas because the goal is to come up with the best writing plan possible. Finally, team members must respect one another's differences. The final document reflecting the work of the team probably will not be completely pleasing to any one team member. Differences are inevitable and demonstrate that we each have our own opinions of what makes good writing. A writing project should not be held captive to any one vision of writing style. The strength of team writing lies in its ability to harmonize different voices into a shared chorus.

V. How should you lead a writing team?

According to Robert Underwood, a technical writer at Lockheed, the leader must first find out as much as possible about the project from the manager who assigned it. That information must be shared accurately with the writing team.

Next, a writing team must be chosen that has all the necessary strengths including: thoroughness and attention to detail, speed in drafting, content knowledge, and organizational abilities. After determining the ideal team size for the project, one extra member should be added. The same people must not be placed together on the same teams time after time, and an effort should be made to involve at least one new writer for each project.

A folder of project information for each participant should be put together for the first meeting. The more information shared from the beginning, the more productive the initial meetings. It's important that team members get to know each other at the first meeting so they begin to trust one another. A bond of good feeling must be established from the beginning.

The leader must not dominate the first meeting if she is to achieve full participation on the part of all members. She should present what she knows about the project as concisely as possible, then open up discussion for the opinions, questions, and suggestions of team members. Such things as why the project is being done, who will read it, and how much time and money the company wants to spend on it should be explained.

By the end of the first meeting, at least three initial decisions are made: when to meet again, what each member will bring to that meeting, and what additional information is needed by the group. The leader does not come up with a working outline or document design at the first meeting because this can discourage fresh thinking by the group.

At the second meeting, the leader listens for interest areas so that she can determine what team members want to do. Once areas of responsibility have been settled, plans for draw-ing up a tentative outline are made. Although this master agenda will change many times, it is important to get some kind of orderly thoughts on paper. Approximate milestones are also set because the resource of time must be considered from the very beginning of the project.

The master outline will be refined at the following meetings, before moving on to the document design, drafting, review, and revision stages. Groupware, which is word processing software designed specifically for team writing, makes work in those areas easier. Using Groupware enables team members to complete their assigned portions of the document while, at the same time, having the work of other members accessible.

During the outlining and drafting stages, the leader keeps in close touch with upper management to make sure the team is heading in the right direction. The first edited draft, or prototype, is circulated among upper managers for their sign-off and revision suggestions.

One or two members of the team usually act as final editors for the last draft. Each page of the document should read as if it were written by one person. The completed document is given to each member for final reading, so that errors in form, content, grammar, mechanics, style, usage, and spelling can be eliminated.

The team leader should invite a senior manager to the final meeting to receive the completed document so that team members share in the sense of accomplishment. It is important that managers have a chance to ask questions and thank the members for their work. Also, the meeting provides an opportunity to clarify the document for management.

VI. Will team writing be involved in your future?

Collaborative writing skills should be practiced in college and in one's career because team writing is so widely established in business and government. Practicing these skills may well determine your effectiveness in your eventual career.

Additional Important Information: In working on a group project, remember to consider the process of your interaction and not just the final product.

Assessment

For Exercise 5, it is a good idea to test students on the "Collaborative Writing" chapter so that they experience the five-step approach completely. If you wish, you can use the same questions they answered as part of Step 4 in Exercise 4.

You may use Exercise 6 to test students, by having them apply the five-step approach to another textbook of your choosing. You may make copies of the overview and preview forms in Chapter 10 for this exercise.

Part 3: Change-of-Pace Readings

Selection 1—"The Dark Menace": Answers

1. e
2. half-asleep; dazed
3. external boundary
4. urging; poking
5. give off; send forth
6. nighttime
7. false

8. bats emit high frequency sounds
    bats can navigate in total darkness
    bats sleep all day
    bats are able to see
    bats use echoes to navigate
    bats can be rabid
    bats are peaceful creatures
    bats do not generally attack humans
    bats are not interested in human hair
    some bats are vampires, but they usually enjoy the blood of animals not humans
 9. burglars
10. c
11. yes; the author sent the dog to attack the bat
12. bats fly into people's hair
13. Bats are not as bad as most people think; there is much misinformation around about bats.

Selection 2—"The Experience of a Lifetime": Answers

1. Near-death or out-of-body experiences can be pleasant and peaceful.
2. It is an experience that we all must confront sooner or later; it is such a mystery.
3. where we go after death
4. euphemisms = the substitution of a word, phrase, or expression that sounds less harsh or offensive than another one
   skeptical = doubtful
   tranquillity = peaceful
5. "I did not do too well on the test," instead of saying "I failed the test" (Answers will vary).
6. back
7. rising
8. the gatekeeper or an angel
9. He was very skeptical before his experience but he certainly believed in them afterwards.

10. He feared death before his experience but was not as frightened of it afterwards. However, he was still in no hurry to die.
11. Answers will vary.
12. Answers will vary.

Selection 3—"The Trajectories of Genius": Answers

1. d
2. Vauvenargues
3. c
4. Fernande Olivier
   Olga Koklova
   Marie-Therese Walter
   Francoise Gilot
   Jacqueline Roque
5. b
6. b
7. Barrio Chino
8. d
9. c
10. f
11. d. 1881
    e. 1900
    f. 1961
    a. 1973
    b. 1886
    c. 1944

Selection 4—"Why Run?": Answers

1. stress fractures
2. Olympic
   Boston
   Marine Corps
   Los Angeles
3. 26 miles, 385 yards

4. menstrual periods
5. g
6. improper (not showing good judgment)
7. to improve health
8. a person who seeks only to meet a personal challenge when running a marathon (one who is satisfied to run in the middle of the pack)
9. strengthens the heart, lungs, and the immune system
   lowers blood pressure
   thins the blood
   elevates the level of the good cholesterol and reduces the bad
   increases energy
   relieves stress
   improves mood
   burns calories
   fights obesity
   helps stop smoking
   offers time to solve problems
10. unpredictable
11. b
    c
    a
12. yes
13. Yes. She is very enthusiastic about marathon running, and she states that she does not intend to give up until she improves her best time.
14. New York
15. Paragraphs will vary.

Selection 5—"With No Parents, Ladeeta, 18, Presses On": Answers

1. Cypress Hills
2. substitute
3. very thin
4. She had seen what drugs had done to her mother and Ladeeta wanted more out of life.

5. 8
6. Butch, Pig, and Charles
7. Because he was thin
8. Because there were middle-class blacks there who spoke and dressed differently
9. Lavelle, Lisa, Lakisha, and Latreece
10. g
    e
    f
    h
    i
    j
    a
    b
    c
    d
11. Answers will vary.
12. Answers will vary.

Selection 6—"The Stono River Rebellion . . .": Answers

1. f
2. e
3. a
4. b
5. f
6. b
   d
   d
   c
   e
   a
   f
7. e

8. ebony regiment
9. d
10. e
11. false
12. c
13. e (1729)
    c (1733)
    h (1734)
    b (1737)
    d (1738)
    f (1739)
    a (1740)
    g (1742)
14. Blacks did not willingly accept slavery and their loss of freedom.

Selection 7—"The Decline and Fall": Answers

1. false
2. false
3. Haldeman and Ehrlichman
4. Saturday Night Massacre
5. Leon Jaworski
6. c
7. c
8. f
9. a
10. b
11. a
12. d
13. a
14. destroy it
15. full disclosure

16.
1) b
2) l
3) e
4) a
5) c
6) j
7) f
8) i
9) k
10) g
11) h
12) d
13) p
14) o
15) q
16) m
17) n

Selection 8—"Young Cassius Clay": Answers

1. 1942
2. 18
3. 18
4. Either he threw it into the Ohio River, or he lost it.
5. This was a speech at a faculty meeting made by Atwood Wilson, who was the principal of Central High School. He stated that "One day our greatest claim to fame is going to be that we knew Cassius Clay, or taught him." This speech was made because Clay had not fulfilled the term paper requirement for graduation. Wilson argued that Clay had unique gifts and was going to be heavyweight champion of the world, and he should not be held to the same rules governing the average student. The speech worked, and Clay was permitted to give an oral presentation instead of a term paper.
6. Columbia Gym
7. He was concerned about raising his blood pressure.

8. River
9. Wrecking crew
10. He fainted.
11. a) unique; original
    b) keep away from; avoid
12. work boots; he ran in them
13. d
14. false
15. a) He gave an oral presentation which was a travelogue on his adventures touring various American cities as an amateur boxer.
    b) Answers will vary.
16. sweet, pillowy, light-skinned black woman with a freckled face, a gentle demeanor, and an easy laugh
17. wild, free-roaming drunk and womanizer; fun-loving; a gifted religious muralist and commercial sign painter
18. unpredictable, witty, mischievous, comical, shy, quiet, playful, happy, fast-talking, confident, energetic, bright
19. 1. f
    2. i
    3. l
    4. n
    5. o
    6. a
    7. e
    8. m
    9. d
    10. c
    11. h
    12. k
    13. b
    14. j
    15. g
20. Answers will vary.

It may be interesting to determine if students notice that the answer to Question 13 cannot *possibly* be choice "e." Ask them about it.

Selection 9—"'A Generation of Clumsy Feeble-Minded Millions' Starved Brains": Answers

1. short-term memory
2. d
3. true
4. b
5. false
6. e
7. e
8. e
9. b
10. false
11. synapses
12. d
13. Cravioto and DeLicardie
14. c
15. e
16. e
17. true
18. e
19. d
20. neurons
21. Paragraphs will vary.

Selection 10—"A Historical Overview of the African American Literary Tradition": Answers

1. The first opportunity African Americans had to give birth to and celebrate the uniqueness of African American culture. It was a very creative literary period for African Americans that provided readers with a slice of African American life.
2. Reconstruction
3. the voyage across the Atlantic Ocean by African slaves
4. the Great Migration and the end of World War I
5. English and Christianity

6. culture
7. cannot read and write
8. Jim Crow
9. rebirth
10. work songs, field hollers, and the folktale
11. because it was actually the *first* opportunity African Americans had to give birth to and celebrate the uniqueness of African American culture
12. *A Leap for Freedom*
13. Charles W. Chesnutt
14. *Our Nig; or, Sketches from the Life of a Free Black;* Harriet E. Wilson
15. the ten percent of African American intellectuals and artists who would lead African Americans in the United States; W. E. B. Du Bois
16. freedom and equality
17. Conservative African Americans believed that the literature written by blacks should "uplift" the race—show African Americans in a positive light. Radical African Americans believed that a "realistic" view of African American life had to be presented because it was art.
18. Claude McKay, Jean Toomer, Countee Cullen, and Langston Hughes
19. Richard Wright
20. Rosa Parks's refusal in 1955 to move to the back of the bus in Montgomery, Alabama
21. *Go Tell It on the Mountain*
22. Gwendolyn Brooks
23. the interconnectedness of family, home, and community as well as a black woman's ability to survive
24. a. prohibited discrimination in voting because of color, religion, or national origin
    b. Pulitzer Prize-winning drama written by August Wilson
    c. prohibited discrimination in public accommodations, schools, and employment
    d. Pulitzer Prize-winning novel written by Toni Morrison

e. wrote the novel: *The Women of Brewster Place*
f. opposed to any concept that separated African American artists from their community; directly related to the quest of African Americans for self-determination
25. The Harlem Renaissance took place primarily in New York City, while the Black Power movement took place throughout the country.

Assessment

If you wish to give students some practice in taking timed tests, the first five selections are particularly suitable for that purpose. Simply set a reasonable time limit for the reading of each selection and the answering of the corresponding comprehension questions. Also, if practical, you may choose to have students attempt to answer the questions without looking back at the reading material.

Because there is such a wide variety of comprehension questions for the selections in this part, students will also get considerable test-taking practice. In fact, toward the end of the semester some of the selections can actually serve as tests to evaluate student progress in the development of the various comprehension skills covered in this textbook. When reading the selections and answering the questions, students should be reminded to apply all of the skills that they have been taught throughout the semester.

The first five selections are relatively short and, therefore, should be given during the first half of the semester; the remaining selections should be assigned during the second half of the semester because they are longer and more difficult. In short, students need sufficient time to develop their reading skills before attempting the last five selections.

Some of the reading selections along with the corresponding questions can be used to assess student comprehension skills. In fact, Selections 8, 9, and 10 could serve as reading tests, provided you set appropriate and reasonable times for their completion.

Finally, it is very important that students realize that the various skills that have been presented are tools to be applied and not the outcome itself. Thus, by applying these tools, students can locate and understand information on which they will be tested in their various college courses.